American Regional Cuisine

Third Edition

THE
INTERNATIONAL
CULINARY
SCHOOLS SM
at The Art Institutes

THE ART INSTITUTES

MICHAEL F. NENES, MBA, CEC, CCE

Photography by Ron Manville

WILEY

Library of Congress Cataloging-in-Publication Data:
Nenes, Michael F.
American regional cuisine; Michael F. Nenes; photography by Ron Manville—3rd ed. p. cm.
Rev. ed. of: American regional cuisine 2nd ed. 2007.
ISBN: 978-1-118-52396-4

Printed in the United States of America

10 9 8 7 6 5 4 3 2 1

Contents

American Regional Cuisine, Third Edition, is written with great pride in tribute to the abundant culinary resources, cultural diversity, and rich food history of North America.

AMERICAN REGIONAL CUISINE AND FARM TO TABLE

"Farm to table" typically means all products are raised on farms or ranches that are within a one-day drive or less of the food-service establishment. Because local products do not have to travel far to reach the consumer, the produce can be picked when it is ripest. When a fruit or vegetable is given the time to completely ripen, it fully develops and retains its vitamins and minerals, lending it a more vibrant flavor. Connecting to the sources of our food is a meaningful part of enjoying the meal. Buying locally helps support the family farmers and ranchers who raise our food. So, we circle back to where American regional cuisine started.

PRINCIPLES AND FOUNDATIONS

North America is a nation of immigrants; only Native Americans can claim North America as their ancestral home. Other Americans or their ancestors came here, creating what many call "the melting pot." They brought with them the traditions of their homeland, which includes agricultural practices, food preferences, and cooking methods. Cuisine in different parts of the United States developed independently. Each region was influenced by the nationality of colonists who settled in the area and by the ingredients locally available. American regional cuisine combines a unique local history and culture with distinct regional ingredients. Regional cuisines reflect the characteristics of the local farmers, ranchers, cheese makers, chefs, and people. Regional cuisine evolves along with the community, dishes absorb and reflect much of the environment, and it is always changing.

The principles and foundations of cooking were developed and practiced in Europe, Asia, Africa, and other countries long before the development of American regional cuisines as we know them today. The European immigrants who came to America applied their basic culinary skills to the ingredients at hand. In the 1900s, as the palate of the typical American became more sophisticated, many European-trained chefs immigrated to the United States to take jobs in the growing restaurant and hotel industries. In time, Americans began to cook professionally, and in many cases they trained under these European chefs. Thus, even today, French is the language of cooking taught to students of the culinary arts. A glossary of cooking terms used in this book can be found at the back of the book in the Basic Culinary Vocabulary section.

The new edition of *American Regional Cuisine* addresses the basics of "sustainability agriculture" or what every chef should know. In the 1990 Farm Bill, the U.S. Congress defined "sustainable agriculture" to have these qualities:

- Satisfy human food and fiber needs.

- Enhance environmental quality and the natural resource based upon which agricultural economy depends.

- Make the most efficient use of nonrenewable resources and on-farm resources, and integrate, where appropriate, natural biological cycles and controls.

- Sustain the economic viability of farm operations.

- Enhance the quality of life for farmers and society as a whole.

Sustainability practices ensure that the land used to raise farm products is healthy and available for the future. Sustainable methods include important practices like biodiversity, water conservations, and environmental protection. We all should embrace and support these practices.

Professional cooking involves following recipes. However, great cooks must understand the foundations of cooking. Great cooks practice accurate culinary techniques and resist the enticement to take shortcuts. The practice of safe and sanitary cooking is not only a necessity but also a professional lifestyle. Great cooks believe in the concepts of lifelong learning. Great cooks embrace "farm to table," supporting where and whenever possible locally grown farm products.

The chapters that follow present the cuisines of 11 culinary regions of the United States. These regional chapters are presented in the order that follows the arrival of the first colonists and the approximate routes they took as they explored and settled what eventually became the United States. The states covered in these chapters have been selected based on the similar cultures and backgrounds of their residents and their cuisines, as well as on how the indigenous ingredients are utilized in that cooking.

Each recipe in the *Third Edition* of *American Regional Cuisine* was selected and tested for its representation of the region. Consideration of the menus and recipes included using a variety of techniques and ingredients, plus the availability of ingredients. Methods and techniques have been listed in clear-cut steps and follow a logical progression for the completion of the recipe.

KEYS TO SUCCESS

1. To produce great food, you must start with high-quality ingredients. Substandard ingredients will not yield great or even good results.

2. Some ingredients are highly specific to a region and may be difficult to obtain elsewhere. These recipes are preceded by Chef Tips, which indicate suitable substitutions.

3. All herbs should be fresh unless specified as dried.

4. All butter called for in recipes should be unsalted unless specified otherwise.

5. Citrus juice should be squeezed from fresh fruit rather than reconstituted from concentration.

6. Cooking times are approximations. The altitude, type of cookware used, and amount of heat applied are all variables that affect cooking time. Professional cooks understand that the times are a guide and doneness is determined by various methods.

7. When possible, white and black pepper should be ground fresh to the level of coarseness called for in the recipes. Ground pepper loses strength over time, making it difficult to judge the quantity needed.

Recipes are guidelines, road maps for the cook. Judgment, knowledge, and skill level will influence the final product. Always read a recipe from start to finish before starting the cooking process. These recipes introduce you to the different flavor profiles and ingredients of a specific region. It is important to respect the ingredient, technique, and cooking method so the final product represents the intended results.

INSTRUCTOR SUPPORT MATERIALS

Lecture PowerPoints and an *Instructor's Manual* are also available to qualified adopters of this book. It contains lecture notes for each chapter along with expanded definitions of the terms contained in the text, and questions to support and encourage classroom discussion. To access these password protected resources, visit www.wiley.com/go/ai.

WILEYPLUS LEARNING SPACE

A place where students can define their strengths and nurture their skills, *WileyPLUS Learning Space* transforms course content into an online learning community. *WileyPLUS Learning Space* invites students to experience learning activities, work through self-assessment, ask questions and share insights. As students interact with the course content, each other, and their instructor, *WileyPLUS Learning Space* creates a personalized study guide for each student. Through collaboration, students make deeper connections to the subject matter and feel part of a community.

Through a flexible course design, instructors can quickly organize learning activities, manage student collaboration, and customize your course—having full control over content as well as the amount of interactivity between students.

WileyPLUS Learning Space lets the instructor:

- Assign activities and add your own materials

- Guide your students through what's important in the interactive e-textbook by easily assigning specific content

- Set up and monitor group learning

- Assess student engagement

- Gain immediate insights to help inform teaching

Defining a clear path to action, the visual reports in *WileyPLUS Learning Space* help both you and your students gauge problem areas and act on what's most important.

Acknowledgments

The International Culinary Schools at The Art Institutes wish to thank the following contributors for their effort on behalf of *American Regional Cuisine*:

Author Michael F. Nenes, MBA, CEC, CCE, Assistant Vice President of Culinary Arts, The International Culinary Schools at The Art Institutes. Chef Nenes began his career with The Art Institutes in 1992 at The Art Institute of Houston as its first academic director of culinary arts. He assumed his current role in 2004, overseeing Culinary Arts curriculum, kitchen and culinary facilities design, and new product development. Before joining the Art Institutes, Chef Nenes owned and operated successful restaurants in Texas, Alaska, and Colorado. The author of *American Regional Cuisine*, 2nd ed., *International Cuisine*, and *Foundations of Professional Cooking: A Global Approach*, Chef Nenes has also competed internationally and nationally. The International Culinary Schools at The Art Institutes have 40 locations across North America, which has allowed Chef Nenes over the last ten years to travel to and experience firsthand all 11 culinary regions.

Thanks to Co-Author Lois Nenes, M.Ed., who has 20 years' hospitality experience and 20 years as a teacher, for her tremendous amount of research, writing, editing, and support; she had to become part explorer, part student, and part teacher. Every effort was made to find information that could be supported by least two documented sources. Lois was a supportive colleague, and we both enjoyed the second *American Regional Cuisine* adventure.

Chef Nenes handled the food styling, for our photographer Ron Manville. Ron is a culinary photographer who has worked with the ACF Culinary Olympic Teams, as well as with some of the top culinary professionals in America. His elegant photography will be instrumental in the success of this book. Ron's creativity was extremely helpful, and his years of experience allowed us to take simple food and make it look exciting.

In addition, we are grateful for the contributions of The International Culinary Schools at the Art Institutes across the country. The recipes were tested by the students at a number of schools across the country.

The Art Institute of Atlanta

The Art Institute of Austin, a branch of The Art Institute of Houston

The Art Institute of California—Hollywood, a campus of Argosy University

The Art Institute of California—Inland Empire, a campus of Argosy University

The Art Institute of California—Los Angeles, a campus of Argosy University

The Art Institute of California—Orange County, a campus of Argosy University

The Art Institute of California—Sacramento, a campus of Argosy University

The Art Institute of California—San Diego, a campus of Argosy University

The Art Institute of California—San Francisco, a campus of Argosy University

The Art Institute of California—Silicon Valley, a campus of Argosy University

The Art Institute of Charleston, a branch of The Art Institute of Atlanta

WileyPLUS Learning Space

An easy way to help your students learn, collaborate, and grow.

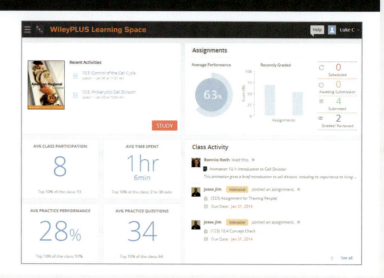

Personalized Experience

Students create their own study guide while they interact with course content and work on learning activities.

Flexible Course Design

Educators can quickly organize learning activities, manage student collaboration, and customize their course—giving them full control over content as well as the amount of interactivity among students.

Clear Path to Action

With visual reports, it's easy for both students and educators to gauge problem areas and act on what's most important.

Instructor Benefits

- Assign activities and add your own materials
- Guide students through what's important in the interactive e-textbook by easily assigning specific content
- Set up and monitor collaborative learning groups
- Assess learner engagement
- Gain immediate insights to help inform teaching

Student Benefits

- Instantly know what you need to work on
- Create a personal study plan
- Assess progress along the way
- Participate in class discussions
- Remember what you have learned because you have made deeper connections to the content

We are dedicated to supporting you from idea to outcome.

WILEY

The Art Institute of Charlotte, a campus of South University

The Art Institute of Colorado

The Art Institute of Dallas, a campus of South University

The Art Institute of Fort Lauderdale

The Art Institute of Houston

The Art Institute of Houston—North, a branch of The Art Institute of Houston

The Art Institute of Indianapolis

The Art Institute of Jacksonville, a branch of Miami International University of Art & Design

The Art Institute of Las Vegas

The Art Institute of Michigan

The Art Institute of Ohio—Cincinnati

The Art Institute of Philadelphia

The Art Institute of Phoenix

The Art Institute of Pittsburgh

The Art Institute of Pittsburgh—Online Division

The Art Institute of Portland

The Art Institute of Raleigh—Durham, a campus of South University

The Art Institute of Salt Lake City

The Art Institute of San Antonio, a branch of The Art Institute of Houston

The Art Institute of Seattle

The Art Institute of St. Louis

The Art Institute of Tampa, a branch of Miami International University of Art & Design

The Art Institute of Tennessee—Nashville, a branch of The Art Institute of Atlanta

The Art Institute of Tucson

The Art Institute of Vancouver

The Art Institute of Vancouver (The International Culinary School at The Art Institute of Vancouver)

The Art Institute of Virginia Beach, a branch of The Art Institute of Atlanta

The Art Institute of Washington, a branch of The Art Institute of Atlanta

The Art Institute of Wisconsin

The Art Institutes International—Kansas City

The Art Institutes International Minnesota

The Illinois Institute of Art—Chicago

The Illinois Institute of Art—Schaumburg

The Cuisine of
New England

The New England region is known for the rocky coastlines of Maine, the White Mountains of New Hampshire, the rolling green mountains and dairies of Vermont, and the fertile farms and orchards of Connecticut. From New England's rivers, bays, and oceans comes seafood of great variety and high quality. The hills and valleys of New England are home to some of America's oldest fruit orchards and vegetable farms. Sugar maple trees and fiddlehead ferns are abundant. The swampy bogs found in Cape Cod and Nantucket make this area home to the cranberry. Perhaps more than any other of the area's natural resources, the Atlantic cod is recognized as a symbol of the region's natural heritage. This species is so much a part of the early history of the settlement of the coastal regions that a model of the "sacred cod" hangs in the Massachusetts statehouse.

Connecticut   "The Nutmeg State." The state shellfish is the Eastern oyster, the state animal is the sperm whale, the state bird is the American robin, the state flower is the mountain laurel, and the state song is "Yankee Doodle."

Maine   "The Pine Tree State." The state animal is the moose, the state fish is the landlocked salmon (a freshwater fish available only to sports fishermen), the state insect is the honeybee, and the state flower is the white pine cone and tassel.

Massachusetts   "The Bay State." The state fish is the cod, the state tree is the American elm, and the state bird is the chickadee.

New Hampshire   "The Granite State." The state saltwater fish is the striped bass, the state freshwater fish is the brook trout, the state tree is the white birch, and the state animal is the white-tailed deer.

Rhode Island   "The Ocean State." The state shell is the quahog, a clamshell that Native Americans used as money; the state bird is the Rhode Island Red chicken; and the state tree is the red maple.

Vermont   "The Green Mountain State." The sugar maple tree is the state tree, and its sap is gathered at the beginning of spring in an activity known as "sug'rin"; the sap is then boiled down to make delicious maple syrup. The state fishes are the brook trout and walleye pike, the state flower is the red clover, and the state insect is the honeybee.

HISTORY AND MAJOR INFLUENCES

THE FIRST COLONISTS

Most people who initially came to the New World hoped to find treasure of one kind or another and return home. But in the New England region, religious motives brought the first settlers. A small group of English separatists, the Pilgrims, arrived in 1620 and founded the Plymouth (Bay) Colony. Unprepared for the hardships of their first winter, their concern was survival. With help from the Native Americans, the Pilgrims lived through the winter.

Native American influence on colonial cookery was incalculable—primarily in terms of the kinds of produce used, leading off with maize, which the settlers called "Indian corn." One tribe of natives, the Wampanoag, shared their seeds of native corn plants and instructed the settlers in how to plant and fertilize their crop by inserting a tiny fish along with each seed. The harvested corn could be steamed, roasted, or dried and pounded into cornmeal. Cornmeal "mush" became a staple of the colonists' diet and was served hot or cold, with milk and butter. The colonists learned to adapt their English traditional recipes, substituting cornmeal for their hearth cakes—puddings with a dif-ferent flavor, but a similar cooking method. Americans now have johnnycakes, boiled and baked Indian puddings, and other English recipes using Indian corn. This use of maize is the most impor-tant and original aspect of American cookery, and the nation is known for its many corn recipes.

In addition to corn, Native Americans subsisted on beans and squash. This "triad" of corn, beans, and squash was referred to as the "three sisters." Kidney beans, green beans, snap beans, butter beans, lima beans, navy peas, and pole beans were planted. Many varieties of squash, including acorn, zucchini, pumpkins, and gourds, were adopted by the colonists. The squash could be eaten fresh or could be dried and stored. The squash seeds could be dried and used as well. When combined, the vegetables were known as "succotash," a term that today describes a mixture of corn with any type of beans and squash.

The Native Americans taught these newcomers how to hunt and fish, and how to cure and smoke their food to preserve it through the winter. Bean pods could be left on the vine until they were thoroughly dried, and then the colonists learned to cook dried beans and depended on them as a staple food through the winter. The Indians of New England flavored their beans with maple sugar and bear fat, and slow-cooked them in underground pits inside deer hides. This preparation evolved into today's baked beans that are very slowly cooked in a bean pot with salt pork and molasses. The Puritans' observance of the Sabbath led to the widespread practice of making beans on Saturday to be eaten on Sunday.

NEW IMMIGRANTS

In the 1880s, when immigrants, particularly those from Ireland, Italy, and Portugal, began to arrive en masse in New England, the culinary customs they brought from their homelands were incorpo-rated into the regional cuisine and cooking style. Single-pot dishes such as meat and seafood stews, which were commonly eaten in Europe, were adapted to the local ingredients. Braised and pickled beef, a mainstay of Britain and Ireland, became the popular dish called New England Boiled Dinner.

Today, with more than 14 million people (though only 5 percent of the U.S. population), New England reflects many of the elements that make up the country's demographic fabric: heavily settled urban cores, expanding suburbs, struggling industrial towns, fast-growing recreational and retirement areas, and isolated rural villages. In recent years New England's population has grown as a result of more immigration. While New England is less racially diverse than the rest of the country, there are newer immigrants from Vietnam and Cape Verde. Massachusetts is home to the third largest Haitian community in the United States, after New York and Florida.

EARLY FARMERS

Native New England ingredients formed the basis of the developing cuisine. Root vegetables such as beets, celeriac, carrots, parsnips, rutabagas, turnips, onions, and white and sweet pota-toes saw them through the winters. Apples were brought over by the English colonists, and over

Maine lobster, also known as the American lobster, is found in the North Atlantic from Labrador to North Carolina, with Maine contributing to more than half of all lobsters caught in the United States. In 17th- and 18th-century America, they were so abundant in the northeast that they were often used as fertilizer. Laws were even passed forbidding people to feed servants lobster more than twice a week. However, improvements in the U.S. transportation infrastructure in the 19th and 20th centuries brought fresh lobster to distant urban areas, and its popularity grew.

Maine lobster is distinguished from the "spiny" lobster, or rock lobster, caught along the southern Atlantic coast and the coast of California, by its heavy claws, which are the enlarged first pair of its legs; spiny lobsters have long antennae and uniformly smaller legs. Live Maine lobster is available year-round, with the bulk of the catch harvested in the summer into the fall. June and July are the peak molting months. Lobsters grow by molting, or shedding their shells. Just after they molt, they are soft and fragile until their new shell has hardened. It takes about 25 molts over five to seven years for a lobster to grow to minimum legal size, 1 pound. Newly molted lobsters are called "soft-shell" lobsters. It is important to be aware of the quality and price of these lobsters, as soft-shell lobsters have less meat in proportion to total body weight than hard-shell lobsters. Hard-shell meat is firmer, while soft-shell meat is softer and tends to contain more water.

The New England states have very strict laws governing lobstering. In Maine, it is illegal to sell lobsters under and over a certain size. Lobstermen use a special gauge to accurately measure the length of the lobster's carapace (body).

The legal minimum length of the carapace is 3¼ inches. Lobsters under this length are called "shorts" or "snappers" and must be thrown back into the ocean. Minimum sizes are enforced to make sure that lobsters are mature enough to breed at least once before they are harvested. The maximum legal length of the carapace is 5 inches; these lobsters are called "jumbo." The maximum size limit is regulated to protect the breeding stock. A minimum-size lobster will weigh around 1 pound, while a maximum-size lobster will weigh between 2 and 4 pounds. Lobsters are referred to in the industry by different names depending on its weight. Market sizes range from "chickens" (1 to 1⅛ pounds) to "jumbos" (over 3½ pounds). The most plentiful and most popular size of a Maine lobster is between 1¼ and 1½ pounds. Other terminology regarding lobsters includes:

CORAL   The roe inside the female lobster that, when cooked, turns from black to orange. The coral is frequently chopped and used in the stuffing for baked lobster or eaten plain with steamed or boiled lobster.

CULL   A lobster with only one claw.

PAQUETTE   A female lobster with black, fertilized eggs under the tail.

TOMALLEY   The liver of the lobster. Many New Englanders consider tomalley a delicacy.

Opinions vary on how best to cook lobster. Some say steaming is superior because the gentle heat will not toughen the meat. Others say boiling seals in the flavor. Baking is another option, but the lobster should be quickly boiled or steamed beforehand.

150 varieties were planted. They established apricot, plum, and pear orchards and cultivated strawberries, blueberries, blackberries, and raspberries. The early settlers of New England also brought many animals with them to their new homeland. As livestock was useful and easy to feed and care for, they could be found on nearly every New England farm. Farmers raised cattle for milk and beef, sheep for mutton and wool, chickens for eggs and meat, and oxen and horses for pulling carts and plows. Pigs were widely owned because they could fend almost entirely for themselves by foraging in the woods for food. Wheat and rye could be planted once the livestock was available to plow the rocky land. The colonists brought their techniques of stone-ground milling for their grains. Cider and ale were the main beverages of the early settlers. Hard fermented cider, the standard drink for both adults and children, was generally made from apples, although pears were also used. Wines from mulberries, cherries, and grapes were also produced.

THE INFLUENCE OF THE SEA ON THE ECONOMY

Eventually, settlers arrived who understood fishing. Coming mainly from Italy and Portugal, they discovered the immense resources of the Grand Banks, a series of underwater plateaus near the province of Newfoundland, Canada. Two ocean currents meet in the Grand Banks, the cold Labrador Current and the warm Gulf Stream. The Grand Banks have the most productive fisheries in the world, yielding cod, swordfish, scallop, and lobster. Also popular are the major flatfish—halibut, flounder, fluke, and dabs. Monkfish, eels, wolffish, sea trout, perch, and sea bass are less familiar but readily available. Small ocean fish like mackerel, porgies, butterfish, and smelts are also in abundant supply. Swordfish, shark, tuna, bluefish, Atlantic salmon, and striped bass come north in the spring and leave before winter arrives. Shellfish such as lobsters, crabs, scallops, oysters, clams, mussels, periwinkles, sea urchins, and even shrimp live in the icy waters.

In New England, the cooking of the earlier era was plain, relying on simple ingredients and skilled hands. But today the culinary traditions of New England grow ever richer as more cultures are integrated and add diversity to the cuisine.

SUSTAINABLE FISHING CONCERNS

The health of the oceans is directly connected to our demand for seafood and the way people catch and farm seafood. Overfishing—catching fish faster than they can reproduce—may be the single biggest threat to ocean ecosystems. In the past decade, Atlantic populations of halibut, bluefin tuna, and yellowtail flounder have joined the list of endangered species. The cod fishery, once a backbone of the North Atlantic economy, collapsed completely in the early 1990s. The breeding population of Atlantic bluefin tuna has been declining steeply and may disappear completely in a few years.

Many of the fish and other animals caught in fishing gear are thrown away as unwanted bycatch. The bycatch of fishery resources—marine mammals, sea turtles, seabirds, and other living marine resources—has become a central concern of the commercial fishing industries, resource managers, conservation organizations, scientists, and the public.

ALTERNATIVE FISHING PRACTICES

Aquaculture, the practice of farm-raising fish and shellfish, will soon surpass wild fisheries as the main source of seafood for the world. Open-net pens or cages enclose fish such as salmon in offshore coastal areas or in freshwater lakes. The disadvantages are that waste from the fish passes freely into the environment, polluting wild habitat; the fish can escape and compete with wild fish for natural resources; and diseases and parasites can spread to wild fish populations.

Ponds enclose some fish in a coastal or inland body of fresh or salt water. Shrimp, catfish, and tilapia are commonly raised in this manner.

In the United States, farmers use raceways to raise rainbow trout. Raceways allow farmers to divert water from a waterway, like a stream or well, so that it flows through channels containing fish. Farmers usually treat the water before directing it back into a natural waterway.

Recirculating systems raise fish in tanks in which the water is treated and recycled through the system. Almost any finfish species, such as striped bass, salmon, and sturgeon, can be raised in recirculating systems. Recirculating systems address many environmental concerns associated with fish farming—fish cannot escape, and wastewater is treated—but they can be costly to operate and rely on electricity or other power sources.

Shellfish aquaculture involves growing shellfish on beaches or suspending them in water by ropes, in plastic trays, or in mesh bags. Oysters, mussels, and clams are filter feeders and require clean water to thrive. Filter feeders can actually filter excess nutrients out of the water.

ENDANGERED FISH

According to the International Union for Conservation of Nature's (IUCN) Red List of endangered species, 1,414 species of fish, or 5 percent of the world's known species, are at risk for extinction.

Bluefin Tuna The most notable of endangered fish bluefin tuna occupies most of the northern Atlantic Ocean. One of the fastest fish in the sea, this fish can grow to a length of 10 feet and weigh more than 1,400 pounds. As these fish migrate thousands of miles across the ocean, so far any efforts to control harvests have not been successful. Chosen by the World Wildlife Fund (WWF) as the sixth most threatened species in the world, sea or land.

Acadian Redfish These fish grow to about 20 inches in length and can live as long as 50 years. Like other overfished species, the Acadian redfish has been subject to pirate fishing, or fishing done in violation of environmental law.

Atlantic Halibut   Found in the North Atlantic Ocean, the Atlantic halibut is the largest of the flat fish species. With a 50-year life span, it can reach a length of 9 feet and weigh up to 1,000 pounds. The IUCN classifies it as endangered, and its numbers are not expected to recover in the near future. This has prompted the United States to ban Atlantic halibut fishing in its coastal waters.

Chilean Sea Bass   Another fish species that has been overfished. Native to the South Pacific and South Atlantic Oceans, it is sometimes called Patagonian toothfish. It became extremely popular in restaurants, causing an increase in demand. Chilean sea bass is a long-lived (up to 50 years), slow-growing fish. Smaller sea bass are likely younger and may not have spawned yet. As fishers caught smaller sea bass, healthy replenishment of the population became unlikely. By the early 2000s, hundreds of American chefs joined a campaign to "Take a Pass on Chilean Sea Bass," with the hope of giving the fishery time to recover. Today, import of Chilean sea bass into the United States is highly regulated by the National Marine Fisheries Service, but illegal fishing continues.

Intervention is also being implemented by organizations such as the Blue Ocean Institute and the Monterey Bay Aquarium. Many concerned national, state, and local organizations publish seafood guides to help consumers make informed choices when buying seafood. And federal legislation now requires fish sellers to identify the source of their seafood. Some retail outlets advertise a commitment to sustainability by raising awareness and selling only products from well-managed fisheries.

Typical New England Ingredients and Dishes

Anadama Bread   A yeast bread made from cornmeal and molasses.

Apple   About 40 varieties of apples are commonly grown in New England. The most popular today are McIntosh, Cortland, New England Red Delicious, Empire, and Rome. Apples have a long and vital tradition in New England. Many varieties were discovered here and have been grown for centuries. The New England apple industry is still largely family owned and orchards are an important community resource.

Barbecue   To a New Englander, "barbecue" means to grill quickly over a fire made from charcoal briquettes, lump charcoal, or hardwood, or simply to cook on a gas or propane grill. In this region, the terms "barbecue" and "grill" are used interchangeably.

Blueberry   In Maine, there is a thriving industry for processing both wild and cultivated blueberries. Before the arrival of Europeans to North America, the Native Americans gathered and dried the fruit for use in winter. The most popular variety is the highbush blueberry because of the larger size of its berries. Also popular is the wild lowbush blueberry, with smaller fruit that is prized for its intense flavor and color.

Bluefish   A round saltwater fish ranging in size from 3 to 6 pounds, common to the coast of Cape Cod and Nantucket in the summer. The bluefish has a blue-silver skin and dark, oily flesh. It is well suited for smoking, broiling, and sautéing, but it must be used quickly, as its freshness decreases rapidly. It is known as a sportsman's "trophy fish" because of its fierceness and fighting nature.

Boston Brown Bread   A traditional colonial sweet bread served on Saturday evenings with baked beans. Boston brown bread is made from cornmeal, molasses, and both rye and whole wheat flours. It is steamed in a large can or mold.

Boston Baked Beans   A dish of navy beans baked a long time with molasses and salt pork or bacon.

Boston Cream Pie   A pie with two layers of white cake, custard filling, and chocolate topping. Considered a pie instead of a cake because colonists did not have cake pans and baked this in a pie pan. Boston cream pie is also considered a pudding pie cake.

Chowder   From the French *chaudeau*, literally meaning "hot water," the term broadly applies today to a hot soup. In this region, it refers to a seafood soup such as New England clam chowder, a creamy mix of clams, onions, and potatoes. (New England clam chowder differs from Manhattan clam chowder, in that the latter has a tomato base and sometimes vegetables, and from Vermont clam chowder, which is simply a clear broth with clams, onions, and potatoes.)

Cider   An alcoholic beverage made from apples. It was common until the late 19th century, when the temperance movement campaigned against alcohol consumption. Early settlers consumed cider and beer instead of the unreliable and sometimes polluted local well water.

Clams   Hardshells, or quahogs, are the hard-shell gray clams that vary in size, from small littlenecks, to cherrystones, to chowder clams. Littlenecks are the choice for raw service; they are mild, sweet, and briny. Clams are slow growers. Littlenecks—the most tender, most expensive, and most sought after—are two to three years old. Cherrystones are five to six years old. Large chowder clams can be 30 years old. Soft-shell clams have an oval shell that is thin and brittle. These clams average 1½ to 3 inches in length, and their shells cannot close completely because of a protruding siphon. The main commercial sources of both types of clams are Maine and Cape Cod. The soft-shell clam has delicate meat that is sweet and slightly salty. The shell should be clean and the siphon firm and plump, not flaccid and dry—it should retract when touched. The siphon is covered with a dark membrane that is removed before the cooked clam is eaten. Softshells are not eaten raw, but are used for steaming or frying.

Clambake   A traditional outdoor cooking method used for festive occasions along the coastal regions of New England. The clambake is typically done on a beach, where a pit is dug in the sand and lined with rocks. It typically takes 2 to 2½ hours to prepare the fire, which is built on top of the rocks to get them to cooking temperature, then the ashes of the fire are removed from the pit. Cleaned seaweed is laid down to protect the food from the heat of the hot rocks. Regional seafood such as lobster, clams, and mussels are placed on top of the seaweed. Side dishes such as potatoes, corn on the cob, onions, and lemons are added as well. The food is then covered with more seaweed. A liquid such as beer is poured on top to provide steam for the cooking process. A sheet of canvas protects the contents and the pit is covered with a bed of sand. The cooking time is roughly 45 minutes, after which the steamed food is dug up and served. Today, most people cook this dish in a large pot.

Cobbler   A baked, unlined, deep-dish fruit pie with a biscuit or piecrust topping.

Cod   A fish so important to New England that the region's largest peninsula, Massachusetts's Cape Cod, was named after it. This fish is in a family that includes haddock, pollock, hake, and hoki. Market size is 2½ to 10 pounds. Large cod weigh 10 to 25 pounds; jumbos are 25 pounds and over. The term "scrod" generally refers to cod under 2½ pounds. Raw Atlantic cod is translucent, ranging from white to pinkish. The lean meat has a mild, clean flavor and large, tender flakes.

Common Crackers   Round, nuggetlike crackers originally from Vermont. Country stores that sold cheese provided these crackers to their customers in "cracker barrels." They are typically eaten with aged cheese or crumbled into a bowl of clam chowder.

Cornmeal   Regular cornmeal is ground between metal rollers and the hull and germ are removed so the resulting texture is finer. It also may be enriched to return nutrients that are lost. Stone-ground is ground between two stones. The hull and germ of the corn kernel are usually left on, so the texture is coarser and the meal usually has a more noticeable "corn" flavor. It also is more perishable, so it should be stored in the refrigerator or freezer to keep it from getting rancid.

Concord Grape   A robust and aromatic grape from a native species found growing in the rugged New England soil. It ripens early, escaping the killing frosts. Concord grapes were used in the first unfermented grape juice known to be produced by Dr. Thomas Welch. It is also used for grape jelly and wine.

Cranberry   A fruit from the northern bogs and one of the few fruits native to North America. Cape Cod and the island of Nantucket are known for their cranberries.

Fiddlehead Fern   The edible, young, coiled frond of a fern that emerges in spring, so named because it looks like a violin scroll. In New England, fiddleheads are available for about two weeks in April and early May.

Indian Pudding   A pudding made with cornmeal, milk, and molasses.

Johnnycake (Journey Cake)   An unleavened cornmeal pancake made without eggs or butter, so-named because it could be carried on long trips in a traveler's saddlebag and baked along the way. Cornbread, also known as "hoecake," "ashcake," and "spidercake," was a staple of any traveler during this period, since cornbread didn't spoil as easily as other breads.

Mackerel   A saltwater fish with a rich, pronounced flavor. The meat is soft, flaky, and moist. The outer bands of dark, strong-tasting meat along the midline may be cut out for a milder flavor. Immature mackerel, called "tinkers," are available in spring and weigh less than a pound. They are a traditional seasonal treat in New England.

Maple Sugar   The crystallized form of maple syrup.

Maple Syrup   By tapping the sap of sugar maple trees and boiling it down to a thick syrup and then to a sugar, Native Americans were able to produce this sweet treat and use it for flavor and for trade. It takes 60 gallons of sap to produce 1½ gallons of syrup. Real maple syrup differs markedly from maple-flavored syrups, which may contain 10 percent or less of actual maple syrup.

Molasses   A syrup derived during the processing of sugarcane into sugar. Molasses was first imported to America from the West Indies. It is commonly found in two varieties: light and dark. Light molasses is used as a syrup, while dark or blackstrap molasses is used primarily as an ingredient.

Mussel   A bivalve mollusk found in shallow coastal waters. Blue mussels from New England have a rich, sweet taste, like a blend of oysters and clams. At one time held in low esteem, blue mussels grow both wild on rocks and pilings and are farmed. Maine is the largest U.S. producer. Mussels are farmed on ropes or in mesh tubes suspended from rafts. Farmed mussels have thin, dark shells, while wild mussels have thicker, silvery shells. Mussels have beards, or byssus threads, which they use to anchor themselves to a growing medium. The beard should be removed prior to cooking. Bags or containers of mussels should display the license number of the shipper to assure they have been purchased from certified growers who harvest in approved, clean areas.

New England Boiled Dinner   This traditional meal is similar to many one-pot meals. Meat, fresh or cured, is simmered for hours, and then vegetables are added. The meat flavors the vegetables, and they both flavor the broth. The New England boiled dinner uses gray or salt-cured brisket of beef as well as parsnips and beets. A regular corned brisket is a good substitution.

Oyster   A bivalve mollusk found in shallow coastal areas. The native East Coast oysters are named according to the bay or town they are associated with—Pemaquids, Wellfleets, and Sheepscotts are a few. The large Belon oyster, also called the "European flat," was brought to America from France and thrives in New England waters. Oysters in New England are enjoyed on the half shell, smoked, in turkey stuffing for Thanksgiving, and in casseroles.

Periwinkle   Small, black or gray snail-like marine mollusk found attached to rocks and seawalls in New England coastal waters. Periwinkles usually are cooked in salted boiling water for 5 to 10 minutes, or until the black cap, used as a lid by the mollusk, can be lifted and removed easily. Periwinkles are extracted with a needle or a sharp toothpick, and served with lemon or garlic butter.

Popover   An American variation of English Yorkshire pudding, popovers are a type of muffin or bread made by pouring a batter of eggs, milk, and flour into butter that has been heated in a muffin pan. They puff up when baked and form a crisp crust and moist center.

Pumpkin   A winter squash introduced to the colonists by the Native Americans. This long-keeping squash is one of the foods that helped the colonists survive their first winter in the New World.

Red Flannel Hash   The leftovers from a New England boiled dinner are chopped and mixed with beets to make a fried mush for the next morning's breakfast. The hash is cooked slowly to form a crusty bottom and served with a poached egg on top.

Scallops   A family of bivalves with fan-shaped shells. The adductor muscle, which allows scallops to "swim" by clicking their shells together, is eaten. This mobility helps scallops escape pollutants that immobile bivalves like mussels, clams, and oysters can't avoid. There are three types of scallops in this region. They are:

Bay Scallops   Small scallops that average 70 to 100 per pound. Mild and sweet, bay scallops are considered the best-tasting of the scallops.

Cape Scallops   Found around Nantucket Island during the winter months, cape scallops are noted for their sweet flavor and are best served raw.

Sea Scallops   Large scallops that range from 20 to 40 per pound. Since sea scallops die out of water, they are always shucked at sea and kept on ice. New Bedford, Massachusetts, is the largest sea scallop port in the country. Sea scallops are farmed in New England, but production is limited. Sea scallops have a sweet, rich taste that ranges from mild to briny. Always remove the little moon-shaped strap that held the muscle to the shell.

Sea Urchin   A green, saltwater animal that looks like a spiny pincushion. It is abundant along the New England coast; the center, soft part that is eaten is referred to as "urchin roe." To serve, cut around the mouth, or bottom, of the urchin using wire cutters or scissors. Rinse gently and remove the viscera that surround the creamy golden roe attached to the top of the urchin. Invert, place on crushed ice, and serve with toast and lemon or lime wedges. The roe can also be used to flavor and garnish sauces.

Shrimp   Maine shrimp are relatives of the northern European prawn. They are small, about 50 to 60 count per pound, and sweet. They are available only from November to March.

Turkey   A large fowl indigenous to the New World. The conquistadors took them to Europe; from there, they were introduced in other parts of the world. Today's domesticated turkeys differ from wild turkeys, with the exceptionally large breasts that breeding produces.

Vermont Cheddar Cheese   A firm yellow or orange cheese made from cow's milk. One of the most difficult and most expensive cheeses to make, owing to the need for consistent milk quality and the process of cheddaring, whereby curds are stacked to force out the whey. True Cheddar cheese is made only in the summer months from the milk of one herd, from one specific farm. Other Cheddar cheese is called "factory Cheddar." It ranges from mild to extra sharp.

Menus and Recipes from
the Cuisine of New England

MENU ONE

New England Clam Chowder

Marinated Tomato and Zucchini Salad with Deep-Fried Potato-Crusted Sea Scallops

New England Boiled Dinner with Horseradish Sauce

Peach and Blueberry Cobbler

MENU TWO

Clams Casino

Butternut Squash Soup with Bay Scallops and Mushrooms

Roast Turkey Breast with Giblet Gravy and Cranberry Sauce

New England Bread Dressing

Glazed Turnips

Mashed Sweet Potatoes

Green Beans with Fried Onions

Gingerbread

MENU THREE

Mini Lobster Rolls

Vermont Country Salad

Poached Haddock with Mussels and Julienne of Vegetables

Sautéed Chicken with Apples and Pears

Browned Butter Cauliflower

Snickerdoodles

OTHER RECIPES

Roast Turkey Roulade

Cod Cakes with Tartar Sauce

Boston Baked Beans

Boston Brown Bread

Bluefish with Clams

New England Clam Chowder

4 servings

CHEF TIP: Clams naturally burrow in the sand; the outside of the shell must be scrubbed and the clams should be purged. To purge, cover the clams with salt water (⅓ cup/2.3 ounces/64 grams salt to 1 gallon/3.785 L water) and let sit for 1 to 2 hours. Adding ¼ cup/2 ounces/56 grams cornmeal to the soaking water helps expel the sand. If clams do not open after cooking, discard them; they were not alive and may be contaminated with bacteria or contain toxins.

AMOUNT	MEASURE	INGREDIENT
10	16 ounces/448 g	Cherrystone clams, washed
or		
1 cup	8 ounces/224 g	Shucked clams, chopped
2 cups	16 ounces/470 ml	Water
or		
1½ cups	12 ounces/325 ml	Clam juice
¼ cup	2 ounces/56 g	Salt pork or bacon, in ¼-inch/6 cm dice
½ cup	2 ounces/56 g	Onion, in ¼-inch/6 cm dice
½ cup	2 ounces/56 g	Celery, in ¼-inch/6 cm dice
1½ teaspoons	1.5 g	Fresh thyme, chopped
1 tablespoon	⅓ ounce/10 g	All-purpose flour
2 cups	16 ounces/470 ml	Milk, hot
4 cups	16 ounces/453 g	All-purpose potatoes, peeled, in ¼-inch/ 6 cm dice
½ cup	4 ounces/117 ml	Heavy cream, warmed
2 tablespoons	6 g	Fresh parsley, chopped
½ teaspoon, or to taste	2 ml	Tabasco
½ teaspoon, or to taste	2 ml	Worcestershire sauce
		Salt and white pepper

PROCEDURE

1. In a 3- to 4-quart (3 to 4 L) saucepan, steam the whole clams, using the 2 cups/16 ounces/470 ml water until they open; do not overcook or they will be tough. Strain the broth through a filter or cheesecloth and reserve. (If not using whole clams, substitute the 1½ cups/12 ounces/325 ml clam juice for the broth in the soup.)

2. Remove clam meat from the shells, chop, and reserve. (If not using whole clams, substitute the 1 cup/8 ounces/224 g chopped clams.)

3. In a 3- to 4-quart (3 to 4 L) saucepan over low heat, sauté the salt pork or bacon until the fat is rendered, 3 to 5 minutes. Turn up the heat to medium high, and crisp and brown the salt pork. Remove and place on a paper towel to drain.

4. Add the onion and celery to the fat in the pan, and cook slowly until translucent, 2 to 3 minutes. Add the thyme; cook 1 minute.

5. Stir in the flour and cook over low heat 8 to 10 minutes to make a blond roux.

6. Slowly add reserved broth or clam juice and warm milk, incorporating to a smooth consistency. Bring to a simmer, and cook 15 minutes.

7. Add the potatoes, cover the pot, and cook for 10 to 15, or until potatoes are just tender.

8. Add reserved clams and the warm cream; bring to a simmer, cook 3 to 5 minutes.

9. Add remaining ingredients and correct seasoning and consistency with additional water or clam broth if necessary.

10. To serve, ladle into a warm soup bowl and garnish with the crisp salt pork or bacon.

New England Clam Chowder

Marinated Tomato and Zucchini Salad with Deep-Fried Potato-Crusted Sea Scallops

Marinated Tomato and Zucchini Salad

AMOUNT	MEASURE	INGREDIENT
For the Dressing		
1 tablespoon	⅓ ounce/10 g	Shallot, minced
1 teaspoon	5 ml	Dijon mustard
2 tablespoons	6 g	Fresh basil leaves, chopped
¼ cup	2 ounces/56 ml	Extra-virgin olive oil
2 tablespoons	1 ounce/28 ml	Vegetable oil
2 tablespoons	1 ounce/28 ml	Red wine vinegar
		Salt and black pepper
For the Salad		
2 cups	16 ounces/448 g	Plum tomatoes, peeled, seeded, cut into wedges
2 cups	8 ounces/224 g	Zucchini, julienned
½ cup	1½ ounces/42 g	Red onion, very thinly sliced
1 cup	2 ounces/56 g	Romaine leaves, chopped
½ cup	56 g	Watercress, washed, dried
2 tablespoons	½ ounce/14 g	Parmesan cheese, freshly grated

PROCEDURE

1. Make the dressing. Combine the shallot, mustard, basil, and olive oil; mix well.

2. Add the vegetable oil, vinegar, salt, and pepper; stir well and allow to rest 1 hour to develop flavors.

3. Make the salad. Marinate the tomatoes, zucchini, and onion in three-fourths of the dressing for 1 hour.

4. Just before serving, toss the romaine and watercress with remaining dressing, then divide among 4 chilled plates.

5. Arrange vegetables on salad greens and sprinkle with Parmesan cheese.

Marinated Tomato and Zucchini Salad with Deep-Fried Potato-Crusted Sea Scallops

Deep-Fried Potato-Crusted Sea Scallops

 **CHEF TIP:** Place the scallops in a colander and rinse well. Using several sheets of paper towel, blot excess moisture off the scallops; they need to be very dry to brown well.

AMOUNT	MEASURE	INGREDIENT
1 tablespoon	½ ounce/15 ml	Vegetable oil
4	2 ounces/56 g	Jumbo sea scallops
		Salt and pepper
2 quarts	64 ounces/2 liters	Water
1 tablespoon	½ ounce/14 g	Kosher salt
4 medium	6 to 8 ounces each/168 to 224 g	Russet potatoes, peeled
1 quart	32 ounces/1 liter	Ice water
¼ cup	1 ounce/28 g	Potato starch or cornstarch
2		Eggs, beaten with a pinch of salt
2 cups	16 ounces/480 ml	Corn oil, for frying

PROCEDURE

1. Heat a 10-inch (25.4 cm) sauté pan (nonstick preferable) over medium heat. Add the vegetable oil. Remove the small muscle attached to each scallop. Pat the scallops dry and season with salt and pepper. Place scallops down in hot pan, give them room. Don't move the scallops for at least 30 seconds. You need a good, dark sear. The scallop will release easily off the bottom of the pan when the sear is achieved. The key is high heat and not too much oil. Turn the scallops and repeat on the other side. Caramelize both sides but scallops should remain rare in the center. Remove scallops from pan, cover, and chill in refrigerator.

2. Add the salt to the water and bring to a boil. Cut the potatoes with an Oriental turning vegetable slicer fitted with the fine blade. (Or cut potato into 1/16-inch/0.15 cm shreds lengthwise, keeping the strands as long as possible.) Drop potato strands into water and boil for 30 seconds. Remove pot from the heat and immediately strain potatoes, then shock in the ice water. Drain and spread potato strands on a dry towel for 15 to 20 minutes or until completely dry.

3. Place potato starch in a small bowl. Place the beaten egg in another small bowl. Place about ¼ cup (1 ounce/28 g) potato strands in the palm of one hand and lightly sprinkle with a little potato starch. Dip each scallop into the potato starch, shake to remove excess starch, and then apply egg, which must completely coat the scallop. Place scallops in the center of the potatoes, encasing in potato strands. Firmly shape potato around scallops. It is best to complete the encasing procedure 1 hour in advance of cooking and chill the scallops to allow the egg to set.

4. Heat the corn oil in a 1-quart (1 L) saucepan to 350°F (176°C). One at a time, place potato-coated scallops on a slotted spoon and slowly lower into the hot oil. When the potato strands are cooked sufficiently to set the potato starch, remove spoon and deep-fry scallops until crisp and golden brown, 2 minutes. Turn scallops as needed to fry evenly. Transfer the scallops to paper towels to drain excess fat. (Two scallops may be fried at the same time; be careful not to lower oil's temperature or the potato will not get crisp.)

5. Plate the salad and nestle a scallop onto the greens on each.

New England Boiled Dinner

CHEF TIP: When potatoes are tournéed, they often are named according to their size. Cocotte potatoes are about 1½ inches (3.8 cm) long, weight ½ to ¾ ounce (15–20 g). Anglaises are 2¼ to 2½ inches (5.5–6 cm) long, weight 1¼ to 1½ ounces (35–45 g). Chateau potatoes are 2½ to 2¾ inches (6–6.5 cm), weight 2 to 2¼ ounces (55–65 g).

AMOUNT	MEASURE	INGREDIENT
1 pound	448 g	Raw corned beef brisket, trimmed
2		Garlic cloves, peeled
1 tablespoon	3 g	Pickling spices
3 to 4	16 ounces/448 g	Carrots, pared and shaped (tourné), 2 per serving
8	16 ounces/448 g	Red Bliss potatoes, cut in half if large, shaped (cocotte), 2 per serving
2 to 3	6 ounces/448 g	Turnips, pared and shaped (tourné), 2 per serving
8	8 ounces, 224 g	Pearl onions, peeled
About ½ head	16 ounces/448 g	Green cabbage, cut into 4 wedges
1 tablespoon	3 g	Fresh parsley, chopped
		Cheesecloth

PROCEDURE

1. Place the corned beef in a large pot with enough cold water to cover it by 1 inch (2.5 cm); add the garlic and the pickling spices tied in cheesecloth, and bring to a boil.

2. Lower the heat and cover; simmer very gently 2 to 3 hours or until the meat is fork-tender.

3. About 30 minutes before the meat is done, add the carrots; 5 minutes later, add the potatoes; 5 minutes later, add the turnips and onions. Continue simmering until the vegetables are tender, 25 to 30 minutes; they should hold their shape.

4. Remove corned beef and any tender vegetable to a pan or bowl, adding enough of the cooking broth to just cover the meat. Wrap the container with foil to keep warm. Remove the pickling spices and discard.

5. Add the cabbage, cover, and cook until tender, 8 to 10 minutes.

6. Drain the vegetables and reserve the liquid.

7. Slice corned beef on an angle against the grain into 1/4-inch (.6 cm) slices.

8. Place the corned beef in a large bowl with hot vegetables and cooking liquid. Garnish with the parsley.

9. Serve each portion with Horseradish Sauce (recipe follows).

New England Boiled Dinner

Horseradish Sauce, Version I

4 servings

✦ **CHEF TIP:** Horseradish has a spicy flavor and was widely used in conserving canned foods for the winter. It originated in southeastern Europe and western Asia. It is resistant to the low temperatures as well as to droughts. Besides the root, horseradish has large edible leaves. The Japanese condiment wasabi, traditionally prepared from the wasabi plant, is often made with horseradish because of the scarcity of the wasabi plant.

AMOUNT	MEASURE	INGREDIENT
2 tablespoons	1 ounce/28 g	Prepared horseradish
1 cup	8 ounces/240 ml	Sour cream
1 tablespoon	½ ounce/15 ml	Lemon juice
Dash		Tabasco
1 teaspoon	5 g	Salt

PROCEDURE   Combine the ingredients, mix until smooth, and chill.

Horseradish Sauce, Version II

4 servings

AMOUNT	MEASURE	INGREDIENT
2 tablespoons	1 ounce/28 g	Prepared horseradish
¼ cup	2 ounces/60 ml	Dijon mustard
2 teaspoons	10 ml	Lemon juice
½ cup	4 ounces/120 ml	Whipping cream

PROCEDURE

1. Combine the horseradish, mustard, and lemon juice.

2. Beat the cream until soft peaks form. Fold in horseradish mixture.

3. Cover and chill 1 hour.

Peach and Blueberry Cobbler

CHEF TIP: New England peaches are ripe and juicy in late summer. Not a large crop, chefs purchase local fruit in Connecticut, Maine, New Hampshire, and Massachusetts. Maine produces 25 percent of all lowbush blueberries in North America. Wild blueberries are the official fruit of Maine.

AMOUNT	MEASURE	INGREDIENT
For the Peaches		
1½ cups	9 ounces/252 g	Ripe peeled peaches, sliced
1 cup	5 ounces/140 g	Blueberries, picked over
1 tablespoon	9 g	Sugar
For the Shortcake		
1 cup	4 ounces/112 g	All-purpose flour, sifted
2 tablespoons	18 g	Sugar
2 teaspoons	8 g	Baking powder
¼ teaspoon	2 g	Salt
4 tablespoons	2 ounces/56 g	Unsalted butter
1		Egg, lightly beaten
2 tablespoons	1 ounce/30 ml	Milk

PROCEDURE

1. Preheat the oven to 350°F (175°C).

2. Prepare the fruit. Toss the peaches and blueberries with sugar to coat evenly. Place the fruit in a baking dish.

3. Make the shortcake. Sift together the flour, sugar, baking powder, and salt.

4. Cut the butter into small pieces about the size of a hazelnut, and add to the flour mixture. Mix gently until it begins to look like cornmeal.

5. Whisk the egg and milk together. Add liquid to the flour mixture and mix just until dough sticks together; on a lightly floured surface, knead gently by hand for about 30 seconds.

6. On a lightly floured surface, roll out the dough to ¼ inch (.6 cm) thick and cut into 8 small or 4 large biscuits to cover the top of the fruit.

7. Bake for 25 to 30 minutes or until the fruit is tender and the shortcake is lightly browned.

8. Allow the cobbler to cool slightly before serving. Serve warm with cream, whipped cream, or ice cream.

Peach and Blueberry Cobbler

Clams Casino

4 servings

✦ **CHEF TIP:** To open clams, hold a clam with the hinged side against a heavy cloth over a bowl. Insert an oyster or clam knife between the shell halves. Gently twist the knife to pry open the shell and release the juices. Holding the clam firmly, move the knife around the clam, cutting the muscle at the hinge. Gently twist to pry apart the shell. Cut the clam meat from the shell. It's best to freeze the clams 15 to 20 minutes before attempting to open. Remove from the freezer and allow to warm for 3 to 5 minutes. As the clams warm up, the muscle relaxes and the shells will open slightly, making it easier to insert the clam knife.

AMOUNT	MEASURE	INGREDIENT
¼ cup	2 ounces/56 g	Bacon, in ¼-inch (.6 cm) dice
2 tablespoons	1 ounce/28 g	Shallots, minced
1 tablespoon	12 g	Garlic, minced
¼ cup	1 ounce/28 g	Red bell pepper, in ¼-inch (.6 cm) dice
¼ cup	1 ounce/28 g	Green bell pepper, in ¼-inch (.6 cm) dice
1 teaspoon	1 g	Fresh flat-leaf parsley, minced
1 teaspoon	5 ml	Lemon juice
½ cup	4 ounces/112 g	Unsalted butter, melted
1 cup	4 ounces/112 g	Dried bread crumbs
		Salt and black pepper
24	32 ounces/896 g	Littleneck or cherrystone clams
As needed		Rock salt
2		Lemons, cut in half, wrapped in cheesecloth

PROCEDURE

1. Preheat the oven to 400°F (205°C).

2. In a 10-inch (25.4 cm) sauté pan, cook the bacon over medium heat until fat is completely rendered and bacon is crisp.

3. Add the shallots, garlic, and peppers to the bacon and sauté over medium heat for approximately 2 to 3 minutes, until peppers are tender.

4. Add the parsley, lemon juice, butter, and bread crumbs; combine well and season to taste. Cool the bread-crumb mixture, set aside.

5. Open the clams with a clam knife and discard the top halves of the shells. Loosen the meat from the lower shells with the clam knife. Leave the clams in the shell. (Alternatively, steam the clams for about 5 minutes until their shells just begin to open. Set aside to cool. When cool enough to handle, remove the top shells and discard. Slide a knife under each clam to loosen it in the shell.)

6. Place clams on a baking sheet and top each clam with 1 tablespoon (½ ounce/15 ml) of the bread-crumb mixture.

7. Bake clams until they are thoroughly cooked and bread-crumb mixture is crisp, approximately 5 to 8 minutes.

8. To serve, evenly spread rock salt on warm plates (the rock salt anchors the clams in place). Place 6 clams on each warmed plate.

9. Garnish each portion with a lemon half wrapped in cheesecloth.

Butternut Squash Soup with Bay Scallops and Mushrooms

4 servings

Bay scallops are mild and sweet, often considered by chefs as the preferred scallop available in the North America. The meat is translucent when raw, appearing milky to pink in color. When cooked, the meat becomes opaque. Bay scallop meat is sweet, plump, and firm when cooked correctly. It is important to not overcook scallops or they will become tough and chewy.

AMOUNT	MEASURE	INGREDIENT
2 tablespoons	1 ounce/30 ml	Butter
3 cups	16 ounces/448 g	Butternut squash, peeled, in 1-inch (2.5 cm) dice
1 cup	6 ounces/168 g	Onion, in ¼-inch (.6 cm) dice
2 teaspoons	.32 ounce/9 g	Garlic, minced
½ tablespoon	¼ ounce/7 g	Grated fresh ginger
		Salt
½ teaspoon		Ground cinnamon
¼ teaspoon		Ground cumin
¼ teaspoon		Ground turmeric
⅛ teaspoon		Cayenne pepper
1 cup	8 ounces/240 ml	Chicken or vegetable stock
¼ cup	2 ounces/60 ml	Dry white wine
½ cup	4 ounces/120 ml	Apple cider
1 tablespoon	½ ounce/15 ml	Fresh lime juice
1 tablespoon	½ ounce/14 g	Brown sugar
2 tablespoons	1 ounce/60 ml	Heavy cream
1 tablespoon	¼ ounce/7 g	Parmesan cheese, grated
1 tablespoon	7 g	Chopped fresh tarragon and parsley

PROCEDURE

1. Over medium heat, melt the butter in a 2- to 3-quart (2 to 3 L) saucepan. Add the squash, onions, garlic, ginger, salt, cinnamon, cumin, turmeric, and cayenne. Cook, stirring frequently, until onions are translucent and soft, 6 to 8 minutes.

2. Add the stock, wine, cider, lime juice, and brown sugar. Stir to combine, bring to a boil, return to a simmer, and cook until squash is tender, 18 to 20 minutes.

3. Stir in the cream and Parmesan. Puree the soup using a food processor or standing or immersion blender until smooth; work in batches, if necessary. Strain and return to heat, correct seasoning, and bring to a simmer.

4. To serve, arrange equal portions of Sautéed Scallops and Mushrooms (recipe follows) in the center of each warm soup bowl and pour soup around. Sprinkle with the chopped herbs.

Butternut Squash Soup with Bay Scallops and Mushrooms

Sautéed Scallops and Mushrooms

4 servings

AMOUNT	MEASURE	INGREDIENT
1 cup	8 ounces/224 g	Bay scallops
2 tablespoons	1 ounce/30 ml	Olive oil
2 tablespoons	1 ounce/30 ml	Butter
½ cup	2 ounces/56 g	Leeks, white part only, julienned
½ cup	2 ounces/56 g	Wild mushrooms (shiitake or chanterelles), in ½-inch (1.2 cm) dice
1 teaspoon	.15 ounce/4.5 g	Garlic clove, minced
		Salt and pepper

PROCEDURE

1. Place the fresh or thawed scallops in a colander and rinse well. Pat dry with paper towels. (It is necessary to remove as much moisture from the surface; they need to be fairly dry to brown properly.)

2. Heat a 10-inch (25.4 cm) sauté pan (nonstick preferable) over medium-high heat. Add half the oil, then add half the butter; wait until the butter melts but does not brown, and then add scallops in a single layer. Sauté scallops until nicely brown on all sides, about 1 minute. Transfer to a holding vessel.

3. In the same pan, add the remaining oil and butter. When butter has melted, add the leeks and cook until soft, 1 to 2 minutes. Add the mushrooms and sauté until most of the moisture has cooked off, 8 to 10 minutes. Add the garlic, and cook 30 seconds to a 1 minute. Return scallops to the mixture and correct seasoning.

Roast Turkey Breast with Giblet Gravy and Cranberry Sauce

4 servings

Roast Turkey Breast

AMOUNT	MEASURE	INGREDIENT
1	2 to 3 pounds/907–1.36 kg	Bone-in turkey breast half
¼ cup	2 ounces/60 ml	Butter, softened
		Salt and pepper

1. Preheat the oven to 325°F (163°C).

2. Pat the turkey dry with paper towels. Coat breast with the butter. Season with salt and pepper.

3. Place breast on a flat roasting rack in a shallow roasting pan. Roast for 30 to 40 minutes. Remove from oven and brush with pan drippings. Return to oven and roast 20 to 30 minutes, or until a meat thermometer inserted into the thickest part reaches 165°F (74°C).

4. Remove from oven and let stand 15 minutes. To carve, cut along the breast bone and ribs to lift out the meat. Cut meat crosswise into ½-inch (1.3 cm) slices. Serve with Giblet Gravy and Cranberry Sauce (recipes follow).

Giblet Gravy

AMOUNT	MEASURE	INGREDIENT
1 tablespoon	½ ounce/14 g	Turkey giblets
		Turkey neck and wing tips
2 cups	16 ounces/480 ml	Turkey or chicken stock
2 tablespoons	1 ounce/28 g	Butter, melted
¼ cup	1 ounce/28 g	All-purpose flour
		Salt and white pepper

PROCEDURE

1. While the turkey is roasting, simmer the turkey giblets, neck, and wing tips in the stock for 1 hour. Remove giblets and dice. Strain stock.

2. Melt the butter in a 2- to 3-quart (2 to 3 L) saucepan. Add the flour and make a pale roux.

3. Combine roasting pan juices and giblet stock to make 2½ cups (20 ounces/600 ml). Add to the pale roux and bring to a simmer. Whisk vigorously until smooth, simmer on low heat for 20 to 30 minutes, and skim the sauce as necessary.

4. Correct the seasoning and add diced giblets as garnish.

New England Bread Dressing

✦ CHEF TIP: For light texture, do not pack dressing into baking pans or inside a bird. Stuffing that is baked separately is normally called "dressing."

Chefs typically do not stuff chickens and turkeys in production kitchens. Baking the dressing separately yields better results, for the following reasons: (1) stuffing inside a bird is a breeding ground for bacteria that cause food poisoning, (2) the stuffing needs additional time to heat thoroughly, which results in overcooked poultry, (3) stuffing poultry and removing the dressing after it is roasted is impractical, time-consuming, and disorderly.

AMOUNT	MEASURE	INGREDIENT
¼ cup	2 ounces/56 g	Butter
1 cup	4 ounces/113 g	Onion, in ¼-inch (.6 cm) dice
½ cup	2 ounces/56 g	Celery, in ¼-inch (.6 cm) dice
½ cup	3 ounces/85 g	Ham, cooked, in ¼-inch (.6 cm) dice
½ cup	3 ounces/85 g	Chicken meat, cooked, in ¼- inch (.6 cm) dice
¼ cup	2 ounces/56 g	Sage sausage, cooked, chopped
3 cups	3 ounces/85 g	Bread (day-old), in 1-inch (2.5 cm) cubes
2		Eggs
½ teaspoon	½ g	Dried sage, crumbled
⅛ teaspoon	⅛ g	White pepper
⅛ teaspoon	⅛ g	Dried thyme
⅛ teaspoon	⅛ g	Mace
⅛ teaspoon	⅛ g	Dried marjoram
½ teaspoon	4 g	Salt
¼ cup	2 ounces/60 ml	Chicken stock

PROCEDURE

1. Preheat the oven to 375°F (190°C)

2. In a 10-inch (25.4 cm) sauté pan, heat the butter over medium-high heat, then sauté the onion and celery until very soft, 3 to 5 minutes.

3. Add the ham, chicken, and sausage; cook 5 minutes, stirring occasionally.

4. Transfer to a bowl and mix in the bread cubes; cool.

5. Beat the eggs with the spices, salt, and stock.

6. Stir eggs into bread-cube mixture. Add more stock if necessary; the dressing should be moist but not soggy. Place dressing in a greased 3-quart shallow (or other appropriate pan) baking dish.

7. Bake uncovered until top is brown and dressing reaches 165°F (74°C) internal temperature.

Cranberry Sauce

✦ **CHEF TIP:** White cranberries are the same species as the familiar red ones, except that they are harvested about three weeks earlier, before they become crimson. Some say the white berries are smoother and milder than the red berries.

AMOUNT	MEASURE	INGREDIENT
½ cup	3½ ounces/100 g	Sugar
2 tablespoons	1 ounce/28 ml	Orange juice
¼ cup	2 ounces/55 ml	Water
3 cups	8 ounces/226 g	Cranberries, fresh or frozen
Pinch		Ground cinnamon

PROCEDURE

1. Combine the sugar, orange juice, and water in a pan and bring to a boil.

2. Add the cranberries and cinnamon. Simmer until cranberries burst, approximately 15 minutes. Simmer for 5 more minutes or until reduced to desired consistency.

3. Remove from heat, cool, and refrigerate.

Glazed Turnips

4 servings

AMOUNT	MEASURE	INGREDIENT
3 cups	12 ounces/340 g	Turnips, peeled, in 1-inch (2.5 cm) dice
½ cup	4 ounces/115 ml	Chicken stock
2 tablespoons	1 ounce/28 ml	Unsalted butter
2 tablespoons	1 ounce/28 ml	Maple syrup
		Salt and white pepper

PROCEDURE

1. Combine the turnips in a 2- to 3-quart (2 to 3 L) saucepan with the chicken stock, butter, and maple syrup.

2. Bring to a simmer and cover the pan. Stir occasionally. Simmer until the liquid has evaporated (10 to 12 minutes); do not overcook turnips. If turnips cook before liquid has reduced, remove and continue to reduce the liquid to a glaze, then return turnips and toss to coat.

3. Season with salt and white pepper.

Mashed Sweet Potatoes

AMOUNT	MEASURE	INGREDIENT
5 cups	20 ounces/567 g	Sweet potatoes, peeled, quartered
½ teaspoon	4 g	Salt
6 tablespoons	3 ounces/90 ml	Heavy cream, heated
¼ cup	2 ounces/56 g	Butter, softened

PROCEDURE

1. In a 4- to 5-quart (4 to 5 L) pot, cover the sweet potatoes with water and season with salt. Bring to a boil, reduce the heat, and simmer until fork-tender, approximately 25 minutes.

2. Drain sweet potatoes and let cool briefly. Put them through a food mill, then into a bowl.

3. Add the cream and butter to sweet potatoes. Mix and correct seasoning.

Green Beans with Fried Onions

4 servings

AMOUNT	MEASURE	INGREDIENT
2 cups	8 ounces/226 g	Green beans, trimmed
½ cup	2 ounces/56 g	Onion, thinly sliced
2 cups	16 ounces/480 ml	Corn oil, for frying
½ cup	2 ounces/56 g	All-purpose flour
		Salt and black pepper
2 tablespoons	1 ounce/28 g	Unsalted butter
1 cup	2½ ounces/70 g	White mushrooms, sliced

PROCEDURE

1. Cook the green beans in boiling salted water until tender. Shock beans in an ice-water bath and reserve.

2. Soak the onion slices in ice water for 1 hour.

3. Heat the oil in a deep-fryer to 375°F (190°C).

4. Drain and dry onion slices thoroughly. Combine the flour and salt and pepper. Toss the onion slices in the seasoned flour until coated. Shake off the excess flour. Deep-fry the onion slices until golden brown and crisp, 1 to 2 minutes.

5. In a 10-inch (25.4 cm) sauté pan, melt the butter and sauté the mushrooms over medium-high heat until tender, golden brown and caramelized, 4 to 5 minutes.

6. Add the reserved beans to the mushrooms and heat through.

7. Top beans with the fried onions just before serving.

Gingerbread

CHEF TIP: For a spicy gingerbread, add up to ½ teaspoon ground black pepper to the dry ingredients. The ground ginger can be replaced with 1 tablespoon grated fresh ginger for even more moistness and added zing. Mix the grated ginger in with the butter.

AMOUNT	MEASURE	INGREDIENT
½ cup	4 ounces/120 ml	Butter
½ cup packed	4 ounces/112 g	Brown sugar
1 cup	11½ ounces/345 ml	Molasses
1		Egg
1½ cups	11 ounces/308 g	All-purpose flour
1 teaspoon	2 g	Ground ginger
½ teaspoon	1 g	Ground cinnamon
¼ teaspoon	½ g	Ground cloves
½ teaspoon	2 g	Salt
1 teaspoon	4 g	Baking soda
1 cup	8 ounces/240 ml	Hot water
1 cup	8 ounces/240 ml	Heavy cream, whipped

PROCEDURE

1. Preheat the oven to 350°F (175°C).

2. Line an 8-inch (20.3 cm) square baking pan with parchment paper. Butter and flour parchment and sides of pan, or spray both with nonstick baking spray.

3. Cream the butter and brown sugar until light and fluffy. Beat in the molasses and egg.

4. Sift the flour and spices together and then sift over the mixture; blend until smooth.

5. Dissolve the baking soda in hot water, and then add gradually stirring into batter; the mixture will be thin.

6. Pour the batter into the baking pan and bake for 40 to 45 minutes, or until a toothpick inserted in center comes out clean and the cake is light and springy.

7. Serve warm with whipped cream.

Mini Lobster Rolls

4 servings

 CHEF TIP: The flavor of garlic becomes rich, sweet, and smoky after roasting.

AMOUNT	MEASURE	INGREDIENT
1		Head of garlic, outer papery layers removed
1 tablespoon	½ ounce/15 ml	Olive oil
		Salt and pepper
4 quarts	4 liters	Water
½ cup	2 ounces/56 g	Celery, roughly chopped
1		Lemon, cut in half
½ cup	2 ounces/56 g	White onion, roughly chopped
1¼ to 1½ pound	20 to 24 ounces/560 to 672 g	Lobster
¼ cup	2 ounces/60 ml	Mayonnaise
¼ cup	1½ ounces/42 g	Green onion, finely chopped
¼ cup	1 ounce/28 g	Celery, minced
1 tablespoon		Fresh tarragon, chopped
1 tablespoon	½ ounce/15 ml	Dijon mustard
½ teaspoon		Old Bay seasoning
3 tablespoons	1½ ounces/45 ml	Butter, softened
4	1¾ to 2 ounces/48 to 56 g each	Soft dinner rolls, top-split
½ cup	1 ounce/28 g	Arugula

PROCEDURE

1. Preheat the oven to 350°F (176°C). Cut the top off the head of garlic, exposing the cloves. Drizzle with olive oil, season with salt and pepper. Wrap in foil and roast in the oven for 40 to 45 minutes, or until the garlic is soft and fragrant. Remove from oven, unwrap, and allow to cool. Separate the cloves and squeeze the roasted garlic from the skins or pass through a food mill. Reserve ½ tablespoons (¼ ounce/8 ml) for recipe.

2. Combine the water, celery, lemon, and onion in a 6-quart (6 L) pot and bring to a boil. Plunge lobster in head first. Allow water to return to a simmer, and cook for 5 minutes. Remove pot from heat. Leave lobster in hot water for 2 more minutes.

3. Plunge lobster into an ice water bath to stop the cooking. When lobster is cool enough to handle, break apart the tail and claws and remove the meat. Reserve the lobster shell for another use. Cut lobster meat into about ¼-inch (.6 cm) pieces. Place in a mixing bowl and chill until needed.

4. Combine the mayonnaise, green onion, celery, tarragon, mustard and seasoning; mix well to combine. Fold in lobster meat.

5. Place the butter and roasted garlic in a small bowl and mix until smooth.

6. Split the dinner rolls and spread the garlic butter evenly on the cut sides. Place rolls on a baking pan and toast in the oven until golden, 3 to 5 minutes. Remove from oven and allow to cool until warm. Evenly distribute the lobster mixture on the bottom halves of the buns, place the arugula on the lobster, and finish with the top halves of the rolls.

Vermont Country Salad

AMOUNT	MEASURE	INGREDIENT
1 tablespoon	½ ounce/15 ml	Maple syrup
2 tablespoons	1 ounce/30 ml	Apple cider vinegar
½ teaspoon		Dijon mustard
½ teaspoon	.07 ounces/2.4 g	Garlic clove, minced
¼ cup	2 ounces/60 ml	Olive oil
		Salt and pepper
¼ cup	2 ounces/56 g	Bacon crumbles, rendered from 5 ounces (140 g), cooked until crisp
2 cups	4 ounces/112 g	Mesclun (baby field greens)
1 cup	4 ounces/112 g	Whole wheat croutons
½ cup	2 ounces/56 g	Cheddar cheese, shredded

PROCEDURE

1. In a medium bowl, combine the maple syrup, cider vinegar, Dijon mustard, and garlic; mix well. Add the oil in a steady stream, whisking constantly. Season with salt and pepper and set aside.

2. In a large bowl, combine the bacon, mesclun, croutons, cheese, and enough salad dressing to coat ingredients. Toss to combine.

3. To serve, mound on chilled plates and serve immediately.

Vermont Country Salad

Poached Haddock with Mussels and Julienne of Vegetables

4 servings

✦ **CHEF TIP:** Mussels are not traditionally served raw and the method for cleaning them is similar to that used for clams. Mussels do not live long after the shaggy beards have been removed, so the beards are normally removed just before cooking.

AMOUNT	MEASURE	INGREDIENT
½ cup	2 ounces/56 g	Celery, julienned
½ cup	2 ounces/56 g	Carrot, julienned
½ cup	2 ounces/56 g	Zucchini, julienned
4 pieces	4 ounces/112 g each	Haddock or cod fillet
24	16 ounces/448 g	Mussels, cleaned and debearded
¾ cup	6 ounces/180 ml	Dry white wine
½ cup	2 ounces/56 g	Leeks, julienned
½ cup	4 ounces/120 ml	Heavy cream
¼ teaspoon		Freshly grated nutmeg
2 tablespoons	1 ounce/30 ml	Butter
2 tablespoons	7 g	Fresh parsley, chopped
		Salt and pepper

PROCEDURE

1. Separately but in the same salted boiling water, blanch the celery, carrot, and zucchini until tender but still firm, 1 to 3 minutes. Drain and shock each in an ice water bath, then drain again. Reserve 1¼ cups (10 ounces/300 ml) cooking water.

2. Bring 1 cup (8 ounces/240 ml) cooking water, wine, and leeks to a simmer in a large pot. Add the mussels, cover, and steam 5 minutes, until they have opened. Remove mussels from cooking liquid. Strain liquid into a 10- to 12-inch (25.4 to 30.5 cm) sauté pan. Remove mussels from shells.

3. Add the fish fillets to the cooking liquid, bring to a simmer, cover, and poach 6 to 8 minutes or until flaky. Transfer fish to a holding dish.

4. Reduce the fish cooking liquid to ½ cup (4 ounces/120 ml). Add the cream and reduce by half or to nappe consistence. Add the nutmeg and correct seasoning. Whisk in the butter, combining well. Return mussels to the pan, heat thoroughly (do not boil), and add the parsley.

5. In a separate pan, combine remaining 2 ounces/60 ml vegetable cooking liquid with julienne vegetables and heat thoroughly, then correct seasoning.

6. Plate a fish fillet on each plate, coat with sauce, and top with julienned vegetables.

Poached Haddock with Mussels and Julienne of Vegetables

Sautéed Chicken with Apples and Pears

CHEF TIP: The Rhode Island Red chicken is dual purpose. This breed yields up to 120 eggs per year, but the chickens are mainly raised for meat production.

AMOUNT	MEASURE	INGREDIENT
¼ cup	2 ounces/56 g	Kosher salt
1 quart	1 liter	Cold water
1 tablespoon		Whole black peppercorns
¼ cup	.33 ounce/10.5 g	Fresh thyme sprigs
¼ cup	.33 ounce/10.5 g	Fresh marjoram sprigs
¼ cup	.33 ounce/10.5 g	Fresh sage sprigs
4		Bay leaves
4	5 ounces/140 g each	Skinless, boneless chicken breasts, tapped to even thickness
As needed		All-purpose flour
6 tablespoons	3 ounces/90 ml	Butter
¼ cup	1 ounce/28 g	Celery, in ¼-inch (.6 cm) dice
½ cup	2 ounces/56 g	Onion, in ¼-inch (.6 cm) dice
1 cup	6 ounces/168 g	Ripe pear, pared, cored, cut into ¼-inch (.6 cm) wedges
1 cup	6 ounces/168 g	Granny Smith apple, pared, cored, cut ¼-inch (.6 cm) wedges
1 cup	8 ounces/240 ml	Chicken stock
¼ cup	2 ounces/60 ml	Sweet apple cider
		Salt and pepper
2 tablespoons	½ ounce/14 g	Green onion, minced

PROCEDURE

1. Combine the cold water, kosher salt, peppercorns, herb sprigs and bay leaves in a pot. Bring to a boil and remove from heat, then chill completely. Add the chicken and let it sit in the brine for 2 hours or longer. Remove chicken from brine and rinse in cold water. Pat dry.

2. Heat a 10- to 12-inch (25.4–30.5 cm) sauté pan over medium-high heat. Add 2 tablespoons (1 ounce/30 ml) of the butter. Dredge chicken in the flour and shake to remove excess, then add to pan. Sauté until brown on both sides, 4 minutes total, but not cooked through. Remove chicken from pan.

3. Add the celery and onion to the pan the chicken was cooked in, and over medium heat cook 3 minutes or until onion is soft and translucent. Add 2 tablespoons (1 ounce/30 ml) butter and the fruit, and cook 5 to 6 minutes or until lightly browned. The pear and apple should be cooked but not soft.

4. Return chicken to pan, and add the stock and cider; cover, bring to a simmer, and cook over low heat 5 to 6 minutes or until chicken is cooked through. Do not overcook the chicken or the meat will be dry.

5. Remove and loosely cover chicken to keep warm. Reduce the liquid in the fruit-vegetable mixture to a glaze, thick and syrupy, 3 to 5 minutes. Add remaining 2 tablespoons (1 ounce/30 ml) butter to the pan, whisk to combine into the sauce, and check seasoning.

6. Plate the chicken and sauce, and distribute the vegetables and fruit evenly. Sprinkle with the green onions.

Sautéed Chicken with Apples and Pears

Browned Butter Cauliflower

AMOUNT	MEASURE	INGREDIENT
½ cup	4 ounces/120 ml	Butter
2 cups	12 ounces/336 g	Cauliflower, in pea-size florets (½ head)
¼ cup	1½ ounces/42 g	Shallots, minced
2 tablespoons	.48 ounce/14 g	Garlic, minced
1 tablespoon	.28 ounce/7 g	Chives, minced
		Salt and pepper

PROCEDURE

1. Heat a 10-inch (25.4 cm) sauté pan over medium heat. Melt the butter and heat until the milk solids caramelize and the butter has a nutty odor, 1 minute.

2. Add the cauliflower and sauté until al dente, 3 to 5 minutes. Add the shallots and garlic, and sauté 1 minute.

3. Add the chives, correct the seasoning, and serve.

Snickerdoodles

CHEF TIP: Snickerdoodles are drop cookies; they have been cited in print from at least 1889. No knows who came up with the name, but we do know that they have been popular in New England for centuries. *The Joy of Cooking* claims that snickerdoodles are probably German in origin, and that the name is a corruption of the German word for "snail dumpling." Snickerdoodles are characterized by a cracked surface; this cookie may be crisp or soft, depending on preference.

AMOUNT	MEASURE	INGREDIENT
2 cups	12 ounces/336 g	All-purpose flour
¼ teaspoon		Baking soda
¼ teaspoon		Cream of tartar
Pinch		Salt
½ cup	4 ounces/120 ml	Butter, softened
2 tablespoons	1 ounce/30 ml	Vegetable shortening
1½ cups	12 ounces/336 g	Sugar
1		Large egg
2 tablespoons	1 ounce/30 ml	Milk
½ teaspoon		Vanilla extract
1 tablespoon		Ground cinnamon

PROCEDURE

1. Preheat oven to 375°F (190°C)

2. Sift together the flour, baking soda, cream of tartar, and salt.

3. In a mixer bowl with the paddle attachment, combine the butter, shortening, and 1 cup (8 ounces/224 g) of the sugar for about 2 minutes. Scrape down the sides of the bowl and add the egg, then beat well to combine. Add the milk and vanilla a little at a time. Add the dry ingredients, and beat to just combine—do not overmix. Chill the dough for 1 hour.

4. Line a baking sheet with a silicone baking mat or parchment paper.

5. Form the dough into 1-inch (2.5 cm) balls. Combine the remaining ½ cup (4 ounces/112 g) sugar with the cinnamon. Roll the chilled dough balls in the cinnamon sugar. Place about 2 inches apart on the prepared baking sheets, then lightly flatten balls with the sugared bottom of a measuring cup.

6. Bake cookies until set in the center and beginning to crack (they will just begin to color a light brown), 8 to 10 minutes, rotating the baking sheets after 5 minutes. Begin to check for doneness after 7 minutes.

7. Transfer the baking sheets to a wire rack to cool for 2 to 3 minutes before transferring the cookies to the rack to cool completely.

Roast Turkey Roulade

4 to 8 servings

AMOUNT	MEASURE	INGREDIENT
1	2 to 3 pound/907–1.36 kg	Skin on, bone-in turkey breast half
		Salt and pepper
For the Filling		
1¼ cups	6 ounces/170 g	Turkey leg meat, trimmed, cubed
1		Egg white
		Salt and white pepper
1 teaspoon	1 g	Fresh thyme, chopped
1 teaspoon	1 g	Fresh parsley, chopped
To Roast		
1 cup	4 ounces/113 g	Onion, peeled, roughly chopped
½ cup	2 ounces/56 g	Celery, roughly chopped
½ cup	2 ounces/56 g	Carrot, peeled, roughly chopped
2 cups	16 ounces/470 ml	Chicken stock
		Salt and black pepper

PROCEDURE

1. Remove the skin from the turkey breast, being careful to keep the skin in one piece. Lay out the skin in a rectangle on a covered sheet pan and put in the refrigerator or freezer to chill.

2. Bone the turkey breast and reserve the bones. Butterfly the breast into a rectangle. Place between two pieces of parchment paper or plastic film; tap the breast gently with a mallet until it is approximately ¼ inch (.6 cm) thick, then season and chill 15 to 20 minutes.

3. Make the filling. Place the leg meat and any breast trimmings in a chilled food processor bowl. Add the egg white and chop until smooth. Add the seasoning and herbs, and combine well. Cook a small portion to taste for seasoning and adjust, if necessary.

4. Preheat the oven to 450°F (232°C).

5. Place the sheet pan with the turkey skin on counter and remove cover. Lay the turkey meat onto the turkey skin. Top the breast meat with the leg meat, leaving a ½-inch (1.2 cm) margin on all sides.

6. Making one roll, roll up the turkey in the skin to form a tight roll. The skin should surround the outside of meat only. Truss the roll as you would a roast. Season to taste.

7. Prepare the roast. Chop the reserved turkey bones and place bones and chopped vegetables in a roasting pan. Place the turkey roll on top and roast for 15 minutes to sear the skin. Turn the oven down to 350° (176°C), add the stock to the pan, and roast until the turkey reaches an internal temperature of 165°F (74°C).

8. Remove roast from the oven. Place on a platter and keep warm. Strain the pan juices and use to make Giblet Gravy (page 25). Serve with Cranberry Sauce (page 27).

(Bottom to top) Green Beans with Fried Onions, Mashed Sweet Potatoes, Roast Turkey Roulade, Giblet Gravy and Cranberry Sauce, Glazed Turnips

Cod Cakes with Tartar Sauce

Cod Cakes

AMOUNT	MEASURE	INGREDIENT
1	8 ounces/226 g	Codfish fillet
2 cups	12 ounces/340 g	All-purpose potatoes, peeled, cooked, mashed
1 teaspoon	1 g	Fresh parsley, minced
1 teaspoon	1 g	Chives, minced
	Pinch	Mace
		Salt and white pepper
1		Egg
½ cup	2 ounces/56 g	Dry bread crumbs
2 tablespoons	1 ounce/28 ml	Heavy cream
¼ cup	2 ounces/56 g	Clarified butter
1 teaspoon	1 g	Fresh parsley, minced, for garnish

PROCEDURE

1. Poach the codfish until just cooked; drain and cool. Chop into ½-inch (1.2 cm) pieces.

2. Add the mashed potatoes, parsley, chives, mace, and white pepper and mix well. Add the egg and mix again. Adjust consistency with heavy cream.

3. Form into 8 patties about ¾ inch (1.9 cm) thick. Dip both sides of each patty into the bread crumbs to coat.

4. Heat the clarified butter in a 10-inch (25.4 cm) sauté pan and fry patties about 4 minutes on each side, until brown and crisp.

5. Drain on paper towels, garnish with parsley, and serve with Tartar Sauce (recipe follows).

For Codfish Balls

Prepare the ingredients as above but roll the mixture into 1-inch (2.54 cm) balls.

Fry in hot oil and serve as hors d'oeuvre.

Tartar Sauce

AMOUNT	MEASURE	INGREDIENT
½ cup	4 ounces/113 g	Mayonnaise
2 tablespoons	1 ounce/28 g	Dill pickles, finely diced
2 tablespoons	1 ounce/28 g	Capers, finely diced
1		Egg, hard-boiled, chopped
1 tablespoon	½ ounce/15 ml	Lemon juice
		Salt and black pepper
Dash		Worcestershire sauce
Dash		Tabasco

PROCEDURE

1. Mix the mayonnaise, dill pickles, capers, hard-boiled egg, and lemon juice in a bowl. Blend until all ingredients are thoroughly incorporated.

2. Season to taste with salt, pepper, Worcestershire sauce, and Tabasco. Chill before serving.

Boston Baked Beans

CHEF TIP: The Native Americans of New England slow-cooked their beans in pits, seasoned with maple sugar and bear fat and wrapped in deer hides. The Puritans' belief in minimal work on the Sabbath led to the widespread practice of making beans on Saturday night, to be eaten on Sunday.

AMOUNT	MEASURE	INGREDIENT
1 cup	8 ounces/226 g	Dried navy beans, pea beans, or other small white beans
¾ cup	4 ounces/113 g	Salt pork, rind removed
2		Garlic cloves, minced
½ cup	3 ounces/85 g	Ripe tomato, peeled, seeded, diced
½ teaspoon	3 g	Salt
1 teaspoon	2 g	Black pepper
2 tablespoons	½ ounce/14 g	Dry mustard
¼ cup	2 ounces/55 ml	Molasses
¼ cup	2 ounces/56 g	Brown sugar
1		Bay leaf
1½ tablespoons	¾ ounce/23 ml	Cider vinegar
1 cup	4 ounces/113 g	Onion, in ½-inch (1.2 cm) dice

PROCEDURE

1. Rinse the beans, pick over to remove any small stones, and cover with cold water. Let stand overnight. Drain.

2. Add half the salt pork to the beans in a 2- to 3-quart (2 to 3 L) pot, add water to cover, cover, and simmer until beans are tender, about 1 hour.

3. Drain beans, reserving the liquid. Dice the salt pork. Set the beans aside.

4. Preheat the oven to 300°F (149°C).

5. Place 2 cups (16 ounces/470 ml) cooking liquid (add water if necessary to reach this amount) in a large saucepan with the garlic, tomato, salt and pepper, mustard, molasses, brown sugar, bay leaf, and vinegar. Simmer 2 minutes.

6. Cut the remaining salt pork into thin slices and score crosswise so they will not curl during cooking.

7. Line the bottom of a 2-quart (64 ounces/2 L) bean pot or casserole with the diced pork and the onion. Place the beans on top.

8. Pour the simmered mixture over. Top with the sliced salt pork. Cover and bake for 3 hours, checking occasionally to be sure the liquid is just barely covering the beans. After 2 hours, remove the cover and cook for 1 hour more. Remove the strips of salt pork and the bay leaves, and stir the pot before serving.

Note: By precooking the beans, you should save 2 to 3 hours of cooking time. Traditionally, step 2 is not done.

Boston Brown Bread

AMOUNT	MEASURE	INGREDIENT
½ cup	2½ ounces/70 g	Bread flour
½ cup	2¼ ounces/63 g	Whole wheat flour
½ cup	3 ounces/83 g	Cornmeal
1 teaspoon	4 g	Baking soda
½ teaspoon	3 g	Salt
⅓ cup	3 ounces/85 ml	Molasses
½ cup	4 ounces/115 ml	Buttermilk
½ cup, scant	2½ ounces/70 g	Raisins

PROCEDURE

1. Preheat the oven to 350°F (175°C). Butter a 1-quart (32 ounces/1 L) pudding mold or a 1-pound (453 g) coffee can.

2. Combine the flours, cornmeal, baking soda, and salt. Stir in the molasses and buttermilk. Fold in the raisins.

3. Fill the mold or coffee can with the batter. It should come about two-thirds of the way up. Cover the top with foil and tie securely with a string to make it airtight. Place in a deep pan and fill the pan with boiling water to come halfway up the side of the mold.

4. Place in oven and steam for 2 hours, checking the water level after 1 hour. Add more water if needed. Check for doneness by sticking a skewer into the bread; it will come out clean when done.

5. Remove string and foil, and allow bread to cool for 1 hour before unmolding. Serve warm.

Bluefish with Clams

CHEF TIP: Bluefish has a distinctive taste, and it takes well to strong flavors. Small mackerel can be substituted for bluefish.

AMOUNT	MEASURE	INGREDIENT
4	4 to 6 ounces/113–170 g each	Bluefish fillets, skin on
2 tablespoons	1 ounce/28 ml	Vegetable oil
		Salt and black pepper
3 tablespoons	1½ ounces/42 ml	Olive oil
2		Bay leaves
6		Garlic cloves, finely minced
1 cup	6 ounces/170 g	Onion, in ¼-inch (.6 cm) dice
¼ cup	2 ounces/55 ml	Dry white wine
¼ cup	2 ounces/55 ml	Fish stock or water
24	32 ounces/907 g	Littleneck clams, scrubbed
1 teaspoon	5 g	Fresh rosemary, chopped
1 teaspoon	5 g	Fresh basil, chopped
¼ cup	28 g	Fresh flat-leaf parsley
6 tablespoons	3 ounces/84 g	Unsalted butter

PROCEDURE

1. Preheat the broiler or oven to 400°F (205°C).

2. Trim the bluefish and remove any scales or bones. Rub the fillets with vegetable oil and season with salt and pepper.

3. Lay the fillets on a broiler pan and broil until just done, 5 to 7 minutes.

4. Heat the olive oil in a medium saucepan over medium heat and add the bay leaves. When the bay leaves begin to brown, add the garlic and onion. Cook until the onion 3 to 4 minutes, or until lightly browned.

5. Turn the heat to high and add the wine and stock. When the liquid begins to boil, add the clams and cover the saucepan.

6. When the clams open, remove them from the pan. Remove the bay leaves and add the rosemary, basil, and parsley. Swirl in the butter, and season with more pepper. (The clams provide enough salt.)

7. To serve, place one fillet on each plate, place 6 clams around the fillet, and spoon the pan sauce over both.

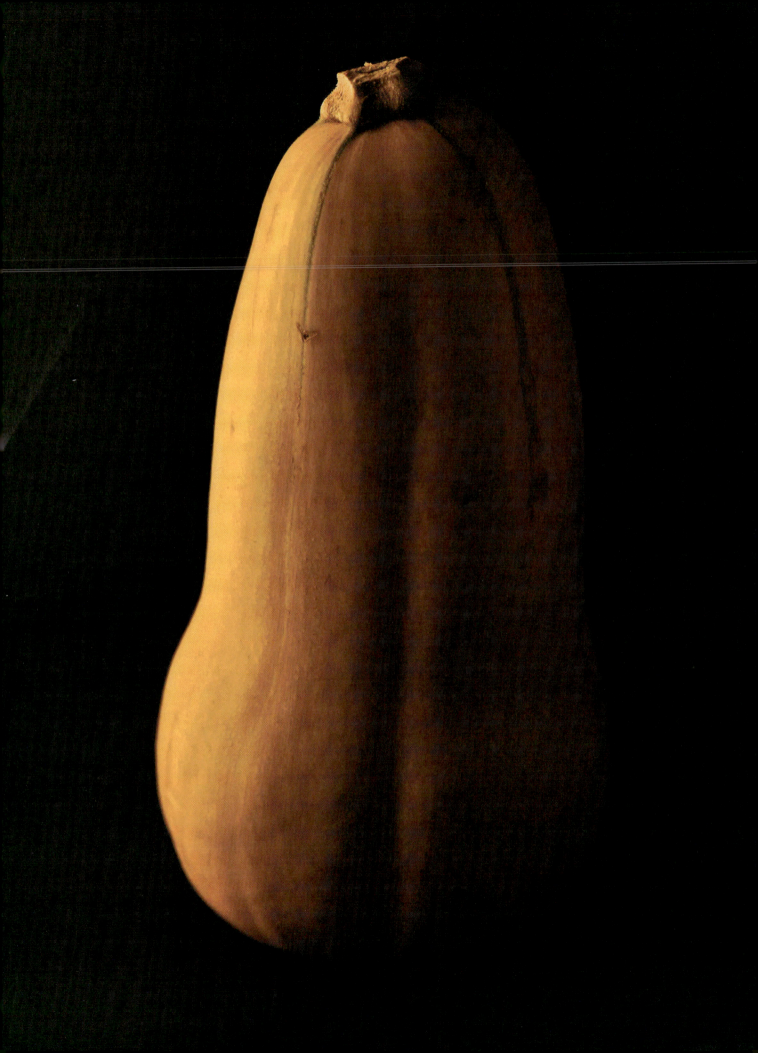

The Cuisine of the
Mid-Atlantic

The Mid-Atlantic region, with its mild climate, abundance of river valleys with rich soil, and extensive coastline, was a perfect environment for the orchards and farms established by the early settlers who emigrated to American from England, Germany, the Netherlands, and other Western European countries. People from all over the world who have been attracted to the large cities of the Mid-Atlantic have, over the years, played an important role in the cuisine of this region.

New York   The apple is the state fruit of "The Empire State," so it makes sense that the apple muffin is the state muffin. The state tree is the sugar maple.

New Jersey   "The Garden State" has the brook trout as its state fish and its state tree is the red oak.

Pennsylvania   "The Keystone State" adopted the ruffed grouse as its state bird; its state tree is the hemlock.

Delaware   Known as "The First State," Delaware chose the blue hen as the state bird. The state flower is the peach blossom, and sweet goldenrod is the state herb.

Maryland   The Maryland blue crab is the state crustacean of "The Old Line State." The rockfish is the state fish.

Virginia   While the state is often referred to as "Old Dominion," "Virginia Is for Lovers" is the popular state slogan. The oyster is the state shell.

West Virginia   Known as "The Mountain State," West Virginia has the golden delicious apple as the state fruit. The sugar maple is the state tree, and the honeybee is the state insect.

Throughout the 1600s and 1700s, additional British colonies were founded in the New World, each for a different reason. Together, the colonies represented a wide variety of people, skills, motives, industries, resources, and agricultural production. This diversity continues to be seen in the distinct features found in each area of the Mid-Atlantic states.

NEW YORK, AMERICA'S FIRST "MELTING POT"

New York's ethnic heritage began in the 17th century, when it was founded as New Amsterdam colony by the Dutch. Before long the colony's population reached 1,000, and its residents spoke more than 15 different languages. For many immigrants, the new colony meant religious freedom. New York's first religious refugees were French Huguenots who settled in what is now considered the Catskills. Religious persecution in the 18th century brought a wave of German immigrants who settled in the Hudson and Mohawk valleys. Later, pogroms in Eastern Europe brought hundreds of thousands of Jewish people to New York City.

Other immigrants arrived later in search of a better living. A potato famine in Ireland sent thousands of Irish people to New York in the mid-19th century. These Irish laborers helped build the Erie Canal and the state's first railroads. In the early 20th century, Italian immigrants settled in central New York State. Poles, Lithuanians, Romanians, and Russians were drawn to the industrial towns of Buffalo, Syracuse, and Schenectady.

Today, the diverse ethnic makeup of New York City significantly influences the city's cuisine. The Italian and Chinese influences are seen throughout the city but especially in Little Italy and Chinatown, whereas the Lower East Side remains the traditional home of Russian, Polish, German, and Ukrainian Jews, who introduced the delicatessen to America. Just north of Central Park in Manhattan is Harlem, where the culinary influences of African Americans, Caribbeans, and Puerto Ricans are seen. Queens has one of the largest foreign-born populations of any county in the United States. The many ethnic enclaves are attractive to immigrants looking to live among people of the same background.

Originally a haven for Italians, Germans, and other working-class immigrant populations, the borough of Queens now includes large numbers of Koreans, Chinese, South Asians, those from Caribbean nations, Africans from all different countries, and people from India, Pakistan, and Bangladesh. Russian immigrants are concentrated in Brooklyn's Brighton Beach, which is sometimes called Little Odessa.

New York State is one of the top dairy producers in the nation. Dairy products account for over half of the state's total farm income, with more than 10,000 dairy farms in operation. New York farmers also raise beef cattle, hogs, pigs, sheep, chickens, turkeys, and ducks. Apples are New York's major fruit, and there are over 3,000 apple orchards in the state.

NEW JERSEY, "THE GARDEN STATE"

New Jersey's official nickname derived from its having so many farms. The name dates back to its early European settlers, who were so pleased with the fertile soil that they wrote letters to family in Europe, calling their new home a "garden spot." Rich soil and plentiful rain make this state one of the most productive farmlands in the nation. New Jersey ranks among the top ten states in its production of blueberries, peaches, lettuce, tomatoes, and apples.

Indeed, food products are one of the state's leading enterprises. Popular brand-name food items made in New Jersey include M & M's candy, Campbell's soups, Oreo cookies, Lipton tea, Heinz ketchup, and Budweiser beer. Along the coast, the fishing industry is also active. New Jersey, once known as the "Clam State," is still a leading producer of clams. The catch off New Jersey's shore also includes scallops, swordfish, tuna, squid, lobster, and flounder.

PENNSYLVANIA

Pennsylvania, and Philadelphia in particular, are known as the birthplace of American independence; *Philadelphia* is Greek for "City of Brotherly Love." Toward the end of the 17th century, William Penn, a member of the Society of Friends (also known as the Quakers), was granted the right to begin a North American colony as a Quaker province. He invited Europeans seeking religious freedom to settle in his colony, and many people, beginning with the Mennonites, accepted his invitation. The Mennonites were followed by the Amish and the Moravians, who first arrived in Philadelphia. These German-speaking people soon became known as the best farmers in the region. Over time, many of these settlers continued their migration west; however, those who remained in Pennsylvania became known as the "Pennsylvania Dutch." Called "Dutch" owing to a mispronunciation of the name of their language, *Deutsche,* they settled in and around Lancaster, where their descendants still live today.

In a life marked by simplicity and peace, these people prepare food referred to as "plain and plenty." Homemade bread, dumplings, doughnuts, and chicken pot pie are specialties. Hearty soups and stews utilize all foods. Home gardens provide fresh fruits and vegetables, and excess from the garden is preserved as pickles, preserves, relishes, and fruit butters.

Food is one of Pennsylvania's most important products. The Hershey factory is the world's biggest producer of chocolate. The world's largest pretzel factory is located near Lancaster, and Lancaster's Central Market is the country's oldest continuously operating farmers' market. Milk is the state's most important farm product, and Pennsylvania is one of the country's leading dairy states. Apples, peaches, cherries, and grapes grow well in the region. Pennsylvania leads the nation in the production of mushrooms, and Kennett Square houses the world's largest mushroom facility. White button mushrooms and exotic mushrooms such as portobellos, chanterelles, and cepes are harvested; Pennsylvania hosts an annual Mushroom Festival in the Brandywine Valley each September.

MARYLAND AND DELAWARE

When the colonists arrived in the Mid-Atlantic region, they discovered that over 40 rivers flowed into the Chesapeake Bay, where the mix of fresh and salt water was home to an amazing quantity and variety of seafood. The colonists quickly learned from the Native Americans how to gather oysters and blue crabs from the Chesapeake Bay, which in the local language meant "great shellfish bay." Oysters, a familiar food to the European settlers, were found in such quantities that not only was the meat consumed but the shells were used for brickmaking and for lining paths. Maryland's waters still produce more oysters than any other state, and the total commercial seafood catch drives the state's economy.

OYSTERS

Two-thirds of the nation's oyster harvest is of Eastern oysters. They are harvested from natural beds and farmed along the East Coast. Because of different conditions in coastal areas—nutrients in the water, salinity levels, temperature, and so on—oysters vary in taste from one location to the next; hence, they often bear the name of the region where they were grown as a means of distinguishing their flavor. The Blue Point oyster is originally from Long Island Sound, but this is now a generic term for all Atlantic oysters. Other names include Chesapeake Bay, Chincoteague, Kent Island, Pine Island, St. George, and Cape Cod oysters.

Oyster farming has been practiced for years in Long Island Sound, Delaware Bay, and the Chesapeake Bay. Harvesters try to avoid the parasites that often destroy natural beds by growing them under controlled conditions in commercial hatcheries. Oysters are typically consumed only during months that have the letter *r* in them—generally the cooler months. Although oysters are edible in the non-*r* months, this is their spawning season and the production of glycogen is excessive at this time, giving the meat a milky appearance, bland taste, and flabby texture.

Oysters are tender creatures and should never be heated too quickly or for too long. As soon as the mantle starts to curl, the oyster is done. Though oysters are often served on the half shell, people in high-risk health categories, such as the young, the elderly, or people with chronic illnesses, should avoid raw shellfish. Oysters may be baked, fried, grilled, sautéed, smoked, or steamed.

Note: Chefs in commercial restaurants should never buy oysters that do not bear the harvester's name, address, date, and certification number, and they should keep the tag for at least 90 days. In the event of a food-borne illness determined to be caused by eating raw oysters, inspectors will be able to use the tag to trace the origin of the harvest and take appropriate actions. The liquid in which shucked fresh oysters are packed should be clear. To test for live oysters, tap the shell; it should close. A sulfur odor indicates a dead oyster.

Historically, the main occupation of Delaware citizens has been agriculture. The original settlers concentrated on growing wheat and corn, and in the early 1800s the area was known for its peach trees. Unfortunately, in the late 1800s a disease killed more than half of those trees. The next agricultural milestone was laid in 1920 by Cecile Steele of Sussex County. She started raising chickens for retail sale instead of just for their eggs. Today, broiler chickens are the state's most valuable agricultural product, and Perdue Farms, which is headquartered in nearby Maryland, is the nation's second largest poultry producer. Breeder Frank Perdue was known for successfully crossbreeding chickens, as well as for having developed a special all-natural feed that combines corn and soybeans with minerals from ground oyster shells and marigold petal extract. Although the marigold petal extract does not add vitamins to the chicken's diet, it is responsible for its distinctive yellow-gold skin color. The company processes approximately 50 million pounds of chicken and turkey per week, and the industry continues to grow.

VIRGINIA AND WEST VIRGINIA

In its earliest years, Virginia's entire economy was plantation-based. Early plantations lay along one of the state's major rivers, and the tobacco grown on that land was shipped to England. Luxury goods and other items that the colony could not produce were imported from Europe. Tobacco was the mainstay of the state, and even after the Civil War it was tobacco that kept Virginia's economy alive for many years. But as early as the 1840s, newcomers to Virginia had begun to show local farmers that they didn't have to depend on tobacco. Gradually, the Tidewater region became a major source of fresh fruits and vegetables for the nation. This truck farming continued because it did not require slave labor. Today, Virginia remains a major producer of potatoes, peanuts, and apples.

During the 19th century, many Scotch Irish and Germans arrived in what is present-day West Virginia by way of Pennsylvania. Later, immigrants from Ireland and eastern and southern Europe came to the state. Because West Virginia has very little flat land, growing crops is difficult. Livestock is the leading agricultural product, and broiler chickens bring the greatest income. Apples and peaches are grown in the eastern panhandle, and West Virginia farmers were first in the nation to produce Golden Delicious apples.

POULTRY AND EGG LABELING

Poultry and egg labels can be complicated to understand. Some of the more familiar labels are:

Certified Organic: The birds are uncaged inside barns or warehouses, and are required to have outdoor access. They are fed an organic, all-vegetarian diet free of antibiotics and pesticides, as required by the U.S. Department of Agriculture's National Organic Program. Compliance is verified through third-party auditing.

Free-Range: Typically, free-range hens are uncaged inside barns or warehouses and have some degree of outdoor access, but there are no requirements for the amount, duration, or quality of outdoor access and they can engage in many natural behaviors such as nesting and foraging. There are no restrictions regarding what the birds can be fed. There is no third-party auditing.

Animal Welfare Approved: The highest animal welfare standards of any third-party auditing program. The birds are cage-free and continuous outdoor perching access is required. They must be able to perform natural behaviors such as nesting, perching, and dust bathing. Animal Welfare Approved is a program of the Animal Welfare Institute.

Cage-Free: As the term implies, hens laying eggs labeled as "cage-free" are uncaged inside barns or warehouses, but they generally do not have access to the outdoors. They can engage in many of their natural behaviors such as walking, nesting, and spreading their wings. There is no third-party auditing.

Free-Roaming: Also known as "free-range," the USDA has defined this claim for some poultry products, but there are no standards in "free-roaming" egg production. This essentially means the hens are cage-free. There is no third-party auditing.

United Egg Producers Certified: The overwhelming majority of the U.S. egg industry complies with this voluntary program of the United Egg Producers.

Vegetarian-Fed: These birds' feed does not contain animal by-products.

Heritage Poultry

The common trait of heritage poultry breeds is their flavor and texture. Heritage chicken breeds can only be raised naturally, which takes three times longer, but the main idea of consuming heritage poultry breeds is to prevent their genetic erosion.

- **The Barred Plymouth Rock:** This chicken's lineage is 150 years old. It was the first chicken to be included in the American Poultry Standards of Perfection list, slightly smaller breasted than the Dark Cornish.

- **The Dark Cornish:** Also called "Indian Game," it provided the genes for many of the modern commercial breeds. It was originally developed for its meat which is dark and not unlike pheasant.

- **Heritage Turkey:** Large corporations have dominated turkey production and breeding since the 1960s, choosing the Broad Breasted Whites because of high breast meat production in a short period. Raising Heritage Breeds is more costly and time-consuming than raising White Breasted Toms. While supermarket turkeys grow to an average of 32 pounds over 18 weeks, Heritage birds take anywhere from 24 to 30 weeks to reach their market weight. Most breeds of heritage turkey were developed in the United States and Europe over hundreds of years and include the Standard Bronze, Bourbon Red, Jersey Buff, Slate, Black Spanish, Narragansett, and White Holland.

POULTRY PROCESSING: WATER IMMERSION VS. AIR CHILLING

After cleaning and inspection, the USDA requires chickens to be chilled in order to inhibit the grown of microorganisms that can cause spoilage. After chickens are slaughtered, cleaned, and inspected, they must be chilled before being packed or further processed. This can be done in one of two ways: immersion in cold water or by air-chilling.

The most popular method in the United States has been to water-chill birds. Immersion in a tank of chlorinated ice-cold water—known as a chiller—is considered the fastest and most effective way of getting the birds down to 40°F or below. Water is considered the most efficient conducting medium for removing animal heat, and modern chillers are efficient, quick and economical. Chickens typically spend 45 minutes to an hour in the chiller and are moved through it by paddles or other devices. The baths are heavily chlorinated, as required by the USDA, and each bird can absorb 2 to 12 percent of its weight in this water as it cools. The liquid seen when the package of a conventionally processed chicken is opened is most often drainage from the water bath. Companies are required to declare on the package the approximate level of moisture retained.

A number of chicken processors have recently embraced the air-chilled method, which has been used in Europe for more than 40 years. Each bird is individually chilled over the course of about three hours. Birds are moved into carefully monitored, temperature-controlled chambers where cold air is misted on them. The birds move over a mile or more on tracks in these special chambers as they cool down. Each chicken is still sprayed inside and out with a chlorine rinse as required by the USDA, but air-chilled chickens do not absorb water as water-chilled chickens do, and when packaged can be labeled with the statement, "No water added." One question consistently asked about the differences between air-chilled vs. immersion-chilled has to do with food safety. There have been studies showing air-chilling chicken does a better job of eliminating microorganisms on raw chicken, compared to immersing birds in chlorinated ice water.

 ## Typical **Mid-Atlantic** Ingredients and Dishes

Angel Food Cake   A light puffy cake made without yeast or egg yolks, and leavened with beaten egg whites. Considered to be from the thrifty Pennsylvania Dutch as a sensible use of leftover egg whites.

Apple Butter   A butterlike spiced apple spread made by the Pennsylvania Dutch. This type of spread can be made with any fruit, but making apple butter is often a traditional Pennsylvania Dutch fall social event involving women.

Bagel   A small, round yeast bread with a hole in the center. The only bread dough to be boiled and then baked, which results in a chewy texture. Bagels may be made with a variety of ingredients or toppings, and today are fashioned by machine and cooked in a modified process.

Beef on Weck   A sandwich of thinly sliced, very lean roast beef served on a German caraway-seed roll encrusted with salt, topped with the beef juices, and accompanied with horseradish. The German name for the roll is *kummelweck,* which is shortened in the name for the sandwich.

Beefsteak Tomato   A tomato of any variety that grows to at least 3 inches in diameter. Large beefsteak tomatoes are prized for their excellent balance of sweetness and tartness, achieved by being vine-ripened during the hottest days of summer.

Beet Egg   An Amish preparation in which eggs are hard-boiled in a seasoned liquid derived from cooked beets. When done, the eggs turn a purplish-red color. Beet eggs were considered to be the first use of colored eggs for the Easter holiday, a tradition brought to America by the first Amish immigrants.

Bialy   A chewy round roll made from wheat flour, salt, yeast, and water. It has an indentation in the center, sprinkled with either chopped onion or poppyseed, and is baked until crisp and golden brown. The name derives from the Polish town of Bialystock.

Blue Crab   A common species of crab found in abundance in the Chesapeake Bay, harvested April through December. Blue crabs are marketed and sold in both their hard- and soft-shell stages. The meat from the crab is available as large pieces (lump) from the body, smaller pieces (flake) also from the body, and darker small pieces (claw) from the legs and claw. The following terminology is associated with blue crabs:

> **Apron**   The flap located on the underside of the body. The apron is pried away from the body to remove the intestinal vein, which is normally pulled out.
>
> **Dead Man's Fingers**   The spongy yellow matter found in the crab's body. The gills and intestines, along with the dead man's fingers, should be discarded.
>
> **Jimmies**   Male crabs, considered a little meatier than female crabs.
>
> **Peelers**   Crabs that have grown their new soft shell underneath and have split the hard shell on top. The new shell will begin to harden within a few hours if the crab is left in the water after molting.
>
> **Soft Shell**   The stage when the crab begins to molt and shed its shell. Both male and female crabs lose their shells and form new ones as they grow. Blue crabs molt up to 22 times before reaching full maturity, between 5 and 7 inches across. Soft-shell crabs are graded by the size of the shell span. Hotel crabs are 4 to 4½ inches, prime crabs are 4½ to 5 inches, jumbo crabs are 5 to 5½ inches, and whale crabs are 5½ inches and larger. Soft-shell crabs are generally pan-fried and eaten whole.
>
> **Sooks**   Female crabs.
>
> **Tomalley**   The yellow-colored liver. The tomalley is edible and considered by many to be a delicacy.

Boova Shenkel   A Pennsylvania Dutch beef stew with potato dumplings. The literal translation is "boys' legs" for the dumplings that resemble short, thick legs.

Borscht   A beef, beet, and cabbage soup of Russian and Polish origin, popular among Jewish people. Served hot or cold, garnished with a dollop of sour cream.

Button Mushrooms   The most common mushrooms consumed in America. They are recognized by a firm white exterior and smooth skin.

Challah   A traditional Jewish braided white yeast bread. This holiday bread is enriched with eggs and sprinkled with poppyseeds.

Chicken   The different names for chickens refer to stages of growth, and sometimes to the cooking method. They are:

> **Poussin**   A baby chicken weighing 14 to 18 ounces.

Hen　An egg-laying female not used for cooking until egg production has ended. Good for broths, stock, and soup.

Pullet　A young female used for meat. Often sold as broilers (weighing from 1¼ to 2½ pounds) or as fryers (from 2½ to 3½ pounds).

Roasters　Young males not sold as broilers and fryers, often raised to be roasters (4 to 6 pounds).

Capons　Males that have been castrated. They are plump and juicy and weigh between 7 and 12 pounds.

Roosters or cocks　Males that are used primarily for breeding. They can be used for broths, stocks, and soups.

Chicken Pot Pie　A Pennsylvania Dutch chicken stew similar to Southern chicken and dumplings. The dumplings are flat squares made from a dough that resembles pie dough and are boiled in a pot of broth, then added to stew.

Clams　Surf clams are the clam variety most frequently found in New Jersey and New York. Too big and too coarse to be eaten whole like other clams, these are processed and are often the "fried clams" featured on menus. The meat is also ground or chopped and used for chowders, bisques, and sauces.

Crab Boil　A special mix of herbs and spices used to season blue crabs when steaming them.

Crab Cake　A patty of crab meat mixed with fresh bread crumbs, eggs, herbs, and spices. It may be pan-fried or sautéed.

Fastnacht　A rectangular piece of dough slit down the center and deep fried, much like a doughnut. It may be filled with jam or topped with molasses.

Foie Gras　The "fat liver" of ducks and geese. The Moulard duck is especially bred for its liver, and in the Mongaup Valley in the Catskill Mountains of New York, this prized duck is now raised to provide America's first French-style foie gras.

Funnel Cake　A crisp, squiggly pastry made by pouring batter through a funnel into hot fat, then swirling it into strips. Funnel cakes are typically sprinkled with powdered sugar or topped with molasses or syrup. Pennsylvania Dutch farmers eat these as a midmorning snack.

Gyro　A Greek-American sandwich made from slices of rotisserie-roasted, seasoned lamb, served in the pocket of pita bread. Sold at Greek lunch counters in New York City and pronounced "JEER-o."

Kosher　Food prepared according to strict Jewish dietary laws. According to kosher laws, meat and milk may not be eaten together at the same meal; even separate dishes, pots, pans, and utensils must be used. Also, consuming pork or shellfish is prohibited. In order for meats to be deemed kosher, the animals must be slaughtered a certain way, under the supervision of a rabbi.

Kugel　A baked noodle or potato pudding served on the Jewish Sabbath.

Latke　A Jewish fried pancake usually made from grated potatoes and traditionally served at Chanukah.

Lebkuchen　A Pennsylvania Dutch spiced drop cake made especially at Christmastime.

Lox　A salt-cured (but not smoked) side of salmon, sliced paper-thin and frequently served on a bagel half spread with cream cheese.

Maryland Stuffed Ham　A ham larded with a mix of cabbage, onions, mustard, hot pepper, and other seasonings, wrapped tightly in a cloth bag, covered with water, and simmered for several hours. The ham is cooled, the bag is cut away, and the ham is served, usually cold, the next day. This is a dish found in southern Maryland and served at Easter.

Matzo　A plain unleavened bread in thin sheets, traditional at the Jewish Passover.

New York Cheesecake　A dense cream cheese cake with a graham cracker crust, sometimes topped with fresh fruit.

Pastrami   Beef brisket that has been brine-cured and seasoned for one to three weeks, then smoked and finally steamed. Served sliced on rye bread, often with mustard.

Philadelphia Pepperpot   A soup of tripe, pepper, and seasonings.

Philly Cheese Steak   A sandwich of shaved slices of rib eye steak and grilled onions, served on a hard roll topped with Cheez Whiz. Additional toppings include relish, peppers, ketchup, and hot sauce.

Pumpernickel   A rye bread with the addition of molasses or caramel to give its dark brown color.

Reuben Sandwich   A grilled sandwich of corned beef, Swiss cheese, sauerkraut, and Russian dressing on rye bread.

Rivel   Rice-shaped bits of dough, formed by rubbing a ball of pasta dough through a sieve, cooked in simmering broth.

Rye Bread   Jewish-style rye bread is a mixture of rye grain and wheat flour, and uses a sourdough starter as a leavening agent, giving it a distinctive, slightly sour flavor. German-style rye bread contains only rye flour; caraway seeds may be either sprinkled on top of the dough or mixed into it before baking.

Sauerbraten   Beef roast that has been cured with sugar and vinegar, then braised, served in a gravy thickened with crushed gingersnaps. The long marinating makes a flavorful, tender roast. A Mennonite and Amish dish.

Schmaltz   A Yiddish-American term for rendered chicken fat. It may be used as a cooking ingredient or flavored with apples, onions, and seasonings and used as a spread.

Schmear   A Yiddish term for a dab or smear of a condiment like cream cheese spread on a bagel, or mustard on a roll.

Schnitz und Kneppe   A Pennsylvania-Dutch dish of smoked ham with dried apples and dumplings.

Scrapple   A pan pudding of boneless pork simmered with cornmeal or buckwheat flour and flavored with sage. The pudding is chilled, sliced, and pan-fried until golden brown.

Shad   A member of the herring family, a coastal and river fish with a rich, oily flesh and delicate flavor. Boning shad can be tedious, owing to the "floating ribs" that lie in two rows paralleling the backbone on each fillet. Available in the spring, when the fish returns from the ocean to spawn. The annual yield of shad has decreased at an alarming rate owing to pollution.

Shad Roe   The roe produced by shad just before spawning. Considered a delicacy with a distinctive, nutty flavor, it can be poached, pan-fried, or sautéed.

Shoofly Pie   The most famous of all Pennsylvania Dutch pies. Also referred to as pie cake or molasses, it is a crumbly mixture of brown sugar, flour, cinnamon, and butter baked over a layer of molasses in a pie shell.

Stromboli   A specialty of Philadelphia, this sandwich is pizza dough folded over a variety of ingredients, usually mozzarella cheese and sliced pepperoni.

Smithfield Ham   Ham that is cured and smoked via a patented process, a product of Smithfield, Virginia. The hams are cured for 6 to 12 months; before they can be used, they must be soaked in water for 12 to 24 hours to remove excess salt.

Smoked Sable   A smoked black codfish found in New York City–style delicatessens, it is sliced thin and served on bread with onions, black olives, and sweet butter.

Tzimmes   Any of a wide variety of Jewish-American casserole dishes made of various sweetened vegetables or fruits.

Vichyssoise   A creamy potato and leek soup served cold.

Waldorf Salad   A salad of apples, celery, and walnuts, with a mayonnaise dressing.

Menus and Recipes from the
Cuisine of the Mid-Atlantic States

MENU ONE
Oysters with Roasted Mushroom Mignonette

Egg, Cucumber, and Tomato Salad

Chicken with Farro and Artichokes

Steamed Brook Trout, Tarragon Sauce, Red Beets, and Pea Puree

Croquette Potatoes

Applesauce Cake with Caramel Glaze

MENU TWO
Vichyssoise

Sautéed Soft-Shell Crabs on Fennel and Arugula Salad

Roast Long Island Duck Breast with Parsnip Puree and Spiced Blueberry Sauce

Roasted Potatoes and Pearl Onions

Angel Food Cupcakes with Whipped Vanilla Cream

MENU THREE
Spicy Crab Soup with Crab Puffs

Waldorf Salad

Buffalo Chicken Wings

Braised Short Ribs

Buttered Homemade Noodles

Red Swiss Chard and Spinach Sauté

Ginger Pound Cake with Warm Cranberries

OTHER RECIPES
"Shaker-Style" Turkey Cutlets

Beets, Belgian Endive, and Feta Salad

Spaghetti Squash

Navy Bean Soup

Beef Pot Pie with Rich Biscuit Topping

Oysters with Roasted Mushroom Mignonette

4 servings

 CHEF TIP: Farm-raised oysters start as seeds (baby oysters that are only about 2 millimeters in length). Two pounds (32 ounces/896 g) contain around 800,000 oysters. In eighteen months those oysters weigh around 250,000 pounds (113,636 kg).

AMOUNT	MEASURE	INGREDIENT
6	1 ounce/28 g	Fresh shiitake mushrooms, stems removed, caps cleaned
½ cup	4 ounces/120 ml	Vegetable oil
¼ cup	1 ounce/28 g	Shallots, minced
¼ cup	2 ounces/60 ml	Dry white wine
¼ cup	2 ounces/60 ml	Champagne vinegar
		Salt and pepper
12		Oysters on the half shell
2 tablespoons	½ ounce/14 g	Green onions, minced

Oysters with Roasted Mushroom Mignonette

1. Preheat the oven to 350°F (176°C).

2. Lightly coat half the mushrooms with a little of the vegetable oil. Roast in the oven until tender, 10 to 15 minutes. Let mushroom cool and cut into ⅛-inch dice.

3. Combine diced mushrooms with the shallots, wine, vinegar, and seasoning. Set mignonette aside.

4. Cut the remaining mushrooms into thin slices (1/16 inch).

5. Heat the remaining oil in an 8-inch (20.3 cm) sauté pan over medium-high heat. Fry the mushroom slices until golden brown, 2 to 3 minutes. Drain the mushrooms on paper towels.

6. To serve, top each oyster with 1 teaspoon mignonette and garnish with equal portions of fried mushrooms and green onions.

Egg, Cucumber, and Tomato Salad

4 servings

AMOUNT	MEASURE	INGREDIENT
½ teaspoon	2 g	Black pepper
⅛ teaspoon	1 g	Salt
1	5 g	Garlic clove, minced
3 tablespoons	1½ ounces/45 ml	Olive oil
1 tablespoon	½ ounce/15 ml	Red wine vinegar
1 tablespoon	½ ounce/15 ml	Lemon juice
¼ cup	1 ounce/28 g	Green onions, finely diced
4		Eggs, hard-cooked, sliced
½ cup	2 ounces/56 g	Celery with leaves, in ¼-inch (.6 cm) dice
½ cup	2 ounces/56 g	Cucumber, peeled, seeded, in ¼-inch (.6 cm) dice
6 (¼ cup)	1 ounce/28 g	Red radishes, sliced
1 head	6 ounces/170 g	Boston (Bibb) lettuce, shredded
2	7 ounces/196 g	Tomatoes, ripe, thinly sliced (16 slices)

PROCEDURE

1. Mix the pepper, salt, garlic, olive oil, vinegar, lemon juice, and green onions for the dressing.

2. Combine the eggs, celery, cucumber, radishes, and lettuce and lightly toss with enough dressing to just coat.

3. Fan 4 tomato slices on each plate and drizzle with remaining dressing.

4. Place an equal amount of lettuce mixture on top of the tomatoes and serve.

Egg, Cucumber, and Tomato Salad

Chicken with Farro and Artichokes

✦ **CHEF TIP:** Farro is the oldest cultivated grain in the world. Farro is able to grow in poor soil conditions and is naturally resistant to fungus. The grain looks like a plump barley grain, and it has a chewy, firm texture. Because it has a low yield compared to other grains, it lost popularity over the years. Farro is a distinct cousin of modern wheat and is similar in texture and taste to spelt. Farro remains a popular food in Italy, parts of Europe, Asia, and the Middle East. When harvested, Farro is divided into three grades: long, medium, and cracked. Most recipes call for farro to be soaked overnight; the soaking softens the hull, floats any debris to the surface, and makes the final product a little more tender. Soaking reduces the cooking time as well; however, if farro is not soaked it can still be cooked and enjoyed. Typical cooking time to properly cook farro ranges from 20 to 40 minutes, boiled in a 2:1 ratio of water to farro. Simmer, covered, for 25 to 35 minutes, then drain off any unabsorbed liquid. Farro can be interchanged in recipes calling for barley, spelt, or quinoa.

AMOUNT	MEASURE	INGREDIENT
For the Farro		
2 tablespoons	1 ounce/28 g	Butter
¼ cup	1 ounce/28 g	Celery, in ¼-inch (.6 cm) dice
½ cup	2 ounces/56 g	Carrot, in ¼-inch (.6 cm) dice
1 cup	4 ounces/112 g	Onion, in ¼-inch (.6 cm) dice
		Salt
1		Fresh rosemary sprig
1		Fresh thyme sprig
1		Fresh marjoram sprig
1½ cups	6¾ ounces/189 g	Farro
For the Chicken		
3 cups	24 ounces/720 ml	Water or chicken or vegetable stock
4	5 ounces/140 g each	Boneless skin-on chicken breast halves, with the wing attached
		Salt and pepper
½ cup	4 ounces/120 ml	Olive oil
2 cups	16 ounces/480 ml	Chicken stock
1		Fresh thyme sprig
1		Fresh rosemary sprig
4	¾ ounce/21 g	Garlic cloves, thickly sliced
6	12 ounces/336 g	Baby artichokes, cooked and quartered
1 tablespoon	½ ounce/15 ml	Fresh lemon juice
1 tablespoon	3 g	Fresh thyme, chopped
1 tablespoon	3 g	Fresh parsley, chopped

(continued) →

1. Make the farro. In a 2- to 3-quart (2 to 3 L) pot, heat the butter over medium heat. Add the celery, carrot, onion, and a pinch of salt; cook until vegetables begin to soften, 3 to 4 minutes.

2. Tie the rosemary, thyme, and marjoram sprigs together in a piece of cheesecloth to make a sachet. Add the farro and the sachet to the cooked vegetables and toss to coat. Add the water and bring to a boil. Reduce to a simmer, cover, and cook until all the liquid has been absorbed and the grain is swelled and tender, 15 to 25 minutes. Add additional liquid, if necessary. Keep warm.

3. Make the chicken. Preheat the oven to 375°F (190°C).

4. Season the chicken lightly on both sides with salt and pepper. Heat a 10- to 12-inch (25.4–30.5 cm) sauté pan over medium-high heat, then add 2 tablespoons (1 ounce/30 ml) of the olive oil. When the oil is hot, add the chicken skin side down and cook until the skin is golden, 4 to 5 minutes without moving the pieces (this helps the skin to brown and crisp). It is important to not crowd the pan or the skin will not sear correctly. Turn the chicken over and cook 2 minutes more.

5. If working in batches, return all the chicken to the pan, add the stock, herb sprigs, and garlic. The liquid should reach only half way up the chicken breast; it is not necessary to use all the stock. Bring the mixture to a simmer, then transfer to the oven and bake until chicken is cooked, 8 to 10 minutes.

6. While the chicken is cooking, heat the remaining 6 tablespoons (3 ounces/90 ml) olive oil in a 10-inch (25.4 cm) sauté pan over medium-high heat, and sauté the artichoke quarters until golden, 2 to 3 minutes. Add the lemon juice, then correct the seasoning. Keep warm.

7. Remove the chicken from the pan. Remove the herb sprigs from the pan and discard. Taste and correct the seasoning of the broth, and reduce slightly to a sauce.

8. To serve, spoon equal portions of farro and artichoke onto each plate. Place the chicken breasts on top and spoon the sauce around. Sprinkle with the chopped thyme and parsley.

Chicken with Farro and Artichokes

Steamed Brook Trout, Tarragon Sauce, Red Beets, and Pea Puree

4 servings

Brook trout are the only trout native to much of the eastern United States, actually a native North American char. The brook trout is the state fish for eight states: Michigan, New Hampshire, New Jersey, New York, Pennsylvania, Vermont, Virginia, and West Virginia. The meat is tender and white with a mild, delicate, and sweet taste.

AMOUNT	MEASURE	INGREDIENT
Tarragon Sauce		
3 tablespoons	1½ ounces/42 g	Butter
¼ cup	1 ounce/28 g	Green onions, minced
		Salt and pepper
Pinch		Confectioners' sugar
6 tablespoons	3 ounces/90 ml	Dry vermouth
1 cup	8 ounces/240 ml	Fish stock
2 tablespoons	½ ounce/14 g	Fresh tarragon, chopped
2 teaspoons		Tarragon vinegar
Red Beets		
1 cup	4 ounces/112 g	Red beets, cooked, peeled, very thinly sliced
3 tablespoons	1½ ounces/45 ml	Olive oil
1 tablespoon	½ ounce/15 ml	Champagne vinegar
1 tablespoon	½ ounce/15 ml	Vegetable stock or water
1 tablespoon	¼ ounce/7 g	Green onions, minced
1 teaspoon		Chives, minced
		Salt and pepper
Roasted Pearl Onions		
12	6 ounces/168 g	Pearl onions, peeled
2 tablespoons	1 ounce/28 g	Butter, melted
Pea Puree		
1 cup	5 ounces/140 g	Green peas
2 tablespoons	1 ounce/28 g	Butter
¼ cup	1 ounce/28 g	Green onions, minced
2	10 g	Garlic cloves, minced
¾ cup	6 ounces/180 ml	Heavy cream
Trout		
4	4 ounces/112 g each	Brook trout fillets, skinless, boned (remove bones with tweezers)
2 tablespoons	1 ounce/30 ml	Olive oil
		Salt and pepper

(continued) →

1. Make the tarragon sauce. Heat a 1-quart (1 L) saucepan over medium heat and melt 1 tablespoon (½ ounce/14 g) of the butter. Add the green onions and cook for 1 minute. Add the salt, pepper, and sugar, then deglaze with the vermouth and add the stock. Cook until liquid is reduced by half, 3 to 4 minutes. Add all but 1 teaspoon of the tarragon leaves, simmer 2 minutes, then strain the sauce. Add vinegar, correct the seasoning, and whisk in the remaining 2 tablespoons (1 ounce/30 ml) butter and the remaining tarragon. Keep warm.

2. Make the beets. Marinate the beets in a bowl with the oil, vinegar, stock, green onions, chives, and salt and pepper for 30 to 45 minutes at room temperature.

3. Prepare the onions. Preheat the oven to 350°F (176°C). Toss the pearl onions with the melted butter and roast until tender, 30 to 45 minutes. It is important to turn the onions every 15 minutes so they brown evenly. Keep warm.

4. Make the pea puree. Blanch the peas in boiling salted water, drain, and shock in cold water. Drain well again. Melt the butter in a 1-quart (1 L) saucepan over medium heat, then sauté the green onions and garlic for 1 minute. Add peas and the cream, then cook 1 minute or until mixture is hot. Puree with a hand blender or blender until smooth. (If the puree is too dense, add a little stock or water.)

5. Prepare the trout. Coat the fillets with olive oil and season with salt and pepper. Place the fillets on the steamer rack and cover the steamer. When the water begins to boil, steam for about 4 minutes. Do not overcook.

6. Serve the trout immediately with the tarragon sauce spooned over the fillets. Garnish with the pea puree, roasted pearl onions, and sliced beets.

Steamed Brook Trout, Tarragon Sauce, Pea Puree, Red Beets, and Roasted Pearl Onions

Croquette Potatoes

AMOUNT	MEASURE	INGREDIENT
3 cups	16 ounces/453 g	Russet potatoes, peeled, quartered
2 tablespoons	1 ounce/28 g	Butter, softened
1		Egg yolk
		Salt and white pepper
½ cup	2 ounces/56 g	All-purpose flour
2		Eggs, beaten with a pinch of salt
3 cups	3 ounces/85 g	Dried bread crumbs
		Vegetable oil, for deep-fat frying

PROCEDURE

1. Place the potatoes in a large pot with cold water, bring to a boil, turn down the heat, and simmer for about 30 minutes, until potatoes are tender.

2. Drain and dry the potatoes, then run them through a food mill. Add the butter and egg yolks. Season with salt and pepper.

3. Shape the croquettes as required. Croquette potatoes are traditionally shaped by placing the mashed potato in a pastry bag with a large round tip and piping long logs onto a half-sheet pan dusted with flour. Cool. Cut the logs into 1½ inch (3.6 cm) long cylindrical shapes, roll cylinders on the floured pan to coat with flour and to keep from altering the shape. Then place in the egg wash, and coat with bread crumbs. It is easier to bread the cylinder-shaped potatoes if they are chilled at least 30 minutes before placing them in the egg wash.

4. Heat the oil to 375°F (190°C) and deep-fry until golden brown, 2½ to 3 minutes. Drain on paper towels and serve immediately.

Applesauce Cake with Caramel Glaze

Makes one 10-inch cake

AMOUNT	MEASURE	INGREDIENT
For the Cake		
1 cup	8 ounces/224 g	Unsalted butter, at room temperature
2 cups	16 ounces/448 g	Brown sugar, packed
1		Egg
3 cups	13 ounces/364 g	All-purpose flour
2 teaspoons	8 g	Baking soda
¼ teaspoon	2 g	Salt
1 teaspoon	2 g	Ground cinnamon
1 teaspoon	2 g	Ground nutmeg
1 teaspoon	2 g	Ground cloves
2 cups	17 ounces/510 ml	Applesauce, unsweetened
2 cups	12 ounces/336 g	Raisins
1 cup	4 ounces/112 g	Walnuts, coarsely chopped
For the Glaze		
1 cup	8 ounces/224 g	Brown sugar, packed
¼ cup	2 ounces/56 g	Unsalted butter
¼ cup	2 ounces/60 ml	Evaporated milk

PROCEDURE

1. Preheat the oven to 350°F (175°C). Grease and flour a 10-inch (25.4 cm) tube pan.

2. Make the cake. Cream the butter until smooth. Gradually add the brown sugar, beating until light and fluffy. Add the egg; beat well.

3. Sift together 2½ cups (10 ounces/280 g) of the flour, the baking soda, salt, and spices. Add to the creamed mixture in batches, alternating with the applesauce. Beat well after each addition.

4. Dredge the raisins and walnuts in the remaining flour; fold into the batter.

5. Pour the batter into the prepared pan. Bake for 1 hour and 15 minutes or until cake tests done.

6. Cool cake in pan 15 minutes, then invert onto a cake rack to cool completely.

7. Prepare the glaze. Combine the brown sugar, butter, and milk. Heat, stirring constantly, until the mixture comes to a boil and the sugar is dissolved.

8. Continue cooking, stirring constantly, until the mixture reaches soft-ball stage (238°F/114°C). If a thermometer is not available, spoon a few drops of the hot sugar into a bowl of very cold water. Check the hardness of the cooled sugar with your fingertips. The balls of sugar will be soft and flexible when pressed between the fingertips. If you remove the ball of sugar from water, it will flatten after a few moments in the hand. Remove from the heat, and beat about 5 minutes or until thick.

9. Drizzle the hot sauce over the cooked cake.

Vichyssoise

4 servings

CHEF TIP: Russet potatoes are too starchy and can make the soup mealy. Red Bliss may make the soup gluey and gelatinous. Remember the potatoes handle a lot of salt and the soup is served cold, which requires more seasoning than a hot soup. Always taste and adjust before serving.

Most food historians generally attribute the creation of this cold soup in 1917 to Louis Diat, chef at the Ritz-Carlton Hotel in New York. There are, however, some conflicting facts that make this story interesting. Was Mr. Diat the first to make French-style cream of leek and potato soup? Culinary evidence suggests not. Recipe 696 in Escoffier's *Guide Culinaire* (circa 1903) provides instructions for *purée parmentier*. The difference? Mr. Escoffier's soup was served hot; Mr. Diat's vichyssoise was served cold. If there is a connection to Vichy (beyond the name), it has not been preserved for posterity.

AMOUNT	MEASURE	INGREDIENT
¼ cup	2 ounces/56 g	Unsalted butter
3 cups	12 ounces/336 g	Leeks, white part only, ½-inch (1.2 cm) rough slices
½ cup	2 ounces/56 g	White onions, in ½-inch (1.2 cm) dice
2 cups	10 ounces/280 g	All-purpose potatoes (such as Yukon Gold), peeled, ½-inch dice
3 cups	24 ounces/720 ml	Chicken stock
¾ cup	6 ounces/180 ml	Milk
1 cup	8 ounces/240 ml	Heavy cream
⅓ cup	½ ounce/14 g	Chives, snipped
		Salt and white pepper

PROCEDURE

1. Over medium heat melt the butter in a 2- to 3-quart (2 to 3 L) saucepan and add the leeks and onions. Cook slowly, browning them very lightly.

2. Add the potatoes and chicken stock and bring to a simmer. Simmer until the leeks and potatoes are very tender, approximately 45 minutes.

3. Puree the soup in a food processor, blender, or food mill, and then run through a fine strainer.

4. Return puree to the heat and add the milk and ½ cup (4 ounces/120 ml) of the cream. Season to taste and return to a boil. Strain again through a fine strainer.

5. Let cool, then add remaining cream. Chill thoroughly before serving, garnished with snipped chives. Correct seasoning before serving.

Sautéed Soft-Shell Crabs on Fennel and Arugula Salad

4 servings

✦ **CHEF TIP:** To clean soft-shell crabs, use sharp scissors or a knife to snip off the "face" of the crab, from behind the eyes—this will kill the crab instantly. Flip the crab over and you will see a triangular "tail" piece folded up against the body of the crab. Unfold it and snip it off, too. Turn the crab right side up and unfold each of the sides. Remove the sandbags and gills either with your scissors or with your hands. Soft-shell crabs are one of America's favorite seafood delicacies. While all crabs shed their shells to grow, only a few species of crab can actually be eaten in this form. The blue crab is the only commercially available soft-shell product. The scientific name, *Callinectes sapidus*, is derived from Latin and Greek (*calli* = beautiful; *nectes* = swimmer; *sapidus* = savory). The translation is not only accurate but also surprisingly poetic.

AMOUNT	MEASURE	INGREDIENT
1	16 ounces/448 g	Fennel bulb
6 tablespoons	3 ounces/90 ml	Olive oil
3 tablespoons	1½ ounces/45 ml	Fresh lemon juice
1 tablespoon	3 g	Fresh flat-leaf parsley, chopped
½ teaspoon		Lemon zest
4	3 ounces/84 g each	Soft-shell crabs, prime grade, cleaned
½ cup	2 ounces/56 g	All-purpose flour
		Salt and pepper
¼ cup	2 ounces/60 ml	Vegetable oil, for sautéing
1 tablespoon	5 g	Garlic, minced
1 cup	2 ounces/56 g	Arugula, washed and dried

PROCEDURE

1. Wash the fennel, remove the fronds, and cut out the bottom core. Using a mandolin or sharp knife, slice the fennel bulb paper thin.

2. Combine the olive oil, lemon juice, parsley, and lemon zest. Toss the dressing with the sliced fennel.

3. Dredge the crabs in seasoned flour; shake off excess flour.

4. Heat a 10- to 12-inch (25.4–30.5 cm) sauté pan over medium-high heat. Add enough oil to coat the pan, add the garlic and sauté 30 seconds.

5. Add crabs to the pan, with more oil if necessary. Cook until golden brown, 2 to 3 minutes. Turn crabs over and cook an additional 2 minutes or until nicely browned. When done, there should be very little or no oil left in the pan and the crabs should be covered with garlic and flour scrapings.

6. Toss the arugula with the fennel and divide among 4 plates. Place 1 crab on each salad.

Roast Long Island Duck Breast with Parsnip Puree and Spiced Blueberry Sauce

AMOUNT	MEASURE	INGREDIENT
Parsnip Puree		
3 cups	18 ounces/504 g	Parsnips, peeled, in 1-inch (2.5 cm) dice
2 cups	16 ounces/480 ml	Heavy cream
1 cup	8 ounces/240 ml	Whole milk
2 tablespoons	1 ounce/28 g	Butter
		Salt and pepper
Blueberry Sauce		
½ cup	2 ounces/56 g	Granny Smith apple, peeled, quartered, cored, and chopped
½ cup	2 ounces/56 g	Onion, roughly chopped
2 cups	10 ounces/280 g	Fresh or frozen blueberries
½ cup, packed	3½ ounces/98 g	Brown sugar
¼ cup	2 ounces/56 g	Granulated sugar
1 tablespoon	10 g	Fresh ginger, minced
1 tablespoon	10 g	Garlic, minced
2		Star anise, whole
1 teaspoon		Lime zest, grated
1 teaspoon		Orange zest, grated
½ cup	4 ounces/120 ml	Red wine vinegar
1 teaspoon		Sriracha sauce
Duck Breast		
4	5 ounces/140 g each	Duck breasts, boneless, skin on
		Salt and pepper

PROCEDURE

1. Prepare the parsnip puree. Combine the parsnips, cream, milk, and butter in a 2- to 3-quart (2 to 3 L) saucepan. Bring to a boil, return to a simmer, and cook over low heat until the parsnips are tender, 14 to 16 minutes. Drain parsnips and reserve liquid.

2. Puree the parsnips in a food processor or through a food mill, adding enough cooking liquid to make a smooth puree. Correct seasoning and keep warm.

3. Make the blueberry sauce. Puree the apple and onion in a food processor or finely chop by hand. In a 2- to 3-quart (2 to 3 L) saucepan over medium heat, combine the apple-onion mixture with the blueberries, brown and granulated sugars, ginger, garlic, star anise, zests, and vinegar. Bring to a boil, then turn to a simmer and cook until sauce begins to thicken, about 30 minutes. After 20 minutes it will still appear to be very thin, but it will thicken. Strain and correct seasoning. (If sauce is too thin after straining, return to heat and cook to desired consistency.)

4. Prepare the duck breasts. Use a sharp knife to score the duck skin in a crisscross pattern. Be careful not to cut through the skin into the meat. Season with salt and pepper. Place breasts skin side down in a heavy-bottomed 10- to 12-inch (25.4–30.5 cm) sauté pan. Start with a cold pan, cooking over low heat and rendering the fat until the skin is golden brown and crisp, approximately 15 minutes.

5. Turn the duck breast, and cook to medium rare. Remove from the pan and allow to rest in a warm place for 10 minutes.

6. Pour off excess fat from the pan, then add blueberry sauce to deglaze pan. Add Sriracha sauce and correct seasoning.

7. Slice the duck breast thinly on the diagonal and serve immediately with parsnip puree, blueberry sauce, and Roasted Potatoes and Pearl Onions (recipe follows).

Roast Long Island Duck Breast with Parsnip Puree and Spiced Blueberry Sauce, and Roasted Potatoes and Pearl Onions

Roasted Potatoes and Pearl Onions

4 servings

AMOUNT	MEASURE	INGREDIENT
12	12 ounces/336 g	Red potatoes
12	6 ounces/168 g	Pearl onions, peeled
1 tablespoon	½ ounce/14 g	Unsalted butter, melted
3 tablespoons	1½ ounces/45 ml	Balsamic vinegar
½ teaspoon	3 g	Salt
		Black pepper
4		Fresh thyme sprigs

PROCEDURE

1. Preheat the oven to 350°F (175°C).

2. Starting at the top of each potato, pare away a ¼-inch (.6 cm)-thick band of skin in a spiral. This not only makes them look appealing but also allows the vinegar to penetrate during the slow cooking process.

3. Combine the pearl onions and potatoes in a baking dish just large enough to hold them.

4. Add the butter and vinegar, and toss to coat. Add the salt and pepper. Bury the thyme springs in the vegetables.

5. Bake for 1 hour or until tender, stirring the vegetables every 15 minutes. (It is important to turn the vegetables every 15 minutes if they are to brown evenly.)

Angel Food Cupcakes with Whipped Vanilla Cream

Makes 12 cupcakes

AMOUNT	MEASURE	INGREDIENT
Cupcakes		
½ cup plus 2 tablespoons	3 ounces/84 g	Confectioners' sugar
⅓ cup	1½ ounces/42 g	All-purpose flour
⅛ teaspoon		Salt
½ cup	4 ounces/120 ml	Egg whites (4 large eggs), at room temperature
½ teaspoon		Cream of tarter
¼ cup	2 ounces/56 g	Granulated sugar
½ teaspoon		Vanilla extract
Whipped Cream		
1 cup	8 ounces/240 ml	Heavy cream
1 tablespoon	½ ounce/14 g	Granulated sugar
½ teaspoon		Vanilla extract

PROCEDURE

1. Preheat the oven to 350°F (176°C). Line a cupcake tin with liners.

2. Make the cupcakes. Sift together the confectioners' sugar, flour, and salt.

3. Beat the egg whites until frothy, add the cream of tartar, and beat at medium speed until soft peaks form, 4 to 5 minutes.

4. Gradually add the granulated sugar with the mixer on medium speed and beat until opaque with soft peaks. Mix in the vanilla.

5. Fold the dry ingredients into the egg whites in three increments.

6. Scoop the batter into the cupcake molds. Bake 16 to 18 minutes or until tops are golden brown. Let cool, then remove cupcakes from mold.

7. Prepare the whipped cream. Whip the heavy cream with the granulated sugar and extract until soft peaks form. Use to frost the cupcakes.

Angel Food Cupcakes with Whipped Vanilla Cream

Spicy Crab Soup with Crab Puffs

4 servings

Spicy Crab Soup

AMOUNT	MEASURE	INGREDIENT
2 tablespoons	1 ounce/28 g	Unsalted butter
½ cup	2 ounces/56 g	Onion, in ½-inch (1.2 cm) dice
½ cup	2 ounces/56 g	Celery, in ½-inch (1.2 cm) dice
1 cup	4 ounces/112 g	Potato, in ¼-inch (.6 cm) dice
2 cups	12 ounces/336 g	Tomatoes, peeled, seeded, in ½-inch (1.2 cm) dice
½ cup	2 ounces/56 g	Corn kernels
2 cups	16 ounces/0.473 L	Chicken stock
1 teaspoon	2 g	Old Bay seasoning
½ teaspoon	3 g	Salt
¼ teaspoon	2 g	Black pepper
1 cup	6 ounces/168 g	Lump crab meat, picked of shell
½ cup	2 ounces/56 g	Green peas
1 teaspoon	5 ml	Lemon juice

PROCEDURE

1. Heat the butter in a 10- to 12-inch (25.4–30.5 cm) sauté pan over medium-high heat. Add the onion and cook until soft and translucent, 2 to 3 minutes. Add the celery and cook 3 minutes. Add the potato, tomatoes, corn, and chicken stock. Add the seasonings and cook 25 minutes, or until the potatoes are completely cooked.

2. Add the crab meat and peas, then simmer 2 to 3 minutes.

3. Correct the seasoning with salt, pepper, and the lemon juice. Serve with Crab Puffs (recipe follows).

Crab Puffs

AMOUNT	MEASURE	INGREDIENT
½ cup	3 ounces/84 g	Claw crab meat, picked of shell
¼ cup	1 ounce/28 g	Cheddar cheese (sharp), grated
1 tablespoon	3 g	Green onion, minced
½ teaspoon	2.5 ml	Worcestershire sauce
½ teaspoon	1 g	Dry mustard
½ cup	4 ounces/120 ml	Water
¼ cup	2 ounces/56 g	Unsalted butter
⅛ teaspoon	1 g	Salt
½ cup	2 ounces/56 g	All-purpose flour
2		Eggs

1. Preheat the oven to 400°F (205°C). Line a baking sheet with parchment.

2. Combine the crab, cheese, green onions, Worcestershire sauce, and mustard and mix well.

3. In a 2- to 3-quart (2 to 3 L) saucepan, combine the water, butter, and salt over medium-high heat and bring to a boil. Immediately remove from heat and add the flour, beating until mixture leaves the sides of the pan and forms a ball.

4. Add the eggs, one at a time, beating thoroughly after each addition.

5. Thoroughly blend in the crab mixture.

6. Drop by small teaspoonfuls onto baking sheet. Bake 15 minutes, then reduce heat to 350°F (175°C), and bake 10 minutes longer.

Spicy Crab Soup with Crab Puffs

Waldorf Salad

CHEF TIP: Created in 1896 by maître d'hôtel Oscar Tschirky, the famous "Oscar of the Waldorf" at New York's Waldorf-Astoria Hotel, the original version of this salad contained only apples, celery, and mayonnaise. Chopped walnuts later became an integral part of the salad.

The simple salad has become victim of too many ingredients, including sugar, whipped cream, grapes, dates, raisins, and so on. Well-flavored ripe apples do not need to be sweetened. Use Red Delicious, Winesap, or any other eating apple.

AMOUNT	MEASURE	INGREDIENT
3 cups	12 ounces/346 g	Apples, unpeeled or peeled, cored, julienned
1 tablespoon	½ ounce/15 ml	Lemon juice
1 cup	4 ounces/112 g	Celery, julienned
½ cup	2 ounces/56 g	Walnuts, toasted and chopped
¼ cup	2 ounces/60 ml	Mayonnaise
		Lettuce leaves, for garnish

PROCEDURE

1. Combine the apples and lemon juice; make certain the apples are well coated so they will not turn dark.

2. Add the celery and walnuts.

3. Stir in the mayonnaise; use just enough to bind the ingredients together—no more.

4. Arrange the salad on lettuce and serve immediately.

Buffalo Chicken Wings

CHEF TIP: Buffalo wings are so ingrained in our national food culture now that it is hard to remember life before wings. From their origin in 1964 to today, they have been a prime example of a food that incorporates many cultural traits. For example, thrift (wings, after all, come from the part of the chicken most people throw away or use only for soups and stocks), ingenuity (the preparation uses simple, at-hand materials to make a new item), and eating with your hands (there is a child-like satisfaction in eating with your fingers, especially when there is a flavorful sauce to lick off). Buffalo wings offer something for almost everyone, and that's why they spread so rapidly from their home in Buffalo, New York, to become part of our national food culture.

AMOUNT	MEASURE	INGREDIENT
Chicken Wings		
12–14	3 pounds/1.36 kg	Chicken wings
6 cups	1.4 L	Vegetable oil, for frying
¼ cup	2 ounces/56 g	Unsalted butter
3 tablespoons	1½ ounces/45 ml	Hot sauce such as Franks or Tabasco
2 tablespoons	1 ounce/30 ml	Cider vinegar
		Salt
Blue Cheese Dressing		
½ cup	4 ounces/120 ml	Mayonnaise
¼ cup	2 ounces/60 ml	Yogurt
½ cup	2 ounces/56 g	Blue cheese, crumbled
2 cups	8 ounces/224 g	Celery sticks, in ¼ × ¼ × 2½ inch (.6 × .6 × 6.4 cm) lengths

PROCEDURE

1. Make the wings. Cut off the chicken wing tips, reserving for another use, and halve the chicken wings at the joint.

2. Heat the oil to 375° to 380°F (190°–193°C). Pat wings dry, and fry until cooked through, golden and crisp, 5 to 8 minutes. Drain on paper towels.

3. Combine the butter, hot sauce, vinegar, and salt over medium heat, and warm until butter is melted. Add chicken wings and toss to coat.

4. Make the dressing. Combine the mayonnaise and yogurt, and stir in the blue cheese; dressing will not be smooth.

5. Serve chicken wings warm or at room temperature, with celery sticks and dressing.

Buffalo Chicken Wings, Celery Sticks, Blue Cheese Dressing, and Vinegar Hot Sauce

Braised Short Ribs

AMOUNT	MEASURE	INGREDIENT
	3 pounds/1.36 kg	Beef short ribs, bone-in English-style, trimmed of excess fat and silverskin
		Salt and black pepper
		Flour, for dusting
¼ cup	2 ounces/60 ml	Vegetable oil
1½ cups	6 ounces/168 g	Onions, in ½-inch (1.2 cm) dice
¾ cup	3 ounces/84 g	Carrots, peeled, in ½-inch (1.2 cm) dice
¼ cup	2 ounces/56 g	Celery, in ½-inch (1.2 cm) dice
1 teaspoon	5 g	Garlic, minced
2 tablespoons	½ ounce/14 g	All-purpose flour
½ cup	3 ounces/84 g	Tomato, peeled, seeded, in ½-inch (1.2 cm) dice
1½ cups	12 ounces/360 ml	Dry red wine
2 cups	16 ounces/480 ml	Beef stock
1 tablespoon	3 g	Fresh thyme leaves, chopped
1 teaspoon	1 g	Fresh rosemary leaves, chopped
2		Bay leaves
1 teaspoon	5 g	Tomato paste

PROCEDURE

1. Preheat the oven to 350°F (175°C).

2. Season the beef ribs with salt and pepper. Dust with flour and shake off excess.

3. Heat the oil in a large braising pan or Dutch oven over high heat. Brown short ribs on all sides; transfer to platter.

4. Reduce heat to medium and cook the onions and carrots in same pan until golden brown. Add the celery and cook until soft. Add the garlic and cook until fragrant, about 30 seconds.

5. Stir in the flour until vegetables are coated, about 1 minute. Add the tomato, wine, beef stock, thyme, rosemary, bay leaves, and tomato paste. Bring to a boil and return short ribs; ribs should be almost covered with liquid. Return to a boil, cover, then place in oven. Simmer until ribs are tender, about 2 hours.

6. Remove ribs from pot; remove excess vegetables that may cling to meat; discard loose bones that have fallen away from meat.

7. Strain the braising liquid, pressing out liquid from solids; discard solids. Let the liquid to sit for 10 minutes to give the fat a chance to separate and rise to the top, then degrease.

8. In a large saucepot, return the braising liquid to a boil, lower heat, and simmer to reduce to desired consistency (nappe); correct seasoning.

9. Place short ribs in sauce and cook, partially covered, until ribs are heated through.

10. Divide ribs and sauce among serving plates.

Buttered Homemade Noodles

4 servings

AMOUNT	MEASURE	INGREDIENT
4		Eggs
1 teaspoon	5 g	Salt
3½ cups	14 ounces/392 g	All-purpose flour
½ cup	4 ounces/120 ml	Cold water
4 tablespoons	2 ounces/56 g	Unsalted butter
2 tablespoons	6 g	Fresh parsley, chopped
		Salt and black pepper

PROCEDURE

1. Beat the eggs and salt together.

2. Place the flour in a bowl; make a well in the center. Combine the eggs with half the water and place in the well.

3. Working from the center outward, gradually mix in the surrounding flour with a wooden spoon or spatula. Combine to make stiff dough.

4. Turn dough out onto a floured work surface and knead vigorously with the heel of the hand, adding droplets of water to unblended bits. Dough should just form a mass—the pasta machine will do the rest. Cover and rest 20 to 30 minutes.

5. Cut the dough in half and cover one piece with plastic. For the other piece, flatten into a cake the size of your palm. Pinch one edge so it will fit into the pasta machine.

6. Set the smooth rollers to their widest opening. Crank the dough through, fold dough in half end to end, and crank through several more times until dough is smooth and a fairly even rectangle; as necessary, brush the dough with flour before passing it through rollers, since it will stick to the machine if it is too damp.

7. When the dough is smooth, reset the rollers to the next lower setting and crank it through, then to the next lower, and the next. By this time, the dough will be long; you may want to cut it in half. Continue rolling until it achieves the correct thickness for noodles (⅛ inch or .3 cm).

8. Hang each strip as it is finished to dry briefly (but not to stiffen)—4 to 5 minutes.

9. Repeat the process with the remaining dough piece.

10. For each strip of dough, dust the top with a little flour and roll it up like a jelly roll. Slice the dough crosswise into noodles ¼ inch (.6 cm) thick.

11. Cook the noodles in boiling salted water for approximately 2 to 3 minutes or until tender. Drain thoroughly.

12. Heat the butter over medium heat. Add the noodles and toss to coat with melted butter and heated thoroughly.

13. Add the parsley, salt, and pepper and toss to incorporate.

Red Swiss Chard and Spinach Sauté

AMOUNT	MEASURE	INGREDIENT
6 cups	12 ounces/336 g	Red Swiss chard, ribs removed, washed thoroughly
6 cups	12 ounces/336 g	Spinach leaves, ribs removed, washed thoroughly
2 tablespoons	1 ounce/30 ml	Olive oil
¼ cup	1 ounce/28 g	Onion, minced
1 tablespoon	½ ounce/14 g	Garlic, minced
4 tablespoons	2 ounces/56 g	Unsalted butter
		Salt and black pepper

PROCEDURE

1. Bring about 3 quarts (96 ounces) of salted water to a boil.

2. Blanch the chard for 2 minutes and the spinach for about 30 seconds. Drain and refresh in ice water; squeeze the leaves dry by hand.

3. Heat a 10- to 12-inch (25.4–30.5 cm) sauté pan over medium-high heat. Add the oil and cook the onion for 3 minutes. Add the garlic and cook 1 minute more. Add the butter and let melt.

4. Add the spinach and chard. Cook until the liquid from the greens has evaporated and the chard is tender, 5 to 7 minutes. Adjust seasoning.

Ginger Pound Cake with Warm Cranberries

Ginger Pound Cake

AMOUNT	MEASURE	INGREDIENT
2 cups	8 ounces/224 g	All-purpose flour
½ teaspoon	2 g	Baking powder
¼ teaspoon	2 g	Salt
1 cup	8 ounces/224 g	Unsalted butter, at room temperature
½ teaspoon	2.5 g	Orange zest, minced
1¼ cups	9 ounces/252 g	Sugar
3		Eggs, at room temperature
2 tablespoons	¼ ounce/7 g	Fresh ginger, grated
½ cup	4 ounces/120 ml	Milk

PROCEDURE

1. Preheat the oven to 350°F (175°C). Butter and lightly flour a 9-inch × 5-inch (23 cm × 13 cm) loaf pan or line it with parchment paper.

2. Sift together the flour, baking powder, and salt.

3. Cream the butter and zest until light and fluffy, about 5 minutes. Gradually add the sugar and beat until the mixture is fluffy again.

4. Add the eggs one at a time, being sure that they are well incorporated after each addition. Mix in the ginger.

5. Add the flour mixture alternately with the milk, beginning and ending with the flour.

6. Pour the batter into the pan and bake for 1½ hours, until a skewer inserted in the center comes out clean.

7. Serve cake warm with Warm Cranberries (recipe follows).

Warm Cranberries

AMOUNT	MEASURE	INGREDIENT
¾ cup	5 ounces/140 g	Sugar
¾ cup	6 ounces/180 ml	Water
1	7 ounces/196 g	Orange
3 cups	8 ounces/224 g	Cranberries

(continued) →

1. Combine the sugar and water over medium heat and bring to a boil, making sure all the sugar is dissolved.

2. Cut a 2-inch (5 cm) zest strip from the orange using a vegetable peeler; do not include any of the bitter, white pith. Juice the orange.

3. Add the zest, orange juice, and the cranberries to the syrup and reduce to a low simmer. Simmer for 6 to 8 minutes or until the cranberries begin to pop, but do not overcook. The berries should be soft but still retain their shape.

4. Remove from the heat and leave cranberries in the syrup to cool.

Ginger Pound Cake with Warm Cranberries

"Shaker-Style" Turkey Cutlets

4 servings

AMOUNT	MEASURE	INGREDIENT
8	3 ounces/84 g each	Turkey cutlets
		Salt and black pepper
4 tablespoons	2 ounces/56 g	Unsalted butter
1 tablespoon	15 g	Shallot, in ¼-inch (.6 cm) dice
½ cup	4 ounces/115 ml	Dry white wine
1¼ cups	10 ounces/293 ml	Fond de veau de lie (brown stock)
1 cup	6 ounces/170 g	Tomato, peeled, seeded, in ¼-inch (.6 cm) dice
1 tablespoon	3 g	Fresh parsley, chopped

PROCEDURE

1. Pound the turkey cutlets to approximately ¼ inch (.6 cm) thick. Pat dry. Season to taste with salt and pepper. Dredge cutlets in flour and shake off the excess.

2. Heat a 10- to 12-inch (25.4–30.5 cm) sauté pan over medium-high heat and add 2 tablespoons (1 ounce/28 g) of the butter. Sauté the cutlets approximately 2 to 3 minutes on each side, until golden brown. Cutlets may need to be sautéed in separate batches; do not overload the pan or they will steam not sauté. Remove and keep warm.

3. Discard the excess fat from the pan and return pan to medium-high heat. Add the shallots and cook 1 minute, stirring often.

4. Add the wine and scrape up the pan drippings, reducing liquid by half.

5. Add the brown stock and reduce to sauce (nappe) consistency. Add the tomato and cook for 1 minute or until hot.

6. Return cutlets to the pan and reheat, then remove to plates, 2 cutlets per serving.

7. Stir the remaining 2 tablespoons (1 ounce/28 g) butter into pan drippings, correct the seasoning, and add the parsley. Spoon sauce over cutlets.

Beets, Belgian Endive, and Feta Salad

4 servings

CHEF TIP: If walnut oil is unavailable, use olive oil and 1 teaspoon Dijon-style mustard.

AMOUNT	MEASURE	INGREDIENT
4 cups	16 ounces/453 g	Beets, mixed red and golden, if available, whole
7 tablespoons	3½ ounces/98 ml	Walnut oil
2 tablespoons	1 ounce/28 ml	Tarragon vinegar
		Salt and black pepper
¼ cup	1 ounce/28 g	Walnuts, chopped
2	4 ounces/112 g	Belgian endive, firm and white
1 cup	2 ounces/56 g	Feta cheese, crumbled

PROCEDURE

1. Preheat the oven to 400°F (205°C).

2. Leaving on the tails and 1 inch (2.5 cm) of the stem on the beets, rinse them, put them in a baking pan with ¼ inch (.6 cm) water, cover, and bake until tender when pierced with a knife, 25 to 40 minutes depending on the size of the beets.

3. Cool beets, then peel and dice into ½-inch (1.2 cm) cubes.

4. Mix 6 tablespoons of the oil, the vinegar, salt, and pepper.

5. Toss beets in half the vinaigrette. Toss the walnuts with remaining walnut oil, salt, and pepper. Transfer to a baking pan.

6. Reduce the oven to 350°F (175°C). Bake the walnuts for 5 to 7 minutes or until they smell toasty. Let cool.

7. Just before serving, quarter the endive, cut out the cores, and break into leaves.

8. Arrange endive leaves in a spoke pattern on individual plates. Spoon beets in the center. Lightly dress endive with vinaigrette, then sprinkle the feta cheese over the salad and top with walnuts.

Beets, Belgian Endive, and Feta Salad

Spaghetti Squash

CHEF TIP: There are several ways to cook spaghetti squash:

Bake it.   Pierce the whole shell several times with a large fork or skewer and place in baking dish. Cook squash in preheated 375°F (190°C) oven approximately 1 hour or until flesh is tender.

Boli it.   Heat a pot of water large enough to hold the whole squash. When the water is boiling, drop in the squash and cook for 20 to 30 minutes, depending on its size. When a fork goes easily into the flesh, the squash is done.

Microwave it.   Cut the squash in half lengthwise; remove seeds. Place squash cut sides up in a microwave dish with ¼ cup (2 ounces, 55 ml) water. Cover with plastic wrap and cook on high for 10 to 12 minutes, depending on size of squash. Add more cooking time if necessary. Let stand covered, for 5 minutes.

Once the squash is cooked, let it cool for 10 to 20 minutes so it will be easier to handle. Cut in half (if it wasn't already) and remove the seeds. Pull a fork lengthwise through the flesh to separate pulp into long strands. You can do these steps ahead of time.

AMOUNT	MEASURE	INGREDIENT
¼ cup	2 ounces/56 g	Unsalted butter
½ small	2 pounds/907 g	Spaghetti squash, cooked
		Salt and black pepper

PROCEDURE

1. Melt the butter over medium heat.

2. Add the strands of spaghetti squash and cook until heated thoroughly.

3. Season to taste with salt and pepper.

Navy Bean Soup

4 servings

AMOUNT	MEASURE	INGREDIENT
3¼ cups	1½ pounds/680 g	Navy beans, picked over
¼ cup	2 ounces/56 g	Bacon, in ¼-inch (.6 cm) dice
1 cup	4 ounces/112 g	Carrot, in ¼-inch (.6 cm) dice
1 cup	4 ounces/112 g	Celery, in ¼-inch (.6 cm) dice
1½ cups	6 ounces/170 g	Onions, in ¼-inch (.6 cm) dice
1 tablespoon	15 g	Garlic, minced
½ teaspoon	½ g	Fresh sage, chopped
1 teaspoon	1 g	Fresh thyme, chopped
3 cups	24 ounces/705 ml	Chicken stock
1	5 ounces/140 g	Smoked ham hock
1 tablespoon	3 g	Chives, minced

PROCEDURE

1. Soak the beans in water overnight and drain.

2. Cook the bacon over low heat until almost crisp. Add the carrot, celery, and onions; cook 5 minutes. Add the garlic, cook 1 minute. Add the herbs.

3. Add the chicken stock, ham hock, and beans and bring to a simmer. Cook until the beans are tender, 45 to 60 minutes.

4. Remove the ham hock, cut off meat into small bits, and return meat to soup, discarding the bone.

5. To thicken the soup, crush some of the beans. Taste and adjust seasoning, then garnish each serving with chives.

Beef Pot Pie with Rich Biscuit Topping

4 servings

 **CHEF TIP:** The pot pie—the real, old-fashioned American pot pie made of chicken, veal, or a combination of meats and fowl—was made in a large, black iron kettle using leftover stew. Strips of dough were placed in the greased kettle, the cooked meat and uncooked vegetables were put in with broth around them, and biscuits were placed on top. The cover was weighted down, and the whole mass was simmered for an undetermined length of time. Today's individual pot pies with a savory top crust are not only more appealing to the eye but also more appetizing to the palate. Biscuits, plain or with herbs and special flavors, are used mostly in making New England pot pies. Southerners are more apt to make pot pies with a rich pastry topping.

AMOUNT	MEASURE	INGREDIENT
Pot Pie		
2 cups	12 ounces/340 g	Cooked beef, in ¾-inch (1.9 cm) dice
¾ cup	3 ounces/85 g	Carrots, in ½-inch (1.2 cm) dice, parboiled
8	4 ounces/112 g	Pearl onions, peeled, parboiled
1½ cups	8 ounces/224 g	All-purpose potatoes, peeled, in ½-inch (1.2 cm) dice, parboiled
1 cup	2½ ounces/70 g	White mushrooms, sliced, sautéed
3 tablespoons	1½ ounces/42 g	Chicken fat or butter
3 tablespoons	½ ounce/14 g	All-purpose flour
1¼ cups	10 ounces/300 ml	Beef stock
¾ cup	6 ounces/180 ml	Light cream or half-and-half
		Salt and black pepper
Biscuit Topping		
2 cups	8 ounces/224 g	All-purpose flour, sifted
2½ teaspoons	10 g	Baking powder
¾ teaspoon	4 g	Salt
6 tablespoons	3 ounces/84 g	Unsalted butter, cold, in ½-inch (1.2 cm) dice
⅔ cup	5 ⅓ ounces/155 ml	Milk

PROCEDURE

1. Make the pot pies. Arrange the beef and vegetables in four individual 6–8 ounce (168–224 g), lightly buttered, ovenproof casseroles.

2. Melt the chicken fat and blend in the flour; cook 3 minutes, stirring.

3. Add the beef stock and whisk to a smooth consistency; let cook 10 minutes.

4. Add the cream and cook 5 minutes; correct consistency by reducing or adding more stock. Correct seasoning and pour over beef and vegetables.

5. Make the biscuit topping. Preheat the oven to 425°F (220°C).

6. Combine the flour, baking powder, and salt. Mix the cold butter into the flour until the mixture looks like coarse cornmeal. Stir in the milk and mix until it starts to form a ball.

7. On a lightly floured surface, knead gently for 30 seconds to shape into a ball (takes about 15 turns). Roll or pat the dough to a ⅓-inch (.8 cm) thickness. Cut dough to fit tops of casseroles or into diamond shapes. (Do not immerse biscuit dough in liquid, or the topping will not brown well.)

8. Bake pot pies about 25 minutes, or until browned and heated through.

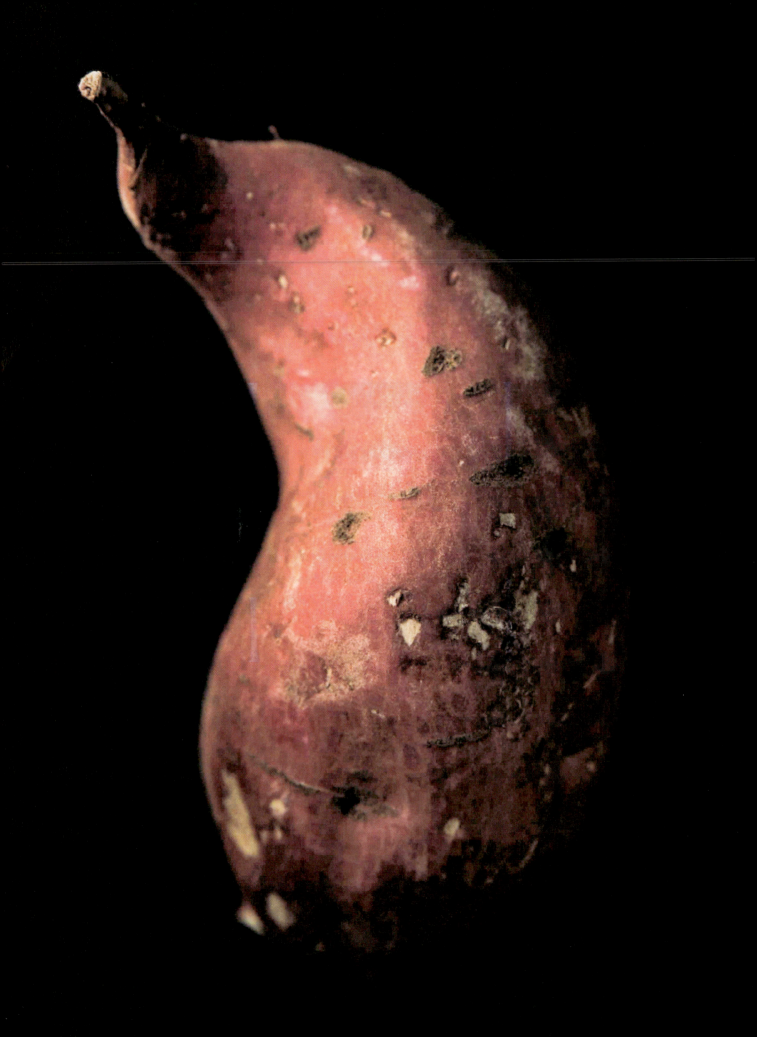

The Cuisine of
the **South**

Southern hospitality. It's big family Sunday dinners, fish frys and fish boils, barbecues, oyster roasts, and public feasts. Throughout the region's history, Southern hospitality has meant open doors, welcoming smiles, and a feast for family, friends, and strangers. Southern cooking came from a blend of English, Native American, and African influences, with a mix of French and Spanish. Today it represents the comfort food that has survived the conflicts of an emerging nation.

Alabama   "The Yellowhammer State," named after the nickname for the state bird, a colorful woodpecker called the northern flicker. The blackberry is the state fruit, and the State Barbeque Championship takes place in Demopolis at Christmastime.

Arkansas   "The Natural State," where the state fruit and the state vegetable are the South Arkansas vine-ripe pink tomato.

Georgia   "The Peach State." Georgia is known for producing the highest-quality peaches. The state vegetable is the Vidalia onion. Peanuts are the state's largest cash crop.

Kentucky   "The Bluegrass State." The Kentucky spotted bass is the state fish, and the state flower is goldenrod.

Mississippi   "The Magnolia State," where the town of Belzoni is known as the Catfish Capital of the World.

North Carolina   "The Tarheel State." The Scuppernong grape is the state fruit, and the state vegetable is the sweet potato.

South Carolina   "The Palmetto State." The sabal palmetto is the state tree; one can sit under a palmetto tree sipping iced tea—the state hospitality beverage.

Tennessee   "The Volunteer State." Tennessee river pearls are the state gem. The state tree is the yellow poplar, or tulip tree.

HISTORY AND MAJOR INFLUENCES

The roots of Southern cuisine predate the arrival of the English and Spanish in the Americas. As in most other areas of the United States, Native Americans of the region heavily influenced the cuisine. When the settlers founded Jamestown, in the Virginia Colony, they encountered the Powhatan tribe of the Algonquian Native Americans, and they shared a dish of succotash, venison, and berries. The Native Americans' diet included meat and seafood cooked over open fires, thought of by many as the original barbecue. Game stews, sweet potatoes, squash, pumpkins, and corn were also staples of this region.

NEW SETTLERS

After the Carolinas were founded in 1670, the first wave of settlers moved south and west, eventually crossing the Appalachian Mountains into Kentucky. The Great Philadelphia Wagon Road, called the Philly Road, was completed in the 1750s; it linked Philadelphia to South Carolina. The immigrants traveling down the Philly Road were typically of Irish, Scottish, Welsh, English, and German descent. From Augusta, Georgia, wagons left the Philly Road and followed the nation's second road, the Upper Federal Road, through Georgia and Alabama to bring goods to market towns like Columbus, Mississippi. A second wave of immigrants split off from the Philly Road in North Carolina in the 1790s to settle in the Blue Ridge Mountains and the valleys and plateaus of Tennessee.

THE OLD SOUTH

The Old South can be defined as the states of the pre–Civil War period from 1820 to 1860, and they were North Carolina, South Carolina, Georgia, Mississippi, and Alabama. Arkansas became part of the United States with the Louisiana Purchase in 1803, and it received statehood in 1836. Its tie to the South was its main crop, cotton. During the antebellum period, the main cash crop in all of the Southern states, from North Carolina to Texas, was cotton. The tobacco and cotton plantations led the economic growth of the South and, in turn, provided the materials for the industrialization of the North.

THE NEW SOUTH

The Reconstruction era began after the Civil War. Cotton plantations, small family farms, subsistence farming, and sharecropping defined the region's economy. By 1900, the expansion of Southern railways, cotton textiles, tobacco and forest products, and the iron, steel, and coal industries were benchmarks of the New South. During the 1920s, cotton was still the region's main cash crop, others being rice, sugar, and tobacco. The cultivation of apples, peaches, peanuts, pecans, and soybeans also began about this time. President Roosevelt's New Deal in 1933 allowed Southern farmers to replace 50 percent of the topsoil depleted by cotton acreage with soybeans, peanuts, hay, wheat, and truck crops. Truck crops included fruits such as peaches, apples, grapes, watermelon, cantaloupe, and blueberries.

WHEN RICE WAS KING

The introduction and successful cultivation of rice was a significant development in colonial South Carolina. From the mid-1700s to the late 19th century, South Carolina was the nation's leading rice producer, and rice was exported by the ton. Rice cultivation, which required intensive labor, provided the basis for an extensive slave-based plantation economy. Charleston was an affluent port serving wealthy plantation owners in rice production. Rice became a staple used frequently in the cooking of the Low Country—an area of swampy marshes, inlets, and bayous that extends from Orangeburg to the coast and the length of the state from the North Carolina border to Georgia's Savannah River. Southerners added rice to casseroles, soups, breads, and puddings. Although the production of cotton and tobacco eventually surpassed that of rice in South Carolina in the first half of the 19th century, rice culture had a significant impact on the landscape, economy, and society. The Civil War, hurricanes, and the end of slavery took their toll on the rice industry in South Carolina, and by the end of the 1800s, most rice production had moved to Texas, California, Arkansas, and Mississippi.

SOUTHERN PLANTATIONS

The agricultural economy and much of life in the South revolved around plantations. Magnificent estate houses and extensive gardens reflected the gracious living, hospitality, and elegance of plantation life. A complete plantation complex as it existed in the 18th and 19th centuries functioned as a small, self-sustaining town. The mansion for the owner and his family was generally flanked by outbuildings, including the overseer's house, slave quarters, summer kitchen, smokehouse, icehouse, poultry house, cotton barn, and corn house. Slaves raised crops, tended livestock, and cultivated gardens. The smokehouse was an integral component of every plantation, and cured ham represents one of the original elements of the Southern diet. Poultry was also an important part of the Southerner's diet. Most plantations kept a variety of domesticated fowl, including chickens, ducks, geese, pigeons, and turkeys. Chickens were the most popular, and Southern fried chicken is a mainstay of the traditional Sunday dinner. Wealthy planters enjoyed the finest of everything and served elegant, elaborate, labor-intensive meals to their guests. They had the financial resources to import costly spices, wines, and fine European foods. Controversial as it was, this lifestyle became known as "Southern hospitality," and even those who lived in humble circumstances prided themselves on being gracious and welcoming to guests.

THE AFRICAN INFLUENCE

The food and style of cooking in the South was profoundly influenced by the African slaves brought to America. Not only did African American slaves introduce many now basic foods, such as okra, yams, black-eyed peas, collard greens, sesame seeds, and watermelon, they also brought cooking techniques from West Africa, such as deep-fat frying. Working as plantation cooks both during and after slavery, they were considered to be even better cooks than the French chefs who had been brought to America. Southern food replaced the plain, bland English cooking and African Americans developed much of what is now thought of as Southern regional cooking. But the slave cooks had to be creative and inventive when they cooked for their own families. They were provided only the waste products after preparing the finer cuts of meat for their owners. Pork was the staple meat of the region, and it was rendered into lard; the hog's skin was fried and called "cracklings." Other ingredients commonly used by slaves included hoofs, ears, tails, brains, and intestines.

With food supplies limited to the vegetables they could grow, and only a limited amount of free time for hunting or fishing, slaves relied on their African traditions to combine complementary ingredients with small portions of meat stretched to flavor vegetable dishes. The term "soul food" referred to food made with feeling and care, and that came from the soul, or one's memory. Recipes were typically handed down through the generations by word of mouth. When millions of African Americans migrated to northern industrial cities in the 20th century, soul food became a way to recognize and celebrate their African American identity.

For many years, Fripp Island, St. Helena's Island, and the nearby Sea Islands were cut off from mainstream South Carolina. As a result, a small group of freed African American slaves, known as "Gullahs," were able to preserve their culture. The Gullahs came from what is now Sierra Leone in West Africa. Most notable was their language: a mixture of contemporary English, older English, and African. They developed their own music and their own rice and fish dishes, and they wove grass baskets that were both sturdy and colorful. Food in this culture took the form of one-pot meals and are represented today by recipes such as Frogmore stew, a blend of shrimp, blue crab, sausage, potatoes, and corn. Red rice, hoppin' john, okra soup, shrimp and grits, pilau, peanut soup, and red beans and rice have their origins in these islands as well.

MOUNTAIN COOKING

When the first pioneers came to the Southern Appalachian Highlands that now are made up of the states of Kentucky, Tennessee, and Alabama, they faced a constant struggle against known and unknown dangers. But the hardy English, Scotch, Irish, Germans, and others tamed the wilderness and left their mark on the region. Industrious and ingenious, these early settlers cultivated fruit, berries, and nuts, as well as grew vegetables, collected honey, and had livestock. By necessity, tastes were simple, food was plain, and thrift was a natural way of life.

With neighbors living miles apart, trails rugged, and communications slow, they learned to make the most of what they had on hand. Cooking was done by early settlers in open fireplaces and brick ovens, and was more an art than a science. Fruits and vegetables were preserved in brine or sugar, or both, in order to have foods for the winter months. A great variety of sweet-and-sour preserves, pickles, chow-chows, and relishes were put out at every meal. Ducks, quail, doves, wild turkeys, and geese were the most sought-after game birds. Other small quarry such as rabbit, squirrel, and raccoon were also used and often roasted, fried, stewed, or smothered in a sauce or gravy.

BARBECUE

Within the debate of what constitutes barbecue, all cooks agree that true barbecue is slow cooking distinguished by the cut of meat and the technique used to cook it. In the Carolinas, pork is the traditional barbecue meat. Generally, the whole hog or shoulder is pit-cooked using direct heat. Slow-cooking at a low temperature ensures that the pig is cooked thoroughly. The resulting pulled and chopped pork may be served with a sauce based on vinegar, water, salt, and pepper. Tomato sauce or ketchup may be added depending on the cook's preferences.

HUMANE TREATMENT OF FARMED ANIMALS

There is high consumer demand for humanely raised meat (beef, pork, and chicken) and other animal products. The demand is clear enough that many food service operators have taken steps to ensure that the animals used in their products have been humanely treated. Individual states have passed specific laws protecting farm animals, and the federal government continues to have hearings on issues surrounding the humane treatment of animals.

Third-Party Certification Programs

Third-party verified humane certification programs have comprehensive standards developed by animal welfare organizations that focus on the needs of the animals. The labels are approved by the USDA for use on products and compliance in independently verified. Some of these programs include:

American Humane Certified (dairy, eggs, chicken, turkey, beef, bison, goat, lamb, pork, veal). The first humane food certification program in the United States, American Humane Certified (previously known as "Free Farmed") is administered as a program of the American Humane Association. Its auditing process includes 24/7 video monitoring of all live areas, including transportation and slaughter facilities.

Certified Humane (dairy, eggs, chicken, turkey, beef, goat, lamb, pork). This humane food certification program is administered by Humane Farm Animal Care and endorsed by many animal advocacy organizations. Species-specific standards require a nutritious diet without antibiotics or hormones, and that animals be raised with shelter, resting areas, sufficient space, and the ability to engage in natural behaviors. The program requires that indoor housing systems (when permitted for poultry and pigs) adhere to strict air quality and lighting standards in addition to those that meet the animals' behavioral and physiological needs.

Food Alliance Certified (dairy, eggs, chicken, beef, bison, goat, lamb, pork). A comprehensive certification program for sustainable farms and food-handling facilities that ensures safe and fair labor conditions, better treatment of animals, wildlife habitat protection, and stewardship of the ecosystem. It ensures humane animal treatment by requiring animals to have access to sunlight, fresh air and water, pasture (where appropriate), adequate food and shelter, enough space to engage in natural and social behaviors, and minimal fear and stress during handling, transport and slaughter. The use of growth hormones and nontherapeutic antibiotics is prohibited.

Memphis barbecue also relies on pork, especially the ribs and shoulder. The meat is smoked over indirect heat and then finished over direct heat. With parts rather than the whole hog, cooking requires less time, space, and fuel. There is considerable debate in this region as to whether the meat or ribs are better when coated with a tomato-based sauce during the cooking process, resulting in a wet or sticky barbecue, or seasoned and served with sauce on the side, known as "dry barbecue."

Texans depend on beef for their barbecue, and the preferred cut is the brisket. Long, slow cooking over indirect heat results in very tender meat that is cut across the grain, rather than pulled or chopped. The meat may be seasoned with a dry rub, but the smoke is what provides the flavor. A wet mop is a sauce that is used during cooking and does not include sugar or tomato sauce, which might burn during cooking. A savory, slightly sweet tomato-based sauce is served on the side, with pickles and sliced onions. Glazed pork ribs or sausage with sauce on the side may also be included in a traditional Texas barbecue.

Tradition in Kansas City (Missouri) calls for both beef and pork (especially the ribs) cooked over indirect heat, but the emphasis is on the sauce. The preference is for a thick, tomato-based sauce with a sweet-and-sour flavor. The sauce is brushed on the meats as a finishing coat during cooking, as well as served on the side. Traditional dishes to serve with barbecue include beans, coleslaw, and potato salad. The style of potato salad, whether mayonnaise-based or mustard-based, the type of slaw—grated, chopped, or shredded—with a creamy or vinegar dressing using red or green cabbage, and the choice of sweet or savory beans depends on the cook and the region and further individualizes a barbecue meal.

SOUTHERN LIVING

Rich or poor, native or immigrant, the South's style of cooking made food a central feature of Southerners' lives. Throughout the region's history, Southern hospitality has revolved around Sunday dinners and public feasts, and the tradition of getting together is taken seriously. It is worth noting that what the rest of the country refers to as "lunch," Southerners call "dinner" and their evening meal is called "supper." No matter the purpose, Southerners are known for their abundant food and timeless, gracious hospitality.

Typical Southern Ingredients and Dishes

Ambrosia   A chilled salad or dessert made with diced fruit, nuts, marshmallows, and coconut.

Benne Wafer   Benne is another name for sesame seed, the main ingredient in this crisp, nut-flavored cookie.

Bibb Lettuce   A small, round lettuce with loosely formed heads and soft, buttery-textured leaves. It is named for Judge Jack Bibb, who developed it in his greenhouse in Frankfort, Kentucky, in 1865. It is also known as "limestone lettuce" because the alkaline limestone soil of the area was credited with helping produce this lettuce.

Biscuit   A small, round quick bread leavened with baking powder or baking soda and cream of tartar. Biscuits should be tender, light, and flaky and are usually served for breakfast, smothered in gravy, or as an accompaniment to fried chicken at dinner.

Black-Eyed Peas   Also known as cowpeas, these small, tan beans with a distinctive black eye were brought to America by African slaves. They are sold fresh, dried, frozen, and canned.

Brunswick Stew   This stew traditionally used squirrel as its primary meat. Today, it may contain smoked pork or chicken and is sometimes seasoned with a ham bone. Brunswick stew is hearty and thick, somewhere between soup and stew in consistency. The traditional vegetables included are tomatoes, onions, celery, carrots, potatoes, lima beans, and corn.

Burgoo   A thick stew made from barbecued meat or mutton and vegetables. Burgoo is often associated with Kentucky.

Butter Bean   A regional name for the lima bean.

Catfish   A freshwater, bottom-feeding fish found in the rivers and lakes of the South. The wild variety has been replaced by the farm-raised variety, now popular across America. Belzoni, Mississippi, is famous for its high-quality, farm-raised catfish, which have a fresh, subtle taste and no fishy odor. Traditional catfish recipes call for the fish to be dredged in cornmeal and fried, served with hush puppies and coleslaw on the side.

Chicken Country Captain   A traditional Low Country dish made by simmering chicken in tomato gravy flavored with curry. It is served over rice.

Chitterling   The small intestine of a hog. After being cleaned, chitterlings are simmered until tender, then fried, added to soups, or served with sauce. They are also used as a casing for sausage.

Chow-Chow   A relish that typically includes cabbage and green tomatoes, which are boiled in pickling brine and flavored with a hint of mustard.

Corn   The Native Americans introduced this staple to the colonists. At the time, corn was tough and required slow cooking to become edible. Now every part of the corn plant is used. The kernels are the most versatile part—used whole in side dishes and popcorn, cooked in ground forms such as cornmeal and cornstarch, and transformed into corn syrup, bourbon, and whiskey. The stalks and cobs are fed to cattle and other animals. The husks are the only authentic wrap for tamales. Corn is primarily a summer crop, but it is readily available throughout the year, frozen and canned. White cornmeal is used more often than yellow in the South, but the two can be interchanged in recipes.

Cornmeal   Ground dried corn kernels. The old-fashioned grinding technique involved water-powered stone mills. The modern approach employs steel rollers. Both methods can be controlled to vary the texture of the resulting meal. Cornmeal is sold in several color varieties—white, yellow, and blue—each of which has its own characteristic flavor.

Corn Pone   The word apone is Native American, meaning "baked." These cakes are made from water and cornmeal and are baked in ashes. From this simple recipe an assortment of breads was developed, including hush puppies, spoonbread, cracklin' bread, johnnycakes, and hoecakes.

Country Ham   A dry ham that is salt-cured for up to three months, then aged for up to 12 months. Country hams are produced in Virginia, Kentucky, Tennessee, North Carolina, and Georgia. After the curing process, the salt is rinsed off and the ham is slowly smoked over a hardwood fire before being aged. The salt used to cure country ham draws out the moisture in the meat, yielding a firm, flavorful finished product.

Cowpeas   A broad category of peas that includes black-eyed peas and purple-hulled peas.

Cracklings   The crisp fried, brown skin of roasted pork. Cracklings are sold packaged and eaten as a snack. They are also used as an ingredient in cornbread.

Deviled   In the South, "deviled" indicates a dish that contains mustard, Worcestershire sauce, Tabasco, and peppers. Deviled eggs are a common appetizer or hors d'oeurve.

Divinity   A regional confection made from white fudge, corn syrup, or molasses combined with stiffly beaten egg whites.

Fatback   A fresh, unsmoked, and unsalted layer of fat from a hog's back.

Frogmore Stew   Named after a town on St. Helena Island, South Carolina, Frogmore stew is a Gullah dish of crab, shrimp, sausage, and corn cooked with spicy seasonings.

Greens   The edible leaves of plants such as collard, mustard, turnip, beet, watercress, poke sallet (or pokeweed), spinach, kale, ramps, and dandelion. Greens are usually sautéed with salt pork or bacon or steamed.

Grits   Ground from hominy to a course, medium, or fine texture, grits are typically made into a soft, savory cornmeal mush. Grits are often served as a breakfast, but also as a side dish. Shrimp and grits is a traditional Carolina dish.

Hoecakes   Also referred to as "johnnycakes," these flat griddle cakes are made from cornmeal, salt, and boiling water. It is said they were created by slaves, who cooked the mixture on their hoe under the hot sun while they worked in the fields.

Hominy   Corn kernels boiled in a lye solution, then hulled, washed, and dried. Hominy is usually sold whole in cans. It is an ingredient commonly found in succotash. When ground, hominy is referred to as "hominy grits."

Hoppin' John   Made from black-eyed peas cooked with salt pork and combined with rice. This dish was a staple of the African slaves who populated the plantations, especially those of the Gullah country of South Carolina. Hoppin' john was traditionally served on New Year's Day to ensure good luck and prosperity, but it is now served year-round. Collard greens and cornbread usually accompany Hoppin' john. The greens are said to represent money and the cornbread signifies gold.

Hush Puppies   A cornmeal dumpling that is deep-fried. They are the traditional accompaniment to fried catfish.

Muscadine   A native American grapevine that grows well in the Southeast. It is eaten as a fruit but was the grape used for the first American-made wine made in North Carolina.

Okra   A vegetable brought to America by African slaves, who used it in stews, soups, or as a side dish. It can be prepared by several methods—frying, boiling, stewing, and baking. Okra's characteristic property is that, when cooked, it exudes a gooey substance that acts as a thickening agent. Okra is available frozen, canned, breaded, and frozen breaded.

Oyster Roast   A popular Low Country event similar to a clambake in the Northeast. Bushels of oysters are dumped into a roasting kettle and covered with a burlap sack, and then placed over hot coals to cook. Once cooked, the oysters are served on newspaper-lined picnic tables.

Peanuts   South Americans cultivated this groundnut over 5,000 years ago. The plants were taken from South America to Africa by Spanish explorers; African slaves, in turn, brought the high-protein peanuts to North America, and slave traders used the peanuts to provide sustenance to the Africans on the long overseas voyage. Today, peanuts are grown primarily in the South. The peanuts grown in Georgia are used primarily for peanut butter and peanut oil. The peanuts grown in Virginia are for eating raw or as cocktail nuts.

Pecans   This relative of the hickory nut has a fat content of over 70 percent, which is higher than any other nut. The trees were brought east from Texas by Thomas Jefferson to his Monticello estate in Virginia. Most pecans are grown in Georgia now, but they can also be found in Oklahoma, Texas, and Virginia.

Pilau   A rice dish associated with South Carolina. Long-grain rice is simmered in an aromatic broth until cooked and nearly dry. Some pilaus call for meat or seafood in a manner similar to Spanish paella.

Poke Sallet   The leaves of the perennial pokeweed plant, which grows wild in the eastern United States. The plant can reach a height of 10 feet and bears small, white flowers that become purple berries. The berries and roots are poisonous. The young leaves must be washed, boiled, and then washed again. Once cooked, poke sallet resembles spinach but tastes like asparagus.

Potlikker   The liquid left over from a meal of greens, field pea, pork, or other items. Often served as a broth, potlikker was a staple among the field hands of the South.

Ramps   A wild onion that resembles a large scallion. Found between February and June over a considerable range—from the Carolinas to Canada—it has an assertive garlic and onion flavor. Ramps are used both raw and cooked.

Red-Eye Gravy   This gravy is made from pan drippings and flecks of ham, a few spoonfuls of coffee, and water. It is cooked until thick and is usually served with ham, biscuits, or cornbread, or used as a sauce with grits or other breakfast food.

Salt Pork   A salt-cure layer of fat from a hog's sides and belly. Salt pork should be blanched before using.

She-Crab Soup   A flour-thickened cream soup prepared exclusively from immature female crabs, resulting in a superior flavor. The roe (crab eggs) is usually added to enhance the flavor. Hard-boiled eggs can be substituted for the crab roe.

Silver Queen Corn   A hybrid corn that is sweet, tender, and white in color. It is the preferred corn in the South.

Spoonbread   A type of cornbread that is similar to a soufflé.

Succotash   A dish Native Americans served to the first American colonists. It is a cooked dish of lima beans, corn kernels, sweet peppers, and, sometimes, meat. The name is derived from a Native American word meaning "boiled whole kernels of corn."

Sweet Potato   A large edible root found by European colonists in America; despite its name, it is not sweet. Sweet potatoes belong to the morning glory family and come in two varieties. The first has light yellow skin and pale yellow flesh; its texture is crumbly. The second variety has a thicker, dark orange skin and an orange, sweet flesh that cooks to a moist texture. Prepare them by baking, boiling, sautéing, or frying.

Vidalia Onion   Sweet onion brought from Texas and grown only in a small number of counties around Vidalia, Georgia. The sulfur-deficient soil in this region yields a milder, sweeter onion than those grown in Texas or Hawaii. The peak growing season is late spring, and every onion is set, clipped, harvested, and sized by hand.

Menus and Recipes from
the Cuisine of the South

MENU ONE

Curried Peanut Soup with Scallions and Quail

Crispy Fried Eggs with Country Ham and Red-Eye Vinaigrette

Seared Triggerfish with Toasted Orzo and Roasted Tomato Sauce

Slow-Cooked Greens

Peach Cobbler

MENU TWO

Shrimp with Pimiento Cheese Grits

Fried Chicken Thighs with Pickled Okra and Stewed Tomatoes

Carolina Pulled Pork Barbecue Sandwich

Sandwich Slaw

Potato Salad

Peanut Brittle

Benne Wafers

MENU THREE

Caramelized Watermelon and Mixed Greens with Shallot-Citrus Dressing

Pecan-Encrusted Catfish with Succotash of Corn, Hominy, and Baby Lima Beans

Pan Roasted Chicken Breast with Haricots Verts, Caramelized Onions, Sweet Potato Fritters,
and Sweet Tea Lemon Jus

Banana Pudding

OTHER RECIPES

Southern Buttermilk Biscuits

Tomato Aspic on Bibb Lettuce Salad

Hush Puppies

Hoppin' John Salad with Pecan Vinaigrette

Fried Green Tomatoes with Blue Cheese

Roasted Tomato Sauce

Frogmore Stew

Curried Peanut Soup with Scallions and Quail

4 servings

 CHEF TIP: The curry in the recipe represents the influence the British and the West Indies had on the cuisine. The peanut plant probably originated in Peru or Brazil, as South Americans made pottery in the shape of peanuts and decorated jars with peanuts as far back as 3,500 years ago. Africans were the first people to introduce peanuts to North America, beginning in the 1700s. Peanuts were used mainly for oil, food, and as a cocoa substitute. Their popularity grew in the late 1800s, when the circus wagons traveled across the country and vendors called "Hot Roasted Peanuts!" to the crowds. In the early 1900s, peanuts became a significant agricultural crop when the boil weevil threatened the South's cotton crop. Peanuts are the 12th most valuable cash crop grown in the United States, according to the American Peanut Council.

AMOUNT	MEASURE	INGREDIENT
2	4 ounces/112 g each	Semi-boneless quail
		Salt and pepper
3 tablespoons	1½ ounces/44 g	Butter
½ cup	2 ounces/56 g	Celery, in ¼-inch (.6 cm) dice
1 cup	4 ounces/112 g	Onion, in ¼-inch (.6 cm) dice
1 teaspoon	3 g	Curry powder
½ teaspoon		Ground cumin
¼ teaspoon		Ground coriander
¼ teaspoon		Ground turmeric
¼ teaspoon		Cayenne, or to taste
½ cup	4 ounces/112 g	Creamy peanut butter
1 quart	1 L	Chicken or vegetable stock
½ cup	2 ounces/56 g	Pecans, toasted, coarsely chopped
½ cup	4 ounces/120 ml	Heavy cream
¼ cup	1 ounce/28 g	Peanuts, roasted, unsalted, coarsely chopped
¼ cup	1 ounce/28 g	Green onions, minced

PROCEDURE

1. Preheat the oven 425°F (232°C). Season the quail with salt and pepper, then roast until the breasts are well browned, 15 to 20 minutes. Let cool, then remove the meat from the bones and shred into small pieces.

2. Melt the butter in a 2- to 3-quart (2 to 3 L) heavy saucepan over medium heat. Add the celery and onion, and sauté 5 to 6 minutes, until onion is soft and translucent. Blend in curry powder, cumin, coriander, turmeric, and cayenne, then cook, stirring, 1 minute.

3. Add the peanut butter, stir to combine, and whisk in the stock. Bring to a boil over medium heat, reduce heat to a simmer, and cook, uncovered, stirring occasionally for 20 minutes.

4. Add the pecans and cook 2 minutes. Remove from the heat and allow to cool for 10 minutes.

5. Puree the soup using a food processor or blender. The soup will still be lumpy. If you want the soup silky, strain through a fine sieve. Return soup to the pan, add the cream, bring to a simmer, and adjust the seasoning.

6. Ladle the soup into a warm soup bowl and sprinkle on the quail meat, chopped peanuts, and green onions.

Curried Peanut Soup with Scallions and Quail

Crispy Fried Eggs with Country Ham and Red-Eye Vinaigrette

4 servings

✳ CHEF TIP: "Red-eye" normally refers to coffee—for example, a red-eye drink may have a shot of espresso in it. Southern red-eye gravy is made with coffee.

AMOUNT	MEASURE	INGREDIENT
For the Red-Eye Vinaigrette		
¼ cup	2 ounces/60 ml	Cider vinegar
1 teaspoon		Honey
2 tablespoons	1 ounce/30 ml	White wine vinegar
6 tablespoons	3 ounces/90 ml	Vegetable oil, preferably grapeseed
4 teaspoons	1¾ ounces/52 ml	Rendered ham fat or bacon fat
2 teaspoons	10.5 g	Sugar
2 teaspoons		Instant coffee granules
2 teaspoons	10 ml	Lemon juice
For the Eggs		
½ cup	2 ounces/56 g	Red onion, thinly sliced
½ cup	2 ounces/56 g	All-purpose flour
¼ teaspoon		Black pepper
2		Eggs, lightly beaten with 1 table-spoon (½ ounce/15 ml) water
½ cup	2 ounces/56 g	Panko (Japanese-style bread crumbs), finely ground
4		Eggs
		Vegetable oil, for deep-frying
4 cups	8 ounces/224 g	Watercress
½ cup	3 ounces/84 g	Queso fresco or very mild feta cheese, crumbled
4 slices	2 ounces/56 g each	Country ham, warmed in a small amount of fat

PROCEDURE

1. Make the vinaigrette. Combine all the ingredients and whisk well to dissolve the sugar and coffee granules. (This makes 1 cup/8 ounces/240 ml dressing.) Set aside.

2. Soak the red onion slices in ice water for 15 minutes. Drain.

3. Make the eggs. Bring a large pot of water to a boil. Add about 2 tablespoons (1 ounce/ 28 g) salt. Carefully place the eggs in their shells in the boiling water and boil exactly 5 minutes. Transfer the eggs to an ice water bath to cool, then remove from the ice water and immediately peel.

4. Coat the eggs in the flour, then dip in the beaten egg and roll in the bread crumbs.

5. Heat the oil to 350°F (175°C) and fry the eggs until golden brown, about 3 minutes. (The yolks should be runny when the eggs are later broken open.)

6. Assemble the salad. Toss the watercress with 3 tablespoons (1½ ounces/45 ml) of the vinaigrette. Divide among 4 plates, and top each with red onion slices, some Pickled Mushrooms (recipe follows), and cheese. Top with a slice of warm ham and a fried egg, and drizzle with additional vinaigrette.

Pickled Mushrooms

AMOUNT	MEASURE	INGREDIENT
1 cup	8 ounces/240 ml	Rice wine vinegar
½ cup	4 ounces/120 ml	Cider vinegar
½ cup	4 ounces/112 g	Sugar
¼ cup	2 ounces/60 ml	Honey
1 tablespoon	3 g	Fresh thyme leaves
1		Bay leaf
3 cups	12 ounces/336 g	Button mushrooms, washed, stems removed, cut into quarters

PROCEDURE

In a 2-quart (1 L) saucepan, combine the vinegars, sugar, honey, thyme, and bay leaf. Bring to a boil over medium heat, stirring to dissolve sugar. Pour the hot liquid over the mushrooms. Cover; refrigerate until cool. Drain before serving.

Crispy Fried Eggs with Country Ham and Red-Eye Vinaigrette

Seared Triggerfish with Toasted Orzo and Roasted Tomato Sauce

4 servings

CHEF TIP: Triggerfish is abundant in South Carolina coastal waters during the fall months. It is one of the best sustainable substitutes for grouper and snapper at that time of year. However, it has a lot of pin bones, so often it is best to cut the fillets into smaller pieces, then cut out the bones in the middle.

AMOUNT	MEASURE	INGREDIENT
2 cups	12 ounces/336 g	Plum tomatoes, cored and halved lengthwise
1 tablespoon	5 g	Garlic, minced
5 tablespoons	2½ ounces/75 ml	Olive oil
2 tablespoons	1 ounce/30 ml	Sherry vinegar
1½ cups	6 ounces/168 g	Uncooked orzo
2 cups	16 ounces/480 ml	Chicken or vegetable stock
		Salt and pepper
1 tablespoon	3 g	Fresh flat-leaf parsley, finely chopped
½ teaspoon		Red pepper flakes
1 cup	4 ounces/112 g	Asparagus, trimmed and cut on bias in ½-inch (1.2 cm) lengths, blanched
4	4 ounces/112 g each	Triggerfish fillets, pin bones removed, each cut in half

PROCEDURE

1. Preheat the oven to 300°F (148°C).

2. Toss the tomatoes with the garlic and 1 tablespoon (½ ounce/15 ml) olive oil. Line a baking sheet with aluminum foil. Lay the tomatoes cut side down on the foil. Roast for 1¼ to 1½ hours, until tomatoes have partially dried but still have some of their juices. Let cool for 10 minutes.

3. Transfer the tomatoes to a blender or food processor. Add the sherry vinegar and puree; if necessary, add a little water to thin the puree to desired thickness.

4. Heat 1 tablespoon (½ ounce/15 ml) olive oil in a 2- to 3-quart (2 to 3 L) saucepan over medium heat. Add the orzo and cook until golden brown, stirring often, about 5 minutes. Add the stock, bring to a boil, and reduce to a simmer. Cover and cook until all the liquid is absorbed, about 10 minutes, and the orzo is tender. Add 1 tablespoon (½ ounce/15 ml) olive oil, the parsley, asparagus, red pepper flakes, and salt and pepper. Mix well.

5. Pat the fish pieces dry with paper towels. Season with salt and pepper. Heat a 10- to 12-inch (25.4–30.5 cm) sauté pan over medium heat; add 2 tablespoons (1 ounce/30 ml) olive oil. When the oil is very hot, add the triggerfish pieces. Sear until golden brown, about 2 minutes, then turn over and sear the second side for 2 minutes. The fish should feel firm to the touch; do not overcook or the fish will be dry.

6. Place the orzo on a warm plate, top with the fish pieces, and spoon the tomato sauce over and around.

Slow-Cooked Greens

4 servings

CHEF TIP: Greens are nutritious powerhouses, loaded with beta-carotene and respectable amounts of vitamin C, calcium, and fiber. Collard, mustard, and turnip greens belong to the cruciferous family, which also includes broccoli, cabbage, and cauliflower.

AMOUNT	MEASURE	INGREDIENT
2 bunches	24 ounces/672 g total	Mixed greens (turnip greens, collards, mustard greens, beet greens, kale, sorrel)
¾ cup	6 ounces/168 g	Bacon, in ¼-inch (.6 cm) dice
½ cup	2 ounces/56 g	Celery, in ¼-inch (.6 cm) dice
2 cups	8 ounces/224 g	Onions, in ¼-inch (.6 cm) dice
1 cup	4 ounces/112 g	Green bell pepper, in ¼-inch (.6 cm) dice
1	6 ounces/168 g	Ham hock
2 tablespoons	1 ounce/30 ml	Red wine vinegar
⅛ teaspoon		Red pepper flakes
1 cup	8 ounces/240 ml	Water
		Salt and black pepper

PROCEDURE

1. Pick over the greens to remove any tough stems, veins, and yellow leaves. Wash two or three times to remove all the grit, and drain thoroughly.

2. Cut greens into 2-inch (5 cm) pieces.

3. In a pot large enough to accommodate all the greens, cook the bacon over medium-high heat until fat has been rendered and bacon is brown but not crisp, 3 to 5 minutes.

4. Add the celery, onions, and bell pepper and cook 5 minutes.

5. Reduce the heat to medium and add the greens. Cover and cook, stirring occasionally, until greens are wilted, about 10 minutes.

6. Add the ham hock, vinegar, and red pepper flakes; cover and cook 5 minutes.

7. Add the water, cover, and simmer for 1½ hours or until tender, stirring occasionally.

8. Remove the ham hock. Pull the meat from the bone. Coarsely chop meat and stir into greens. Cook 5 minutes longer. Taste and correct the seasoning.

Peach Cobbler

CHEF TIP: A cobbler is a home-style baked fruit dessert, usually made with a top crust. The crust and/or topping will have different versions depending on the region of the country. Cobblers might have been originally made with a biscuit topping; when the biscuits were dropped onto the fruit in small rounds, it likely gave the appearance of a cobbled road, hence the name. Cobblers can also be made with cake batter or cookie dough toppings.

AMOUNT	MEASURE	INGREDIENT
For the Pastry		
1½ cups	6 ounces/168 g	All-purpose flour
¾ teaspoon	4 g	Kosher salt
½ teaspoon	3 g	Sugar
½ cup	4 ounces/112 g	Unsalted butter, in ½-inch (1.2 cm) pieces, cold
¼ cup	2 ounces/60 ml	Milk, very cold
For the Filling		
4 cups	24 ounces/672 g	Peaches, firm but ripe, peeled, in ½-inch (1.2 cm) slices
¼ cup	2 ounces/56 g	Sugar, plus some to sprinkle on top
1 tablespoon	7 g	All-purpose flour
⅛ teaspoon	1 g	Salt
¼ teaspoon	1 g	Freshly grated nutmeg
2 tablespoons	1 ounce/28 g	Butter
		Melted butter or milk, for brushing

PROCEDURE

1. Preheat the oven to 425°F (220°C). Grease a 9 × 13-inch (22.5 × 32.5 cm) baking pan.

2. Make the pastry. Combine the flour, salt, and sugar. Cut in the butter with fingertips or a pastry blender until it resembles coarse meal. Stir in the milk with a rubber spatula or fork until the dry ingredients are just moistened. Let dough rest for 1 minute, then transfer to a well-floured surface.

3. Roll the dough into a rough 6 × 10-inch (15 × 25 cm) rectangle. With the long edge of the dough facing you, fold in both short ends of the dough so that they meet in the center; then fold the dough in half crosswise, forming a package of dough four layers thick. Once again, roll the dough into a rectangle ¼ inch (.6 cm) thick.

4. Using a lightly greased and floured 2-inch (5 cm) or smaller cutter, stamp out, with one decisive punch per round, four rows of three dough rounds each, cutting them close together to generate as few scraps as possible. Dip the cutter into flour before each new cut. (Scraps may be re-rolled if necessary.)

5. Make the filling. Toss the peaches with the sugar, flour, salt, and nutmeg. Spread in the prepared pan and dot with half the butter.

6. Place the dough rounds on top but not touching; brush the dough with melted butter or milk. Sprinkle a little sugar over the top of the dough.

7. Bake 10 minutes, then reduce heat to 375°F (190°C) and bake 10 to 12 minutes longer, until the top is deep golden brown and the filling begins to bubble.

8. Cool on a rack until warm; may be served with whipped cream or ice cream.

Peach Cobbler

Shrimp with Pimiento Cheese Grits

4 servings

CHEF TIP: Pimiento cheese is traditional mixture of grated sharp Cheddar, mayonnaise, and diced pimiento. It is the "pâté of the South" or the "Caviar of the South." When it first appeared in the early 20th century, it was a filling for finger sandwiches. The original version was quite different, having originated as a way to combine two new products of the North's industrial food manufacturing: cream cheese and canned pimientos.

Pimiento Cheese Grits

AMOUNT	MEASURE	INGREDIENT
4 cups	32 ounces/960 L	Water
1 cup	6 ounces/168 g	Coarse stone-ground white grits
½ cup	4 ounces/120 ml	Heavy cream
1 tablespoon	½ ounce/14 g	Butter
½ cup	3 ounces/84 g	Roasted red bell pepper, in ¼-inch (.6 cm) dice
1 cup	4 ounces/112 g	Sharp Cheddar cheese, shredded
		Salt and pepper

PROCEDURE

1. Bring the water to a boil in a 2- to 3-quart (2 to 3 L) pot, then slowly pour in the grits, stirring constantly. Reduce the heat to low and continue to cook, stirring often so the grits do not settle to the bottom and scorch. Cook 8 to 10 minutes or until the grits plump. Cook an additional 20 to 25 minutes, stirring frequently but not constantly.

2. Add the cream, butter, roasted red pepper, and cheese. Cook, stirring, until cheese has melted and the flavor of the pepper develops with the grits, about 10 minutes. Correct the seasoning with salt and pepper, then keep covered and warm. (If grits become too thick, adjust the consistency with warm water.)

Shrimp and Sauce

AMOUNT	MEASURE	INGREDIENT
6 tablespoons	3 ounces/84 g	Butter
2 cups	12 ounces/336 g	Peeled and deveined medium shrimp (20–25 count)
		Salt and pepper
¼ cup	1 ounce/28 g	Shallots, minced
1 teaspoon		Fresh thyme, chopped
½ cup	2 ounces/56 g	Carrot, peeled, in ¼-inch (.6 cm) dice
½ cup	2 ounces/56 g	Celery, peeled, in ¼-inch (.6 cm) dice
½ cup	2 ounces/56 g	Onion, in ¼-inch (.6 cm) dice
¼ cup	2 ounces/60 ml	Dry white wine
1 cup	6 ounces/168 g	Tomato, peeled, seeded, in ¼-inch (.6 cm) dice
1 tablespoon	3 g	Fresh flat-leaf parsley, chopped
1 tablespoon	½ ounce/15 ml	Lemon juice

PROCEDURE

1. Heat 2 tablespoons (1 ounce/30 ml) of the butter in a 10-inch (25.4 cm) sauté pan over medium-high heat. Season the shrimp with salt and pepper and sear in the pan on all sides, 1 to 2 minutes; do not overcook. Remove and set aside.

2. In the same pan, add 2 more tablespoons (1 ounce/30 ml) butter and sauté the shallots and thyme for 1 minute. Add the carrot, celery, and onion, and cook 2 to 3 minutes, stirring frequently. Deglaze the pan with the wine and add the tomato. Cook 4 to 5 minutes or until liquid has reduced by half.

3. Return shrimp to the pan, stir in the parsley and lemon juice, and bring to a simmer. Stir in the remaining 2 tablespoons (1 ounce/30 ml) butter. Correct the seasoning.

4. Place ½ cup grits on each plate and spoon the shrimp and sauce over.

Shrimp with Pimiento Cheese Grits

Fried Chicken Thighs with Pickled Okra and Stewed Tomatoes

4 servings

✦ **CHEF TIP:** For a true Southern pan-fried chicken, combine 1 pound (448 g) lard, ½ cup (4 ounces/120 ml) butter, and ½ cup (4 ounces/112 g) diced country-style ham. Simmer over low heat for 30 minutes, skimming as needed, until the butter is clarified. Strain and use for frying the chicken.

Brining the poultry (soaking in a saltwater solution) before cooking serves two purposes: it helps the flesh retain moisture and it seasons the meat all the way through. To make the brine, stir kosher salt into cold water until dissolved, in the proportion of ¼ cup (56 g) salt to 1 quart (1 L) water. (Don't use table salt in this formula or it will be too salty.)

For best results, prepare the Pickled Okra and Stewed Tomatoes before you fry the chicken.

Fried Chicken Thighs

AMOUNT	MEASURE	INGREDIENT
4	4 ounces/112 g	Chicken thighs, boneless and skinless, brined if desired
1 cup	8 ounces/240 ml	Buttermilk
1 cup	4 ounces/112 g	All-purpose flour
2 tablespoons	²/₃ ounce/18 g	Cornstarch
⅛ teaspoon		Cayenne pepper
⅛ teaspoon		Dry mustard
		Salt and black pepper
As needed		Vegetable oil, for frying

PROCEDURE

1. If chicken was brined, drain and rinse.

2. Soak chicken in buttermilk for 1 hour at room temperature or 4 hours in the refrigerator.

3. Combine the flour, cornstarch, cayenne, mustard, and salt and pepper in a bowl. (Remember, the brined chicken may have enough salt already.) Remove the chicken from the buttermilk and drain. Dredge in the flour mixture, and then pat well to remove all excess flour. Let sit until the flour is pastelike. (This is crucial for crisp chicken.)

4. Heat the oil to 335°F (168°C) in a deep pot or deep-fryer. Add the chicken pieces, skin side down; do not overcrowd the pan—fry in batches, if necessary. Cook 4 to 6 minutes on each side, until the chicken is golden brown and cooked through.

5. Drain on a rack and over paper towels.

6. Place ½ cup (3 ounces/84 g) Stewed Tomatoes (recipe follows) on each plate. Place a hot chicken thigh on top of the tomato mixture and garnish with Pickled Okra (recipe follows).

Stewed Tomatoes

AMOUNT	MEASURE	INGREDIENT
1 tablespoon	½ ounce/14 g	Unsalted butter
1 tablespoon	¼ ounce/7 g	Shallots, minced
1 cup	6 ounces/168 g	Tomato, peeled, seeded, in ¼-inch (.6 cm) dice (heirloom variety, if possible)
1 cup	6 ounces/168 g	Green tomatoes, peeled, seeded, in ¼-inch (.6 cm) dice
½ teaspoon		Jalapeño pepper, minced
1 tablespoon	3 g	Fresh flat-leaf parsley, chopped
2 teaspoons		Fresh mint, chopped
1 tablespoon	½ ounce/15 ml	Chicken stock

PROCEDURE

1. Heat a 10- to 12-inch (25.4–30.5 cm) sauté pan over medium heat. Add the butter and shallots, and cook 2 minutes, stirring occasionally.

2. Add the red and green tomatoes, cook 3 to 4 minutes, then add the jalapeño, parsley, mint, and chicken stock. Cook 2 minutes.

Pickled Okra

AMOUNT	MEASURE	INGREDIENTS
2 cups	8 ounces/224 g	Okra
3 tablespoons	1¼ ounces/35 g	Coarse salt
1 cup	8 ounces/240 ml	Water
1½ cups	12 ounces/360 ml	White vinegar
1 tablespoon	½ ounce/14 g	Sugar
1		Bay leaf
1 tablespoon	7 g	Pickling spice
2 cups	12 ounces/336 g	Onions, in ½-inch (1.2 cm) slices

PROCEDURE

1. Place the okra in a colander. Add 1½ tablespoons (18 g) salt and toss to combine. Let okra drain in sink for 10 minutes. Prepare an ice water bath.

2. Combine the remaining salt, the water, vinegar, sugar, bay leaf, pickling spice, and onions in a nonreactive 2- to 3-quart (2 to 3 L) heavy saucepan. Bring to a boil over medium heat, stirring until the sugar has dissolved.

3. Rinse okra under cold running water to remove salt. Transfer to a large bowl. Pour the hot brine over the okra. Set bowl in ice water bath and let cool 10 minutes, stirring often.

4. Transfer the cool okra mixture to the refrigerator to cool completely, about 25 minutes.

Carolina Pulled Pork Barbecue Sandwich

AMOUNT	MEASURE	INGREDIENT
For the Dry Rub		
1½ tablespoons	⅓ ounce/10 g	Black pepper
1½ tablespoons	¾ ounce/21 g	Dark brown sugar
1½ tablespoons	⅓ ounce/10 g	Paprika
2 tablespoons	1 ounce/28 g	Coarse salt
½ teaspoon	1 g	Cayenne pepper
1	2 pounds/896 g	Boneless pork shoulder (Boston butt)
For the Mop		
½ cup	4 ounces/120 ml	Cider vinegar
¼ cup	2 ounces/60 ml	Water
1 tablespoon	15 ml	Worcestershire sauce
½ tablespoon	3 g	Black pepper
½ teaspoon	3 g	Coarse salt
1 teaspoon	5 ml	Vegetable oil
1 cup	8 ounces/240 ml	Carolina Barbecue Sauce (recipe follows)
4		Hamburger buns, toasted

PROCEDURE

1. Make the dry rub. Mix the ingredients and sprinkle the dry rub over the pork, pressing it into the meat. Cover and let sit 30 minutes at room temperature.

2. Make the mop. Combine the ingredients and set aside.

3. Prepare the barbecue. If possible, hot-smoke the pork until fork-tender, brushing with the mop every 45 minutes. Alternatively, roast the pork in a 300°F (150°C) oven for 2 to 3 hours or until fork-tender, brushing with the mop every 45 minutes. Meat may be cut into two pieces to facilitate roasting.

4. Remove pork from the smoker or oven and let rest 30 minutes.

5. Pull the meat apart or shred using two forks.

6. Combine the shredded pork with the barbecue sauce in a saucepan, cover tightly, and simmer 20 to 30 minutes. Add more water, if needed.

7. Serve the pork barbecue on toasted buns with Sandwich Slaw and Potato Salad (recipes follow), and offer additional barbecue sauce on the side.

Carolina BBQ Sauce

AMOUNT	MEASURE	INGREDIENT
1 teaspoon	2 g	Dry mustard
1 teaspoon	5 g	Coarse salt
1 tablespoon	¼ ounce/7 g	Sweet Hungarian paprika
1 tablespoon	½ ounce/14 g	Granulated sugar
1 tablespoon	½ ounce/14 g	Brown sugar
½ teaspoon	1 g	Cayenne pepper
½ teaspoon	1 g	Black pepper
²/₃ cup	6 ounces/180 ml	Water
¼ cup	2 ounces/60 ml	Worcestershire sauce
½ cup	4 ounces/120 ml	Red wine vinegar

PROCEDURE

1. Combine the mustard, salt, paprika, sugars, and peppers in a saucepan. Stir in the water; heat to boiling, then remove from heat.

2. Stir in the Worcestershire sauce and vinegar.

Sandwich Slaw

4 servings

AMOUNT	MEASURE	INGREDIENT
2 cups	7 ounces/196 g	Green cabbage, shredded
2 tablespoons	½ ounce/14 g	Onion, minced
2 tablespoons	1 ounce/28 ml	Cider vinegar
2 tablespoons	1 ounce/30 ml	Mayonnaise
1	5 g	Garlic clove, minced
2 teaspoons	⅓ ounce/10 g	Sugar
1 teaspoon	2 g	Black pepper
		Salt

PROCEDURE

Mix the cabbage, onion, vinegar, mayonnaise, garlic, sugar, pepper, and salt in a bowl and refrigerate for 1 hour. Place a generous portion on each sandwich or serve alongside.

Carolina Pulled Pork Barbecue Sandwich with Slaw, Potato Salad, and Carolina BBQ Sauce

Potato Salad

 **CHEF TIP:** All-purpose potatoes have moderate moisture and starch. This type of potato tends to hold its shape after cooking.

AMOUNT	MEASURE	INGREDIENT
2		Eggs, hard-cooked
3 cups	18 ounces/504 g	All-purpose potatoes, cooked, peeled, in 1-inch (2.5 cm) cubes
½ cup	2 ounces/56 g	Celery, in ¼-inch (.6 cm) dice
¼ cup	1 ounce/28 g	Green onions, chopped
⅓ cup	2 ounces/56 g	Bread-and-butter pickles, chopped
½ cup	2 ounces/56 g	Red onion, in ¼-inch (.6 cm) dice
½ cup	2 ounces/56 g	Red bell pepper, in ¼-inch (.6 cm) dice
¾ cup	6 ounces/180 ml	Mayonnaise
1 teaspoon	5 ml	Worcestershire sauce
1 teaspoon	5 ml	Dijon mustard
		Salt and pepper

PROCEDURE

1. Separate the yolks from the whites of the hard-cooked eggs. Mash yolks and chop whites.

2. In a large bowl, combine the chopped egg white, potatoes, celery, green onions, pickles, red onion, and bell pepper.

3. Combine the egg yolks with the mayonnaise, Worcestershire sauce, and mustard; mix well. Pour over the potato mixture and stir gently to coat with the dressing.

4. Correct the seasoning with salt and pepper. Chill before serving.

Peanut Brittle

Makes 2 pounds (907 g)

✦ **CHEF TIP:** This great treat came out of the South in the late 19th century, when people were searching for new products and ideas for using the peanut crop.

AMOUNT	MEASURE	INGREDIENT
2 cups	14 ounces/392 g	Sugar
½ cup	6 ounces/180 ml	Light corn syrup
½ cup	4 ounces/120 ml	Water
1 cup	5 ounces/140 g	Raw peanuts
½ teaspoon	3 g	Salt
1 tablespoon	½ ounce/14 g	Unsalted butter
⅛ teaspoon	1 g	Baking soda
½ teaspoon	2 ml	Vanilla extract

PROCEDURE

1. Grease a shallow pan or coat with cooking spray.

2. In a 2- to 3-quart (2 to 3 L) heavy saucepan over medium heat, combine the sugar, corn syrup, and water, stirring to dissolve the sugar.

3. Continue to cook to soft-ball stage (238°F/114°C). If a thermometer is not available, spoon a few drops of the hot sugar into a bowl of very cold water. Check the hardness of the cooled sugar with your fingertips. The balls of sugar will be soft and flexible when pressed between the fingertips. If you remove the ball of sugar from the water, it will flatten after a few moments in the hand.

4. Add the peanuts and salt; cook, stirring constantly, until the mixture reaches the hard-crack stage (300°F, 149°C). Or, sugar spooned into very cold water will form hard, brittle threads that break when bent. The sugar is very hot; allow the syrup to cool in the cold water for a few moments before touching it.

5. Remove from heat and stir in the butter, baking soda, and vanilla.

6. Pour the mixture into the prepared pan and cool.

7. When hardened, break into irregular 2-inch (5 cm) pieces. Store in an airtight container.

Benne Wafers

AMOUNT	MEASURE	INGREDIENT
1 cup	4 ounces/112 g	White sesame seeds
¾ cup	6 ounces/168 g	Butter, melted
1½ cups	12 ounces/336 g	Brown Sugar
1		Egg
1 teaspoon	5 ml	Vanilla extract
1 cup	4 ounces/112 g	All-purpose flour
¼ teaspoon		Salt
¼ teaspoon		Baking powder

PROCEDURE

1. Preheat the oven to 375°F (190°C). Line a baking sheet with parchment or use a silicone mat.

2. Place the sesame seeds on an ungreased baking sheet and toast for 8 to 10 minutes, until light brown. Leave oven on.

3. In a large bowl, combine the melted butter, brown sugar, egg, vanilla, flour, salt, and baking powder; mix well. Add the sesame seeds and mix well.

4. Drop by ½ teaspoon 1½ inches (3.8 cm) apart onto the prepared baking sheet. Bake for 4 to 6 minutes, until light brown.

5. Let the cookies cool 2 minutes, then move to a wire rack to cool completely. Store cooled cookies in an airtight container.

Peanut Brittle and Benne Wafers

Caramelized Watermelon and Mixed Greens with Shallot-Citrus Dressing

4 servings

 **CHEF TIP:** Look for watermelons with a bright skin; dullness may indicate it is old. Examine for the "field spot"—a large splotch of creamy to yellow skin or even an orange color. This indicates the melon was allowed to sit in the field, maturing and producing sugar. Avoid melons where the field spot is white, pale green, or nonexistent. The melon should be heavy for its size, which indicates it is juicy.

To prep, cut the watermelon into 1-inch (2.5 cm) thick slices, which will make it easier to caramelize.

AMOUNT	MEASURE	INGREDIENT
For the Dressing		
1½ tablespoons	¾ ounce/21 g	Shallots, minced
1 teaspoon	5 ml	Dijon mustard
½ teaspoon	3 ml	Honey
2 tablespoons	1 ounce/30 ml	Cider vinegar
1 tablespoon	½ ounce/15 ml	Orange juice
1 tablespoon	½ ounce/15 ml	Lime juice
¼ cup	2 ounces/60 ml	Extra-virgin olive oil
¼ cup	2 ounces/60 ml	Vegetable oil
		Salt and black pepper
For the Salad		
1½ tablespoons	⅓ ounce/10 g	White sesame seeds
¼ teaspoon	1 ml	Roasted sesame oil
2 cups	11 ounces/308 g	Watermelon, seeded, in 1-inch (2.5 cm) pieces, rind reserved for pickling or another use
2 tablespoons	1 ounce/30 ml	Vegetable oil
2 cups	4 ounces/112 g	Watercress leaves
1 cup	2 ounces/56 g	Arugula
¼ cup	½ ounce/14 g	Fresh flat-leaf parsley
½ cup	2 ounces/56 g	Green onions, sliced
¼ cup	1 ounce/28 g	Chervil tops (or fresh oregano)
½ cup	3 ounces/84 g	Cucumber, in 12 ribbons

PROCEDURE

1. Make the dressing. In a blender, combine all the ingredients except the oils and salt and pepper. Blend until smooth, then slowly add the oils to make an emulsion. Correct the seasoning with salt and pepper.

2. Prepare the salad. In a small sauté pan, toast the sesame seeds in the sesame oil until lightly toasted.

(continued) →

3. Dry the melon pieces on two or three layers of paper towels and press additional towels on top. The surface of the melon needs to be somewhat dry to caramelize without splattering.

4. Heat a heavy 10- to 12-inch (25.4–30.5 cm) skillet over medium-high heat until very hot. Add 2 tablespoons (1 ounce/30 ml) oil to just coat the pan. When the oil "shimmers," remove the melon from the paper towels and carefully lay it in the pan. Sear until you start to smell a sweet, caramel smell, then lift out with a spatula; the melon should have a dark brown side (it is okay to sear only one side). Work in batches, as necessary. Place seared melon in the freezer for 5 minutes to stop the cooking, then in the refrigerator to chill and firm up.

5. Trim the watermelon rind and cut into 1-inch (2.5 cm) pieces.

6. Combine half the sesame seeds in a large bowl with the watercress, arugula, parsley, green onions, and chervil. Toss with half the dressing.

7. Toss the cucumber ribbons with 1 tablespoon (½ ounce/15 ml) of the dressing. Roll the ribbons individually so they form a loose cylinder shape.

8. Toss the chilled watermelon cubes with the remaining dressing.

9. Divide the greens evenly among cold plates, top with the seared watermelon and garnish with the cucumber ribbons.

10. Sprinkle with the remaining sesame seeds.

Caramelized Watermelon and Mixed Greens

Pecan-Encrusted Catfish with Succotash of Corn, Hominy, and Baby Lima Beans

4 servings

✦ **CHEF TIP:** For best results, give the breading time to firm up before pan-frying. If you put breaded food immediately into hot oil, the breading may fall off.

Pecan-Encrusted Catfish

AMOUNT	MEASURE	INGREDIENT
1 cup	4 ounces/112 g	Pecans, chopped
⅓ cup	2 ounces/56 g	Fine-ground cornmeal
½ cup	2 ounces/56 g	Dried bread crumbs
2 tablespoons	6 g	Fresh parsley, chopped
4	4 ounces/112 g each	Catfish fillets
		Salt and white pepper
1 cup	4 ounces/112 g	All-purpose flour
1		Egg, lightly beaten with 1 tablespoon (15 ml) water
To taste		Salt and white pepper
1 cup	4 ounces, 112 g	All-purpose flour, for dredging
As needed		Vegetable oil, for pan-frying

PROCEDURE

1. Place the pecans, cornmeal, bread crumbs, and parsley in a food processor and blend until chopped. (This can be as fine as you like.)

2. Season the catfish with salt and pepper and dip the fillets in flour; shake off excess, then dip in the egg wash and let excess drip off. Place fillets in the pecan cornmeal mixture, pat and turn until completely breaded, then refrigerate for 1 hour to set the breading.

3. Heat the oil to 350°F (175°C) in a 10- to 12-inch (25.4–30.5 cm) skillet.

4. Pan-fry the fillets 2 to 3 minutes on the first side, then turn and cook 1 to 1½ minutes more on the other side, until golden brown; drain on paper towels.

Succotash of Corn, Hominy, and Baby Lima Beans

AMOUNT	MEASURE	INGREDIENT
2 cups	5 ounces/141 g	Baby lima beans
2 tablespoons	1 ounce/28 g	Bacon, in ¼-inch (.6 cm) dice
2 tablespoons	1 ounce/28 g	Butter
1 cup	5 ounces/141 g	Fresh corn kernels, cut from cob
3 tablespoons	1 ounce/30 g	Shallots, chopped
1 cup	6 ounces/170 g	Hominy, drained
2 tablespoons	1 ounce/30 ml	Dry white wine or chicken stock
½ cup	4 ounces/120 ml	Heavy cream
		Salt and black pepper
1 tablespoon	3 g	Fresh parsley, chopped

PROCEDURE

1. Parboil the lima beans 1 minute, until just tender; drain.

2. Over medium heat, render the bacon until crisp, 3 to 5 minutes.

3. Add half the butter to the pan, then add the shallots and cook for 2 minutes or until soft. Add the corn, and cook 3 minutes or until corn is tender.

4. Add the hominy and lima beans; stir to combine.

5. Add the wine; cook 3 to 5 minutes or until liquid is almost gone.

6. Add the cream and cook to reduce until it begins to thicken.

7. Stir in remaining butter, season with salt and pepper, and toss in the parsley.

Pecan-Encrusted Catfish with Succotash of Corn, Hominy, and Baby Lima Beans

Pan-Roasted Chicken Breast with Haricots Verts, Caramelized Onions, Sweet Potato Fritters, and Sweet Tea Lemon Jus

4 servings

 **CHEF TIP:** Conventional processed chicken parts are dunked in iced chlorinated water to bring down the chicken's temperature after it's been slaughtered. Air-chilled chicken are sprayed with chlorinated water inside and out, and then rapidly cooled in cold air chambers. Air-chilled chickens cost significantly more, but chefs claim the result is a better-tasting bird that retains its natural flavors and boasts a crisper skin when roasting or sautéing.

Pan-Roasted Chicken Breast

AMOUNT	MEASURE	INGREDIENT
2 tablespoons	1 ounce/30 ml	Olive oil
4	5 ounces/140 g each	Air-chilled chicken breast halves, boneless, skin on
		Salt and pepper
2 cups	16 ounces/480 ml	Sweet tea, freshly brewed
1 tablespoon	½ ounce/15 ml	Lemon juice
2 tablespoons	1 ounce/28 g	Butter, cold

PROCEDURE

1. Preheat the oven to 400°F (204°C).

2. Brush a 10- to 12-inch (25.4–30.5 cm) oven-safe sauté pan with the olive oil. Season the chicken breasts. Lay the chicken skin side down in the cold pan and place the pan on the stove over medium-high heat. (This method yields in a crisper skin.) Let the chicken brown for 3 minutes, then place in the oven without flipping and roast for 6 to 8 minutes or until the internal temperature reaches 155°F (68°C). Remove chicken from pan and keep warm.

3. Discard any rendered grease and place the sauté pan over high heat. Deglaze with the tea and lemon juice, scrape the bottom of the pan and reducing the liquid by half. Remove pan from heat and whisk in the butter. Correct the seasoning.

Haricots Verts

AMOUNT	MEASURE	INGREDIENT
1 tablespoon	½ ounce/15 ml	Olive oil
¼ cup	1 ounce/28 g	Country ham, diced
1 cup	4 ounces/112 g	Haricots verts, trimmed and blanched
1 cup	8 ounces/224 g	Caramelized Onions (page 122)
		Salt and pepper

PROCEDURE

1. Heat a 10- to 12-inch (25.4–30.5 cm) sauté pan over medium-high heat. Add the olive oil and ham. Allow the ham to render for 2 minutes, then add the onions and cook 2 to 3 minutes.

2. Add the beans to the pan and sauté until heated through. Season with salt and pepper and serve.

Pan-Roasted Chicken Breast with Haricots Verts, Caramelized Onions, Sweet Potato Fritters, and Sweet Tea Lemon Jus

Caramelized Onion

AMOUNT	MEASURE	INGREDIENT
2 tablespoons	1 ounce/28 g	Vegetable oil
1 tablespoon	½ ounce/14 g	Butter
3 cups	18 ounces/504 g	Yellow medium onions, sliced ⅛ inch/0.125 cm thick
¼ cup	2 ounces/60 ml	Chicken stock

PROCEDURE

1. Heat a 10- to 12-inch (25.4–30.5 cm) sauté pan over medium-high heat. Add the oil; when fat is hot and begins to ripple, add the onions.

2. Stir the onions untl they are coated with oil. Add the butter and continue to stir until butter coats the onions.

3. Reduce heat to medium low and cook, stirring, for 10 minutes.

4. Let cook for 30 to 45 minutes, stirring occasionally. The trick is to allow the onions to brown; if you stir too often, they will not brown. Continue to cook and scrape the pan until the onions are a rich brown color. At the end of the cooking process, add the stock to deglaze the pan.

Sweet Potato Fritters

AMOUNT	MEASURE	INGREDIENT
As needed		Vegetable oil, for deep-frying
¼ cup	1 ounce/28 g	All-purpose flour
		Salt
½ teaspoon		Baking powder
1		Egg, separated
1 tablespoon	½ ounce/14 g	Butter, melted
1 cup	8 ounces/224 g	Mashed sweet potatoes
1 teaspoon	3 g	Sugar
½ cup	4 ounces/120 ml	Milk

PROCEDURE

1. Heat the oil to 365°F (185°C) in a deep pot.

2. Sift the flour, salt, and baking powder together.

3. Beat the egg white to stiff peaks.

4. Combine the melted butter, sweet potato, sugar, milk, and egg yolk in a bowl. Mix in the dry ingredients, then fold in the egg white.

5. Drop by tablespoons (½ ounce/14 g) in the hot oil and cook until browned, about 2 minutes, then remove and drain on paper towels.

Banana Pudding

AMOUNT	MEASURE	INGREDIENT
For the Custard		
1 cup	8 ounces/240 ml	Milk
1 cup	8 ounces/240 ml	Heavy cream
½		Vanilla bean
6		Egg yolks
⅓ cup	2½ ounces/70 g	Sugar
2 tablespoons	1 ounce/28 g	All-purpose flour
Pinch		Salt
1 teaspoon	5 ml	Vanilla extract
For the Meringue		
6		Egg whites, room temperature
¼ teaspoon	2 ml	Vanilla extract
½ cup	3½ ounces/98 g	Sugar
For the Filling		
2 cups	8 ounces/224 g	Angel food cake, in 1-inch (2.5 cm) cubes, lightly toasted, or vanilla wafers
2	13 ounces/364 g	Bananas, in ½-inch (1.2 cm) slices

PROCEDURE

1. Preheat the oven to 400°F (205°C).

2. Make the custard. In a 2- to 3-quart (2 to 3 L) nonreactive saucepan, combine the milk, ½ cup (4 ounces/120 ml) of the cream, and the vanilla bean. Heat to just below a simmer, cover, and remove from heat; let sit for 15 minutes to develop the vanilla flavor, then remove vanilla bean, wipe off, and retain for another use.

3. Whisk together the egg yolks, sugar, flour, and salt until smooth.

4. Whisk the warm milk into the egg yolk mixture, pour back into the saucepan, and return pan to the heat. Cook until the custard thickens and begins to bubble, then cook for 1 minute more. (It should be thick at this point.)

5. Strain the custard through a fine-mesh sieve into a bowl and immediately whisk in the remaining cream and the vanilla extract.

6. Make the meringue. Beat the egg whites until they begin to froth, then add the vanilla. Continue beating until they make soft peaks. Gradually add the sugar a tablespoon at a time, and beat until egg whites are moist and very glossy.

7. Assemble the pudding. Spoon a thin layer of custard into the bottom of a 4-cup (32 ounces/ 960 ml) ovenproof baking container. Top with a layer of cake cubes and some sliced bananas. Spoon more custard over and continue layering, ending with custard on top.

8. Top the pudding with the meringue, making sure there is a good seal at the edges of the baking pan.

9. Bake for 5 minutes, until golden brown. Serve warm or at room temperature.

Banana Pudding

Southern Buttermilk Biscuits

4 servings

AMOUNT	MEASURE	INGREDIENT
2 cups	8 ounces/224 g	All-purpose flour
¼ teaspoon		Baking soda
1 tablespoon	½ ounce	Baking powder
1 teaspoon	5 g	Salt
6 tablespoons	3 ounces/84 g	Butter, very cold, in chunks
1 cup (approximately)	8 ounces/240 ml	Buttermilk

PROCEDURE

1. Preheat the oven to 450°F (232°C).

2. Combine the flour, baking soda, baking powder, and salt in a bowl.

3. Cut the butter into the dry ingredients until it resembles coarse meal.

4. Add the buttermilk, and mix just until combined (about 30 seconds). If mixture appears too dry, add a little more buttermilk; the dough should be on the wet side.

5. Turn the dough out onto a floured work bench. Gently pat the dough until it is about ½ inch (1.2 cm) thick. Fold the dough five times.

6. Press the dough to 1 inch (2.5 cm) thick. Use a round cutter to cut biscuits. Place on an ungreased baking sheet. If you want soft biscuits, allow them to touch; for "crusty" sides, place biscuits 1 inch (2.5 cm) apart. (Biscuits placed close together rise higher.)

7. Bake 10 to 12 minutes, until light golden brown. Do not overbake.

Tomato Aspic on Bibb Lettuce Salad

4 servings

 CHEF TIP: The traditional accompaniment is mayonnaise.

Tomato Aspic

AMOUNT	MEASURE	INGREDIENT
2 cups	12 ounces/336 g	Tomatoes, peeled, seeded, roughly chopped
½ cup	2 ounces/56 g	Onion, in ¼-inch (.6 cm) dice
½ cup	2 ounces/56 g	Celery, in ¼-inch (.6 cm) dice
1		Garlic clove, smashed
2		Bay leaves
3		Whole peppercorns
2		Whole cloves
1 teaspoon	6 g	Kosher salt
1 cup plus 2 tablespoons	9 ounces/270 ml	Water
½ tablespoon	7 g	Sugar
½ tablespoon	7 ml	Cider vinegar
½ tablespoon	7 ml	Lemon juice
1 tablespoon	9 g	Unflavored gelatin

PROCEDURE

1. Make the base. Combine the tomatoes, onion, celery, garlic, bay leaves, peppercorns, cloves, half the salt, and 1 cup (8 ounces/240 ml) water in a 2- to 3-quart (2 to 3 L) nonreactive pan. Bring to a simmer, uncovered, over medium heat. Simmer for 20 minutes or until tomatoes have broken down (to maintain a fresh flavor, do not cook longer than necessary).

2. Strain through a fine-mesh strainer, pressing gently to extract all the juice. Measure to have 2 cups (16 ounces/480 ml) liquid. Add the sugar, vinegar, and lemon juice, tasting and adjusting depending on the ripeness and flavor of the tomatoes; tomatoes vary greatly in sweetness and acidity. Also, aspic is a cold dish, and cold temperature will dull the seasoning slightly. When mixture is seasoned correctly, return to a simmer.

3. Mix in the remaining 2 tablespoons (1 ounce/30 ml) water and let soften. Add the gelatin mixture to the simmering tomato juice and stir for 2 minutes.

4. Remove from the heat, and strain into a bowl over ice water, stirring constantly until the liquid cools and begins to thicken. (This is an important step to ensure an even color and texture.) However, do not chill until it starts to set or you will have lumpy aspic. If it gets away from you, just reheat gently and chill.

5. Pour the tomato mixture into four 4-ounce (120 ml) lightly oiled molds. Cover and refrigerate several hours until set.

Bibb Lettuce Salad

AMOUNT	MEASURE	INGREDIENT
1½ tablespoons	¾ ounce/23 ml	Lemon juice
1 tablespoon	½ ounce/15 ml	Red wine vinegar
1 tablespoon	½ ounce/14 g	Sugar
1 teaspoon	5 g	Dijon mustard
¼ cup	2 ounces/60 ml	Olive oil
		Salt and black pepper
2 heads	8 ounces/226 g	Bibb lettuce

PROCEDURE

1. Combine the lemon juice, vinegar, sugar, and mustard in a small bowl; whisk until blended.

2. Slowly whisk in the olive oil. Season with salt and pepper.

3. Toss the lettuce with enough vinaigrette to lightly coat.

4. Place lettuce on individual chilled plates. Remove the aspic from the molds and place one on each serving.

Hush Puppies

Makes about 15 to 20

✦ **CHEF TIP:** Hush puppies are an essential component of fried-fish plates in the South. There are many stories about how they were named, the most common referring to the scraps of fried corn dough thrown to hungry hounds to "hush" them.

AMOUNT	MEASURE	INGREDIENT
As needed		Vegetable oil, for deep-frying
1 cup	6 ounces/168 g	Fine-ground cornmeal
1 tablespoon	8 g	All-purpose flour
½ teaspoon	2 g	Baking soda
½ teaspoon	2 g	Baking powder
½ teaspoon	3 g	Kosher salt
¼ cup	1 ounce/28 g	Onion, grated or finely minced
2 tablespoons	6 g	Green onion, green part only, minced
1		Egg yolk
1 cup	8 ounces/240 ml	Buttermilk
2		Egg whites

PROCEDURE

1. Preheat the oil in a deep pot or a deep-fryer to 350°F (175°C).

2. Combine the cornmeal, flour, baking soda, baking powder, and salt in a large bowl; whisk to blend well.

3. Add the onion, green onion, egg yolk, and buttermilk; stir to combine (mixture should be the consistency of loose mashed potatoes; if necessary, add more buttermilk).

4. Whip the egg whites to soft peaks. Fold into cornmeal mixture.

5. Drop the mixture by rounded tablespoons into the hot oil. Dip the spoon in a container of water after each hush puppy is dropped in the oil. Cook to golden brown, about 1 to 2 minutes, turning to ensure even cooking.

6. Drain on paper towels to drain. Serve immediately.

Hoppin' John Salad with Pecan Vinaigrette

4 servings

AMOUNT	MEASURE	INGREDIENT
For the Salad		
½ cup	3 ounces/84 g	Uncooked long-grain white rice, cooked to yield 2 cups cooked rice
2½ cups	13 ounces/364 g	Raw black-eyed peas, cooked to yield 6 cups cooked peas, chilled
½ cup	2 ounces/56 g	Red bell pepper, seeded, in ⅛-inch (.3 cm) dice
½ cup	2 ounces/ 56 g	Green beans, blanched, shocked, and cut into 1½-inch (3.8 cm) lengths on bias
½ cup	2 ounces/56 g	Green onions, chopped
For the Vinaigrette		
2 tablespoons	1 ounce/30 ml	Cider vinegar
½ teaspoon	2 g	Brown sugar
⅓ cup	1½ ounces/42 g	Pecans, chopped and toasted
½ teaspoon	1 g	Fresh thyme, chopped
½ teaspoon	5 g	Salt
½ cup	4 ounces/120 ml	Vegetable oil
		Salt and black pepper
2 cups	4 ounces/112 g	Mixed baby field greens

PROCEDURE

1. Prepare the salad. Combine the cooked rice, cooked black-eyed peas, bell pepper, green beans, and green onions. Set aside.

2. Make the vinaigrette. Puree all the ingredients except the oil and salt and pepper in a food processor until smooth. Slowly drizzle in the oil, then adjust the seasoning.

3. Assemble the dish. Toss all but 6 tablespoons (3 ounces/84 ml) of the vinaigrette with the rice and black-eyed pea mixture. Toss the mixed greens with the remaining vinaigrette and place as a bed on cold plates. Mold 1 cup (4 ounces/112 g) hoppin' john mixture onto each plate of greens.

Fried Green Tomatoes with Blue Cheese

4 servings

AMOUNT	MEASURE	INGREDIENT
½ cup	4 ounces/120 ml	Buttermilk
1		Egg, lightly beaten
½ tablespoon	8 ml	Tabasco
8 slices	16 ounces/448 g	Green tomatoes or firm red tomatoes, in ¼-inch (.6 cm) slices
½ cup	2 ounces/56 g	All-purpose flour
1 cup	6 ounces/170 g	Medium-ground yellow cornmeal
½ teaspoon	3 g	Salt
⅛ teaspoon	1 g	Black pepper
As needed		Peanut oil, for pan-frying
¼ cup	2 ounces/56 g	Blue cheese, crumbled

PROCEDURE

1. Combine the buttermilk, egg, and Tabasco in a bowl. Place the tomato slices in the mixture and marinate for 30 minutes, turning occasionally.

2. Combine the flour, cornmeal, salt, and pepper.

3. Drain the tomato slices and dredge in the cornmeal mixture.

4. Place the slices on a baking sheet and refrigerate for 30 minutes to allow the breading to dry.

5. Heat the oil in a 10- to 12-inch (25.4–30.5 cm) skillet to 350°F (175°C).

6. Pan-fry the tomato slices for 45 seconds to 1 minute on each side or until they are golden brown. Do not overcrowd the pan or the temperature of the fat will drop and you will end up with greasy tomatoes. Drain on paper towels.

7. To serve, place 2 tomato slices on each warm plate. Spoon on Roasted Tomato Sauce (recipe follows) and sprinkle with blue cheese.

Roasted Tomato Sauce

4 servings

AMOUNT	MEASURE	INGREDIENT
3 cups	16 ounces/448 g	Plum tomatoes, quartered
1 cup	3 ounces/84 g	Red onion, quartered
½ teaspoon	1 g	Fresh thyme, chopped
½ teaspoon	1 g	Fresh rosemary, chopped
1 tablespoon	½ ounce/15 ml	Olive oil
		Salt and black pepper

1. Preheat the oven to 350°F (175°C).

2. Toss the tomatoes, onion, and herbs with the oil. Place on a parchment-lined sheet pan and roast for 45 minutes.

3. Puree in a food processor to desired consistency (slightly lumpy, coarse texture).

4. Correct the seasoning with salt and pepper.

Frogmore Stew

4 servings

AMOUNT	MEASURE	INGREDIENT
1	6 ounces/168 g	Vidalia onion, halved
2	10 g	Garlic cloves, minced
1 tablespoon	¼ ounce/7 g	Old Bay seasoning
1 quart	32 ounces/960 ml	Clam juice
2 cups	16 ounces/480 ml	Water
1 teaspoon	5 g	Salt
2		Ears of corn, shucked, cut into 3-inch (7.6 cm) pieces
6	1 pound/448 g	New potatoes, scrubbed, cut in half
	12 ounces/336 g	Kielbasa or andouille sausage, cut into 1-inch (2.5 cm) pieces
	12 ounces/336 g	Crawfish, whole
	12 ounces/336 g	Medium shrimp, unpeeled (20–24 count)
¼ cup	1 ounce/28 g	Green onions, thinly sliced
½ cup	3 ounces/84 g	Tomato, peeled, seeded, in ¼-inch (.6 cm) dice

PROCEDURE

1. Combine the onion, garlic, Old Bay seasoning, clam juice, water, and salt in a large pot; bring to a boil. Add the corn and cook until tender, about 5 minutes.

2. Reduce the heat to a simmer and add the potatoes and sausage; cook until tender, 6 to 8 minutes more.

3. Add the crawfish and shrimp. Cook until shrimp and crawfish are just done, about 4 minutes.

4. Divide the shellfish, corn, sausage, and potatoes evenly into serving bowls. Ladle the broth evenly over the mixture. Garnish with green onions and tomato.

Floribbean Cuisine

Floribbean cuisine, also known as "new era cuisine," has emerged as one of America's new and most innovative regional cooking styles. The fresh flavors, combinations, and tastes of Floribbean cuisine are representative of the variety and quality of foods indigenous to Florida and the Caribbean Islands.

Regional chefs often make a commitment to using locally grown foods and the fish and seafood of the abundant fresh and salt waters of the area. The cooking style and techniques used in Florida today are highly influenced by those of Cuba, Jamaica, and the Bahamas, but they are lighter, with less frying and fewer oils involved in the preparation. This current movement is, however, only a little more than a decade old. The roots of Floribbean cuisine trace back to the exploration of the New World by the Spanish.

Florida, "The Sunshine State," is one of the world's strongest tourist magnets due to its abundance of sunny days. The state tree is the sabal palm, from which hearts of palm, or swamp cabbage, is harvested. The state reptile is the alligator, which lives in the streams and swamplands. The state freshwater fish is the largemouth bass, and the state saltwater fish is the sailfish. The state beverage is orange juice, and the state flower is the orange blossom.

HISTORY AND MAJOR INFLUENCES

Juan Ponce de Leon first landed on the Atlantic Coast in 1513, and shortly thereafter Spain began to colonize the area, building forts and missions. But with Florida's rough terrain and the Spaniards' supply problems and weakening empire in Europe, all of their expeditions failed. They did, however, establish a settlement at St. Augustine in northeastern Florida in 1565, and this became the first permanent European settlement in the United States. The French disputed Spain's right to Florida, so they began to settle the area, too.

Both sides attacked the other's settlements, often completely destroying them. Farther north, the English became worried that the Spanish and French would threaten the Carolinas and Georgia. When the French and Indian War ended in 1763, Spain gave Florida to England. After the Revolutionary War, England gave Florida back to Spain. Finally, in 1819, Spain sold Florida to the United States.

FLORIDA DEVELOPMENT

During the final quarter of the 19th century, large-scale commercial agriculture in Florida, especially cattle raising, grew in importance. Industries such as cigar manufacturing took root in the immigrant communities of the state. Potential investors became interested in enterprises as diverse as sponge harvesting in Tarpon Springs while the Florida citrus industry grew rapidly. The development of industries throughout Florida prompted the construction of roads and railroads on a large scale. The citrus industry benefited now that oranges could be shipped to the northern states in less than a week. Beginning in the 1870s, residents from the northern states visited Florida as tourists to enjoy the state's natural beauty and mild climate. This tourism industry drove the development of lavish winter resorts, from Palm Beach to Miami Beach, nicknamed the "Gold Coast."

By the early 1900s, Florida's population and per-capita wealth were increasing rapidly, and land developers and promoters marketed the state as a tourist and retirement mecca, resulting in a massive real estate boom in South Florida. This boom ended by 1926, and land prices plummeted. The Great Depression hit the nation and Florida's citrus industry was further devastated by the invasion of the Mediterranean fruit fly. World War II brought an end to the Great Depression and led the reemergence of economic development in Florida. One of the most significant trends of the postwar era has been steady population growth, resulting from large migrations from within the United States and from countries throughout the Western Hemisphere.

LITTLE HAVANA

Florida's most diverse cities are Tampa and Miami. Before the turn of the century, Tampa was the center of the U.S. cigar manufacturing industry. Many of the cigar makers were Cuban Americans, and southern and eastern Europe provided the rest of the workforce. With so many immigrants from Cuba, Spain, and Italy, Tampa developed a mixed Mediterranean and Latin culture.

Florida's current multicultural center is Miami. In 1959, a revolutionary army led by Fidel Castro seized power in Cuba. Castro's political foes and many professionals and businesspeople fled the island-nation, just 90 miles from southern Florida. Many of these Cuban exiles eventually settled in Miami. In 1980, more than 100,000 people left Cuba for Florida and have since developed a Cuban-American economic and political presence in South Florida. Although Cuban Americans now form South Florida's largest ethnic community, other groups have played a significant cultural role as well. Northern Jewish retirees moved to South Florida beaches, and today the region has the second largest Jewish population of any U.S. metropolitan area. Large populations from Haiti, Nicaragua, the Dominican Republic, Brazil, and other Central American countries also exist in Florida. In addition, a Southeast Asian influence is beginning to be seen as more people immigrate to Florida from Indonesia, Cambodia, and Vietnam.

THE PEOPLE, THEIR INGREDIENTS, AND ADAPTATIONS

THE FLORIDA COASTLINE

When the Spanish arrived in Florida in the early 1500s, they brought cattle and pigs with them to the New World. From this introduction of livestock to Florida, the Spanish are given credit for many recipes using meat in a region that formerly depended entirely on fish and game. In return for livestock, the Native Americans taught the Spanish about local fruits and vegetables, including hearts of palm, malanga, yuca, and plantains. Later, the abundant finfish attracted Cuban fishermen to the harbors and bays. They salted and dried their catch, and then shipped it to Havana and other Spanish colonial settlements. Before the Civil War in the 1860s, the commercial red snapper and grouper industry was active, as well as industries developed for harvesting and processing clams, scallops, turtles, oysters, and shrimp. The spiny lobster, actually a large sea crawfish with no claws, is found in the waters off lower Florida's west coast. Stone crabs are trapped and fishermen remove one of the two claws, tossing the crabs back into the water to grow the missing claw back. The conch that is found in the spiraled seashell has sweet but tough meat that is chopped up for fritters and chowders. The conch was so popular in Key West that it was hunted to near extinction, leading to dependence on Costa Rica and the Bahamas for harvest. Greek sponge divers settled at Tarpon Springs in 1905, and other immigrants, including Italians, Chinese, and Cubans, brought their cooking traditions with them.

THE FLORIDA PANHANDLE

Inland toward the center and north of the state, the food is more Southern in character. In the mid-1600s, the Spanish conquistadors brought many thousands of slaves from Africa to Florida and the Caribbean Islands. The slaves brought with them the skills and knowledge to grow, cook, and prepare the types of foods they were familiar with: sweet potatoes, eggplant, sesame seeds, and okra. Many of the regional specialties, like field peas and okra, came from this period. In the mid-1700s, a group of Minorcans—people of Catalan descent from the Spanish Balearic Islands—were brought to the Florida region as indentured laborers. Their foods and cooking influenced the existing Florida cuisine, particularly in the use of peppers.

SOUTH FLORIDA AND THE GOLD COAST

Agriculture has fueled much of the area's economic development. Draining the Everglades uncovered rich soil, permitting the development of sugarcane fields, and helped turn the area southwest of Miami into the winter vegetable capital of the country. Today, Florida is the nation's top producer of sugarcane, and Florida trails only California in the production of fresh vegetables such as tomatoes, greens, beans, and peppers.

Florida is one of the largest producers of citrus fruits in the world, and Florida oranges provide nearly 80 percent of the orange juice consumed in the United States. Florida also produces grapefruit, limes, lemons, and tangerines. Some of the more exotic citrus fruits from the region include kumquats, tangelos, pummelos, and calamondins. Probably the greatest influence on Floribbean cuisine began in the 1950s, with the large migration of Cubans to South Florida. Caribbean and Latin American immigrants have followed the Cubans and have found that many of their native ingredients are indigenous to Florida. They brought with them all of the rice and legume dishes from the Caribbean, like rice and peas, or beans. Coloring foods, such as adding turmeric and saffron to rice, reminded them of the palm oil that is used in West Africa, from where many Caribbean slaves originated. They used cane sugar in oil, caramelized to give a color and flavor to their stews. Dried and smoked ingredients, as well as pickled pork and vegetables, are important in intensifying their foods. Seasoning pastes, salsa, rubs, and hot sauces are used not only for flavor but also to enhance digestion and encourage perspiration in order to cool off in the hot environment. By balancing the hot spices with cool, tropical fruits, this cuisine has captured the attention of the more adventurous American palate.

In the 1980s, a talented group of local chefs recognized these exotic ingredients and the cooking traditions of the immigrant population. With Miami's explosion as a new and exciting

Fishermen use a wide range of gear to land their catch. Every type has its own effects on the ocean. Using the right gear for the right job, the fishing industry can help minimize its impact on the environment. In places where management agencies have enforced the use of better fishing gear, bycatch and habitat damage have been reduced. This includes requiring devices that allow turtles to escape from nets, the use of less harmful "circle hooks," and a movement away from harmful methods such as bottom trawls and dredges.

Pole/troll is considered environmentally responsible and a good alternative to longlining. Fishermen use a fishing pole and bait to target a variety of fish, ranging from open-ocean swimmers like tuna and mahi mahi, to bottom dwellers like cod. With this type of fishing method fishermen have very low bycatch rates.

Traps and pots are used to catch lobsters, crabs, shrimp, sablefish, and Pacific cod. These submerged wire or wood cages attract fish with bait and hold them alive until fishermen return to haul in the catch. Traps and pots are usually placed on the ocean bottom and have lower unintended catch and less sea floor impact than mobile gear like trawls.

Harpooning is a traditional method for catching large predatory fish such as bluefin tuna and swordfish. When a harpooner spots a fish, he thrusts or shoots a long aluminum or wooden harpoon into the animal and hauls it aboard. Harpooning is considered an environmentally responsible fishing method. Bycatch of unwanted marine life is not a concern because harpoon fishermen visually identify the species and size of the targeted fish before killing it.

Trolling is a hook-and-line method that is designed to catch fish that will follow a moving lure or bait, such as salmon, mahimahi, and albacore tuna. Fishing lines are towed behind or alongside a boat. Fishermen use a variety of lures and baits to "troll" for different fish at different depths. Trolling is an environmentally responsible fishing method, as fishermen can quickly release unwanted catch from their hooks because lines are reeled in soon after a fish takes the bait.

Longlines can be set near the surface to catch fish like tuna and swordfish, or when laid on the sea floor, to catch deep dwelling fish like cod and halibut. In this fishing method a central fishing line that can range from one to 50 miles long; this line is strung with smaller lines of baited hooks, dangling at evenly spaced intervals. Nearly 20 percent of shark species are threatened with extinction, primarily as a result of being caught accidentally on longlines. When cast out and left to "soak," longlines attract anything that swims by, from sharks to sea turtles. By sinking longlines deeper or using different hooks, fishermen can reduce the bycatch problem for sea turtles, sharks, and seabirds.

Purse seining is used to catch schooling fish, such as sardines, or species that gather to spawn, such as squid. A large wall of netting is used to encircle schools of fish. Fishermen pull the bottom of the netting closed—like a drawstring purse—to herd fish into the center. There are several types of purse seines and, depending on which is used, some can catch other animals (such as when tuna seines are intentionally set on schools of dolphins). Bycatch also includes young fish that could rebuild populations if they were allowed to grow and breed.

Gillnetting is used to catch sardines, salmon, and cod. Curtains of netting are suspended by a system of floats and weights that can be anchored to the sea floor or allowed to float at the surface. The netting is almost invisible to fish, so they swim right into it. Unfortunately, gillnets can also entangle and kill other animals, including sharks and sea turtles.

Trawls and dredges are designed to catch fish such as pollock, cod, flounder, and shrimp. These nets are towed at various depths to catch fish or shellfish. Trawl nets, which can be as large as a football field, are either dragged along the sea floor or hang midway between the floor and the surface. Bottom trawling can result in high levels of bycatch. The effects of trawling can actually be seen on satellite images taken from space. Dredging is done by dragging a heavy frame with an attached mesh bag along the sea floor to catch animals living on or in the mud or sand; catches include scallops, clams, and oysters. Dredging can damage the sea floor by scraping the bottom and also often results in significant bycatch.

playground for the hip, rich, and famous, they have developed and marketed what has become one of the next acknowledged regional cuisines of America.

LATIN CARIBBEAN INFLUENCE

Latin Caribbean cooking offers complex, flavorful ingredients from diverse cultures. Ingredients introduced by ancient Aztecs, Mayans, and Incas are combined with flavors and recipes of its diverse groups of immigrants, including the Spanish, Portuguese, French, Italians, Middle Easterners, Africans, Chinese, Japanese, and Germans. Cooks from regions that include Cuba, Puerto Rico, and the Dominican Republic flavor their foods with relatively mild seasonings—oregano, tomato, garlic, black pepper, and mild chiles. Rice is a staple and seafood, fruits, and root vegetables like cassava, boniato, and malanga are abundant. Ground meat dishes called picadillo, rice and beans, mofongos (mashed plantain with pork crackling), escabeches, seviches, frijoles, and paella are commonly found. Recipes are flavored with adobos, mojos, coconut milk, and cilantro. Salsas are now the most frequently used condiment in the United States, and are an essential part of Latin regions.

Salsas come in many forms and flavors. Spicy and hot with vegetables such as tomatoes, beans, corn, peppers, and cucumbers, or tart and acidic with fruits like mango, pears, pineapple, and grapefruit, they are used extensively to provide flavor. The word *mojo* comes from the Spanish word *mojado*, which means "wet." Mojos are more liquid in consistency than salsas and are used as sauces or marinades. The heat of the salsas and mojos are adjusted with the choice of peppers, from the fiery Scotch bonnets to the milder banana peppers. By using any of the countless vinegars or fruit juices combined with choices of oils that include olive, walnut, hazelnut, and avocado, salsas and mojos can provide a wide range of flavors. In addition, they have the benefit of being very low in calories and cholesterol, making them healthy alternatives to heavier, cream-based sauces. They require little or no cooking and the fresher, more colorful, and more flavorful the ingredients, the better the salsas and mojos are. These sauces are served with chips, or with any type of meat, fish, or poultry.

Typical Floribbean Ingredients and Dishes

Alcaporado   A Cuban-style beef stew cooked with raisins and olives.

Adobo   An all-purpose seasoning containing garlic, vinegar, oregano, black pepper, and turmeric. Adobos are used as base seasonings to add flavor to stews, sauces, or rice, and to marinate beef, pork, chicken, or fish. The word *adobo* means "marinade" and dry adobos are used as spice rubs or pastes.

Annatto   Small reddish berries (achiote seeds) that serve as a colorant in the cooking of the Caribbean. Mixed with lard or other cooking oils, they give the foods cooked in them an orange-yellow cast. It has been suggested that this method of cooking replaces the red palm oil used in West African cooking. Annatto oil can be drizzled over meat and shellfish, or added to salad dressings.

Arroz con Pollo   A Cuban chicken and rice dish frequently served in South Florida restaurants. It can be served as an entree with a little broth or as a hearty soup.

Arroz Marillo   Cuban-style saffron rice. Typically, long-grain white rice cooked with saffron, but due to the high cost of saffron, turmeric is frequently substituted.

Avocado   Originally from Mexico and considered an aphrodisiac by the Incas and Aztecs, avocados grown in South Florida are called alligator pears because the skin resembles an alligator hide. Florida avocados typically have a higher water content and milder flavor than avocados from California.

Banana Leaf   Found in Latin, Caribbean, and Asian specialty markets, this leaf from the banana tree is used as a wrapper for cooking food in the Florida region. The technique imparts the flavor of the banana to other foods.

Banana Pepper   Also known as the Hungarian wax chile, banana peppers are large, usually 3 to 5 inches in length, ranging in flavor from mild to medium hot. Banana peppers are known for their distinctive waxy texture.

Beans   The most common beans used in Floribbean cooking are kidney beans, preferred by the Haitians; black beans, preferred by the Cubans; and pink beans, found frequently in Caribbean cooking.

Bolichi   A marinated pot roast rolled with hard-boiled eggs, this popular Cuban dish is similar to the South American preparation for pot roast called *matambre*.

Boniato   A tuber similar in appearance to a sweet potato with white or yellow flesh and a somewhat bitter flavor. Drier, fluffier, and a little less sweet than a sweet potato, boniato can be prepared by boiling, baking, deep-frying, roasting, steaming, or sautéing.

Calabeza   A large Cuban squash, also known as a West Indian pumpkin, with a round or pear shape. Larger than a honeydew melon, the skin may be orange, green, or striped. The orange flesh has a flavor similar to pumpkin or butternut squash, but is sweeter and moister. Calebeza is typically sold halved or in slices due to its large size.

Calamondins   Known as an acid orange, the fruit is small and orange, about 1 inch (2.5 cm) in diameter, and resembles a tangerine. The tree is often grown as an ornamental, but the fruit is edible and the juice can be used like lemon or lime juice.

Callaloo   A vegetable similar to kale, Swiss chard, and spinach, brought to South Florida by the African slaves from the Caribbean.

Cassava   Another name for yuca.

Coconut   The large, hairy fruit of the coconut palm tree. The flesh of the fruit is white in color and lines the inside of the shell. When selecting coconuts, shake them to ensure that there is liquid inside the shell.

Coconut Milk   A combination of equal parts water and shredded fresh coconut meat, simmered until foamy. The mixture is then strained though cheesecloth to retain as much liquid as possible. Canned coconut milk makes an excellent substitute for fresh.

Conch   A large mollusk found in the coral reefs off the coast of South Florida and around the Florida Keys. Conch meat has a flavor similar to sweet clams and is typically used to make chowder or fritters. Conch shells are large, attractive, and whorled—the kind that children hold to their ear to hear the sound of the ocean.

Cubanella Pepper   A large, lemon-yellow, mild pepper about the size of a green bell pepper.

Flan   The Cuban-style preparation of flan flavors the traditional French custard with almonds, coconut, or rum. It is frequently served with plantains or black beans.

Grouper   A fish found in the waters of the Caribbean, the Gulf of Mexico, and the North and South Atlantic. There are many species, including black, tiger, yellowmouth, comb, and graysby, ranging in size from 5 to 15 pounds, but sometimes as large as 600 pounds. The flesh is lean, firm, and sweet, making grouper suitable for baking, broiling, frying, poaching, and steaming.

Guava   A round fruit with a flavor similar to strawberries. Usually 2 to 6 inches in diameter, with thick greenish-white, yellow, or red edible skin. It has small seeds embedded in the flesh of the fruit that can be removed by passing the flesh through a sieve. Guava can be eaten raw or cooked in jellies, pastes, or chutneys, or used as a base for glazes and custards.

Hearts of Palm   Also referred to as swamp cabbage, hearts of palm are the tender inner parts of the sabal or cabbage palm tree. They have a white to ivory color and many concentric layers with a delicate flavor reminiscent of an artichoke. They are considered rare and are expensive because the palm tree must be destroyed in order to obtain them. Hearts of palm are served in salad preparations and can be eaten raw or cooked.

Jamaican Pimiento   Also known as allspice, this highly aromatic pea-size berry has a flavor that tastes like a combination of cinnamon, nutmeg, and cloves. When the berries are ground, the spice is known as pimiento.

Jerk Seasoning   A dry seasoning used primarily in the preparation of grilled meat. The ingredients can vary depending on the cook, but it is usually a blend of chiles, thyme, spices (such as cinnamon, ginger, allspice, and cloves), garlic, and onions. Jerk seasoning can be either rubbed directly onto the meat or blended with a liquid to create a marinade. In the Caribbean, the most common meats seasoned in this fashion are pork and chicken.

Key Lime   One of the two main varieties of lime available in the United States. Small, yellowish fruit with a highly aromatic, tart flavor, similar to very tart lemons, Key lime trees were first

Chifles (Fried Plantain Chips)

4 servings

CHEF TIP: Chifles are thin slices of plantain that are deep-fried and sprinkled with salt. These are a traditional treat in many parts of the world. Plantains are eaten in all stages of ripeness; they are bigger and firmer than bananas and lower in sugar content. Green plantains, and often yellow, can be tricky and difficult to peel, especially if they are cold. Bring them to room temperature or soak them in hot tap water for a few minutes to warm them before peeling. To peel, cut off both ends and discard the tips. Hold the plantain firmly against the cutting board and use a paring knife to make a cut down the length of the plantain, cutting only deep enough to pierce the peel. Remove the peel; it will come off in sections.

AMOUNT	MEASURE	INGREDIENT
As needed		Vegetable oil, for deep-frying
2		Green plantains, peeled
		Coarse salt

PROCEDURE

1. Preheat the oil to 360°F (182°C).

2. Using a mandolin or sharp knife, cut the plantains into ⅛-inch (.3 cm) slices on the diagonal.

3. In small batches, fry the plantains for 2 to 3 minutes or until crisp and golden. Remove and drain on paper towels. Sprinkle lightly with salt and serve.

Louisiana's Cajun and Creole Cuisines

Louisiana has been described as a "cultural gumbo" in which each ingredient is identifiable yet all have blended, affecting each other. A complex blend of Native American, French, Spanish, German, English, African, and Italian influences creates a unique regional culture. These people have merged to become the Cajuns and Creoles—the source of Louisiana's culinary heritage. Cajun cooking, earthy and robust, has been described as "country cooking." It is based on food that was indigenous to the area and features one-pot meals that contain a variety of ingredients gathered from the "swamp-floor pantry." Creole cooking, like Cajun, depended heavily on whatever foods were available. But Creole food, unlike Cajun, began in New Orleans. Creole food, or "city food," was created by sharing cooking styles and is considered more sophisticated and complex than Cajun cooking. Though each cuisine represents its own style, the sharing and the evolution continue, and Cajun and Creole cooking differences begin to blur. As these two regional cuisines become more difficult to separate, it is important to remember that food in Louisiana represents a celebration of life, a joy in living, and comes with the admonishment: *Laissez Les Bon Temps Rouler!* ("Let the Good Times Roll!").

Louisiana is known as "the Pelican State," and Louisiana's state bird is the pelican. The pelican has been a symbol of Louisiana since the arrival of early European settlers, who were impressed with the pelican's generous and nurturing attitude toward its young. Louisiana is also known as the "Bayou State" for the many slow, sluggish, small streams that meander through the lowlands and marshes of the southern section of the state, and as the "Creole State" for the people of French and Spanish descent and the culture that they have preserved. The state crustacean is the crawfish, the state reptile is the alligator, and the state freshwater fish is the white perch (also called *sac-au-lait,* or "white crappie"). The state insect is the honeybee, and the state drink is milk.

HISTORY AND MAJOR INFLUENCES

No other state has a more varied or colorful past than Louisiana. The layers of history can be seen in the 18th-century French buildings of the Vieux Carré (New Orleans's French Quarter), with their splendid Spanish courtyards hidden just behind the gates. New Orleans began as a French settlement in 1718, became Spanish in 1762, then French again briefly just after 1800, and with the Louisiana Purchase in 1803, making it American.

EUROPEAN DISCOVERY AND SETTLEMENT

Before the age of European exploration, the region was inhabited by thousands of Native Americans. The largest tribes included the Caddo, the Natchez, the Chitimacha, and the Choctaw. They planted vegetables, hunted game, and fished along the eastern bank of the Mississippi River. The first Europeans to enter the area were from Spain. Among them were Hernando de Soto and his expedition that explored large parts of what is now the southern United States and came though Louisiana in 1542.

FRENCH RULE

The French established their first settlement in Natchitoches in 1686, but they found it difficult to attract settlers to this isolated part of the New World. King Louis XIV asked an organization of traders, called the Company of the West, to manage the colony. Headed by John Law, the Company tried several schemes to attract settlers, including attempts to lure fortune seekers by claiming Louisiana was a land filled with gold and silver. The French government encouraged prisoners and debtors to pay for their crimes by moving to the new colony. Nevertheless, not many people came to Louisiana until 1718, when Jean-Baptiste Le Moyne, Sieur de Bienville, established a port city that he called New Orleans. Located just 110 miles upstream from the mouth of the Mississippi River, New Orleans later became the commercial center of the South and one of the country's most important international ports. The capital of the territory developed a strong character all its own. European settlers brought with them fine clothing and furnishings and established elegant traditions like banquets and balls.

SPANISH RULE

By 1762, France was deep in debt and at war with Britain over control of North America. No longer able to afford to develop the Louisiana territory, France offered it to Spain. For 40 years, Spain helped Louisiana to flourish and added its special flavor to its heritage. The territory's population boomed at this time. New arrivals from Europe joined the original French and Spanish settlers. These Europeans, called "Creoles," were generally wealthy and educated, and they brought with them a variety of celebrated European customs and traditions. Germans established towns and villages in the north-central region of the state. Scots, Irish, and British settlers arrived to settle in Louisiana's northeast. One of the most important groups to come was the Acadians, who established farms along the bayous west of New Orleans. Acadians were French settlers forced to leave Canada by the British during the Seven Years' War (1756–1763, also called the French and Indian War). Some returned to France or went to other colonies, but many chose to settle in southern Louisiana, where they became known as "Cajuns." Slaves brought to work on Louisiana's expanding network of plantations made up the largest group of new residents. Many slaves were brought to the colony directly from the African regions, while others were taken from French islands in the Caribbean. By the beginning of the 1800s, more than 30,000 slaves would live in Louisiana, making up nearly half of its population.

BECOMING AMERICANS

In 1803, the French needed cash to finance another war with Britain. In a deal that would nearly double the size of the United States, President Thomas Jefferson bought the Louisiana Territory from the French for only $15 million. Just nine years later, in 1812, Louisiana became the 18th state to join the Union. Cotton, sugar, and rice were the three most valuable crops in the world during this time, and Louisiana's humid climate and rich soil were perfect for growing all three. More than 1,600 plantations were established. Steam-powered vessels found their way down the Mississippi River all the way from the East Coast to New Orleans. Goods produced throughout the United States could now travel by river to the Gulf of Mexico and from there, sail to international ports. By the mid-19th century, New Orleans was the largest city in the South, the third largest city in the nation, and one of the busiest ports in the world.

A GUMBO SOCIETY

CAJUN COUNTRY, ALSO KNOWN AS ACADIANA

The term *Cajun* describes both a geographical area and the people who live in or come from that region. Forcibly expelled by the British from their homes and farms in Canada during the second half of the 18th century, many Acadians made their way to southern Louisiana, where, over the generations, their descendants have formed the nucleus of Louisiana's Cajun life and culture. Originally farmers, trappers, and fisherman, the Cajuns had to rely on local resources, such as the fish, shellfish, and wild game. Native Americans taught them how to exploit the swamps, bayous, and surrounding forests. The Choctaws, Chitimacha, and Houmas showed them how to use ingredients such as corn, ground sassafras leaves (filé powder), and bay leaves. Wildlife, including alligator, crawfish, and turtles, were used by the Cajuns in their cooking. They depended on their black cast-iron pots. Because of the simple utilitarian kitchen of the traditional Cajun, one-pot meals were practical and common. This is reflected in their jambalaya, grillades, stews, étouffées, fricassées, soups, and gumbos. Because of the frugal nature needed to survive in the Bayou country, nothing was ever wasted by Cajuns, including all portions of butchered meats, stocks, and vegetables. The Cajun people are well known for their hospitality as well. In spite of the tragedy that befell them, they cook with a *joi de vivre*, or love of life. They are also known for the term *lagniappe*, which refers to "something extra and not expected," like a few extra shrimp in the étouffée, or 13 cookies in a dozen (commonly known today as a "baker's dozen"). Cajun French, still spoken today, uses words and grammar derived from traditional French, English, Spanish, African, and Native American languages. Tucked away among the bayous and swamplands of the Atchafalaya Basin, this area is now considered one of the last great wilderness regions of the continental United States.

PLANTATION COUNTRY

Just west of New Orleans, winding along both sides of the Mississippi River, can be found flowing fields of sugarcane. Plantation agriculture flourished in Louisiana in the 18th century. These plantation owners influenced the area in many ways, particularly by teaching their slaves English rather than French. African Americans had a profound influence on the cooking style of the region. When they cooked, they combined ingredients such as rice, beans, and green leafy vegetables with traditional African ingredients such as okra, sweet potatoes, onions, and garlic. They also favored a cooking technique called "slow roasting" and extended this idea of continuous cooking to traditional French roux.

Also, being closer to New Orleans and on major transportation routes, the Germans, Spanish, French, English, and Americans from along the Mississippi River were more cosmopolitan than people in the swamps and on the prairies to the west. A large number of Germans arrived during the Spanish period, settled upriver from New Orleans along the German coast, and provided most of the vegetable crops needed by New Orleans. The Germans also brought pigs, chicken, and cattle. Their extensive knowledge of all forms of butchering helped establish the fine sausage making in South Louisiana. Escaping the lack of economic and social opportunities in Europe, the Italians came to the area as farmers, blacksmiths, and merchants. Famous for their own cooking skills, their influence on the cuisine can be seen in the pasta, red gravies, bread baking, garlic, eggplant, and artichoke dishes.

THE CROSSROADS

Central Louisiana became a meeting place for the many cultures of Louisiana. This is where the Native Americans thrived for centuries. All the tribes cultivated pumpkins, squash, and corn. They used wild berries, nuts, and persimmons in their cooking. Later, the French and the Spanish each ruled this region. Englishmen sought their fortunes here and American settlers flooded in after the Louisiana Purchase. Czech, Lebanese, Afro-Caribbean, Italian, and Syrian cultures contributed to the heritage of this region.

SPORTSMAN'S PARADISE

The forests and rolling hills of northern Louisiana were a hunter's paradise for Native Americans, French trappers, and American settlers of the early 1700s and 1800s. Today there is still opportunity for wild turkey, duck, partridge, and quail hunting. Catfish, both freshwater and pond raised, is abundant.

FOOD AND CULTURAL INFLUENCES

GUMBO

Descended from the French bouillabaisse and renamed from the West African word for okra, *guingombo*, this type of hearty soup or stew is frequently served in the Louisiana region. There are as many recipes for gumbo as there are cooks. Over time, the dish evolved to include hot peppers, contributed by the Spanish settlers; okra, contributed by the Africans; and filé powder, contributed by the Native Americans. Gumbo is the essence of cultural diversity. It blends and balances all the varied ethnic influences that have shaped present-day Louisiana cooking: the Spanish love of rice and spices, the Southern fondness for okra, the French technique of making roux, and the Caribbean art of combining seasonings. In New Orleans and southeastern Louisiana, seafood gumbo is made with shrimp and crabs, and tomatoes are added and cooked in the pot with the gumbo. In southwestern Louisiana, the favorite recipe includes chicken and andouille sausage gumbo thickened with only roux—no okra or tomatoes. Gumbo is traditionally served with or over rice.

THE MUFFULETTA

Many people think the only cultural and culinary heritage of New Orleans is French, Spanish, African, and Creole. When asked to name the quintessential sandwiches of New Orleans, many people will immediately reply "po'boy." But the muffuletta is as New Orleans as the popular po'boys and there's nothing Creole about it. This sandwich is pure Italian, and specifically Sicilian. New Orleans, in its population and its cuisine, owes much to Italy and especially to the Italians who have been coming since the 1880s. The Italian contribution to local culture and cuisine has been considerable; in fact, Creole-Italian refers to one of the local subcuisines. It is said that the muffuletta sandwich was invented by Signor Lupo Salvadore, who opened the now-famous little Italian market called Central Grocery on Decatur Street in the French Quarter in 1906. He created the muffuletta sandwich for a favored customer. It is actually named for the baker of the round Italian bread on which the sandwich is served.

LOUISIANA'S GULF COAST

Louisiana's shores, marshes, bays, and bayous yield a variety of seafood. Blue crabs and oysters are harvested, and in the brackish waters where the Mississippi joins the Gulf of Mexico are some of the most fertile shrimping grounds in the country. Redfish, trout, flounder, and pompano are found farther out in the gulf. South Louisiana is the crawfish capital of the world, supporting a multimillion-dollar-a-year industry. Sometimes called "Louisiana lobster," the crawfish is much

COUNTRY OF ORIGIN LABELING PROGRAM

Country of Origin Labeling, or COOL, is a labeling law that requires retailers, such as full-line grocery stores, supermarkets, and club warehouse stores, to notify their customers of the sources of certain foods. Food products, both imported and domestic, must meet the food safety standards of USDA's Food Safety and Inspection Service and the U.S. Food and Drug Administration. The Agricultural Marketing Service (AMS) of the U.S. Department of Agriculture enforces country of origin labeling regulations for all foods covered under this law. USDA's Food Safety and Inspection Service (FSIS) enforces the labeling requirements for labeling of meat, poultry, and egg products, including covered commodities.

Foods that must be labeled with their country of origin are:

- Muscle cuts of beef (including veal), lamb, pork, goat, and chicken
- Ground beef, ground lamb, ground pork, ground goat, and ground chicken
- Farm-raised fish and shellfish
- Wild-caught fish and shellfish
- Perishable agricultural commodities
- Peanuts, pecans, and macadamia nuts
- Ginseng

There are four country of origin labeling categories depending on where the animal was born, raised, and slaughtered. They are:

1. Meat from animals born, raised, and slaughtered in the United States or from animals present in the United States prior to July 15, 2008.
2. Meat from animals not born in the United States, but raised and slaughtered in the United States.
3. Meat from animals imported into the United States for immediate slaughter.
4. Foreign meat imported into the United States.

Processed food products (such as hot dogs) do not require country of origin labeling. As an example, "processed food" means a retail item derived from a commodity covered under this law that has undergone specific processing, resulting in a change of character (for example, cooking, curing, smoking, restructuring) or has been combined with another food component.

smaller and its color varies with the water in which it lives, as well as its variety. Although it is found in swamps and marshes throughout the state, the best wild populations occur in the overflow basins of the Atchafalaya, Red, and Pearl rivers. Crawfish farms have also been established where the crustaceans are cultivated for local use and for shipment to other states.

NEW ORLEANS

In 1718, Jean-Baptiste LeMoyne, Sieur de Bienville, chose a high spot along the Mississippi River to be the center of the French colony of Louisiana. It was strategically located to control traffic on the Mississippi. It was also a port that allowed immigrants to arrive from other countries. In the 18th century, the Spaniards governing New Orleans named all residents of European heritage *Criollo* (roughly translated from the Portuguese for "native to a region"). The name, which later became *Creole*, is claimed by different groups of people. The traditional New Orleans definition included those who could trace their lineage to aristocratic French or Spanish ancestry. They used the word to imply someone of refined cultural background with an appreciation for an elegant lifestyle.

These people brought not only their wealth and education but also their chefs and cooks. With these chefs came the knowledge of the grand cuisines of France and other parts of Europe. Additional interpretations of Creole include former slaves who often took the same last name as their former owners and traced their lineage in the same fashion. Today, Creole cooking reflects the history of sharing and borrowing among the state's ethnic groups. In addition to the French, Spanish, and Americans, ethnic groups that included Haitians, Caribbeans, Italians, Germans, and Irish made significant contributions to the culture of the city.

Alligator   This large reptile, indigenous to the swamps, rivers, and marshes of Louisiana, is considered a Cajun specialty. High in protein while low in fat and cholesterol, it may be compared to chicken. The choicest cuts of alligator are the tail and jaw sections. Alligator meat needs to be trimmed of all fat and tendons before it is cooked to prevent it from becoming tough.

Bananas Foster   A popular dessert prepared tableside and made famous at Brennan's Restaurant in New Orleans. Bananas are cooked in a mixture of butter, brown sugar, cinnamon, rum, and banana liqueur; it is served hot, right out of the pan, with a scoop of vanilla ice cream. The dish is named after Dick Foster, a political figure and friend of the Brennan family; the restaurant claims to use over 35,000 pounds of bananas each year in the preparation of their classic dessert.

Beignet   French for "fritter." Beignets are diamond-shaped, raised doughnuts without the hole in the middle. They are typically topped liberally with powdered sugar before serving.

Blackened Redfish   A fish preparation invented and popularized by Chef Paul Prudhomme in 1979 in his New Orleans restaurant K-Paul. Chef Prudhomme prepares the fish by seasoning it with a custom blend of Cajun spices and cooking it at a super-hot temperature in a cast-iron skillet. Blackened redfish became so famous that it is now considered the icon of Cajun cooking, and at one time became so popular that redfish was placed on the endangered species list.

Boucherie   A Cajun tradition and communal feast that centers on the slaughter of a pig. In the days before refrigeration, these gatherings were held in the fall or winter, when cooler temperatures allowed time to cure meats before they spoiled. Using "everything but the oink," the cooks prepared cracklings from the skin, headcheese from the brain, and lard from the fat. They used the entrails for sausage casings and made sausages such as boudin blanc, boudin rouge, andouille, and tasso. The organs were used to make a dish called "debris."

Bread Pudding   Considered by many to be the apple pie of Louisiana, this dessert combines the influences of the French, with their bread, and the Germans, with their eggs and dairy products. A number of "authentic" regional recipes for bread pudding exist, but they all start with leftover French bread soaked in milk and eggs, then combined with ingredients such as nuts, raisins, nutmeg, and cinnamon, and baked in an oven. Whiskey sauce or caramel sauce is the traditional topping.

Brown Meunière Sauce   A brown butter sauce, much like the French sauce beurre noisette. It is made by adding demi-glace sauce and cayenne pepper to browned butter, giving it a spicy flavor and a nutty aroma, used to top both meat and fish dishes.

Café au Lait   Coffee made with the addition of ground chicory root and served with steamed milk. It became popular during the Civil War and remains a Louisiana specialty.

Calas   A breakfast fritter like beignets, calas are fried balls of rice and dough that are eaten covered with powdered sugar. The word calas comes from one or more African languages meaning, "fried cake." African American street vendors sold the fresh hot calas in the city's French Quarter, with cries of *"Calas, belles calas tout chauds!"*

Cane Syrup   The concentrated sap of the sugarcane plant, also referred to as "light molasses." Cane syrup is made by crushing sugarcane to extract the juice, treating to remove the impurities, and then boiling to concentrate it. The syrup is then processed to allow the cropping out of the sugar crystals. The technique is progressive so that the first syrup produced—molasses—can yield an additional crop of crystals, or brown sugar. The syrups derived from sugarcane vary in color from light brown to almost black and can be blended from different varieties of cane. Cane syrup is frequently substituted for maple syrup and molasses in Cajun and Creole preparations.

Chicory   The root of a variety of Belgian endive that, when mature, is dried, roasted, and ground. When mixed with coffee beans and brewed, chicory imparts a bittersweet, somewhat nutty flavor to the coffee. Napoleon's troops first added chicory to coffee to stretch their

Menus and Recipes from
the Cuisine of Louisiana

MENU ONE
Chicken and Bacon Hash with Poached Egg and Hollandaise Sauce

Red Beans and Rice

Frog Legs Pinquate

Cajun Omelet

Fried Oyster Po'Boy

Beignets

MENU TWO
Chicken and Andouille Sausage Gumbo

Tomato and Haricots Verts Salad

Fried Fish in Pearly Meal with Remoulade Sauce

Crawfish Étouffée with Rice

Smothered Okra

Bread Pudding with Whiskey Sauce

MENU THREE
New Orleans Shrimp Bisque

Roasted Eggplant and Oysters

Creole Jambalaya

Chicken Maquechoux

Pecan Pralines

OTHER RECIPES
Fried Stuffed Crawfish Heads

Muffuletta

Chicken and Bacon Hash with Poached Egg and Hollandaise Sauce

4 servings

AMOUNT	MEASURE	INGREDIENT
2 cups	8 ounces/224 g	Russet potato, peeled, in ¼-inch (.6 cm) dice
1 tablespoon	½ ounce/15 ml	Olive oil
2 thick slices	2 ounces/56 g total	Bacon, in ½-inch (1.2 cm) dice
1 cup	4 ounces/112 g	Onion, in ¼-inch (.6 cm) dice
½ cup	2 ounces/56 g	Celery, in ¼-inch (.6 cm) dice
1	5 g	Garlic clove, minced
1	4 tablespoons/ 3.5 ounces/98 g	Jalapeño pepper, stemmed, seeded, minced
1½ teaspoons		Fresh thyme, chopped
½ teaspoon		Paprika
¼ teaspoon		Cayenne pepper
		Freshly ground black pepper
1½ cups	6 ounces/168 g	Cooked chicken, shredded
¼ cup	2 ounces/60 ml	Chicken stock
		Salt
½ cup	2 ounces/56 g	Green onions, thinly sliced
2 tablespoons	1 ounce/30 ml	Rendered bacon fat or vegetable oil
		All-purpose flour, for dusting
4		Eggs, poached
2 cups	8 ounces/240 ml	Hollandaise Sauce (see Ch. 7, Bacon Hollandaise Sauce; using 5 oz (150 ml) warm clarified butter instead of bacon fat, follow steps 2 and 3 only)

PROCEDURE

1. In a saucepan, cover the potato with water and add a little salt; bring to a boil, reduce heat to low, and simmer until tender, 12 to 14 minutes. Drain.

2. In a 10- to 12-inch (25.4–30.5 cm) sauté pan, heat the olive oil over medium-high heat. Add the bacon and cook until the fat renders and bacon is lightly browned but still soft, 5 to 6 minutes.

3. Add the onion, celery, garlic, jalapeño, thyme, paprika, cayenne, and black pepper; sauté over medium heat, stirring occasionally, until vegetables are soft and fragrant, 5 to 6 minutes.

4. Add the chicken and stock; cook 3 to 4 minutes. Add the potato and continue to cook, stirring occasionally, until the liquid has been absorbed. Correct the seasoning with the salt and some more pepper.

5. Add the green onions and toss to combine. Spread the hash on a baking sheet and refrigerate until cool.

6. Form the hash into 3- to 4-inch (7.6–10.2 cm) patties, approximately 4 to 5 ounces (112–140 g) each. Refrigerate for 30 minutes.

7. Heat the bacon fat or oil in a 10- to 12-inch (25.4–30.5 cm) cast-iron skillet over medium-high heat. Dust the hash patties with a little flour on both sides, then add them to the skillet and cook until golden brown and crisp, 3 to 4 minutes per side.

8. Top each patty with a poached egg and drizzle with Hollandaise Sauce.

Chicken and Bacon Hash with Poached Egg and Hollandaise Sauce

Red Beans and Rice

AMOUNT	MEASURE	INGREDIENT
2 cups	4 ounces/112 g	Dried red kidney beans, soaked overnight
1 cup	4 ounces/112 g	Onion, in ¼-inch (.6 cm) dice
¼ cup	½ ounce/14 g	Green onion, chopped
¼ cup	1¼ ounces/35 g	Green bell pepper, in ¼-inch (.6 cm) dice
1 tablespoon	3 g	Fresh parsley, minced
1 cup	6 ounces/168 g	Ham, in 1-inch (2.5 cm) cubes
½ cup	3 ounces/84 g	Bacon, in ½-inch (1.2 cm) cubes
1	8 ounces/224 g	Ham hock
½ tablespoon	3 g	Salt
½ teaspoon	3 g	Black pepper
½ tablespoon	6 g	Garlic, minced
Pinch		Cayenne pepper
Pinch		Red pepper flakes
1		Bay leaf, broken into quarters
¼ teaspoon		Dried thyme
Pinch		Dried basil
1¼ quarts	40 ounces/1.2 L	Water or chicken or vegetable stock, cold
2 cups	8 ounces/224 g	Cooked long-grain rice

PROCEDURE

1. Drain the soaked beans. Combine with all the ingredients except the water and rice in a large pot. Add just enough cold water to cover.

2. Bring to a boil over high heat. Reduce the heat to a simmer and cook 2 to 3 hours or until beans are tender and a thick natural gravy has formed. Add 1 cup water toward the end of the cooking if the mixture appears too dry. During cooking, stir frequently and scrape down the sides and across the bottom to prevent scorching.

3. Remove the ham hock and cut meat into ½-inch (1.2 cm) cubes; return to the beans. Remove the bay leaf pieces.

4. In warmed large soup bowls, place ½ cup (2 ounces/56 g) of the rice, then cover with the beans.

Frog Legs Pinquate

AMOUNT	MEASURE	INGREDIENT
16 (4 per serving)	4 ounces/112 g each	Frog legs, quartered
6 tablespoons	1½ ounces/42 g	All-purpose flour
2 tablespoons	1 ounce/30 ml	Vegetable oil
2 tablespoons	1 ounce/28 g	Butter
1 cup	4 ounces/112 g	Onion, in ¼-inch (.6 cm) dice
½ cup	2 ounces/56 g	Celery, in ¼-inch (.6 cm) dice
1 cup	4 ounces/112 g	Green bell pepper, in ¼-inch (.6 cm) dice
2	10 g	garlic cloves, minced
½ cup	4 ounces/112 g	Tomato paste
2 cups	12 ounces/336 g	Tomatoes, peeled, in ¼-inch (.6 cm) dice
1¼ cups	10 ounces/300 ml	Chicken stock
½ teaspoon		Cayenne pepper
1		Bay leaf
1 teaspoon		Tabasco
1 teaspoon		Worcestershire sauce
1 tablespoon	½ ounce/15 ml	Lemon juice
2 tablespoons	¼ ounce/7 g	Fresh parsley, chopped
		Salt and pepper
2 cups	9 ounces/252 g	Steamed rice, hot

PROCEDURE

1. Dust the frog legs with 2 tablespoons (½ ounce/14 g) of the flour.

2. Heat the oil in a 10- to 12-inch (25.4–30.5 cm) skillet until smoking hot, add the frog legs, and brown lightly on all sides, 3 to 4 minutes. Remove frog legs.

3. Add the remaining ½ cup (62.5 g) flour to the pan to make a roux, stirring constantly over medium-low heat until roux is light to medium brown, 7 to 9 minutes.

4. Stir in the butter and add the onion, celery, and green pepper, and cook, stirring, for 3 to 4 minutes. Add the garlic and cook 1 minute more. Add the tomato paste and cook 2 to 3 minutes, stirring constantly.

5. Add the tomatoes, stock, cayenne, bay leaf, Tabasco, and Worcestershire sauce. Bring to a boil, reduce to a simmer, and cook 10 to 12 minutes.

6. Return the frog legs to the sauce and cook 3 to 4 minutes, basting the meat with the sauce. Remove bay leaf.

7. Add the lemon juice and parsley, then correct seasoning with salt and pepper.

8. Spoon the mixture over the steamed rice.

Cajun Omelet

AMOUNT	MEASURE	INGREDIENT
1 cup	6 ounces/168 g	Ham, in ½-inch (1.2 cm) dice
1 cup	6 ounces/168 g	Smoked sausage, in ½-inch (1.2 cm) dice
½ cup	2 ounces/56g	Onion, in ¼-inch (.6 cm) dice
½ cup	2 ounces/56 g	Green bell pepper, in ¼-inch (.6 cm) dice
2	10 g	Garlic gloves, minced
12		Eggs
		Salt and pepper
4 tablespoons	2 ounces/56 g	Butter, clarified
1 cup	4 ounces/112 g	Provolone cheese, grated
2 tablespoons	¼ ounce/7 g	Fresh parsley, chopped
		Tabasco

PROCEDURE

1. In an 8-inch (20.3 cm) skillet, combine the ham and sausage, and sauté for 2 to 3 minutes. Add the onion and green pepper, and cook until vegetables just begin to soften, 2 to 3 minutes more. Add the garlic, cook 1 minute, and remove from heat.

2. Make the omelets one at a time. Whisk together 3 eggs and season with salt and pepper.

3. Heat an 8-inch (20.3 cm) nonstick pan over medium heat. Add 1 tablespoon (½ ounce/14 g) butter. Add the eggs and stir with a wooden or all-temperature spoon, constantly moving the pan back and forth until the eggs have slightly coagulated. Let the eggs finish cooking without moving the pan; do not brown. Tilt the pan and use a spatula or fork to loosen the omelet. Roll the omelet to the center of the pan. Turn the pan handle 180 degrees away from you and tilt the pan toward you. Slide the omelet onto a plate, seam side down. The omelet should be oval shaped.

4. Slit open the omelet and place ½ cup (3–4 ounces/84–112 g) vegetable filling in the opening and around the omelet. Sprinkle ¼ cup (1 ounce/28 g) of the cheese on the omelet and melt under a broiler or salamander. Continue to make remaining omelets, using the remaining butter, vegetable filling, and cheese.

5. Garnish omelets with parsley and serve with Tabasco.

Cajun Omelet

Fried Oyster Po'Boy

✦ **CHEF TIP:** The po'boy sandwich is as diverse as the city it symbolizes. The original sandwich had its origins in the Martin Brothers Coffee Stand and Restaurant in the French Market.

AMOUNT	MEASURE	INGREDIENT
As needed		Vegetable oil, for deep-frying
24	2 cups/16 ounces/448 g	Oysters, shucked
		Salt and black pepper
		All-purpose flour, for dusting
3	6 ounces/180 ml	Eggs, lightly beaten with a little water
2 cups	6 ounces/168 g	Dried bread crumbs
1		French bread loaf, cut into 4 6-inch (15 cm) sections
		Remoulade Sauce (page 198)
2 cups	4 ounces/112 g	Iceberg lettuce, shredded
2	10 ounces/280 g	Tomatoes, in 12 slices total
2		Lemons, cut in half, wrapped

PROCEDURE

1. Heat the oil in a deep-fat fryer to 375°F (190°C).

2. Drain and dry the oysters. Season with salt and pepper; dip them in a light dusting of flour, then shake off excess flour. Dip the oysters in the egg wash, and drain, then coat in bread crumbs. Turn the oysters and pat until the bread crumbs adhere and cover the oysters completely.

3. Fry the oysters until golden brown and crisp, about 2 to 3 minutes. Drain on paper towels.

4. Split the French bread sections lengthwise and warm or toast the halves.

5. Spread the cut sides with a little Remoulade Sauce. Place ½ cup (1 ounce/28 g) lettuce over the sauce, then place 3 tomato slices on each po'boy. Top the tomatoes with 6 fried oysters and close the sandwich.

6. Serve with lemon halves.

Fried Oyster Po'Boy with Remoulade Sauce

Beignets

4 servings

AMOUNT	MEASURE	INGREDIENT
½ cup	3 ounces/84 g	Granulated sugar
4 cups	16 ounces/448 g	All-purpose flour
1 cup	8 ounces/240 ml	Milk, warmed, about 110°F (43°C)
2¼ teaspoons	¼ ounce/7 g	Active dry yeast
½ cup	4 ounces/112 g	Butter, melted
½ teaspoon	3 g	Salt
½ teaspoon		Vanilla extract
		All-purpose flour, for dusting
As needed		Vegetable oil, for deep-frying
1 cup	4½ ounces/126 g	Confectioners' sugar

PROCEDURE

1. Whisk 1 tablespoon (½ ounce/14 g) sugar and 1 tablespoon flour (¼ ounce/7 g) into the warm milk. Sprinkle the yeast over warm milk and allow to dissolve, about 2 minutes, then whisk together. Let the mixture sit until bubbles appear on the surface.

2. Whisk the butter, salt, and vanilla into the milk mixture. Add the remaining flour and remaining sugar, folding to combine. Knead the dough in a mixer fitted with a dough hook at medium speed for 1 to 2 minutes, or by hand on a lightly floured surface for about 5 minutes, or until smooth. Place the dough in a bowl and cover with plastic wrap. Place in the refrigerator for 2 hours.

3. Remove dough from refrigerator and roll out on a floured surface to a thickness of ¼ inch (.6 cm). Cut into 2-inch (5.1 cm) squares, cover loosely with plastic wrap, and allow to rise at room temperature for 1 hour.

4. Heat the oil to 350°F (176°C). Fry the beignets in small batches, turning them every 30 seconds until golden brown, about 2 to 3 minutes. Drain on paper towels and generously dust beignets with confectioners' sugar while still warm.

Beignets Dusted with Confectioners' Sugar

Chicken and Andouille Sausage Gumbo

4 servings

 **CHEF TIP:** Gumbo comes in many varieties, but every version reflects certain fundamental cooking techniques. First, most gumbos have a roux base that is cooked slowly to a rich brown, giving gumbo much of its characteristic thick texture and smoky taste. To prevent the roux from burning once it is done, add the cold vegetables all at once. Filé powder, when used to thicken gumbo, should be added only after the gumbo is finished and removed from the heat. Once filé powder is stirred in, the soup cannot be reheated, as the filé will either turn stringy or solidify at the bottom of the pot. For the best results, let the gumbo stand in the pot for 5 minutes after adding the filé powder.

If this chicken and andouille sausage gumbo is used as a main course, it makes four servings of about 8 to 10 ounces/240 to 300 ml each; if used as an appetizer, it makes eight servings of about 4 to 6 ounces/120 to 180 ml each.

AMOUNT	MEASURE	INGREDIENT
For the Seasoning Mix		
½ teaspoon	3 g	Salt
½ teaspoon	3 g	Black pepper
½ teaspoon	3 g	Cayenne pepper
½ teaspoon	3 g	White pepper
½ teaspoon		Paprika
½ teaspoon		Onion powder
½ teaspoon		Garlic powder
For the Gumbo		
2 cups	12 ounces/336 g	Chicken thigh meat, skin removed, in 1-inch (2.5 cm) pieces
1 cup	4 ounces/112 g	Onion, in ¼-inch (.6 cm) dice
1 cup	5 ounces/140 g	Green bell pepper, in ¼-inch (.6 cm) dice
¾ cup	3 ounces/84 g	Celery, in ¼-inch (.6 cm) dice
1¼ cups	5½ ounces/154 g	All-purpose flour
1½ cups	12 ounces/360 ml	Vegetable oil
7 cups	56 ounces/1.75 L	Chicken stock
1½ cups	8 ounces/224 g	Andouille smoked sausage or any other pure smoked pork sausage, such as Polish sausage (kielbasa), in ¼-inch (.6 cm) cubes
1 teaspoon		Garlic, minced
		Salt and black pepper
2 cups	9 ounces/252 g	Cooked long-grain rice

PROCEDURE

1. Make the seasoning mix. Combine the ingredients and divide in half.

2. Make the gumbo. Toss the chicken with half the seasoning mixture and set aside for 30 minutes.

3. Combine the onion, green pepper, and celery in a bowl.

4. Combine half the flour with the remaining seasoning mixture. Toss the chicken with the flour mixture until well coated.

5. Heat the oil in a 10-inch (25.4 cm) sauté pan over until very hot, 390°F (199°C). Fry the chicken until the crust is brown on all sides and the meat is cooked, about 3 to 5 minutes. Drain on paper towels.

6. Carefully pour the hot oil into a container, leaving as many of the browned particles in the pan as possible. Scrape the pan bottom to loosen any remaining particles.

7. Return ¼ cup (2 ounces/56 ml) hot oil to the pan over medium-high heat. Gradually add the reserved flour. Cook, whisking constantly, until the flour is dark red brown to black, 5 to 6 minutes, being careful not to scorch the roux.

8. Remove pan from the heat and immediately add the vegetables, stirring constantly, until the roux stops getting darker. Return to low heat and cook 5 minutes more, or until vegetables are soft, stirring constantly and scraping the pan bottom well.

9. In a 4-quart (3.78 L) pot, bring the stock to a boil and then reduce to a simmer. Add the roux to the stock a little at a time, stirring until dissolved between each addition.

10. Bring the stock back to a boil, reduce the heat to a simmer again, and add the sausage and garlic. Simmer, uncovered, 30 minutes, stirring often as it begins to thicken.

11. Add the fried chicken and adjust the seasoning with salt and pepper.

12. To serve as a main course, mound a portion of the rice (about ½ cup/2¼ ounces/63 g) in the center of individual soup bowls; ladle about 1¼ cups (10 ounces/293 ml) gumbo around the rice. For serving as an appetizer, place 1 heaping teaspoon (5 ml) of the rice in a cup and ladle about ¾ cup (6 ounces/178 ml) gumbo on top.

Chicken and Andouille Sausage Gumbo with Rice

Tomato and Haricots Verts Salad

4 servings

AMOUNT	MEASURE	INGREDIENT
For the Dressing		
1 tablespoon	½ ounce/15 ml	Mayonnaise
1 teaspoon	5 ml	Dijon mustard
2 tablespoons	1 ounce/30 ml	Red wine vinegar
1 tablespoon	½ ounce/15 ml	Lemon juice
1	5 g	Garlic clove, mashed with a bit of salt
½ cup	4 ounces/120 ml	Olive oil
		Salt and black pepper
For the Salad		
1 cup	4 ounces/112 g	Fennel, in paper-thin slices
1 cup	4 ounces/112 g	Haricots verts, blanched
1½ cups	9 ounces/252 g	Tomatoes, peeled, julienned
1 teaspoon		Chives, chopped
1 teaspoon		Fresh basil, cut in chiffonade

PROCEDURE

1. Make the dressing. Place the mayonnaise, mustard, vinegar, lemon juice, and garlic in a blender. While the blender is running, slowly drizzle in the oil until the dressing is smooth and thick. Adjust seasoning with salt and pepper.

2. Make the salad. Combine the fennel, beans, tomatoes, chives, and basil in a large bowl. Toss the salad with the dressing and serve on chilled plates.

Fried Fish in Pearly Meal with Remoulade Sauce

4 servings

✦ **CHEF TIP:**   Yellow corn flour may be found in most gourmet shops. It may be sold as packaged, pre-seasoned seafood breading, such as Zatarain's Fish Fry. If unavailable in your area, use one-third cornstarch, one-third flour, and one-third yellow cornmeal.

AMOUNT	MEASURE	INGREDIENT
4	12 ounces/336 g each	Whitefish fillet (speckled trout or freshwater bass, grouper, perch, brook trout)
1 cup	8 ounces/240 ml	Milk, cold
As needed		Vegetable oil, for deep-frying
1 cup	4 ounces/112 g	Yellow corn flour
1 cup	6 ounces/170 g	Yellow cornmeal
1½ teaspoons	8 g	Salt
¼ teaspoon		Black pepper
Pinch		Cayenne pepper
1 cup	2 ounces/56 g	Romaine lettuce, coarsely chopped

PROCEDURE

1. Rinse the fillets; remove any obvious bones or skin, and dry the fillets. Cut the fish into strips of ½ × ½ × 2 inches (1.2 × 1.2 × 5 cm); these fish fingers are called *goujonettes.* Lay the fish strips in a pan and add cold milk to just cover. Soak 30 minutes.

2. Preheat the deep-fryer or a deep pot to 375°F (190°C).

3. Combine the corn flour and cornmeal with the salt, pepper, and cayenne, and mix well.

4. Pat the fish dry. Dip the fillets in the seasoned flour to coat evenly, then fry until golden brown, about 2 to 3 minutes. Drain on paper towels.

5. Place the romaine lettuce on plates and top each with a fish fillet. Serve with Remoulade Sauce (recipe follows).

Remoulade Sauce

AMOUNT	MEASURE	INGREDIENT
For the Puree		
1 cup	3½ ounces/98g	Green onions, coarsely chopped
½ cup	2 ounces/56 g	Celery, coarsely chopped
1 tablespoon	3 g	Fresh parsley, coarsely chopped
To Finish the Sauce		
3 tablespoons	1½ ounces/45 ml	Creole mustard
1 tablespoon	¼ ounce/7 g	Paprika
1 teaspoon	5 g	Salt
½ teaspoon	3 g	Black pepper
¼ teaspoon		Cayenne pepper
⅓ cup	2½ ounces/80 ml	White wine vinegar
1½ tablespoons	¾ ounce/21 ml	Lemon juice
1 teaspoon		Fresh basil, chopped
¾ cup	6 ounces/180 ml	Olive oil
¼ cup	¾ ounce/25 g	Green onion, in ¼-inch (.6 cm) dice
2 tablespoons	½ ounce/14 g	Celery, in ¼-inch (.6 cm) dice
1 tablespoon	3 g	Fresh parsley, finely diced

PROCEDURE

1. Make the puree. In a mortar and pestle, or with a blender or food processor, grind the green onions, celery, and parsley to a puree.

2. Finish the sauce. Combine the puree with the mustard, paprika, salt, pepper, and cayenne. Blend well. Add the vinegar, lemon juice, and basil. Blend well again.

3. Gradually add the olive oil, blending constantly to make an emulsion (mayonnaise).

4. Add the diced green onion, celery, and parsley and combine well. Refrigerate for at least 1 hour to combine flavors.

Fried Fish in Pearly Meal with Remoulade Sauce

Crawfish Etouffée with Rice

Crawfish Etouffée

AMOUNT	MEASURE	INGREDIENT
6 tablespoons	3 ounces/84 g	Butter
¼ cup	1 ounce/28 g	All-purpose flour
1 cup	4 ounces/112 g	Onion, in ½-inch (1.2 cm) dice
½ cup	2 ½ ounces/70 g	Green bell pepper, in ½-inch (1.2 cm) dice
½ cup	2 ounces/56 g	Celery, in ½-inch (1.2 cm) dice
1 tablespoon	½ ounce/15 g	Garlic, minced
1½ cups	12 ounces/336 g	Crawfish tail meat
6 tablespoons	3 ounces/84 g	Crawfish fat, or butter
1 teaspoon	5 g	Salt
¼ teaspoon		Black pepper
¼ teaspoon		Cayenne pepper
1 teaspoon	5 ml	Lemon juice
⅓ cup	1 ounce/28 g	Green onion tops, thinly sliced
1 tablespoon	3 g	Fresh parsley, minced
1 cup	8 ounces/240 ml	Fish stock or cold water
2 cups	9 ounces/252 g	Basic Boiled Rice (recipe follows)

PROCEDURE

1. In a heavy 3-quart (3 L) saucepan, melt the butter over low heat. Gradually add the flour and cook over low heat until a medium brown roux is formed, 5 to 7 minutes.

2. Add the onion, green pepper, celery, and garlic. Cook, stirring, until the vegetables are tender, 6 to 8 minutes.

3. Add the crawfish tail meat, crawfish fat, salt, pepper, cayenne, lemon juice, green onion, and parsley; mix well.

4. Add the fish stock or cold water, bring to a boil, and simmer 10 to 15 minutes, stirring frequently. Remove from the heat.

5. Place servings of rice in individual bowls and pour the étouffée over the rice.

Crawfish Etouffée

 CHEF TIP: Firm, fluffy, freshly prepared rice is an essential accompaniment for gumbos, bean dishes, bisques, étouffées, and many other dishes.

AMOUNT	MEASURE	INGREDIENT
1 cup	6½ ounces/182 g	Long-grain rice
2 cups	16 ounces/480 ml	Cold water
1 teaspoon	5 g	Salt
1 teaspoon	5 g	Butter

PROCEDURE

1. Combine the rice, water, salt, and butter in a heavy 3-quart (3 L) saucepan with a tight-fitting lid and bring to a boil over high heat.

2. Stir once with a fork, then cover and reduce the heat to very low. Simmer for 15 minutes; do not lift the cover during the cooking.

3. Let rice stand, still covered, for 5 to 10 minutes longer. Uncover, and fluff the rice gently with a fork.

Smothered Okra

4 servings

AMOUNT	MEASURE	INGREDIENT
2 tablespoons	1 ounce/30 ml	Vegetable oil
1 cup	4 ounces/112 g	Onion, in thin slices
4 cups	13½ ounces/378 g	Okra, stem ends trimmed
¾ cup	4 ounces/112 g	Tomato, peeled, chopped
		Salt and black pepper
⅛ teaspoon		Cayenne pepper
⅛ teaspoon		Chili powder
⅛ teaspoon		Dried thyme

PROCEDURE

1. Heat the oil in a 10- to 12-inch (25.4–30.5 cm) sauté pan over medium-high heat. Add the onion and sauté over low heat until lightly brown, about 3 to 4 minutes.

2. Add the okra, tomato, and seasonings; cover and simmer until the okra is tender, about 6 to 8 minutes. Smaller okra will take less time to cook than larger pods.

Bread Pudding with Whiskey Sauce

4 servings

Bread Pudding

 **CHEF TIP:** This is the classic New Orleans bread pudding. Use half-and-half instead of milk, and an extra egg to make it even richer. You can add different fruits, nuts, and liqueurs, if desired.

AMOUNT	MEASURE	INGREDIENT
2 cups (¼ baguette)	2 ounces/56 g	Day-old French bread, in 1½- to 2-inch (38–5 cm) cubes
1 cup plus 6 tablespoons	11 ounces/330 ml	Milk
1		Egg, lightly beaten
⅓ cup	2½ ounces/70 g	Granulated sugar
1½ teaspoons	7.5 ml	Vanilla extract
1 tablespoon	11 g	Raisins, soaked in Cointreau or Kirsch
1 teaspoon		Ground cinnamon
¼ teaspoon		Grated nutmeg
2 tablespoons	1 ounce/28 g	Dark brown sugar
1½ tablespoons	1½ ounces/44 g	Unsalted butter, in small cubes

PROCEDURE

1. Soak the bread cubes in 6 tablespoons (3 ounces/90 ml) of the milk for 1 hour.

2. Preheat the oven to 300°F (149°C). Butter a 1-quart (32 ounces/1 L) pan.

3. Beat the remaining 1 cup (8 ounces/240 ml) milk, the egg, sugar, and vanilla to combine well. Add the milk-soaked bread, then add the raisins and mix well.

4. Pour the mixture into the prepared pan and sprinkle with the cinnamon, nutmeg, and brown sugar. Top with the butter cubes.

5. Bake for 1 hour, or until set. Allow to cool 30 minutes before cutting.

6. Serve with Whiskey Sauce (recipe follows).

Whiskey Sauce

CHEF TIP: For a nonalcoholic version, add a teaspoon of rum extract or orange or vanilla extract.

AMOUNT	MEASURE	INGREDIENT
¼ cup	2 ounces/56 g	Unsalted butter
¼ cup	1 ounce/28 g	Confectioners' sugar
1		Egg, lightly beaten
¼ cup	2 ounces/56 ml	Bourbon

PROCEDURE

1. In a 1-quart (32 ounces/1 L) pan or a 10-inch (25.4 cm) sauté pan, melt the butter over low heat.

2. When hot but not browned, add the sugar. Beat with a whisk until thick and hot.

3. Remove pan from the heat and whisk in the egg. Beat until emulsified, about 2 minutes. Whisk in the bourbon and serve.

New Orleans Shrimp Bisque

4 servings

✦ CHEF TIP: The basic reason for making a dark roux is for the distinctive taste and texture it lends to the food. This roux taste and texture is characteristic of many dishes that Louisiana Cajuns make. Cooked roux is called "Cajun napalm"; it is extremely hot and sticks to your skin—be very careful to avoid splashing.

AMOUNT	MEASURE	INGREDIENT
For the Roux		
5 tablespoons	2½ ounces/75 ml	Bacon drippings or butter
1 cup	4 ounces/112 g	All-purpose flour
For the Bisque		
2 tablespoons	1 ounce/28 g	Butter
1 cup	4 ounces/112 g	Onion, in ¼-inch (.6 cm) dice
¼ cup	1 ounce/28 g	Green onions, white part only, thinly sliced
3 tablespoons	⅓ ounce/9 g	Green onions, green tops, thinly sliced
2½ tablespoons	¾ ounce/21 g	Celery, in ¼-inch (.6 cm) dice
2 tablespoons	6 g	Fresh parsley, finely minced
1 tablespoon	½ ounce/14 g	Garlic, minced
1 tablespoon	½ ounce/14 g	Salt
¼ teaspoon		Black pepper
½ teaspoon		Cayenne pepper
2		Bay leaves
1 teaspoon		Dried thyme
½ teaspoon		Dry mustard
½ teaspoon		Dried basil
4		Whole cloves
1 cup	8 ounces/224 g	Shrimp, peeled, chopped
2 cups	16 ounces/2 L	Seafood stock or clam juice
1 cup	8 ounces/224 g	Medium shrimp (25–30 count), peeled, whole

PROCEDURE

1. Make the roux. In a 2-quart (2 L) saucepan, heat the bacon fat over low heat and gradually add the flour. Cook to a medium brown roux, 12 to 15 minutes.

2. Make the bisque. In another 2-quart (2 L) saucepan, melt the butter over medium heat and slowly brown the onion and white parts of the green onions, about 10 minutes. The onions must be cooked before the roux is finished.

3. Add the cooked green onions to the roux as soon as the roux is the desired color (rich peanut butter), then add the green onion tops, celery, parsley, garlic, and seasonings and herbs; mix thoroughly, cook 3 minutes.

4. Add the chopped shrimp. Gradually add the stock, stirring constantly to keep smooth. Bring the bisque to a boil, lower the heat, and simmer 30 minutes or more.

5. Add the whole shrimp and simmer 1 minute more. Remove bay leaves.

6. Serve over boiled rice.

Roasted Eggplant and Oysters

4 servings

AMOUNT	MEASURE	INGREDIENT
2 large	2 pounds/896 g	Eggplants
4 cups	16 ounces/448 g	Onions, in ½-inch (1.2 cm) dice
¾ cup	6 ounces/168 g	Unsalted butter
1 cup	6 ounces/168 g	Bacon, in ½-inch (1.2 cm) dice
½ cup plus 4 teaspoons	1½ ounces/42 g	Italian bread crumbs
1 teaspoon	5 g	Salt
½ teaspoon	3 g	Black pepper
1½ pints (2½ dozen)	24 ounces/720 ml	Shucked medium oysters, drained

PROCEDURE

1. Preheat the oven to 425°F (220°C).

2. Pierce the eggplants several times with a fork and place on a baking sheet. Bake eggplants 30 to 45 minutes, or until very tender. Test with a skewer to see if the center is done. Remove from oven and cool. Keep oven on.

3. In a 10-inch (25.4 cm) sauté pan, cook the onions in ¼ cup (2 ounces/56 g) of the butter until glazed, but not brown, 3 to 4 minutes.

4. In another small skillet, fry the bacon until crisp. Remove from the fat, and drain on several layers of paper towels. With a sharp knife, cut off the stem ends of the eggplants and peel them carefully. Discard the skin and chop the flesh into ¾-inch (1.9 cm) cubes. Place in a colander to drain for 30 minutes.

5. Combine the drained eggplant with the sautéed onions. Crumble the bacon into the mixture; add ½ cup of the bread crumbs, the salt, pepper, and oysters.

6. Melt the remaining ½ cup (4 ounces/112 g) butter in a small saucepan.

7. Divide the eggplant pulp and oyster mixture into four equal portions and place in 8-ounce (224 g) ramekins. Pour the melted butter over each portion, then sprinkle each evenly with remaining 4 teaspoons of bread crumbs.

8. Bake ramekins for 20 minutes, or until the mixture bubbles vigorously around the edges and the tops are well browned.

Creole Jambalaya

4 servings

CHEF TIP: One of the secrets of a great jambalaya is the way fat rendered from the chicken or sausage coats and seals the rice, helping it keep its texture during the long cooking while it absorbs the flavors that surround it. This cooking process is similar to the technique for making rice pilaf. Some jambalaya recipes call for the rice to be browned before adding the liquid. By using both dried and fresh herbs, intense and diverse flavors are imparted to the jambalaya. When preparing jambalaya, cook the meats over medium heat, stirring constantly, until they are thoroughly browned. This process takes about 15 minutes. When the meats are browned, remove them from the pan and brown the vegetables in the same manner. Add the seasonings after the vegetables are browned and cook for 5 minutes more to build the flavors on top on one another.

AMOUNT	MEASURE	INGREDIENT
2 tablespoons	1 ounce/30 ml	Vegetable oil
1	2 pounds/0.9 kg	Frying chicken, cut into eighths
4 cups	16 ounces/448 g	Onions, in ½-inch (1.2 cm) dice
⅔ cup	3 ounces/84 g	Green bell pepper, in ½-inch (1.2 cm) dice
¾ cup	2 ounces/56 g	Green onion tops, thinly sliced
1 tablespoon	½ ounce/14 g	Garlic, minced
2 tablespoons	6 g	Fresh parsley, minced
¾ cup	4 ounces/112 g	Baked ham, in ½-inch (1.2 cm) dice
1 cup	6 ounces/168 g	Lean pork, in ½-inch (1.2 cm) cubes
2 cups	12 ounces/336 g	Smoked sausages (Polish, French, garlic), in ½-inch (1.2 cm) slices
2 teaspoons	10 g	Salt
½ teaspoon		Black pepper
¼ teaspoon		Cayenne pepper
½ teaspoon		Chili powder
2		Bay leaves
¼ teaspoon		Dried thyme
⅛ teaspoon		Ground cloves
¼ teaspoon		Dried basil
⅛ teaspoon		Mace
1½ cups	9¾ ounces/276 g	Uncooked long-grain rice
3 cups	24 ounces/705 ml	Chicken stock

PROCEDURE

1. Preheat the oven to 350°F (180°C).

2. In a 3- to 4-quart (3 to 4 L) heavy-bottomed oven-safe pot, heat the oil over medium heat. Add the chicken and brown, about 5 minutes, then remove.

3. Add the vegetables, parsley, ham, and pork. Cook over medium heat, stirring constantly, for about 10 minutes or until everything is brown.

4. Add the sausages and seasonings and herbs; continue to cook over low heat for 5 minutes, stirring occasionally and scraping pan bottom well.

5. Add the rice and increase the heat to medium; cook 5 minutes, or until the rice is lightly browned, stirring and scraping the sides and bottom.

6. Return the chicken to the pot; add the stock. Mix well; bring to a boil. Cover the pot and place in the oven. Cook 35 minutes, stirring occasionally.

7. Uncover the pot and cook 10 minutes more. Raise the heat to medium to allow the rice to dry out, stirring very frequently.

8. Remove the bay leaves and serve immediately.

Creole Jambalaya

Chicken Maquechoux

4 servings

✦ CHEF TIP: Maquechoux is a traditional dish of southern Louisiana. It is thought to be a combination of Acadian French (Cajun) and American Indian cultural influence. The success of the dish requires fresh corn, the pulp and milk giving the dish its distinctive creaminess. The easiest way to milk the corn cobs is to use a Bundt pan. Also, do not cut the entire kernel off the cob. Leaving part of the kernel gives more milk.

AMOUNT	MEASURE	INGREDIENT
For the Chicken		
¼ cup	2 ounces/60 ml	Vegetable oil
1	2 pounds/0.9 kg	Chicken fryer, cut into eighths
For the Maquechoux		
¼ cup	2 ounces/56 g	Unsalted butter
1 cup	4 ounces/112 g	Onion, in ½-inch (1.2 cm) dice
½ cup	2½ ounces/70 g	Green bell pepper, in ½-inch (1.2 cm) dice
½ cup	2½ ounces/70 g	Red bell pepper, in ½-inch (1.2 cm) dice
½ cup	2 ounces/56 g	Celery, in ½-inch (1.2 cm) dice
1¼ cups	8 ounces/224 g	Tomatoes, peeled, in ½-inch (1.2 cm) dice
1 teaspoon	5 g	Salt
½ teaspoon		Cayenne pepper
1 teaspoon		Black pepper
5¼ cups	34 ounces/952 g	Fresh corn kernels, milk reserved
2 tablespoons	1 ounce/28 g	Sugar
½ cup	4 ounces/120 ml	Heavy cream
2 tablespoons	1 ounce/30 ml	Milk

PROCEDURE

1. Prepare the chicken. In a 2- to 3-quart (2 to 3 L) saucepan, heat the oil over medium heat. Brown the chicken parts, turning frequently, for 4 to 5 minutes. Remove and set on a rack to drain. Drain fat from the pan.

2. Make the maquechoix. Melt the butter over medium-high heat in the same pan as used for the chicken. Add the onion, bell peppers, celery, and tomatoes and sauté until the onion is transparent, about 10 minutes.

3. Stir in the salt and peppers. Add the corn kernels and milk from the cobs, the sugar, and cream, and stir well. Reduce the heat to medium and cook until the corn is tender, 10 minutes. Adjust the seasonings.

4. Add the chicken to the corn mixture. Reduce the heat to low and cook chicken 10 to 15 minutes, stirring frequently. Make sure chicken dark meat is cooked; if mixture seems to be drying, add 2 to 3 tablespoons (1–1½ ounces/30–45 ml) milk toward the end of the cooking period. The corn mixture should have the consistency of thick creamed corn.

5. Serve hot, in warmed bowls.

Chicken Maquechoux

Pecan Pralines

AMOUNT	MEASURE	INGREDIENT
1 cup	7 ounces/196 g	Brown sugar
½ cup	3½ ounces/98 g	Granulated sugar
¼ teaspoon		Salt
½ cup	4 ounces/120 ml	Heavy cream
¼ teaspoon		Cream of tartar
1 cup	4 ounces/112 g	Pecan pieces
2 tablespoons	1 ounce/28 g	Butter
½ tablespoon	7 ml	Vanilla extract

PROCEDURE

1. Combine the sugars, salt, cream, and cream of tartar in a 2-quart (2 L) heavy pan. Stir over low heat until the sugar dissolves, wiping the crystals from the sides of the pan with a rubber spatula.

2. Raise heat to medium and cook for 15 minutes or until mixture reaches the soft-ball stage, 234°F to 240°F (112.5–115°C), on a candy thermometer. Continue to cook to soft-ball stage (238°F/114°C). (If a thermometer is not available, spoon a few drops of the hot sugar into a bowl of very cold water. Check the hardness of the cooled sugar with your fingertips. The balls of sugar will be soft and flexible when pressed between the fingertips. If you remove the ball of sugar from water, it will flatten after a few moments in the hand.)

3. Add the pecans. Cook, stirring constantly, for 2 minutes. Remove from heat and add the butter, vanilla, and a pinch of salt. Beat until the mixture looks creamy around edges of pan (this happens very quickly but if you need to speed the process, put saucepan in cold water while beating).

4. Drop the candy from a tablespoon onto waxed paper or baking parchment, leaving about 2 to 3 inches (5 to 7.5 cm) between each. Let cool.

5. Remove pralines from the paper or cut the waxed paper between each and wrap individually.

Pecan Pralines

Fried Stuffed Crawfish Heads

4 servings

✦ **CHEF TIP:** Stuffed crawfish heads are crawfish shells filled with sautéed chopped crawfish meat, vegetables, and bread. Don't try to eat the shells—even good frying won't make them edible.

AMOUNT	MEASURE	INGREDIENT
For the Stuffing		
3 tablespoons	1½ ounces/44 g	Butter
1 cup	4 ounces/112 g	Onion, in ¼-inch (.6 cm) dice
½ cup	2½ ounces/70 g	Green bell pepper, in ¼-inch (.6 cm) dice
¼ cup	1 ounce/28 g	Celery, in ¼-inch (.6 cm) dice
⅓ cup	1½ ounces/42 g	Green onions, in ¼-inch (.6 cm) dice
2 tablespoons	6 g	Fresh parsley, finely minced
¾ teaspoon	4 g	Salt
¼ teaspoon		Black pepper
⅛ teaspoon		Cayenne pepper
⅛ teaspoon		Dried thyme
⅛ teaspoon		Ground allspice
2 cups	12 ounces/336 g	Crawfish meat, chopped
½ cup	1 ounce/28 g	Fresh white bread crumbs, soaked in ¼ cup (2 ounces/6 ml) milk
For the Crawfish		
2		Eggs, lightly beaten
2 tablespoons	1 ounce/30 ml	Water
1 cup	4½ ounces/124 g	All-purpose flour
1 teaspoon	5 g	Salt
½ teaspoon		Black pepper
24		Crawfish shells, cleaned
As needed		Vegetable oil, for deep-frying

PROCEDURE

1. Make the stuffing. Melt the butter over low heat. Add the vegetables and parsley. Sauté until soft and just beginning to brown, about 6 to 8 minutes.

2. Add the seasonings and blend. Add the crawfish meat, then add the soaked bread and toss to combine. Cook over very low heat, stirring constantly, for 8 to 10 minutes.

3. Prepare the crawfish. Beat together the eggs and water; combine the flour and seasonings.

4. Fill the crawfish shells with the stuffing.

5. Dip the stuffed heads in the beaten egg to dampen. Roll in the seasoned flour to coat evenly. Let dry.

6. Heat the oil to 375°F (190°C) in a deep-fryer or deep pot.

7. Fry the stuffed heads until deep golden brown, about 2 to 3 minutes. Drain on paper towels. Serve hot.

Muffuletta

4 servings

AMOUNT	MEASURE	INGREDIENT
For the Olive Salad		
½ cup	2 ounces/56 g	Large pimento-stuffed green olives, slightly crushed, well drained
¼ cup	1 ounce/28 g	Pickled sliced cauliflower
½ teaspoon		Capers, drained
¼ cup	1 ounce/28 g	Celery, in thin diagonal slices
2 tablespoons	½ ounce/14 g	Carrot, in thin diagonal slices
Pinch		Celery seeds
Pinch		Dried oregano
1	5 g	Garlic clove, minced
		Black pepper
¼ cup	1 ounce/28 g	Pepperoncini, drained, left whole
¼ cup	1 ounce/28 g	Greek black olives, chopped
¼ cup	1 ounce/28 g	Cocktail onions, drained, chopped
		Olive oil
For the Sandwich		
1	1½ pounds/672 g	Round loaf Italian bread (6 inch)
	2 ounces/56 g	Mortadella, thinly sliced
	2 ounces/56 g	Ham, thinly sliced
	2 ounces/56 g	Hard Genoa salami, thinly sliced
	2 ounces/56 g	Mozzarella cheese, sliced
	2 ounces/56 g	Provolone cheese, sliced

PROCEDURE

1. Make the salad. Combine all the ingredients and cover with oil. Refrigerate at least 24 hours.

2. Make the sandwiches. Split the bread horizontally. Spread each half with equal parts olive salad and oil from the salad. Place the meats and cheeses evenly on the bottom half and cover with the top half of the bread. Cut into 4 equal pieces.

The Cuisine of the
Central Plains

Known as the land of milk and grain, the Central Plains are the breadbasket and main source of food crops for the United States. The region includes the corn belt and the wheat belt, and has a long history during which cattle "kingdoms" reigned. Expertise in dairy farming has resulted in innovative and extensive cheese making. Meats, game, and poultry are staples of the Central Plains, and the lakes, streams, and rivers of the region supply many varieties of freshwater fish. The cultural diversity of the residents of the Central Plains has added a wealth of culinary knowledge and variety to what we know today as American regional cuisine.

Illinois Known as "The Prairie State," Illinois's rich black soil makes it one of the leading agriculture states in the nation. Farms take up more than 80 percent of the state's total land mass. Corn is Illinois's chief crop, though the state also produces large amounts of soybeans, oats, wheat, and livestock.

Indiana "The Hoosier State," also known as the "Crossroads of America." Corn and soybeans are grown in every county.

Iowa "The Hawkeye State" raises one-fifth of the nation's corn and one-quarter of its pork.

Kansas "The Sunflower State" is the nation's leader in wheat production. Beef is the state's most valuable farm product.

Michigan "The Wolverine State," Michigan is so named because early fur traders were often looking for wolverine fur. Heavily forested, the state is prime land for foraging for the highly prized morel mushrooms in spring.

Minnesota "The Gopher State," where wheat remains a main crop, is a leader in the production of corn, wild rice, dairy goods, and livestock.

Missouri "The Show Me State," where farm products from throughout the Great Plains were processed in Missouri for shipment east, and the stockyards of Kansas City were famous for many years.

Nebraska "The Cornhusker State," where ranching is the most important agricultural industry. Corn is the biggest crop. Nebraska produces about 10 percent of the country's corn.

North Dakota "The Flickertail State." Wheat is the most important crop, and much of North Dakota's wheat goes to making pasta. More waterfowl, like ducks and geese, breed in North Dakota than in any other state.

Ohio   "The Buckeye State," where the rich soil makes Ohio part of the fertile farmland of the corn belt.

South Dakota   "The Mount Rushmore State" produces some of the nation's leading amounts of rye, wheat, and corn. Ranches raise beef cattle and sheep.

Wisconsin   "The Badger State," also known as the "Dairy State," is world famous for its cheese. With over 1 million milk cows, Wisconsin produces more cheese and milk than any other state.

HISTORY OF THE REGION

The first Europeans to travel through the Central Plains were the French fur traders, known as "mountain men," in the 1600s. Although they were not settlers, they did establish outposts in the region. These outposts were significant because only there could the mountain men obtain food and supplies. Typically, the foods available in the outposts were those from the local area. Relatively few changes occurred in the Central Plains over the next century and a half.

In 1803, President Thomas Jefferson purchased the Louisiana Territory from France for $15 million. This event, known as the Louisiana Purchase, included 800,000 square miles of territory west of the Mississippi River to the Rocky Mountains and north to Canada. The United States had little geographic knowledge of the West at the time of the purchase, so President Jefferson selected Meriwether Lewis and William Clark to explore the northern reaches of the new purchase and then to proceed to the Pacific Ocean. Lewis and Clark traveled up the Missouri River from St. Louis, crossed the Rocky Mountains, and descended the Columbia River on the West Coast. They gathered a vast amount of geographic and scientific information, and established diplomatic and trade relations with some Native American tribes. They were later followed by Zebulon Pike and Stephen Long, both of whom explored the central Great Plains area. At that time, the dry, flat, prairie land of the Central Plains offered little to farmers who were used to working on land with plentiful rainfall and having available trees to build houses.

In 1849, gold was discovered in California, and the Oregon and Santa Fe trails opened, signaling the start of the land rush. A few European immigrants and people from other parts of America began to settle in the Great Plains to farm, ranch, build towns, and work on the railroads. The Homestead Act of 1862 further encouraged agricultural expansion. The act offered 160 acres virtually free to any citizen willing to develop the land. Lawmakers hoped that the Homestead Act would lead to agricultural development in the western states. Farming families settled on the millions of acres traveled over by those who had migrated to more inviting places on the Pacific Coast. These hardy families farmed the plains with new techniques and equipment developed after the Civil War.

The federal government, in an effort to contribute to the development of these new farming methods, conducted research in the newly created Department of Agriculture and endowed agricultural colleges. These universities are today many of the Big Ten schools, including Ohio State, Michigan State, and Iowa State. To produce crops in an area that had little rainfall, farmers on the Great Plains used new methods of dry farming and irrigated land close to streams. And while the prairies were covered with wild grasses and wildflowers, it was difficult to farm. These grasses had roots deep in the soil, and plows had a hard time cutting through the tangled roots; farmers struggled just to prepare a few acres of land for planting. In 1838, John Deere, a blacksmith living in Illinois, invented a new steel plow that made it easier to turn the soil. These farmers benefited greatly from the industrial revolution, and inventions and innovations in farm machinery have allowed them to continue to cultivate the land and grow more crops.

THE SCANDINAVIAN INFLUENCE

Between 1820 and 1914, over 2 million Scandinavians immigrated to America. Norwegians were the first to arrive, and they began to work along the East Coast as loggers, fishermen, and farmers. Soon, many moved inland, where they found the weather and lands of the Midwest and Central Plains similar to Norway. Around 1840, the Norwegians settled in the area of the upper Mississippi Valley—specifically, the region that today makes up much of Minnesota and Wisconsin. Following the Norwegians were many immigrants from Sweden and Denmark, who also settled in the Central Plains. As this westward migration took place, the Mississippi River quickly became a dividing line between the "civilized" East and the "untamed" West. The Central Plains, with the Mississippi River running through the middle, lured new residents with hopes of agricultural wealth and great prosperity.

These immigrants from northern Europe who settled throughout the Central Plains first learned how to harvest corn and wild rice from the Native Americans. Native Americans taught them techniques for hunting the abundant wild game of the region, including pheasant, quail, grouse, wild turkey, deer, and buffalo. The settlers also learned how to fish in the many rivers and lakes, which contain walleye, yellow perch, trout, and pike, and are home to many varieties of duck, geese, and other waterfowl. Most important, the vast lands were well suited for farming and for grazing livestock. Rustic stews, breads, and the root vegetables that were the traditional foods of Scandinavians became dietary staples. The Scandinavians brought to the area many other food traditions from the Old Country, such as cheese and sausage making, and smoking fish and meat.

THE EASTERN EUROPEAN INFLUENCE

As western migration continued, people from Eastern Europe began to settle in the Central Plains, which also reminded them of their homelands. Germans, Poles, and Austrians settled in Illinois and Iowa, as well as Minnesota and Wisconsin. They farmed the land and raised dairy cattle as their primary source of income. Wisconsin became a popular destination of German and Swedish immigrants. Cheese production began in Wisconsin in the 1830s, and Cheddar cheese was made in the English tradition while other cheeses from the Old Country, such as brie, ricotta, Limburger, mozzarella, feta, and gouda, were made as well. Two of the three cheeses invented in America—brick and Colby—were first produced in the 1870s. Today, there are over 200 cheese-making plants in Wisconsin alone. Wisconsin is also the number-one dairy state in the country, producing milk, butter, and excellent domestic cheese.

Germans and Bohemians who emigrated to the region brought the art of brewing and their love of beer. The extensive prairies and farmlands of the Central Plains were perfect for growing wheat, oats, barley, rye, and corn, which are the grains used to produce beer. The region's major trade areas of St. Louis, Milwaukee, Chicago, Cincinnati, St. Paul, and Kansas City became homes to America's first breweries. By the end of the 19th century, thousands of breweries had sprung up and began to produce unique beers. The great beer industry went into decline during Prohibition, which began in 1920; by 1933, when Prohibition ended, only 400 of the original breweries were able to reopen for business. Although many of the original brewers no longer operate in Milwaukee, residents still enjoy the traditions and culture that beer brewing left behind.

German immigrants also brought their expertise in sausage making. Not only were they experts in sausage production, they were inventive as well. The German farmers of the Central Plains regions originated sausage varieties such as knackwurst, bratwurst, liverwurst, Mettwurst, and Thuringer, which are still popular products today. They also built smokehouses to smoke hams, bacon, and fish from the region's lakes and rivers.

THE EFFECT OF THE RAILROADS

The growth of railroads encouraged westward expansion more than any other single development. By the mid-1800s, railroads had connected the East with the West, and the Central Plains became a major hub. Railroads were also responsible for the growth of ranching. After the Civil War there was growing demand for beef in the eastern and northern cities. Railroads provided the means of linking supply with demand. Cattle were herded northward out of Texas along the Chisholm and Great Western trails to towns on the Great Plains. There they were loaded into specially built rail cars and carried to slaughterhouses in Kansas City, Chicago, and other urban centers.

By the late 1800s, cattle drives were no longer necessary. As Native American tribes were defeated, cattle ranching spread into the Great Plains states of Kansas, Nebraska, and North and South Dakota. New breeds of cattle that could withstand the harsh conditions could now be fattened on plains grasses and shipped east with relative ease. Ranching became a big business and many of the largest ranches were owned by corporations funded by millions of dollars in stock sold in the East, Britain, and Europe.

CORN AND WHEAT

Corn is the foundation on which ancient civilizations, such as the Maya and the Aztec, were built. Throughout the 19th century, the size of the corn crop increased as the settlers moved into the western territories. In the mid-1800s, a new hybrid, called Reid's Yellow Dent, began to be widely cultivated in the Midwest. By 1882, people were referring to the corn-producing states of the Midwest as the Corn Belt. Over 85 percent of all corn grown is dent corn, or field corn, and is used primarily to feed animals and livestock, making it an important American commodity. From 1877 through 1920, American horticulturists developed many new hybrids that became standard on the country's farms.

In 1950, Dr. J. R. Laughnam of the University of Illinois discovered some very sweet strains of corn. In the 1960s, Dr. A. M. Rhodes, also at the University of Illinois, developed an even sweeter corn. Mature sweet corn is eaten fresh, boiled and buttered. It is found frozen and canned. Corn is also used to make products such as ethanol, corn syrup, and corn oil. Wheat is a grain that was brought to America by the European colonists. It is a grass whose seed belongs to the cereal grains group, and it contains gluten, the basic structure for forming doughs for breads, rolls, and other baked goods. Due to difficulties in cultivation, wheat was not a major crop until the end of the 19th century, when Turkey Red Winter Wheat began to grow well in the Central Plains. The growth and development of wheat crops in the Central Plains are attributed to Mennonite farmers, originally from the Ukraine, who, with land provided by the Santa Fe Railroad in 1875, began farming along the rail lines in Kansas.

KANSAS WHEAT

Six classes of wheat are grown in the United States, and Kansas produces three of them:

Hard Red Winter (98 Percent)   High in protein, with strong gluten. Used for yeast breads and rolls.

Soft Red Winter (1 Percent)   Used for flat breads, cakes, pastries, and crackers.

Hard White (1 Percent)   Used for yeast breads, hard rolls, tortillas, and noodles.

The three main parts of the wheat kernel are the endosperm, bran, and germ:

Endosperm   Constituting about 83 percent of the total kernel mass, this is the source of white flour. Enriched flour products contained added quantities of riboflavin, niacin, thiamin, and iron.

Bran   About 14 percent of the kernel, this part is included in whole wheat flour. Bran is the outer coat and is an excellent source of fiber.

Germ   About 2.5 percent of the kernel, this is the embryo or sprouting section of the seed. It is usually separated because it contains the fat that limits the keeping quality of flours.

THE CONTROVERSY OVER GENETICALLY MODIFIED FOODS

In genetic modification (or engineering; GM) of food plants, scientists remove one or more genes from the DNA of another organism, such as a bacterium, virus, or animal, and "recombine" them into the DNA of the plant they want to alter. Much like developing hybrid species, genetic engineers hope the plant will express the traits associated with the genes. In corn, for example, the genes from a bacterium known as *Bacillus thuringiensis*, or Bt, has been transferred into the DNA of corn. The protein from the Bt genes is able to kill insects, and with this genetic transfer corn is now able to produce its own pesticide.

The GM crop industry and its supporters maintain that GM crops are an extension of natural breeding and do not pose different risks from naturally bred crops. The supporters claim the crops are strictly regulated for safety and can be more nutritious than naturally bred crops. They feel there is a benefit to farmers by increasing crop yields while reducing pesticide use. And finally promoters believe GM crops benefit the environment, reduce energy use, and help problems caused by climate change. However, a large and growing body of scientific and other authoritative evidence shows that these claims may not be true. Other evidence is contradictory and indicates that GM crops are laboratory-made, using technology that differs from natural breeding methods and poses different risks from non-GM crops. These crops are not adequately regulated to ensure safety, and can in fact be toxic, allergenic or less nutritious than their natural counterparts. There is concern that GM crops create problems for farmers, including herbicide-tolerant "superweeds," compromised soil quality, and increased disease susceptibility in crops.

Today, the majority of corn, soybeans, cotton, canola, sugar beets grown in the United States are GM. Fifty percent of papaya grown in Hawaii is GM. A variety of GM fruits and vegetables are being field-tested, including apple, banana, blueberry, carrot, cranberry, eggplant, grape, grapefruit, lettuce, onion, pea, pepper, persimmon, pineapple, plum, potato, squash, strawberry, sweet potato, tomato, and watermelon. Potential GM animals include pigs genetically altered to produce higher amounts of Omega-3 fatty acids. Scientists at the University of Guelph in Ontario, Canada, have genetically altered pigs to produce manure that contains up to 75 percent less phosphorus, which is a leading cause of water pollution. Massachusetts-based Aqua Bounty Farms has genetically engineered salmon to grow twice as fast as conventional salmon. Environmentalists worry the transgenic salmon could escape from fish farm pens and interbreed with wild salmon, threatening the species.

One of the original forces behind westward expansion—farmers looking for better land—was also important in the development of the plains states. The railroads provided a way to transport harvested crops to markets. Men like Adolphus Swift and George A. Hormel developed methods of keeping food refrigerated in railcars so that quality and sanitary conditions could be maintained during the long trip.

CHICAGO, A CITY OF DIVERSITY

Chicago's stockyards emerged in the late 1800s. With them came a huge migration of newly freed slaves from the South, as well as Irish, Italian, and Polish immigrants seeking new opportunities in the fastest growing city of the Central Plains. Small ethnic communities sprang up, providing a great deal of ethnic and cultural diversity. Even though the stockyards are no longer there, ethnic neighborhoods still exist in Chicago. Hispanic, Swedish, Asian, Jewish, Pakistani, Indian, and Arab cultures, to name a few, are vital communities making up Chicago's rich cultural diversity. Small enclaves of Russians, African Americans, Italians, Greeks, and Poles contribute to the cuisine found in Chicago today and have allowed Chicago to grow into one of America's great food cities.

Some of the greatest chefs in the world are in Chicago, including Rick Bayless and Michael Foley. These famous chefs and their restaurants have helped support today's market farmers, who grow and sell crops only for urban markets and restaurants featuring high-quality ingredients. The farmers follow the principle of "farm to table," indicating that their products are usually less than a day off the vine or out of the ground when sold. These people are committed to respecting the region's culture and demand to keep its food sources strong and healthy.

Bigos   A rich and heartily flavored Polish hunter's stew made from fresh pork, bacon, kielbasa sausage, mushrooms, and sauerkraut. The traditional recipe requires three days for preparation.

Black Walnut   The Black walnut is about the same size as the English walnut, but with an oily nutmeat that has an earthy, pungent taste. Grown in Missouri, black walnuts are used more as a cooking ingredient than as a snack nut. These nuts are becoming hard to find and very expensive, owing to the harvesting of the trees for hardwood.

Cheeses

Brick Cheese   One of the three cheeses invented in America this smooth, cow's milk cheese was created in 1877 by John Jossi of Wisconsin. It is formed into bricks that weigh about 5 pounds each, have small holes, and are aged about three months.

Cheddar Cheese   The most popular cheese in America. Wisconsin devotes about half its annual cheese production to the Cheddar variety. Cheddar comes in two colors and many flavors. (Americans west of the Mississippi River seem to prefer their Cheddar an orange color, made by adding annatto seed extract to the milk during production, while Americans east of the Mississippi prefer Cheddar white, or uncolored. The flavors are identical. Flavor variations of Cheddar cheese are based on how long the cheese is aged. Mild Cheddar is aged fewer than four months; aging between four and ten months creates a medium sharp flavor; and more than ten months results in a sharp flavor. The color of the wax found on the Cheddar indicates its age—clear wax for mild cheddar, red wax for medium-sharp, and black wax for sharp.)

Colby Cheese   A granular cheese made by the Steinwand family in the town of Colby, Wisconsin. This is also one of the three cheeses invented in America. (Monterey Jack cheese, discussed in the chapter on California Cuisine, is the third cheese invented in America.) The FDA standards require that it contain not less than 50 percent milk fat.

Maytag Blue Cheese   A blue-veined, tangy, smooth-textured cheese first made by the Maytag family in cooperation with Iowa State University. Containing the milk from Holstein cows, this cheese is aged for six months—nearly twice the time for traditional blue cheese. This is the first artisan cheese in America.

Processed Cheese   The most commonly consumed cheese product in America, it is made by melting various kinds of cheeses with emulsifiers, acids, and flavorings. The cheese is then colored and shaped in a mold that resembles a block of cheese. The most common processed cheese is called American cheese and was invented by James L. Kraft in the early 1900s. It is available sliced prior to packaging and as individually wrapped slices.

Fish

Muskellunge   Also referred to as "muskie," this is the largest of the pike fish and the state fish of Wisconsin. Known to grow as large as 70 pounds, it has very sharp teeth and is a vicious fighter, making it a favorite among anglers.

Pike   There are six species, many of which are found in rivers and lakes. The largest of the pike is the muskie, and the most common is the great northern pike, usually weighing between 4 and 10 pounds.

Smelt   First introduced into the Great Lakes in 1906, the freshwater smelt resembles a very small salmon and is a member of the salmon family. About 7 to 8 inches long, smelt have a fatty, rich mild flavor. They are typically either deep-fried or pan-fried.

Walleye   Also known as "walleye pike," it is actually a perch. This mild-tasting fish with a delicate flesh is also called "yellow pike" or "blue pike."

Whitefish   Considered to be one of the best freshwater fishes in the United States; the meat is fatty, snow white, and flaky. It is a member of the salmon and trout family and is found in the frigid waters of the Great Lakes. Though often poached for a cold presentation, it is also found smoked. The roe of the female is considered as desirable as shad roe.

Yellow Perch   A river and lake fish known for its especially sweet-tasting flesh; not readily available owing to a recent ban imposed to protect the species from extinction.

Fish Boil   A social event at which various kinds of fish are boiled in a huge kettle of water over an outdoor fire. Various whitefish, potatoes, and onions are added to water that has been heavily salted. Just before serving, kerosene is thrown onto the fire, allowing the kettle to boil over and remove the impurities from the broth. Door County, Wisconsin, is famous for this annual Scandinavian feast.

Game Birds   Quail, pheasant, partridge, and turkey are found throughout the Central Plains.

Holupka   A Russian term for stuffed cabbage rolls.

Honey   A major product of the Central Plains, primarily North and South Dakota, which process over 60 million pounds of honey each year. The most popular types of honey are clover and blossom, which are light in color and mildly sweet in flavor. Wildflower honey is much darker than and not as sweet as clover honey. Wildflower honey is excellent for cooking, as it provides dishes a distinct flavor without adding extra sweetness.

Jerusalem Artichoke   This bulb of the perennial sunflower plant is also referred to as a sunchoke. It is usually chopped up raw and used in salad, or may be boiled or steamed.

Juniper Berries   Common among German and Scandinavia settlers, these are used as a seasoning in sauerkraut or in marinades for game and pork. It is also the flavoring in gin.

Kielbasa   A Polish type of cured sausage with garlic flavoring, usually cooked by boiling or grilling.

Lefse   A flat bread of Norwegian origin made by the farm women of western Minnesota. The dough, made from potatoes, is rolled extremely thin with a special rolling pin called a lefse roller. The bread is cooked on a griddle and served with butter and cinnamon sugar.

Lutefisk   A Scandinavian style of prepared fresh cod. To prepare lutefisk, cod fillets are soaked in a lye solution made with the ashes of birch wood. The cod is then air-dried. This method of preserving fish may be primitive, but fish preserved in this manner can remain unspoiled for years in regions with cold climates. To serve, it is softened by simmering in salted water for about ten minutes, and served with a white sauce and potatoes on the side.

Morel   A tan to black mushroom with a cone-shaped, umbrella-capped stem that grows primarily in the deep wooded forests of Michigan. Morels are found growing beneath oak, elm, and ash trees. Their growing patterns are inconsistent and unpredictable, making them scarce as well as expensive. The fresh morel season lasts just a few short weeks from April to May.

Oblaten   The first course of the traditional meatless Polish meal served on Christmas Eve. Also referred to as the "holy wafer," this thin bread is elaborately stamped prior to baking.

Paczki   A filled doughnut of Polish heritage, usually served during Lent. Paczki are traditionally filled with raspberry preserves but may also be made with a variety of fruit fillings.

Persimmon   Also known as a date plum, this Native American fruit grows in southern Indiana, Illinois, and Missouri. About the size of a golf ball, the persimmon has a vibrant orange color with a deep green crown. If not fully ripe, it has an astringent flavor. Most often used for persimmon pudding; it is also used for jams, jellies, and preserves.

Pirogi   A filled dumpling of Eastern European heritage. The flour dough of traditional pirogi may be filled with ground, seasoned pork, sauerkraut, and farmer or cottage cheese, or may be filled with sweet fruit, such as cherries or apples. Pirogis are typically fried in bacon fat or oil.

Popcorn   From the variety called flint corn, popcorn is harvested after it has matured and dried on the stalk. The small hard kernels contain only a small amount of soft starch and a moisture content of about 13.5 percent. The outside, elastic layer resists the buildup of steam until the temperature reaches abound 400°F. The kernel expands and the endosperm violently ruptures. Orville Redenbacher became the world's largest grower of hybrid popcorn after buying an agricultural business in 1952. In 1965, after years of cross-breeding, he finally developed a yellow corn that popped twice as big as others and left very few unpopped kernels.

Rullepolse   A type of cured, spiced, and pressed beef flank made by the Danish descendants of Elk Horn, Iowa.

Sausage   The Central Plains are considered the home of sausage in the United States. Illinois produces and butchers the most hogs, and the Danish, Bavarian, and Scandinavian immigrants have had significant influence on the style of sausage making. Other German and Polish sausages include Sheboygan bratwurst, Usingers Thuringer sausage, Polish sausage, knackwurst, beerwurst, and liverwurst.

Sorghum   A canelike grass plant, originally from Africa, that grows well in the Central Plains. A sweet, dark syrup is extracted from the plant and is used in a fashion similar to molasses or honey. The use of sorghum as a sweetener dates back to the days of the pioneers.

Sunflower   A perennial plant that dates as far back as 3000 B.C. It was a major crop in the Central Plains for Native Americans as well as for the European settlers in the region. Sunflower seeds grown for oil are solid black in color. Sunflower seeds grown for eating are striped. A perennial sunflower variety also produces a bulb that is used as a vegetable, known as Jerusalem artichoke.

Tart Cherry   Grown primarily on the shores of northern Michigan from the variety known as Montmorency cherry. These cherries are light and clear and sometimes called "transparent cherries" or "pie cherries." Very tart and sour, they are sweetened with sugar to make excellent pies, cobblers, and preserves.

Waterfowl   A large number of ducks and geese migrate south for the winter from Canada. Hunting is popular and these birds continue to be a large part of the diet for the residents of the Central Plains.

Wild Rice   Not a true rice, but the grain of a tall aquatic grass grown predominately in Minnesota and Wisconsin. This is the only cereal grain indigenous to North America.

Menus and Recipes from
the Cuisine of the Central Plains

MENU ONE
Roasted Beet and Pickled Rhubarb Salad

Wisconsin Friday Night Fish Fry

Pork Medallions with Pears and Herbed Israeli Couscous

Sautéed Green Beans and Cherry Tomatoes

Sour Cream Coffee Cake

MENU TWO
Wisconsin Cheddar and Beer Soup

Cannellini Beans with Tomatoes and Basil

Roast Chicken with Wild Rice, Walnuts, and Dried Fruit Stuffing

Winter Vegetables with Thyme and Broccoli Florets

Brownie Pudding Cake

MENU THREE
Barley Beef Soup

Garden Lettuce, Watercress, Escarole with Goat Cheese and Sun-Dried Tomatoes

Kansas City Barbecued Ribs

Steak Fries

Macaroni and Cheese

Molasses Cookies

OTHER RECIPES
Planked Whitefish with Green Onion Butter

Mashed Celeriac and Potatoes

Corn and Wild Rice Cakes

Morel Mushrooms with Spinach

Chicago Deep-Dish Pizza

Roasted Beet and Pickled Rhubarb Salad

4 servings

AMOUNT	MEASURE	INGREDIENT
For Pickled Rhubarb		
1 cup	8 ounces/240 ml	Water
¼ cup	2 ounces/60 ml	Rice wine vinegar
¼ cup	2 ounces/56 g	Sugar
1 cup	4 ounces/112 g	Rhubarb, peeled, in thin slices
For Spiced Walnuts		
¼ cup plus 2 tablespoons	3 ounces/90 ml	Water
¼ cup	2 ounces/56 g	Sugar
1		Star anise
1½ teaspoons	3 g	Ground cinnamon
¾ teaspoon	1.5 g	Cayenne pepper
¾ teaspoon	1.5 g	Ground cloves
1 cup	4 ounces/112 g	Walnuts, chopped
For Roasted Beets		
3 medium to small	18 ounces/504 g total	Red or yellow beets, or a combination, tops and bottoms trimmed
2	2 ounces/56 g	Shallots, peeled
4	1 ounce/28 g	Garlic cloves
¼ bunch		Fresh thyme
2 tablespoons	1 ounce/30 ml	Olive oil
		Salt and pepper
For Yogurt Dressing		
3 tablespoons	1 ounce/30 ml	Honey
2 tablespoons	¾ ounce/20 ml	Pomegranate molasses
⅛ teaspoon		Ground cumin
⅛ teaspoon		Smoked paprika
¼ cup plus 2 tablespoons	3 ounces/90 ml	Greek yogurt
		Salt and pepper
2 cups	4 ounces/112 g	Frisée

PROCEDURE

1. Make the rhubarb. Combine the water, vinegar, and sugar in a nonreactive pot and bring to a boil. Pour the hot liquid over the rhubarb. Cover with plastic wrap and allow to cool at room temperature. Refrigerate until needed.

2. Prepare the walnuts. Combine the water, sugar, star anise, cinnamon, cayenne, and cloves in a 2- to 3-quart (2 to 3 L) saucepan over high heat. Bring to a boil, then reduce heat to medium and simmer for 10 minutes. Strain the liquid, combine with the walnuts, and toss to coat.

3. Preheat the oven to 250°F (121°C). Line a baking sheet with parchment.

4. Drain the liquid from the walnuts. Place walnuts on baking sheet and roast until well toasted and caramelized, 15 to 20 minutes. Stir the nuts every 4 to 5 minutes. Let cool, then store in an airtight container. Increase the oven temperature to 350°F (177°C).

5. Make the beets. Toss the beets, shallots, garlic, thyme, and olive oil with salt and pepper in a bowl. Wrap the beets in a piece of foil, then fold and seal. Place on a baking pan and roast until tender, 1½ to 2 hours. Let cool. When cool enough to handle, peel and slice beets as thin as possible.

6. Make the dressing. Combine the honey, molasses, cumin, and paprika in a small saucepan over medium heat. Simmer 4 to 5 minutes, then remove from the heat and let cool about 5 minutes. Strain into a bowl and whisk in the yogurt.

7. To serve, toss the beets with just enough yogurt dressing to coat; adjust the seasoning with salt and pepper. Toss the frisée, pickled rhubarb, and half the walnuts with a little yogurt dressing to coat.

8. Arrange sliced beets on 4 serving plates, place equal portions of frisée on top of the beets. Sprinkle with spiced walnuts.

Roasted Beet and Pickled Rhubarb Salad

Wisconsin Friday Night Fish Fry

4 servings

CHEF TIP: The fish fry may sound like a simple concept—essentially, frying fish!—but it's also a Wisconsin tradition, from supper clubs in the North Woods to trendy restaurants in Milwaukee. You'd be hard-pressed to find a restaurant in this state not cooking fish on a Friday night.

Its interpretation varies widely, but the sides are pretty much consistent: coleslaw, tartar sauce, potato pancakes, rye bread, and applesauce (to spread on top of the pancakes). Depending on which restaurant you visit, the fish is likely beer-battered, pan-fried, or baked. The most popular choices of fish are perch, walleye, and cod. Most of the fish today are deep-fried; deep-frying was not very popular until the 1950s, when commercial deep-fryers were developed and made it possible for small bars and restaurants to offer deep-fried fish. Until then most of the fish for a Friday night fish fry was pan-fried. Pan-frying allowed cooks to prepare the fish in larger batches.

Fried Fish

CHEF TIP: Fish fillets thicker than 1 inch (2.5 cm) tend to take longer to cook and are often mushy in the center.

AMOUNT	MEASURE	INGREDIENT
1		Egg
½ cup	4 ounces/120 ml	Milk
4	4–5 ounces/112–140 g each	Cod fillets or other firm, white fish
⅓ cup	1½ ounces/45 g	All-purpose flour
⅓ cup	2 ounces/56 g	Cracker meal
¼ teaspoon		Cayenne pepper
		Kosher salt
As needed		Vegetable oil, for pan-frying

PROCEDURE

1. Whisk the egg and milk together, then add the cod and set aside for 30 minutes.

2. Combine the flour, cracker meal, cayenne, and salt in a bowl.

3. Heat 1 inch of oil in a heavy-bottom 10-inch (25.4 cm) skillet over medium-high heat until the fat reaches 375°F (191°C).

4. Remove the fish from the milk mixture and dredge in the flour and cracker meal mixture, turning to coat well. Slip the fish into the fat and pan-fry on the first side 2 to 3 minutes, until golden brown. Do not crowd the fish. Turn the fish and pan-fry 2 to 3 minutes on the other side, until golden brown.

5. Serve with Tartar Sauce (page 40), Coleslaw (page 288), and Potato Pancakes with Cinnamon Applesauce (recipes follow).

Potato Pancakes

✦ **CHEF TIP:** There is more than one way to make a potato pancake, across cultural lines and within cultures. For example, Irish cooks make boxty. Boxty can be thin like a crepe or thicker, in a rounded patty or cut into wedges from one large cake. These potato pancakes are made with both grated raw potatoes and mashed potatoes, with flour and buttermilk or milk to bind the mixture. Boxty may also have a leavening agent, such as baking powder or baking soda. On the other hand, Jewish cooks make latkes. Latkes are typically grated potatoes and onions, eggs, and salt, and are often are made with matzo meal instead of flour.

AMOUNT	MEASURE	INGREDIENT
2 cups	12 ounces/336 g	Russet potatoes, peeled, finely grated
2		Eggs
1 tablespoon	½ ounce/14 g	Onion, grated
1 tablespoon	¼ ounce/7 g	All-purpose flour
		Salt and pepper
As needed		Vegetable oil

PROCEDURE

1. Grate the potatoes with a hand grater or in a food processor fitted with the large shredding disk. Rinse off the starch, drain, and using a clean towel or cheesecloth, wring out potato in batches to extract as much liquid as possible. Place in a large bowl.

2. Whisk together the eggs and onion. Combine with the potatoes and stir in the flour and salt and pepper.

3. Heat a ¼ inch (.6 cm) of oil in a 10-inch (25.4 cm) cast-iron skillet over medium heat. When the oil is hot, form the potato mixture into patties 3 to 4 inches (7.6–10.2 cm) wide and ¼ inch (.6 cm) thick, and place in oil. Do not crowd the pan; fry in batches, if necessary. Fry the first side until crusty and golden brown, 3 to 4 minutes. Turn and cook the second side until brown and crisp, another 3 to 4 minutes. Drain briefly on paper towels. Replenish the oil if necessary to maintain the depth so the pancakes brown evenly.

4. Serve with Cinnamon Applesauce (recipe follows).

Cinnamon Applesauce

AMOUNT	MEASURE	INGREDIENT
3 cups	12 ounces/336 g	Apples, peeled, in ¼-inch (.6 cm) dice
½ cup	4 ounces/120 ml	Water
¼ cup (or to taste)	2 ounces/56 g	Sugar
⅛ teaspoon		Ground cinnamon

PROCEDURE

1. Combine apples and water; bring to a boil over high heat. Reduce heat to medium and simmer 20 to 25 minutes or until apples are tender.

2. Add sugar and cinnamon; cook 3 to 5 minutes to dissolve the sugar. Taste for flavor and adjust the sugar and spice if necessary.

Fried Fish Fillet with Potato Pancakes, Applesauce, and Coleslaw

Pork Medallions with Pears and Herbed Israeli Couscous

Pork Medallions

AMOUNT	MEASURE	INGREDIENT
4	5 ounces/140 g each	Pork chops or medallions, ¾ inch (1.9 cm) thick
		Salt and pepper
2 tablespoons	1 ounce/30 ml	Vegetable oil
2 tablespoons	1 ounce/28 g	Butter
1½ cups	6 ounces/168 g	Ripe pears, peeled, in ½-inch (1.2 cm) dice
¼ cup	2 ounces/60 ml	Dry white wine or apple juice
¼ cup	2 ounces/60 ml	Heavy cream
1 tablespoon	½ ounce/15 ml	Dijon mustard
¼ cup	1 ounce/28 g	Maytag blue cheese

PROCEDURE

1. Season the pork with salt and pepper.

2. Heat a 10- to 12-inch (25.4–30.5 cm) sauté pan over medium heat. Heat the oil and add the pork chops. Cook 5 minutes or until well browned. Turn the chops and cook 5 minutes more or until browned and juices run clear. Set chops aside.

3. Drain fat from pan and add the butter and pears, then cook over medium-high heat until browned. Remove pears from pan.

4. Deglaze the pan with the wine. Add the cream and reduce until thick (nappé). Whisk in the mustard and blue cheese.

5. Return pears to the sauce to heat through and correct the seasoning.

6. Serve each chop with sauce and the pears.

Herbed Israeli Couscous

AMOUNT	MEASURE	INGREDIENT
1 tablespoon	½ ounce/15 ml	Vegetable oil
1 cup	6 ounces/168 g	Israeli couscous
2 cups	16 ounces/480 ml	Chicken or vegetable stock
1 tablespoon	3 g	Fresh parsley, chopped
1 teaspoon		Fresh tarragon, chopped
1 tablespoon	½ ounce/15 ml	Fresh lemon juice
		Salt and pepper

PROCEDURE

1. Heat the oil in a 1- to 2-quart (1 to 2 L) saucepan over medium heat. Add the couscous and sauté, stirring constantly, until slightly browned and aromatic, 2 to 3 minutes.

2. Add the stock and bring to a boil. Reduce the heat and simmer until tender, 10 to 12 minutes or until liquid has evaporated.

3. Stir in the parsley, tarragon, lemon juice, and salt and pepper.

Pork Medallions, Pears, and Herbed Israeli Couscous

Sautéed Green Beans and Cherry Tomatoes

4 servings

CHEF TIP: There is only one way to tell if a green bean is cooked—by tasting it. Undercooked green beans are tough and rubbery; overcooked beans are mushy. Beans of different sizes and different ages cook at different rates. Undercooked beans have an earthy taste. Correctly cooked beans are tender to the bite, still bright green and have a sweet taste.

AMOUNT	MEASURE	INGREDIENT
3 cups	12 ounces/336 g	Green beans, trimmed
2 tablespoons	1 ounce/28 g	Unsalted butter
1		Shallot, minced
1	5 g	Garlic clove, minced
1 teaspoon	5 ml	Lemon juice
1 tablespoon	½ ounce/15 ml	Dry white wine
1 cup	5 ounces/140 g	Cherry tomatoes, halved
1 tablespoon	3 g	Fresh tarragon, chopped
		Salt and black pepper

PROCEDURE

1. Cook the beans in boiling salted water for 6 to 8 minutes, until tender. Shock in ice water and drain. Dry well.

2. Heat a 10- to 12-inch (25.4–30.5 cm) sauté pan over medium heat, add the butter, shallot, and garlic, and cook 2 minutes. Add the lemon juice and wine, and cook 1 minute more or until almost dry.

3. Add the beans; cook 1 to 2 minutes or until heated through, then add the cherry tomatoes and tarragon. Cook 1 to 2 minutes or just long enough to heat through.

4. Season with salt and pepper. Serve immediately.

Sour Cream Coffee Cake

6 to 8 servings

AMOUNT	MEASURE	INGREDIENT
1½ cups	12 ounces/360 ml	Sour cream
1 cup	7 ounces/196 g	Granulated sugar
1		Egg
½ cup	2 ounces/56 g	Dried cranberries
½ cup	2 ounces/56 g	Dried cherries, chopped
½ cup	2 ounces/56 g	Dried apples, chopped
2 cups	9 ounces/252 g	All-purpose flour
2 teaspoons	8 g	Baking powder
½ teaspoon	3 g	Salt
1 cup	4 ounces/112 g	Walnuts, black or English, chopped
½ cup, packed	4 ounces/112 g	Light brown sugar
1 teaspoon		Ground cinnamon
¼ cup	2 ounces/56 g	Unsalted butter

PROCEDURE

1. Preheat the oven to 350°F (175°C). Grease a 9-inch (22 cm) springform pan.

2. Combine the sour cream, granulated sugar, and egg. Stir in the cranberries, cherries, and apples.

3. In separate bowl, sift together the flour, baking powder, and salt.

4. Add the flour mixture to the sour cream mixture and stir thoroughly.

5. Scrape batter into prepared pan. Smooth the surface and sprinkle evenly with the walnuts, brown sugar, and cinnamon. Dot with the butter.

6. Bake for 1 hour or until a wooden skewer tests clean. Let cool 10 minutes before unmolding.

Wisconsin Cheese and Beer Soup

4 servings

✦ **CHEF TIP:** When adding cheese to hot liquid, make sure the liquid is 140°–185°F (60°–85°C). If the liquid is too hot, the cheese will curdle rather than melt. This soup is traditionally served with a warm, soft pretzel.

AMOUNT	MEASURE	INGREDIENT
½ cup	4 ounces/112 g	Unsalted butter
½ cup	2 ounces/56 g	Onion, in ¼-inch (.6 cm) dice
¼ cup	1 ounce/28 g	Celery, in ¼-inch (.6 cm) dice
¼ cup	1 ounce/28 g	Red bell pepper, in ¼-inch (.6 cm) dice
½ cup	2 ounces/56 g	All-purpose flour
1 teaspoon	5 ml	Dry mustard
⅛ teaspoon		Paprika
½ teaspoon		Dried thyme
2 tablespoons	1 ounce/30 ml	Worcestershire sauce
1½ cups	12 ounces/360 ml	Beer
2 cups	16 ounces/480 ml	Chicken stock
2 cups	16 ounces/480 ml	Milk
1⅓ cups	8 ounces/224 g	Kielbasa sausage, in ¼-inch (.6 cm) dice
		Salt and white pepper
2 cups	8 ounces/224 g	Wisconsin sharp Cheddar cheese, grated
½ cup	1 ounce/28 g	Green onions, in thin slices

PROCEDURE

1. Heat the butter in a 2- to 3-quart (2 to 3 L) saucepan over medium heat. Add the onion, celery, and bell pepper, and cook 2 to 3 minutes or until the onion is translucent.

2. Add the flour; whisk in to make a roux. Add the mustard, thyme, and Worcestershire and cook 3 minutes.

3. Add the beer and stock; stir vigorously to dissolve the roux, and then simmer for 30 minutes.

4. Heat the milk separately in a saucepan and add to the soup.

5. In a skillet, sauté and render the fat from the sausage. Drain on paper towels, and then add sausage to the soup. Simmer for an additional 5 minutes.

6. Remove soup from the heat and stir in the grated cheese until smooth. Season with salt and pepper, and garnish with the green onions.

Cannellini Beans with Tomatoes and Basil

4 servings

✧ **CHEF TIP:** Cannellini beans are large white beans with a traditional kidney shape. They have thin skins and a tender, creamy flesh. With a slightly nutty taste and mild earthiness, they hold their shape well and are one of the best white beans for salads.

AMOUNT	MEASURE	INGREDIENT
1 cup	7 ounces/196 g	Dried cannellini beans, soaked overnight
1		Bay leaf
2 each		Fresh thyme, marjoram, sage, and parsley sprigs
½ cup	3 ounces/84 g	Red onion, in ½-inch (1.2 cm) dice
½ teaspoon		Champagne vinegar
2 tablespoons	1 ounce/30 ml	Red wine vinegar
2 teaspoons	10 g	Lemon zest
2	2 ounces/56 g	Garlic cloves, minced
		Salt and black pepper
⅓ cup	2½ ounces/80 ml	Olive oil
1½ cups	9 ounces/252 g	Tomatoes, peeled, in ½-inch (1.2 cm) dice
¼ cup	½ ounce/14 g	Fresh basil, chopped

PROCEDURE

1. Drain and rinse the beans. Cover generously with cold water. Add the bay leaf and herb sprigs. Bring to a boil, reduce to a simmer, and cook 20 to 25 minutes or until beans are tender and beginning to open.

2. Blanch the onion in boiling water for 15 seconds. Remove and toss with the Champagne vinegar.

3. Combine the red wine vinegar, lemon zest, garlic, ¾ teaspoon salt, and ¼ teaspoon pepper; whisk in the oil.

4. Drain the beans and toss immediately with the vinaigrette. The hot beans will soak up the flavors. Let cool.

5. Add the tomatoes, onion, and basil to the beans. Marinate for 1 to 2 hours.

6. Correct seasoning and serve at room temperature.

Cannellini Beans with Tomatoes and Basil

Roast Chicken with Wild Rice, Walnut, and Dried Fruit Stuffing

4 to 6 servings

CHEF TIP: Wild rice is not actually rice. It is an annual water-grass seed. It is the only grain native to North America, and it originated in the area of upper Great lakes. Surprisingly, 1 cup uncooked wild rice yields 3 to 4 cups cooked wild rice. It typically takes wild rice twice as long to cook as white rice. Cook until the rice is tender and the kernels pop open.

AMOUNT	MEASURE	INGREDIENT
½ cup	4 ounces/112 g	Unsalted butter
1 cup	4 ounces/112 g	Leek, in thin slices
2 cups	8 ounces/224 g	Onions, in ½-inch (1.2 cm) dice
¾ cup	3 ounces/84 g	Celery, in ½-inch (1.2 cm) dice
1 cup	6½ ounces/182 g	Uncooked wild rice, rinsed in cold water
3 cups	24 ounces/720 ml	Apple cider
2 cups	16 ounces/480 ml	Chicken stock
½ cup	4 ounces/120 ml	Applejack brandy
½ cup	2 ounces/56 g	Green apple, peeled, in ½-inch (1.2 cm) dice
¼ cup	1 ounce/28 g	Dried cherries, diced
¼ cup	1 ounce/28 g	Dried apples, diced
1 cup	4 ounces/112 g	Walnuts, toasted, chopped
4 tablespoons	½ ounce/14 g	Fresh rosemary, chopped
2 tablespoons	¼ ounce/7 g	Fresh thyme, chopped
1	4 pounds/1.82 kg	Roasting chicken
		Salt and pepper

PROCEDURE

1. Preheat the oven to 325°F (163°C).

2. In a 2- to 3-quart (2 to 3 L) saucepan, melt half the butter over medium heat.

3. Add the leek, onions, and celery; sauté until tender, about 4 minutes.

4. Add the wild rice and sauté for 2 minutes. Then add 1 cup (8 ounces/237 ml) of the apple cider, the chicken stock, and brandy. Bring to a boil, cover, and reduce to a simmer. Cook 30 minutes or until tender.

5. Add the green apple and dried fruits. Cover and cook 15 minutes more or until rice is tender.

6. Stir in the nuts and half the rosemary and the thyme. Correct the seasonings and cool stuffing.

7. Combine the remaining butter with the remaining rosemary. Set aside.

8. Season the chicken on all sides with salt and pepper. Loosen the skin from the breasts and spread the rosemary butter over the breast meat under the skin. Then stuff the chicken with the rice mixture; do not pack too tightly.

9. Set the chicken on a rack in a shallow pan. Roast, basting with remaining apple cider, until juices run clear, 1 to 1½ hours.

10. Let stand 10 minutes before serving. Serve with pan drippings and rice stuffing.

Roast Chicken with Wild Rice Stuffing

Winter Vegetables with Thyme and Broccoli Florets

4 servings

AMOUNT	MEASURE	INGREDIENT
1½ cups	6.75 ounces/189 g	Turnips, peeled, in ¼-inch (.6 cm) slices
1½ cups	6.75 ounces/189 g	Rutabaga, peeled, in ¼-inch (.6 cm) slices
1 cup	4 ounces/112 g	Broccoli stalks, peeled, julienned
1 cup	4 ounces/112 g	Carrots, peeled, julienned
3 tablespoons	1½ ounces/44 g	Unsalted butter
1 teaspoon		Fresh parsley, chopped
1 teaspoon		Thyme leaves
		Salt and black pepper

PROCEDURE

1. Bring salted water to a boil in a large pot. Individually cook the vegetables, starting with the turnips, then rutabaga, broccoli, and carrots until just tender, a minute or so. Drain each and set aside.

2. In a 10- to 12-in (25.4–30.5 cm) skillet, heat the butter with the parsley and thyme. Add the vegetables and cook gently to evaporate the water; don't fry the vegetables.

3. Adjust the seasoning with salt and pepper. Serve with Broccoli Florets (recipe follows).

Broccoli Florets

AMOUNT	MEASURE	INGREDIENT
1 cup	2½ ounces/70 g	Broccoli florets, trimmed
1 tablespoon	½ ounce/14 g	Unsalted butter
		Salt and white pepper

PROCEDURE

1. Bring salted water to a boil in a large pot and parboil the broccoli until just before tender. Shock in an ice bath and drain.

2. In an 8- to 10-inch (10.3–25.4 cm) skillet, heat the butter, add the broccoli, and toss to coat. Cook until hot; correct the seasoning with salt and pepper.

Brownie Pudding Cake

AMOUNT	MEASURE	INGREDIENT
1 cup	4 ounces/112 g	All-purpose flour
⅔ cup	3 ounces/84 g	Unsweetened cocoa powder
¾ teaspoon	3 g	Baking powder
¾ teaspoon	4 g	Salt
1 cup	7 ounces/196 g	Granulated sugar
2		Eggs
6 tablespoons	3 ounces/84 g	Unsalted butter, melted, cooled
½ cup	4 ounces/120 ml	Heavy cream
1 teaspoon	5 ml	Vanilla extract
1⅓ cups	10½ ounces/315 ml	Boiling water
¾ cup (packed)	6 ounces/168 g	Light brown sugar

PROCEDURE

1. Preheat the oven to 350°F (175°C).

2. Sift together the flour, ⅓ cup (1½ ounces/42 g) of the cocoa powder, the baking powder, and salt; set aside.

3. In a mixer, using the paddle attachment, beat the granulated sugar and eggs on medium-high speed until very pale and light yellow, 4 to 6 minutes. Reduce the speed to low and add the butter, cream, and vanilla.

4. Add the flour mixture and beat on low speed until just combined, about 30 seconds.

5. Spread batter in an ungreased 8-inch (20 cm) square baking pan.

6. Whisk together the remaining ⅓ cup (1½ ounces/42 g) cocoa powder, the boiling water, and brown sugar; pour over the batter.

7. Bake 35 to 40 minutes or until a wooden skewer tests almost clean. Let stand 15 minutes before serving. May be served with ice cream or whipped topping.

Beef Barley Soup

4 servings

 CHEF TIP: Whole-grain barley is a high-fiber, high-protein grain. When cooked, barley has a chewy texture and nutty flavor. Barley is most often used in soup, but it can be used like other grains, such as couscous or rice.

AMOUNT	MEASURE	INGREDIENT
2 tablespoons	1 ounce/30 ml	Vegetable oil
1 cup	6 ounces/168 g	Lean boneless beef (top sirloin or top round), in ¼-inch (.6 cm) dice
¾ cup	3 ounces/84 g	Carrots, peeled, in ¼-inch (.6 cm) dice
¾ cup	3 ounces/84 g	Celery, in ¼ inch (.6 cm) dice
¾ cup	3 ounces/84 g	Onion, in ¼-inch (.6 cm) dice
1	5 g	Garlic clove, minced
1 cup	4 ounces/112 g	Pearl barley
2 tablespoons	1 ounce/28 g	Tomato paste
⅛ teaspoon		Dried thyme
3 cups	24 ounces/720 ml	Chicken stock
1 tablespoon	½ ounce/15 ml	Worcestershire sauce
½		Bay leaf
		Salt and white pepper
1 teaspoon		Chives, chopped

PROCEDURE

1. In a 2- to 3-quart (2 to 3 L) saucepan, heat the oil over medium heat and cook the meat until it is well browned, about 3 to 4 minutes.

2. Turn down the heat, add the vegetables, and cook 5 minutes.

3. Add the barley and coat with oil. Add the tomato paste and cook 1 minute.

4. Add the tomato paste, thyme, stock, Worcestershire sauce, and bay leaf. Bring to a simmer and cook 30 minutes, until barley is tender. Skim the fat as needed.

5. Remove the bay leaf. Correct the seasoning with salt and pepper, and garnish with chives.

Garden Lettuce, Watercress, Escarole with Goat Cheese and Sun-Dried Tomatoes

4 servings

AMOUNT	MEASURE	INGREDIENT
For the Balsamic Vinaigrette		
2 tablespoons	1 ounce/30 ml	Balsamic vinegar
1 tablespoon	½ ounce/14 g	Garlic, minced
½ teaspoon	3 g	Salt
½ teaspoon		Black pepper
½ cup	4 ounces/120 ml	Olive oil
For the Salad		
1 cup	2 ounces/56 g	Escarole, tender inner leaves
2 cups	4 ounces/112 g	Mixed baby greens
1 cup	2 ounces/56 g	Watercress leaves
1 tablespoon	⅓ ounce/9 g	Sunflower seeds, toasted
2	¼ ounce/7 g	Sun-dried tomatoes packed in oil, drained, thinly sliced
2 tablespoons	1 ounce/28 g	Goat cheese, creamy mild (chèvre or Montrachet)
		Black pepper

PROCEDURE

1. Make the dressing. Combine the vinegar, garlic, salt, pepper, and olive oil.

2. Prepare the salad. Tear the large leaves of escarole into pieces. Toss the escarole, baby greens, watercress, sunflower seeds, and sun-dried tomatoes with enough vinaigrette to just coat the leaves. Start with a little dressing and add more if necessary.

3. Crumble the cheese onto the salad and toss again. Sprinkle with black pepper and serve on chilled plates.

Kansas City Barbecued Ribs

CHEF TIP: If a smoky flavor is not desired, the ribs can be cooked in a combination oven at 275°F (135°C) or a traditional oven at 325°F (162.8°C). Numerous varieties of baby back ribs are available in the market. Some of the region's most notable ribs come from the pork-producing states of Kansas, Missouri, Iowa, and Illinois. To be classified as baby back ribs, the entire rack of ribs should not exceed 1¾ pounds. Larger racks are simply called back ribs.

AMOUNT	MEASURE	INGREDIENT
2 racks	3½ pounds/1.58 kg	Baby back ribs, peeled
For the Seasoning Mix		
½ cup	3½ ounces/98 g	Granulated sugar
¼ cup	1 ounce/28 g	Paprika
2 tablespoons	1 ounce/28 g	Kosher salt
2 tablespoons	1 ounce/28 g	Celery salt
1½ tablespoons	¾ ounce/21 g	Onion powder
1½ tablespoons	¾ ounce/21 g	Chili powder
1 teaspoon	2 g	Ground cumin
1 tablespoon	¼ ounce/7 g	Black pepper
1 teaspoon	2 g	Dry mustard
¼ teaspoon		Cayenne pepper
For the Sauce		
½ cup	4 ounces/112 g	Light brown sugar
½ teaspoon	1 g	Chili powder
½ teaspoon	1 g	Dry mustard
½ teaspoon	1 g	Ground ginger
⅛ teaspoon		Ground allspice
⅛ teaspoon		Paprika
⅛ teaspoon		Mace
⅛ teaspoon		Black pepper
½ cup	4 ounces/120 ml	Cider vinegar
⅓ cup	4 ounces/120 ml	Molasses
1 teaspoon	5 ml	Liquid smoke
2 cups	16 ounces/480 ml	Ketchup
¼ cup	2 ounces/60 ml	Water
		Wood chips for smoking

PROCEDURE

1. Remove the thin, transparent skin from the back side of the rib racks. This is easily done by scraping the corner of the bone on the small side of the rack on the backside. Lift the skin and pull. The skin should separate from the rack in 1 piece.

2. Make the seasoning mix. Combine the ingredients and mix well.

3. Rub the ribs liberally with the seasoning mix. Cover and refrigerate for at least 24 hours or until needed.

4. Make the sauce. Place the ingredients in a 2- to 3-quart (2 to 3 L) saucepot. Bring to a boil, stirring constantly, then turn the heat down to a simmer and simmer for 1 hour.

5. Soak the wood chips and prepare a smoker.

6. Coat the ribs liberally with the barbecue sauce. Place the rib racks in the smoker and smoke for 2 hours at 250°F (122°C), basting every hour with the extra barbecue sauce.

7. Reheat the remaining sauce when serving.

Steak Fries

4 servings

AMOUNT	MEASURE	INGREDIENT
2 large	12 ounces/336 g	Russet potatoes
As needed		Vegetable oil, for deep-frying
		Coarse salt
		Black pepper

PROCEDURE

1. Peel and wash the potatoes. Cut lengthwise into 8 wedges.

2. Parboil the potatoes in boiling salted water for 2 to 3 minutes. Do not overcook or they will not hold their shape when fried. Drain, cool, and dry.

3. Heat the oil to 350°F (175°C) in a deep-fryer or deep pot. Place the potatoes in the hot oil and let them get soft and form a skin, 2 to 3 minutes. Remove from the oil and let the temperature of the oil return to 350°F (175°C). Then, return the potatoes to the hot oil, and fry until potatoes are golden brown and crisp, about 1 to 2 minutes.

4. Drain the potatoes on paper towels and season with salt and pepper.

Kansas City Barbecued Ribs with Steak Fries

Macaroni and Cheese

CHEF TIP: The original homemade recipe is said to include pasta, butter or cream, and Parmesan cheese. American cooks have improvised, using a variety of cheeses, with sharp Cheddar cheese being the most common. Kraft Foods introduced the Kraft Macaroni and Cheese Dinner in 1937, at the end of the Great Depression. In that year alone, 8 million boxes were sold.

AMOUNT	MEASURE	INGREDIENT
2 cups	8 ounces/224 g	Elbow macaroni
¼ cup	2 ounces/56 g	Butter, softened
Dash		Tabasco
1½ cups	12 ounces/360 ml	Evaporated milk, warmed
2		Eggs, lightly beaten
1 teaspoon		Dry mustard, dissolved in a little water
4 cups	16 ounces/448 g	Sharp Cheddar cheese
		Salt and white pepper

PROCEDURE

1. Preheat the oven to 350°F (175°C).

2. Cook the macaroni in boiling salted water, stirring occasionally, until just barely tender, about 6 to 7 minutes.

3. Drain and toss with the butter.

4. Mix the Tabasco with 1 cup (8 ounces/235 ml) milk. Add the eggs, mustard, and 3 cups (12 ounces/340 g) of the cheese. Combine well and check seasoning with salt and pepper. Mix in the macaroni.

5. Transfer to a 2-quart (2 L) baking pan and set in oven. Every 5 minutes, stir in some of the reserved cheese, also adding more evaporated milk as necessary to keep the mixture moist and smooth. When you have incorporated all the cheese, the mixture should be creamy, about 20 minutes.

Molasses Cookies

CHEF TIP: Molasses is the dark, sweet, syrupy by-product made during the extraction of sugars from sugarcane and sugar beets. Up until the 1880s, molasses was the most popular sweetener in the United States because it was cheaper than refined sugar. Unlike other types of sweeteners, it is high in minerals. Molasses has a strong, distinct flavor and has half the sweetening power of white sugar. The largest and most dynamic region for sugar beet production is in or close to the Red River Valley of western Minnesota and eastern North Dakota.

AMOUNT	MEASURE	INGREDIENT
1¼ cups	5 ounces/140 g	All-purpose flour
1 teaspoon	6 g	Baking soda
½ teaspoon	1 g	Ground cinnamon
½ teaspoon	1 g	Ground ginger
½ teaspoon	1 g	Ground nutmeg
½ teaspoon	1 g	Ground allspice
¼ teaspoon		Salt
6 tablespoons	3 ounces/88 g	Vegetable shortening
½ cup (packed)	4 ounces/112 g	Brown sugar
1		Egg
¼ cup	2 ounces/60 ml	Molasses
2 tablespoons	1 ounce/28 g	Granulated sugar

PROCEDURE

1. Sift together the flour, baking soda, cinnamon, ginger, nutmeg, allspice, and salt.

2. In a mixer, using the paddle attachment, beat the shortening on medium speed for 30 seconds. Add the brown sugar and beat until well combined, scraping the sides of the bowl occasionally.

3. Beat in the egg and molasses until combined well, about 30 seconds.

4. Add the flour mixture, beating on low speed just until mixture is combined, 15 to 20 seconds. Cover and chill 1 hour, or until dough is easy to handle.

5. Preheat the oven to 350°F (175°C). Line a baking sheet with parchment.

6. Place the granulated sugar in a small bowl. Shape the dough into 1-inch (2.5 cm) balls. Roll the balls in sugar to coat. Place about 1½ inches (3.8 cm) apart on baking sheet.

7. Bake for 8 to 10 minutes or until bottoms are light brown and tops are puffed; do not overbake. Cool on baking sheet for 2 minutes, then transfer to a wire rack and let cool completely.

Planked Whitefish with Green Onion Butter

4 servings

 **CHEF TIP:** Planking is a method of cooking fish that the settlers of the region learned from the Native Americans. A whole fish is tied to a large piece of driftwood and placed vertically next to a fire, where it cooks slowly until done. Today, planking is accomplished by placing a fish fillet on a soaked plank of wood—usually cedar, which gives off a tasty and unique flavor. The fillet is then cooked, plank and all, on a grill over a fire or even by baking in an oven. The cedar planks used in this preparation are easy to find at a local building supply store. Cedar roof shingles are usually smooth on one side and the perfect shape for a fish fillet of this size. Be sure to purchase the untreated variety, as some shingles come with a chemical fire retardant that leaves an unpleasant aftertaste on the fish. The shingles are inexpensive. It is recommended, for sanitary reasons, that they not be reused. The whitefish called for in this Central Plains recipe can be walleye, pike, or yellow perch. However, the procedure yields excellent results with any type of round fish or large flatfish, such as halibut or turbot. Small flatfish, like sole and flounder, should be avoided, as they are too delicate and tend to absorb too much flavor from the wooden planks.

AMOUNT	MEASURE	INGREDIENT
4		Untreated cedar wood planks or shingles, 4 × 6 × ½ inch (10 × 15 × 1.2 cm)
½ cup	4 ounces/112 g	Butter, softened
1		Egg yolk
2 tablespoons	1 ounce/30 ml	Lemon juice
1 tablespoon	1 ounce/15 ml	Dijon mustard
¼ cup	1 ounce/28 g	Dry bread crumbs
¼ cup	1½ ounces/42 g	Green onions, chopped
2 tablespoons	¼ ounce/7 g	Fresh parsley, chopped
1	5 g	Garlic clove, smashed
¼ cup	2 ounces/60 ml	Vegetable oil
4	4 ounces/112 g each	Whitefish fillets, skinless
		Salt and black pepper

PROCEDURE

1. Soak the cedar planks in water for at least 2 hours.

2. Mix the butter, egg yolk, lemon juice, mustard, bread crumbs, green onions, parsley, and garlic in a food processor. Pulse for 15 to 20 seconds to combine into a paste. Roll the paste into a cylinder about 1 inch (2.5 cm) thick, and wrap in plastic wrap. Refrigerate until firm.

3. Preheat the oven to 425°F (220°C).

4. Dry off the planks and brush with the oil. Place in the oven on a baking sheet for 5 minutes to begin to season the wood.

5. Brush the fish fillets with oil and season with salt and pepper.

6. Remove the paste from the refrigerator and cut into ¼-inch (.6 cm) slices. Place 1 to 2 slices on each fillet. Place the fish on the hot planks and return to the oven. Bake for 6 to 8 minutes (or until opaque and flaky), until the butter has melted into a brown crust. Remove and serve immediately.

Mashed Celeriac and Potatoes

AMOUNT	MEASURE	INGREDIENT
2 cups	10 ounces/280 g	Celeriac, peeled, in 1-inch (2.5 cm) cubes
2 cups	10 ounces/280 g	All-purpose potatoes, peeled, in quarters
3	15 g	Garlic cloves, quartered
		Salt and white pepper
Pinch		Grated nutmeg
2 tablespoons	1 ounce/28 g	Butter

PROCEDURE

1. In a 3- to 4-quart (3 to 4 L) saucepan, combine the celeriac, potatoes, garlic, and salt with water to cover. Bring to a boil. Reduce heat to medium and simmer for 30 minutes or until all ingredients are tender.

2. Drain the vegetables, reserving the liquid.

3. Force the vegetables through a ricer or food mill or mash with a potato masher.

4. Add enough of the cooking liquid to soften the consistency (like mashed potatoes) and return the mixture to a pan over low heat, stirring until heated through. Season with salt, pepper, and nutmeg.

5. Add the butter and serve hot.

Corn and Wild Rice Cakes

4 servings

AMOUNT	MEASURE	INGREDIENT
1½ teaspoons	7 g	Butter
¾ cup	3 ounces/85 g	Leek, white part only, in thin slices
1 teaspoon		Garlic, minced
1 cup	7 ounces/196 g	Cooked wild rice
½ cup	2½ ounces/70 g	Corn kernels, fresh or frozen
1		Egg, lightly beaten
¼ cup	2 ounces/60 ml	Heavy cream
1 tablespoon	3 g	Fresh parsley, chopped
1 tablespoon	3 g	Chives, chopped
¼ teaspoon		Black pepper
½ teaspoon		Salt
¼ cup	1 ounce/28 g	All-purpose flour
As needed		Vegetable oil

PROCEDURE

1. Heat a 10- to 12-inch (25.4–30.5 cm) sauté pan over medium heat. Add butter, leek, and garlic, and cook until leek is soft, 3 to 5 minutes.

2. Place the wild rice in a medium bowl. Add the leek mixture and the corn.

3. Mix the egg and cream until well blended. Add the parsley, chives, and pepper, and salt.

4. Add cream mixture to the wild rice mixture, then stir in the flour to thicken the mixture; you may need to add more or less flour.

5. Form rice cakes using a ⅓ cup (2.66 ounces/78 g) measure. Let chill 30 minutes.

6. Heat the oil in a 10- to 12-inch (25.4–30.5 cm) sauté pan over medium heat, then add the cakes and sauté until lightly browned, about 3 minutes per side.

7. Serve the cake topped with Morel Mushrooms with Spinach (recipe follows).

Morel Mushrooms with Spinach

✤ **CHEF TIP:** If fresh morel mushrooms are unavailable or too expensive, dried morels can be substituted. The dried mushrooms need to be reconstituted prior to using, however. Boil a small pot of water, add the dried mushrooms, cover, and remove from the heat. Steep the mushrooms 4 to 5 minutes, then remove from the hot water, leaving any debris in the water. Generally, the mushrooms expand to 5 times their dried weight, so to get 10 ounces (280 g) of reconstituted mushrooms, use just 2 ounces (56 g) of dried. The water that the mushrooms steep in is flavorful and can be strained and used in a variety of soups and sauces. In addition, a dried forest mushroom mix is available at a very reasonable cost.

AMOUNT	MEASURE	INGREDIENT
6 cups	12 ounces/336 g	Fresh spinach, trimmed
1 cup	4 ounces/112 g	Fresh morel mushrooms, trimmed, large ones halved
6 tablespoons	3 ounces/84 g	Unsalted butter
¼ cup	2 ounces/60 ml	Heavy cream
		Salt and pepper
		Grated nutmeg

PROCEDURE

1. Blanch the spinach in boiling salted water for 1 minute; drain. Refresh in ice water, drain again. Gently squeeze to remove excess water.

2. Brush, lightly wash, and rinse the morels to make sure they are completely clean and free of grit. (If using dried mushrooms, soak 2 ounces (56 g) in warm water for at least 30 minutes. Drain and pat dry.)

3. Melt ¼ cup (2 ounces/56 g) butter in a 10- to 12-inch (25.4–30.5 cm) skillet, add mushrooms, and heat through. Add the spinach, turn heat to high, and cook, stirring, until most of the liquid has evaporated.

4. Add the cream, bring to a boil, and reduce by half.

5. Correct seasoning with salt, pepper, and nutmeg, and stir in remaining 2 tablespoons (1 ounce/28 g) butter.

Chicago Deep-Dish Pizza

4 servings

✤ **CHEF TIP:** One package of active dry yeast is about 2¼ teaspoons (¼ ounce/7 g), if you are using loose yeast instead.

AMOUNT	MEASURE	INGREDIENT
For the Dough		
2¼ teaspoons	¼ ounce/7 g	Active dry yeast
6 tablespoons	3 ounces/90 ml	Warm water (110°F/42°C)
1 teaspoon	5 g	Sugar
6 tablespoons	3 ounces/90 ml	Milk
2 tablespoons	1 ounce/30 ml	Olive oil
1 tablespoon	½ ounce/15 g	Fine-ground cornmeal
½ teaspoon		Salt
3 tablespoons	24 g	Whole wheat flour
1¾ cups	7 ounces/196 g	All-purpose flour
For the Tomato Sauce		
2 tablespoons	1 ounce/30 ml	Olive oil
1 cup	4 ounces/112 g	Onion, in ¼-inch (.6 cm) dice
1	5 g	Garlic clove, minced
3 cups	18 ounces/504 g	Tomatoes, peeled, chopped
¼ cup	2 ounces/56 g	Tomato puree
⅛ teaspoon		Dried basil
⅛ teaspoon		Dried oregano
		Salt and black pepper
For the Topping		
	16 ounces/168 g	Mozzarella cheese, thinly sliced
1 cup	4 ounces/112 g	Cooked Italian sausage, sliced
½ cup	2 ounces/56 g	Red bell pepper, thinly sliced
1 cup	4 ounces/112 g	Mozzarella cheese, shredded
⅓ cup	1 ounce/28 g	Parmesan cheese, grated
2 tablespoons	1 ounce/30 ml	Olive oil

1. Make the dough. Dissolve the yeast in the water and sugar, and set aside in a warm place for about 10 minutes. The yeast should start to foam (bubble up and become creamy looking); if it does not, discard and try again with fresh yeast.

2. Combine the milk, olive oil, and cornmeal. Add the yeast mixture. Add the salt and whole wheat flour; mix well. Gradually add the white flour and work to a soft, pliable dough.

3. Turn out dough onto a lightly floured surface and knead for 5 minutes. Put the dough in an oiled bowl and turn to coat the surface with oil. Cover the bowl and let the dough rise in a warm place until doubled in bulk, 35 to 45 minutes.

4. Punch down the dough, cover again, and allow to double again, about 30 minutes.

5. Preheat the oven to 450°F (225°C). Lightly oil a 9-inch (22 cm) round baking pan that is 1½ inches (3.8 cm) deep.

6. Make the sauce. Heat the oil, add the onion and garlic, and cook over medium to low heat, 3 minutes or until onion is soft. Stir in the tomatoes, tomato puree, basil, oregano, salt, and pepper. Simmer for 15 to 20 minutes, until thick. Do not overcook or you'll lose the taste of the fresh tomatoes.

7. Assemble the pizza. Roll the dough into a 12-inch (30 cm) circle and fit it into the prepared pan. The dough should just cover the bottom and sides of the pan, with no overhang. Prick dough all over with a fork.

8. Place the sliced mozzarella in tile-like layers on the bottom of the pie. Spread the tomato sauce over the cheese, covering completely. Spread the sausage and red pepper over the tomato sauce. Top with the shredded mozzarella and the Parmesan cheese. Drizzle olive oil over the top of the pie.

9. Bake 25 minutes, or until the cheese and crust are golden and the filling is bubbly. Remove from oven and allow to rest for 5 minutes before cutting.

Texas and
Tex-Mex Cuisine

BIG AS TEXAS

A state that is as large as all of New England, New York, Pennsylvania, Ohio, and Illinois combined, Texas has served under six flags and reflects a culture that includes cowboys, rodeos, and ten-gallon hats. It is a region that bred a cuisine described as the only food that is truly native to the United States. A cooking style that merges the Texas and Mexican cultures, Tex-Mex cooking was originally regarded as a poor man's Mexican food based on corn, pinto beans, tomatoes, and chiles. It was developed by people working with primitive kitchens and limited ingredients, and it owes its appeal to the inventiveness of its creators, who were able to make their foods interesting by combining the same ingredients in different ways. Today it has become sophisticated while still adhering to many south-of-the-border traditions.

Additionally, Longhorn cattle, cowboys, chuckwagon cooking, and Lone Star chili come to mind. The beef and chilis we associate with the cuisine of Texas are remnants of the state's Spanish and Mexican heritages. From the famous "bowl of red"—Texas chili—to tacos, fajitas, and salsa, these flavorful introductions influence the eating habits of not only Texans but also of all other Americans.

Texas's "Lone Star State" nickname comes from the symbolism of the star on the 1836 flag, which signified that Texas was an independent republic, and was a reminder of the state's struggle for independence from Mexico. "Friendship" is the state motto. The state tree is the pecan, and the state fruit is the Texas red grapefruit. The state vegetable is the Texas 1015 sweet onion, the state native pepper is the chiltepin, and the state pepper is the jalapeño chile. The state plant is the prickly pear cactus, and chili was proclaimed the state dish by the Texas Legislature in 1977. Rodeo is the official sport of Texas.

HISTORY AND MAJOR INFLUENCES

In 1519, Spain was the first European nation to claim what is now Texas. The Spanish came to Texas in search of a shorter route to the Far East and with hopes of finding treasure while they "civilized" and Christianized the natives. They built their first settlement in Texas: Ysleta Mission in present El Paso, established in 1681. Gradually expanding from Mexico, the Spanish built other missions, forts, and civil settlements for nearly 150 years, until Mexico threw off European rule and became independent in 1821. During that time, those who came to this land survived on game that included buffalo, venison, hogs, and the native wild cattle. They learned to raise gourds, squash, sweet potatoes, and corn. Other small grains such as oats and rye had been imported, while the settlers grew most of the other foods that they consumed.

Planning to expand its base from French Louisiana, France planted its flag in eastern Texas near the Gulf Coast. But the first colony, called Fort St. Louis, was not successful owing to natural and political disasters that included disease and famine. For more than a decade after Mexico became independent, hardy pioneers from the Hispanic south and the Anglo north flowed into Texas, a frontier for both groups. But conflicting social and political attitudes alienated the two cultures. Texans revolted, and they won their independence on April 21, 1836. Those who had come and survived continued to depend on wild game and corn, though many brought familiar breeds of cattle, hogs, sheep, and poultry with them.

During nearly ten years of independence, the Texas republic endured epidemics, financial crises, and continued volatile clashes with Mexico. But it was during this period that unique aspects of the Texas heritage developed. Texas became the birthplace of the American cowboy; the Texas Rangers were the first to use Sam Colt's remarkable six-shooters; and Sam Houston became an American ideal of rugged individualism. In contrast to the Wild West, the eastern coast of Texas had become highly settled, with seaports and plantations. The leading port of Galveston reflected European and Southern influences in its culture and cuisine, and staples such as salt, coffee, sugar, and wheat flour were brought from New Orleans to Galveston.

In 1845, Texas became the 28th state to join the United States of America. But 16 years after Texas joined the Union, the American Civil War erupted. Ignoring the advice of Governor Sam Houston to establish a neutral republic, Texas cast its lot with the doomed Southerners, reaping devastation and economic collapse as did all Confederate states. But two events fixed Texas and Texans as somehow different in the nation's eyes. First, Texas troops on Texas soil won the final battle of the Civil War, not knowing the South had surrendered a month earlier. Second, returning Texans found a population explosion of wild Longhorns, sparking the great trail drives that became one of America's legends. Pushing aside the defeat and bitter reconstruction after the Civil War, the offspring of Texas pioneers marshaled their strengths to secure a future based on determined self-reliance. One of the first successes was the famous Texas Longhorn, providing beef for a growing nation. Newly turned topsoil on vast farm acreage yielded bountiful crops. The 20th century dawned with the discovery of fabulous sources—gushers roaring at a place called Spindletop, near Beaumont in East Texas. By the mid-20th century, modern Texas industries were developing in a climate of advanced technology. Today, Texas horizons continue to expand, reaching up to the limitless reaches of outer space.

 ## THE PEOPLE . . . TEXANS BY CHOICE

DEEP EAST TEXAS

Two distinct economic classes settled in the piney woods of what is known as Deep East Texas. People from Alabama, Georgia, Mississippi, and Louisiana included plantation owners, who brought the tradition of fine foods and Southern hospitality to their Texas plantations. They also brought Cajun and Creole cookery from nearby Louisiana. Shrimp, oysters, crabs, and fish from the Gulf of Mexico were widely available and used in spicy seafood Creoles, gumbos, and jambalayas. Rice crops were grown in the low marshy coastal plains near the Gulf of Mexico. But those who worked on the plantations and in the rice fields were less fortunate, and their meals continued to be limited to wild berries, fruits, edible weeds, wild duck, dove, quail, and other game. While the pines continue to supply a giant lumbering industry and almost all of the state's huge rice crop comes from East Texas, today the real wealth of East Texas is from its immense, rich oil fields and the heavy industry that crowds the Gulf Coast.

CENTRAL TEXAS

Stephen F. Austin settled in central Texas with more than 300 of his loyal followers. Large land grants were available, and Germans wrote home of the opportunities that made Texas seem like an earthly paradise. A steady stream of immigrants left northwestern Germany and established what is known as the "German Belt," which stretched in broad but fragmented clusters across the south-central part of the state. Large numbers of Czechs and Poles joined this immigration as well. These people brought their skills at preparing the foods of their homeland, but they adapted them to the ingredients they found available. Their specialties included sausage making and meat smoking. Indeed, the German method of meat smoking is considered a major force in the origin of Texas barbecue, which comes from this region, and some feel the German treatment of veal à la Wiener schnitzel is the predecessor of the Texas favorite—chicken-fried steak.

WEST TEXAS

Texas ranches were established to raise beef cattle on land granted to Mexican families by the king of Spain. The well-known Texas Longhorns, descendants of the wild cattle left by the Spanish in the 16th century, were popular because they could withstand the extreme weather of the deserts of West Texas. Until the discovery of oil in West Texas, cattle production was the biggest industry in the state. Although the Longhorns were well suited to the region, their meat was not considered the most tender or flavorful. Today, beef is still the primary meat of the region; however, the ranchers prefer to raise Hereford, Brahma, and Angus cattle. Other meats are now being raised in West Texas, including bison, ostrich, emu, axis venison, and antelope.

THE GULF COAST

The Gulf's coastal areas were first settled by Native Americans and fiercely protected by the Karankawas. Galveston was where Cabeza de Vaca, the first European to set foot on Texas soil, landed in 1528, and where pirate chieftan Jean Laffite ruled. Many of the immigrants who settled the rest of Texas and the Southwest entered through this port. Today, on the Gulf Coast, seafood is as much a part of Texas cuisine as are chili and chicken-fried steak. More than 100 million pounds of shrimp, oysters, blue crabs, and finfish, including redfish, red snapper, pompano, flounder, and speckled trout, are harvested annually from the Gulf of Mexico. Natural and manmade oyster reefs are found along the Texas coastline. The American commercial oyster thrives in the bays and estuaries behind barrier islands separating the Texas mainland from the Gulf of Mexico. Here, fresh water and saltwater combine to create the environment oysters need to flourish. Several types of shrimp are caught along the coastline, each named for its color, which is determined by its diet. The two most popular are white shrimp and brown shrimp.

CHUCKWAGON COOKING

The legendary time of the trail drives lasted only about 20 years, from the end of the Civil War to the mid-1880s. In that period, around 10 million cattle were herded from Texas to rail heads in Kansas and Missouri. Many of these cattle went as far as Wyoming, to Chicago, and even into Canada. In the early days of the great trail drives, the cowhand had to make do with what he could carry with him. Texas rancher Charles Goodnight is given credit for the efficient design of the chuckwagon. Using a surplus military wagon, he added a chuck box and tailgate that served as a workstation. This chuck box had shelves and drawers to hold what the cook would need to prepare meals for the day, including a coffee grinder and other cooking utensils to provide hot meals for the dozen or more cowboys and the trail boss. The most essential cooking tool was the cast-iron Dutch oven. This heavy stew pot rested above the coals on three stubby legs. It had a tight-fitting lid with a raised rim. The cook would then pile more hot coals onto the lid. The ability to heat from both above and below allowed for roasting and braising, as well for baking the cowboys' favorite camp bread—the buttermilk biscuit. A large water barrel was attached to the side of the wagon, along with tool boxes, hooks, and brackets. Chuck was the cowboy word for "food" and cooking was usually done over an open fire. The chuckwagon cook was called a "cookie" or "coosie," from the Spanish word *cocinero* (male cook). Favorite meals included grilled steaks, smoked brisket, and biscuits. Mexican music and Mexican food quickly became part of the cowboy culture. Cowboys learned to play the guitar and compose ballads in English that mimicked the sentiments of Spanish love songs. Mexican cowboys introduced their favorite foods—chili, beans, and tortillas—to chuckwagon cooking.

Today's beef options generally fall into four categories: branded beef, certified organic beef, conventional beef, and grass-finished beef.

Branded Beef

Unbranded beef is USDA-approved and simply carries the generic name of the beef cut on the label. Branded Beef carries a specific brand name on the beef label and meets the unique set of specifications set by the branding company such as breed-specific, guaranteed tender, grain-fed, grass-fed, natural, organic, humanely-raised and/or environmentally responsible and can include all USDA quality grades of beef: Select, Choice, and Prime. When the word "certified" appears in the brand name, it means that the specifications such as breed or marbling scores are monitored and verified by an impartial third party such as the Agricultural Marketing Service (AMS) or the Food Safety and Inspection Service (FSIS). This certification helps ensure product consistency.

- "Breed specific" Branded Beef. This type of Branded Beef chooses cattle from a specific breed. Certified Angus Beef and Certified Hereford Beef are examples of breed-based brands. Emerging in popularity over the last few decades has been a trend called "Kobe-styled beef" or American Kobe beef. This umbrella term generally refers to Angus cattle that have been cross-bred with Japanese Wagyu stock. The Japanese government and cattle ranchers have taken issue with this labeling because it enjoys the benefit of the Kobe beef brand while not being authentic Kobe beef.

- "Company specific" Branded Beef. This type of branded program chooses beef from all types of breeds but includes other criteria in terms of grade, marbling, size, types of feed used and/or restrictions on the use of pesticides, antibiotics and growth hormones. Examples would include the Sterling Silver Beef program or Maverick Ranch. Packer brands include Cargill Meat Solution's Sterling Silver Premium Beef, or National Beef's Naturewell Natural Beef, Black Canyon® Preium Reserve, and Imperial Valley Premium Beef.

- "Store branded" Branded Beef. Some grocery store chains are now branding their beef. For retailers, the store-branded beef allows them to differentiate themselves with a product available only at their store. Retailers look at meat products as an area to set themselves apart to help drive product development and improvement. Whatever category a given brand falls into, it will have a number of specific requirements around some variety of attributes

such as grade, age, and process or source verification. Often it will extend a guarantee of satisfaction.

- Natural Beef. All fresh beef is natural according to the United States Department of Agriculture (USDA). The USDA defines Natural Beef as "minimally processed containing no additives." Beef that is labeled "natural" is most likely from companies that are marketing Natural Beef but are emphasizing restrictions on types of feed and/or the use of pesticides, antibiotics and growth hormones. All fresh beef found in the meat case that does not have an ingredient label (a label is added if the product includes a marinade or solution) is Natural.

Certified Organic Beef

The Organic Food Production Act, effective October 2002, established USDA standards for food labeled organic. Organic beef that carries the "USDA Organic" label has been raised and processed in a way that meets strict guidelines that meets USDA National Organic Program (NOP) standards.

For cattle, these standards include:

- Cattle must be fed 100 percent organic feed, but may be provided certain vitamin and mineral supplements. All the feed that the animal receives must also be certified as organically grown grasses and grains and cannot contain any animal by-products.

- Organically raised cattle may not be given hormones to promote growth or antibiotics for any reason. Animals that get sick are treated; however, any animal that is treated with antibiotics is taken out of the NOP.

- Although all cattle have access to pastures for most of their lives, the NOP also requires pasture access for cattle that are being Grain-Finished.

- All organically raised cattle must be raised separate from their conventional counterparts and then processed in certified organic facilities.

Some people confuse organic beef with grass-fed beef. The two categories are not the same, but are not mutually exclusive. Organic beef comes from cattle that are raised without antibiotics or growth hormones, and are fed an organically grown, vegetarian diet. This diet may or may not include grains. Grass-fed beef comes from cattle raised solely on grass, hay, and forage. Grains cannot be included in the diets of grass-fed cattle, but the grass and hay may or may not be organically grown. If the hay and grass in a grass-fed cow's diet is organic, then the beef is both organic and grass-fed. Cattle raised to be turned into grass-fed beef are usually a smaller breed. They grow slower, and have a lower slaughter weight.

Corn Fed Beef, or Conventional Beef

Corn-fed, also known as conventional or grain-fed, is the most widely produced kind of beef in the U.S. Conventional beef assures a consistent, year-round supply of beef at considerably lower prices than branded beef. Corn-fed beef cattle spend most of their lives in range or pasture conditions eating grass. At 12 to 18 months of age, conventional cattle are moved to a feedlot and are usually separated into groups of 100 animals and live in pens. Cattle usually spend four to six months in a feedlot, during which they are fed a diet of corn and/or silage, hay and other grains as well as FDA approved growth hormones to bring them to slaughter weight more quickly and antibiotics to treat, control, and prevent disease. No matter the type of production, U.S. beef is considered among the safest beef in the world due to strong government regulations and enforcement

Grass-Finished Beef

Grass-Finished Beef comes from animals that have been pasture-fed throughout their lives. The majority of Grass-Finished Beef marketed in the U.S. is imported from Australia and New Zealand where grass is in greater abundance than feed corn and can be grown year-round. Grass-Finished Beef is not necessarily Certified Organic Beef. Since cattle may be given FDA-approved antibiotics and/or hormones. The Grass-Finished Beef market is designed to satisfy consumers who prefer the concept of cattle grazing through the final stage of production.

The question of Grass-Finished versus Grain-Finished Beef usually centers on flavor and not how lean the beef is. There are 19 cuts of beef that meet the government labeling guidelines for lean, including Top Sirloin Steak, Top Loin (Strip) Steak, Flank Steak, Rib eye Steak, Tenderloin Steak, and T-Bone Steak. Grass-Finished Beef tends to grade Select (slight intramuscular fat marbling), giving it the same lean profile as Conventional Beef graded Select.

Beef Breeds

The breeds listed below are marketed as premium brands but beef in the county comes from a variety of cattle types. Texas Longhorn, English Hereford, and many other types of cattle can be graded USDA Prime and USDA Choice.

- **Black Angus**: Angus beef is the most popular premium beef in America and can come from either red angus or black angus cattle.

- **Kobe:** Kobe beef is regulated as a geographic indicator by the Japanese government and the Kobe region. True Kobe Beef is produced in the Hyogo prefecture (of which Kobe is the capital) in Japan, from a type of cattle called Wagyu (which roughly translates to "Japanese cow"). It is characterized by bright red meat with pure white, extensively marbled fat. Beer is fed to the cattle during summer months when the interaction of fat cover, temperature and humidity depresses feed intake. Beer stimulates their appetite to keep the cattle on feed in the heat of the summer. Daily massaging is done to relieve stress and muscle stiffness. To be labeled Kobe, beef must not only come from Wagyu cattle but must also be processed in Kobe Japan.

- **American Wagyu** (also called American-Style Kobe): The United States currently has a mix of pure bred Wagyu cattle and cattle that have been cross-bred with Angus cattle. American Wagyu are fed a diet similar to that of Wagyu in Japan. American Wagyu also displays the same characteristics of Kobe beef but since it was not processed in Japan cannot use the name Kobe Beef. Wagyu, like Kobe beef, is known for its marbling characteristics, taste, tenderness, and juiciness.

- **Australian Wagyu:** Wagyu cattle were first imported into Australia in 1991, and Australian cattle companies maintain both pure bred and cross bred herds. The cattle are feed a diet similar to that of Wagyu in Japan and display the same characteristics of Kobe beef and American-Style Kobe beef.

Heritage Beef

Heritage beef comes from pure and cross bred livestock and from rare and endangered breeds. These heritage breeds were originally bred for particular geographical and climatic environments and consumer preferences. In the last few decades, heritage breeds have been mostly ignored in favor of a handful of "super-efficient" cattle breeds promoted by the large agricultural-feed-lot-meat industries. Heritage breeds are not as "efficient," economically speaking, as their industrial counterparts: they will only thrive on pastures as the true herbivores they are. They simply do not respond well to the artificial life of feed-lot cattle.

- **The Red Poll:** These were developed as a dual purpose breed. Small and hardy, a true red with a white mottled face.

- **The Dexter**: First imported to the U.S. in the early 1900s, from Ireland. Because of its small size it requires less pasturing space. Beef from Dexter breeds result in small cuts of prime, dark meat.

SOUTH TEXAS

South Texas was originally cleared by farmers from the Midwest who were attracted by the subtropical climate and long growing season, allowing them to produce two crops in one year on the same land. They planted vegetables, reaping the first agricultural bonanza from valley soil. The Rio Grande Valley produces more than 40 crops—primarily cotton, grain sorghum, sugarcane, fruits, and vegetables. Today, the major food crops grown include cabbage, onions, carrots, peppers, broccoli, citrus fruits, and cantaloupes and honeydew melons. The onion is Texas's top produce crop, one of more than 45 types of produce grown in Texas, the nation's third largest producer of fruits and vegetables. The famous 1015 onion, developed at Texas A&M University specifically for Rio Grande Valley growing conditions, is so sweet and mild it has been voted the sweetest tasting onion in a national competition, and it is tearless. It is named 1015 for the day it is planted—October 15.

The food of the settlers in this South Texas region was based primarily on the cuisine of Mexico and Spain. Tacos, guacamole, enchiladas, burritos, and tortillas became staples. Those, along with fajitas with spicy salsas and fresh flour tortillas, were the start of the first true American regional cuisine.

Typical Tex-Mex Dishes and Regional Foods

Anticucho   A Tex-Mex shish kebab usually made with sirloin chunks marinated with jalapeño and tomato, then skewered and grilled over a mesquite wood fire.

Arroz   Spanish for "rice," the staple of Tex-Mex cooking. Texmati rice is a brand name for a crossbreed of white, long-grain, and the aromatic basmati rice. It is known for its delicious nutty taste and when cooking, it smells like popcorn.

Barbacoa   In Spanish, *barbacoa* means "food cooked over or adjacent to an open fire." In Tex-Mex cooking, it is a Mexican-style shredded beef made from the cow's head. Barbacoa is typically served with pico de gallo and freshly made corn or flour tortillas.

Boracho   A cooking term indicating the inclusion of beer in a recipe—for example, in *frijoles borachos*, which means "beans cooked with beer."

Burrito   A large flour tortilla filled with any number of ingredients that could include meat, beans, or vegetables. The burrito is formed by tucking the ends of the tortilla inside as it is rolled to seal in the filling. They are usually eaten with condiments such as salsa, lettuce, tomato, cheese, and guacamole.

Cabrito   Spanish for "goat." Like cattle and sheep, goats are a major source of revenue on many Texas ranches, but they also run wild throughout parts of the state. Grilled or barbecued, split or butchered, goat is a feature for large gatherings or feasts. Older goat is used for milk and cheese products.

Caldo de Res   A Spanish beef soup with vegetables, often served with corn on the cob that has been cut into thick slices.

Cheeses:

Queso   Spanish for "cheese." In Tex-Mex cooking, Cheddar is the most frequently used cheese. One of the most distinct differences between Tex-Mex and American Southwest foods is the choice of cheese. In American Southwest cuisine, fresh goat cheese, or queso fresca, is used for traditional dishes. In Tex-Mex cooking, Cheddar and Monterey Jack are the cheeses used.

Queso Blanco   Spanish for "white cheese." Queso blanco is the Mexican cheese Monterey Jack was named after. It became popular as an economical product that could be made with little equipment and even when only a small amount of milk was available.

Chicken-Fried Steak   An original Texas recipe made with tenderized round steak or cubed steak coated with egg and flour and pan-fried. Local Texans usually refer to chicken-fried steak by the abbreviation CFS. Chicken-fried steak is traditionally served covered with a white cream gravy and with side dishes of mashed potatoes, green beans, and biscuits.

Chiles   Chiles are considered the premier seasoning in Tex-Mex cooking. Over 7,000 varieties have been identified. The chile (of the genus *Capsicum*) is a member of the nightshade family, which also includes tomatoes and potatoes. The word *capsicum* is a from the Greek word *kapto*, meaning "to bite"—a reference to the chile's intense heat and pungent, biting flavor. This heat source, capsaisin, spreads unevenly throughout the inside of the pod and is concentrated in the ribs of the pod. Aztecs called the peppers *chilli* or *chiltepin*. In 1912, a chemist named Wilbur Scoville measured the heat index of chiles by diluting ground chili in water until the heat dissipated. The result was Scoville units, measured in increments of 100. Scoville units go from 1 to 16 million, the latter of which was Scoville's rating of pure capsaicin, the chemical responsible for the chile's potent heat. A more modern version used by many chile writers is called Scoville Scale, with a rating of 0 to 10. Bell peppers rate a 0 because they contain no capsaicinoid. The habanero rates highest with a 10 on the heat scale. A few of the more popular chiles include:

Anaheim, or Green Chile   These mild green chiles (also called Big Jim or Colorado peppers) are among the most common varieties of chiles (rated 1 or 2 on the heat scale) and are best when roasted and peeled.

Poblano Chile   A dark green chile that tapers down to a point and is 4 to 6 inches long. This chile is most often used for chile rellenos. It's relatively mild, about 3 or 4 on the heat scale. It is also known in its dried form as ancho chile.

Jalapeño Chile   Named after the region of Jalapa, this is the most popular and well known chile in North America. A fairly spicy, small chile that turns from green to red as it matures, as with most chiles, the heat comes mainly from the seeds. The jalapeño is placed at about 5 on the heat scale.

Serrano Chile   Literally meaning "highland" or "mountain," it is a small, fresh, hot chile measuring about 1½ inches long. As it matures, it turns from dark green to red, then to yellow. Usually the smaller a serrano chile is in size, the hotter it is. It is placed at about 6 on the heat scale. The serrano chile is usually used when making pico de gallo.

Cayenne Pepper   Almost always sold in its dried state, this chile is very popular as a powder. It registers about an 8 on the heat scale. Cayenne is used extensively in Cajun and Creole cooking.

Habanero Chile   Closely related to the Caribbean Scotch bonnet, this is the hottest chile known to man. Marble shaped and registering 10 on the heat scale, it comes in a variety of colors, including green, yellow, orange, and red.

The process of drying chiles concentrates their natural sugars and intensifies their flavors. Tex-Mex cooking professionals generally choose to blend their own chili powder by grinding a special mix of dried chiles in a coffee grinder. This technique is used to bring an exact flavor to a given recipe by carefully balancing the different flavors of various chiles. Select dried chiles that are clean and not discolored; they should not be faded, dusty, or broken. Freshly dried chiles will be relatively soft and supple, with a distinct aroma. The more popular dried chiles include:

Ancho Chile   A ripe poblano chile that has been dried. This is the most commonly used dried chile in Tex-Mex cooking. It has an earthy, smoky flavor and is the basis for commercial chili powders and ranks 3 on the heat scale.

Cascabel Chile   About 1½ inches in diameter and shaped like an acorn. Cascabel chiles have a distinctive flavor and are dark orange to red in color. The seeds of the cascabel chile rattle in the pod, which explains the literal translation of its name, "jingle bell." Also known as the "rattler," it is about a 4 or 5 on the heat scale.

Chíltepin Chile   Considered tiny, dried red-orange bullets of fiery heat, they are the Texas state native chile and are rated 9 on the heat scale.

Chipotle Chile   A smoked and dried jalapeño. Chipotle chiles are brick red in color and available fresh as well as canned. They are moderately hot but possess a distinct, complex flavor with no equivalent substitute. The heat of chipotle chiles is placed at about 2 on the heat scale.

Pasilla Chile A dried chilaca, this chile's name means "little raisin." Long, dark, and wrinkled, this is an essential ingredient in many moles. It is about 3 or 4 on the heat scale, with smoky, dried fruit overtones.

Gebhardt's Chili Powder A popular brand of chili powder from San Antonio, Texas. Gebhardt's chili powder features ground dried chiles enhanced with herbs and spices.

Use caution in handling and storing chiles. When handling, wear gloves to protect your hands because the oils in the chiles can cause severe burns. Don't touch your face or eyes. If chiles come in contact with your bare hands, wash your hands thoroughly with soapy water. When grinding dried chiles, beware of the chile dust in the air, which will irritate eyes and throats.

Chile Relleno *Relleno* is Spanish for "stuffed." Authentic Tex-Mex chiles rellenos are fresh, large poblano chiles stuffed with cheese and dipped in egg batter. They are then pan-fried in oil and served with refried beans and rice.

Chili The official state dish of Texas, chili is a Tex-Mex adaptation of an American Southwest dish of meat (usually beef or pork) that is slowly simmered in a sauce made from dried chiles and spices. In Tex-Mex cooking, beans are never included. San Antonio is credited with being the birthplace of today's Texas chili. Back then, the market area was a central point for cattle drives, the army, missionaries, and railroad men. Women of the mission would prepare large kettles of traditional stews or chili and bring them to the plaza to feed the hungry crowds. These ladies were known as "chili queens" and this practice lasted until the early 1940s—until sanitation laws forced them out of business.

Chimichanga A burrito that has been deep-fried.

Chorizo A spicy Mexican sausage made with pork and seasonings. Mexican chorizo is made with fresh pork, while Spanish chorizo calls for smoked pork. The casing is usually removed before cooking.

Churro A light, crisp pastry dough made from cornmeal and sugar. The dough is piped out of a pastry bag into strips and deep-fried until golden brown. Churros are served sprinkled with cinnamon sugar.

Cilantro A highly aromatic herb related to parsley; it is used extensively in Tex-Mex cooking. Cilantro is also referred to as Chinese parsley. The leaves of the herb are usually finely chopped and used as a condiment or as an ingredient in Tex-Mex recipes. The stems can be chopped and used in soups, beans, or anything that is simmered.

Colache A Tex-Mex version of ratatouille, using the procedure of respecting each vegetable's individual cooking time.

Enchilada A corn tortilla rolled with a filling made from cheese, beans, chicken, pork, or beef. Enchiladas are typically smothered with a thin, red, chile sauce, referred to as enchilada sauce, topped with Cheddar cheese, and baked in an oven until the cheese is completely melted.

Escabeche A method of pickling that is frequently used to prepare fish or vegetables. Escabeche is typically served as an appetizer, light entrée, or side dish. It is best served at room temperature after resting under refrigeration overnight. The resting process allows the flavor of the vegetables to fully develop.

Fajita An original Tex-Mex recipe made by grilling marinated skirt steak, then slicing it and serving it with smoked strips of green chiles and tortillas. Fajitas originated along the Rio Grande on the Texas-Mexico border and were typically eaten by cattle wranglers. The skirt steak (the diaphragm muscle of the steer) is the usual cut of meat used for fajitas. Skirt steaks were originally the discards given to the cowboys after cattle were slaughtered. Dramatic, but not authentic, the presentation of fajitas with sizzling bell peppers and onions on a hot, cast-iron plate is an adaptation created to market the menu item.

Flauta A white or yellow corn tortilla stuffed with beef, chicken, or pork. Flautas are rolled and pan- or deep-fried until crisp. They are usually about ¾ inch in diameter and are served two or three to a plate. Flautas may be topped with cheese, sour cream, and guacamole.

Flan   A Tex-Mex dessert similar to French crème caramel. Flan is made either as a pie and cut into slices or in individual cups.

Frijoles   Spanish for "beans." After corn, beans are historically the most important ingredient in the Tex-Mex pantry. The pinto (from the word "painted," owing the brownish pink streaks on the beige bean) is the most used bean in this country.

Guacamole   An avocado mixture made from the fruit's flesh. Guacamole is usually blended with lemon or lime juice, diced onion, and chopped cilantro. It is used as a side dish or condiment in numerous Tex-Mex dishes.

Jícama   A crisp, crunchy root vegetable with a thick brown skin that must be removed prior to use. The flavor of jícama is similar to a mild apple crossed with a potato—this makes it excellent for use in salads and salsas. Some use it in place of water chestnuts. Unlike apples, the flesh of jícama does not turn brown after it is peeled. In Mexico, it is eaten thinly sliced, with a squeeze of lime and a dusting of cayenne.

Mole   Derived from the Aztec word *molli*, meaning a "concoction," "stew," or "sauce." Mole is a complex dish woven together with dried chiles, nuts, seeds, vegetables, spices, and chocolate. Each local area has its own version of mole, from Texas to Arizona to Mexico. The most frequently seen are green mole, made with tomatillos, and red mole, made with pumpkin seeds. Mole is typically made as a sauce and used to braise meat and poultry items.

Nachos   Made with tostadas (a "toasted chip") and the addition of toppings such as beans, meats, or cheese. They may also be served with guacamole and sour cream.

Nopales   The whole paddles or pads of the prickly pear cactus. Nopalitos are cactus pads that have been peeled and cut into julienne. They are available in cans and jars. Some say that cactus pads have a flavor similar to green bell peppers. Others say nopales taste more like green beans. They are commonly used as an ingredient in salads. Nopalitos should be rinsed several times under cold water before using.

Pico de Gallo   The literal translation is "beak of the rooster." Pico de gallo is an uncooked salsa made from tomatoes, onions, serrano chiles, and cilantro, all cut into a very small dice (as if pecked by a rooster).

Ranchero   A Tex-Mex cooking term referring to the addition of tomatoes, bell peppers, and garlic in a recipe. Ranchero is usually used to describe a cooked salsa or a cooking technique, as in frijoles rancheros.

Refried Beans   A well-known recipe frequently served in the Tex-Mex region. Refried beans are commonly referred to as "refritos" and are usually made from pinto beans. The Spanish word *refritos* means "well fried" but is frequently misinterpreted as refried or twice fried. Typically, pinto beans are cooked and drained, and then mashed with hot lard or bacon fat, seasonings, and sometimes chiles. Despite their name, refried beans are fried only once.

Ruby Red Grapefruit   An important crop produced in Texas is the red grapefruit, which began as a mutation of the pink grapefruit tree. Today, all red grapefruits are descendants of the Ruby Red first grown in Mission, Texas, in the 1920s. The Ruby Red grapefruit was the first grapefruit to be granted a U.S. patent. During the 1970s, several important mutations found on the Ruby trees produced fruit even redder than the 1929 Ruby Red grapefruit. Dr. Richard Hensz—of Texas A&M University—spent many years in the laboratory working to produce the reddest grapefruit through mutations caused by ionizing radiation. In 1970, the Star Ruby variety was released, making it the first commercial grapefruit produced by artificial means. Red grapefruit contains high levels of a chemical called lycopene that studies have shown seems to prevent some cancers.

Salsa   The Spanish word for "sauce." In Tex-Mex cooking, it refers to a relish or condiment, a mixture of chopped vegetables, fruits (usually tomatoes), and seasonings that may be cooked or uncooked, is usually not pureed, and is served as an accompaniment to a dish. Salsa that is blended finely in a food processor is usually called "picante sauce." Owing to an increased awareness of nutritional issues, salsas have risen in popularity because they are low in cholesterol, fat, and calories. Salsa has recently replaced tomato ketchup as the best-selling condiment in North America.

Salsa Verde   Made from the tomatillo, a small, green Mexican fruit of the tomato family. Tomatillos are covered with a brown husk. They are used mainly in making fresh and cooked salsas. The tomatillos are simmered and then blended in a food processor with spices.

Taco   A folded, grilled, or deep-fried corn tortilla typically filled with meat such as pork, beef, chicken, and more recently duck or fish. Tacos are usually topped with lettuce, tomatoes, and cheese and served with pico de gallo.

Tamale   A traditional Tex-Mex recipe whose name is derived from the ancient Aztec word *tamalli*. Tamales are made from masa dough and typically are filled with shredded pork or beef. They are usually 5 or 6 inches long and about 1 inch thick. The tamale is wrapped in a soaked corn husk, steamed, and topped with red chili. Tamales are a Hispanic holiday tradition throughout Texas and are always served at Christmas and New Year.

Tortilla   Spanish for "little cakes," which the conquistadors thought the Native American recipe resembled. Before the European colonists introduced wheat flour to the region, tortillas were made exclusively from the corn grown by the Native Americans and were the staple food. In Tex-Mex cooking, tortillas are a thin round made of either corn flour or wheat flour. Once the dough (masa) is made, the tortillas are formed in a tortilla press or hand-shaped by patting the dough. Tortillas are then cooked quickly on a hot skillet or griddle called a comal. They are eaten either by themselves or with other Tex-Mex dishes. Corn tortillas are usually about 6 inches in diameter—much smaller than their flour counterparts, which can be as large as 24 inches around. Tortillas are also used to wrap a variety of Tex-Mex foods, such as beans, meats, and vegetables, and eaten like a taco.

Menus and Recipes from
Texas and Tex-Mex Cuisine

MENU ONE
LBJ Pedernales River Chili

Jalapeño Cornbread

Grilled Quesadillas

Flour Tortillas

Lone Star Chicken-Fried Steak with Cream Gravy

Mashed Potatoes

Black-Eyed Peas

Mexican Wedding Cookies

MENU TWO
Tortilla Soup

Pork Taquitos with Sour Cream, Guacamole, and Pico de Gallo

Tex-Mex Plate:

Crayfish Tacos with Green Chile Sauce

Cheese Enchiladas

Arroz Mexicana

Refried Beans

Flan

MENU THREE
Caldo de Res

Gulf Shrimp Corn Dogs with Cabbage and Radish Slaw

Fried Chicken Livers with Bacon Hollandaise on Petite Rosemary Biscuits

Redfish on the Half Shell with Grilled Red Onion and Frisée Salad

Pecan Squares

OTHER RECIPES
Tex-Mex Fajitas

Braggin' Rights Brisket

Homemade Tamales

Kale Chips

LBJ Pedernales River Chili

4 servings

 **CHEF TIP:** Texas chili, also known as a bowl of red, should be meat, chilies, tomatoes, and not much else—simply perfect. Beans were most likely added to chili to stretch it; they are an easy way to get nutrition.

AMOUNT	MEASURE	INGREDIENT
1 tablespoon, or as needed	½ ounce/14 ml	Vegetable oil
4 cups	1½ pounds/680 g	Beef chuck, trimmed, in ½-inch (1.2 cm) cubes
2 cups	8 ounces/226 g	Onions, in ¼-inch (.6 cm) dice
2	½ ounce/14 g	Garlic cloves, minced
½ teaspoon	1 g	Dried oregano
1 teaspoon	2 g	Ground cumin
1 tablespoon	¼ ounce/7 g	Chili powder
3 cups	18 ounces/705 ml	Tomatoes, peeled, in ¼-inch (.6 cm) dice
2 cups, or as needed	16 ounces/480 ml	Beef stock, hot
		Salt and pepper

PROCEDURE

1. Preheat a heavy 3- to 4-quart (3 to 4 L) saucepot, which should be as tall as its diameter, over medium-high heat and add the vegetable oil to coat the bottom. When the oil is hot, add enough meat to just cover the bottom of the pan and evenly brown on all sides, 5 to 7 minutes. This step may need to be done in small batches. Remove meat and set aside.

2. Remove any excess oil from the pot. Over low to medium-low heat, add the onions and garlic, cooking 4 minutes or until vegetables begin to evenly brown.

3. Add the oregano, cumin, and chili powder and cook 2 minutes. Return the browned beef cubes to the pot and add the tomatoes and stock to just cover. Bring to a boil, then reduce to a simmer and cook 1 to 1½ hours or until the beef is tender. Skim fat as it cooks, adding more stock or water if necessary.

4. Taste and adjust the seasoning with salt and pepper.

Jalapeño Cornbread

AMOUNT	MEASURE	INGREDIENT
2	6 tablespoons/5 ounces/140 g	Jalapeño peppers, minced
2 cups	16 ounces/452g	Cream-style corn
½ teaspoon		Baking soda
½ teaspoon		Salt
1 tablespoon	½ ounce/15 g	Sugar
2		Eggs, lightly beaten
⅓ cup	2.6 ounces/78 ml	Buttermilk
¼ cup	2 ounces/60 ml	Vegetable oil
1 cup	4 ounces/112 g	Cheddar cheese, shredded
2 cups	10½ ounces/400 g	Yellow cornmeal

PROCEDURE

1. Preheat the oven to 400°F (205°C). Heavily grease a 17½ x 12-inch (44.5 cm x 30.5 cm) baking pan.

2. In a large bowl, combine the jalapeño with the corn. Mix in the baking soda, salt, and sugar. Add the eggs, buttermilk, and oil. Then mix in the cheese and cornmeal. Do not overmix.

3. Pour the batter into the prepared pan and bake for 25 to 30 minutes, or until the top is brown and a toothpick inserted in the center comes out clean.

4. Cool in the pan and cut to serve.

LBJ Pedernales River Chili with Jalapeño Cornbread

Grilled Quesadillas

AMOUNT	MEASURE	INGREDIENT
4		Flour tortillas, 8 inches (20 cm) in diameter, homemade if possible (recipe follows)
2 tablespoons	1 ounce/28 g	Butter, melted
2 tablespoons	1 ounce/30 ml	Vegetable oil
2 cups	8 ounces/226 g	Mexican cheese (Oaxaca, Chihuahua, or asadero) or whole milk mozzarella, in thin slices or shreds
4 tablespoons	2 ounces/56 g	Poblano chile, roasted, peeled, ¼ inch (.6 cm) dice
2 tablespoons	¼ ounce/7 g	Fresh cilantro leaves, chopped

PROCEDURE

1. Prepare a grill. Soften the tortillas by heating on the grill for 15 seconds on one side, turn and heat an additional 15 seconds, or until soft.

2. Combine the melted butter and vegetable oil in a small bowl. Brush one side of the tortillas with the butter-oil mixture, turn the tortilla over, and spread ½ cup (2 ounces/56 g) of the cheese on half of each tortilla, leaving a 1-inch (2.5 cm) border.

3. Top each with the chile and cilantro, and fold over.

4. Brush both sides of each tortilla liberally with butter-oil mixture and place on grill. When grill-marked, turn tortillas over and continue to cook until cheese melts.

5. Cut into quarters and serve.

Flour Tortillas

 CHEF TIP: The dough will be very sticky. It will dry out as the dough rests, but, even after resting, it is soft dough, so be sure to dust with additional flour when rolling into tortillas.

AMOUNT	MEASURE	INGREDIENT
2¼ cups	9 ounces/252 g	All-purpose flour
2 teaspoons	4 g	Baking powder
½ cup	4 ounces/112 g	Lard or vegetable shortening
2 teaspoons	10 g	Salt
1 cup	8 ounces/240 ml	Hot water (110°F/43°C)

PROCEDURE

1. Combine 2 cups (8 ounces/224 g) of the flour and the baking powder in a large bowl.

2. Add the lard or vegetable shortening and blend in using a pastry cutter, back of a fork or your hands until it resembles coarse meal.

3. Dissolve the salt in the warm water.

4. Add the salted water slowly to the flour mixture and knead until a soft dough forms, 4 to 5 minutes. Add additional warm water, as necessary. Roll the dough into a ball, cover with plastic wrap, and let rest 30 minutes.

5. Knead the dough for an additional 2 minutes, then divide into 12 equal pieces and form into round balls.

6. Heat a comal or griddle over medium heat.

7. Using a rolling pin, on a surface dusted with the remaining flour, roll out each ball of dough into a round shape, approximately ⅛ inch (0.3 cm) thick and 6 to 7 inches (15.2–17.8 cm) round. Keep the dough balls covered with a towel so they do not dry out while you roll out the others.

8. Place each tortilla on the hot comal or griddle and cook approximately 1 minute on each side or until no longer doughy and have turned light golden. If the tortilla puffs up, poke a small hole to release the steam.

9. Remove from the comal and cover with a towel to keep moist and warm.

Lone Star Chicken-Fried Steak with Cream Gravy

4 servings

 **CHEF TIP:** Chicken-fried steak is traditionally served with "the works"—white cream gravy, mashed potatoes, fresh corn or green beans, and biscuits. In Texas, it is considered "great" if the portion size is large enough to hang over the plate. Chicken-fried steak should be pan-fried; the oil should only cover a little more than half way up the side of the steaks when they are cooking.

Lone Star Chicken-Fried Steak

AMOUNT	MEASURE	INGREDIENT
2		Eggs
½ cup	4 ounces/115 ml	Milk
1 cup	4 ounces/112 g	All-purpose flour
1 teaspoon	5 g	Salt
¼ teaspoon	1 g	Black pepper
4	4–5 ounces/112–140 g each	Beef round steaks, trimmed, ¼-inch thick
As needed		Vegetable oil, for frying

PROCEDURE

1. Combine the eggs and milk in a small bowl.

2. In another bowl, combine the flour, salt, and pepper.

3. Dredge the steaks in the flour, then dip into the egg mixture, then back in the seasoned flour again, lightly shaking off excess.

4. Heat the oil in a heavy, deep 10- to 12-inch (25.4–30.5 cm) sauté pan to a temperature of 350°F (175°C). Add the steaks; do not overload the pan or the temperature of the oil will drop, resulting in a greasy final product—fry in batches if necessary. Fry steaks for 4 minutes on one side, or until golden brown, then turn over and fry on the other side until golden brown, another 4 to 5 minutes. Adjust the heat as necessary while cooking. Pan-fried items should be turned only once.

5. Drain steaks on paper towels and serve with Cream Gravy (recipe follows).

Cream Gravy

 **CHEF TIP:** The American history of cream gravy goes back hundreds of years, when people didn't have the ingredients to make complex meat-stock gravies, but there was always flour, milk, and pepper on hand to add to pan drippings. It was considered a wonderful way to stretch a meal during the Depression. Gravy is based on the drippings of cooked meat and is prepared quickly. Sometimes it may be called country gravy or white gravy. Cracked black peppercorns are the traditional seasoning; however, chipotles, jalapeños, or cayenne or chili powder may also be used to season the gravy.

AMOUNT	MEASURE	INGREDIENT
2 tablespoons	1 ounce/28 ml	Fat with pan drippings
2 tablespoons	½ ounce/15 g	All-purpose flour
2 cups	16 ounces/480 ml	Warm milk (whole or 2 percent)
		Salt and pepper

PROCEDURE

1. Place the drippings in pan (if possible, from pan used to fry the steaks) over medium-high heat. When hot, stir in the flour. Remove from the heat and whisk in the warm milk.

2. Return pan to low heat and whisk until thickened and smooth, scraping the bottom of the pan. Cook 5 to 10 minutes. (Traditionally it is only cooked until thick, 3 to 5 minutes, but cooking longer helps remove the starchy flour taste.) Gravy making is an inexact science; it is supposed to be thick, but if it's too thick, thin with additional milk or water, added a little at a time. Consistency should be pourable, not a thick paste.

3. Season with salt and pepper. Don't skimp on the pepper.

Lone Star Chicken-Fried Steak with Cream Gravy

Mashed Potatoes

 CHEF TIP: Mashed potatoes can be made by either baking or boiling the potatoes. When boiling, do not cut the potatoes too small, as they will become waterlogged and prevent the finished mashed potatoes from being light and fluffy, which is the desired texture. The best way to check the doneness of boiled potatoes is to insert the tip of a paring knife or skewer into one of the bigger parts of potato. Lift the knife and potato out of the water. If the potato slides off, the potatoes are correctly cooked. If the potato remains on the knife, the potato needs to cook longer. If the potato crumbles when the knife is inserted, the potatoes are overcooked. A ricer is a culinary tool frequently used to mash potatoes.

AMOUNT	MEASURE	INGREDIENT
5 cups	1½ pounds/680 g	Russet potatoes, peeled, quartered
½ cup	4 ounces/120 ml	Warm heavy cream or whole milk
¼ cup	2 ounces/56 g	Butter, softened
		Salt and white pepper

PROCEDURE

1. Cover the potatoes with cold water, add salt, bring to a boil, and reduce to a low simmer. Simmer until tender, approximately 25 minutes. Drain potatoes and return to the pot. Cook over low heat for approximately 3 minutes to dry them.

2. Combine the cream and butter in a saucepot and heat until hot but not boiling.

3. Run the potatoes through a small food mill or ricer set over a warm pot to catch the potato.

4. Blend the cream and butter mixture into the potato, adjusting the consistency as desired. Mashed potatoes should be soft and moist, but hold their shape without being runny. Season to taste with salt and white pepper.

Black-Eyed Peas

✦ **CHEF TIP:** Do not add salt or acid to the beans until they are cooked, as ingredients will lengthen the cooking process and harden the skins.

AMOUNT	MEASURE	INGREDIENT
1 cup	6 ounces/170 g	Dried black-eyed peas
¼ cup	2 ounces/56 g	Bacon, in ½-inch (1.2 cm) dice
½ cup	2 ounces/56 g	Onion, in ½-inch (1.2 cm) dice
1	5 g	Garlic clove, minced
1¼ cups	10 ounces/280 ml	Water
1		Fresh thyme sprig
1 piece	2 ounces/56 g	Salt pork
		Salt and black pepper

PROCEDURE

1. Soak the black-eyed peas overnight in water or do a quick-soak. (Quick-soak: cover peas with water, bring to a boil, and simmer 2 minutes; remove from the heat and let soak in hot liquid, covered, for 1 hour.) Drain the peas.

2. In a 3- to 4-quart (3–4 L) pot over medium heat, render the bacon until almost crisp, about 3 minutes.

3. Add the onion and garlic, and cook about 4 minutes more, or until the onion is soft. Add the black-eyed peas, water, thyme, salt pork, and salt and pepper, adding more water if necessary to cover the peas.

4. Leave pot uncovered. Bring to a boil, reduce to a simmer, and cook 45 to 60 minutes, or until the black-eyed peas are tender.

5. Remove the salt pork and serve.

Mexican Wedding Cookies

Makes about 3 dozen cookies

CHEF TIP: The dough will look light and fluffy because air bubbles are incorporated into the fat. When a mixture is overcreamed, creamed too fast, or the fat is too warm, the fat starts to break down and release previously creamed-in air bubbles. The results may be a dense, flat, and flavorless product.

AMOUNT	MEASURE	INGREDIENT
1 cup	8 ounces/226 g	Unsalted butter, softened
½ cup, plus additional for rolling	2 ounces/56 g	Confectioners' sugar, sifted
1 tablespoon	½ ounce/15 ml	Vanilla extract
2¼ cups	10 ounces/280 g	All-purpose flour
1½ teaspoons	7 g	Salt
¾ cup	3 ounces/85 g	Pecans, finely chopped

PROCEDURE

1. With a mixer, cream the butter and ½ cup (2 ounces/56 g) sugar until light and fluffy. Add the vanilla.

2. Sift the flour and salt together. Gradually add the flour and pecans to the creamed mixture, beating on low speed after each addition until well blended. Chill the dough for 1 hour.

3. Preheat the oven to 350°F (175°C).

4. Roll the dough out into 1-inch (2.5 cm) balls. Place on an ungreased cookie sheet.

5. Bake until set, but do not brown, approximately 15 minutes.

6. Let cookies cool 5 minutes, then while still warm, roll in additional confectioners' sugar until evenly coated. Cool cookies on wire rack.

Mexican Wedding Cookies

Tortilla Soup

4 servings

 CHEF TIP: This soup was originally created in order to use leftover tortillas.

AMOUNT	MEASURE	INGREDIENT
2 cups	8 ounces/226 g	Onions, quartered
3 cups	18 ounces/504 g	Plum tomatoes, halved
6 tablespoons	3 ounces/90 ml	Vegetable oil
1½	3 ounces/84 g	6-inch (15.2 cm) corn tortilla, cut into short strips
3	15 g	Garlic cloves, minced
1		Ancho chile, stemmed, seeded, toasted, finely chopped
1		Bay leaf
2 teaspoons	4 g	Ground cumin
5 cups	40 ounces/1.2 L	Chicken stock
6 tablespoons	3 ounces/90 ml	Tomato sauce
		Salt and pepper
1 cup	4 ounces/112 g	Cooked chicken meat, julienned
½ cup	2 ounces/56 g	Cheddar or Monterey jack cheese, shredded
½ cup	2 ounces/56 g	Corn tortilla, julienned and fried until crisp

PROCEDURE

1. Preheat grill; grill should be hot. Rub the onions and tomatoes with half the oil and grill on all sides until well charred, 15 to 20 minutes. (Can also be done on a baking sheet under the broiler.)

2. Put the tomatoes and onions in a blender or processor and blend until smooth.

3. Heat the remaining oil. Add the tortilla strips, garlic, and chile and sauté for 3 to 4 minutes.

4. Add the bay leaf, cumin, and stock; bring to a boil. Stir in the tomato-onion mixture and add the tomato sauce. Simmer for 30 minutes.

5. Season and strain through a coarse strainer. Taste and adjust seasoning with salt and pepper.

6. Heat the soup and serve. Garnish with the chicken, cheese, and crisp tortilla strips.

Tortilla Soup

Pork Taquitos with Sour Cream, Guacamole, and Pico de Gallo

4 servings

✦ **CHEF TIP:** Flautas and taquitos are very similar and the terms are used interchangeable depending on the location. A taquito is usually made with corn tortillas and flautas, which mean "flutes," are usually made with flour tortillas, though both are deep-fried. However, you can find taquitos made with flour tortillas and flautas made with corn. The Mexican street-food vendors may call them tacos dorados (fried tacos, literally, "golden tacos"). Taquitos are always shorter than flautas and usually served as an appetizer. Plus, one of the keys to their success is that they can be fried to order.

Pork Taquitos

AMOUNT	MEASURE	INGREDIENT
2 cups	16 ounces/480 ml	Vegetable oil
12	7 ounces/196 g	6-inch (15.2 cm) corn tortillas
2 cups	10 ounces/280 g	Pork Deshebrada (recipe follows)
2 cups	4 ounces/113 g	Iceberg lettuce, shredded
½ cup	4 ounces/120 ml	Sour cream

PROCEDURE

1. Heat a 10-inch (25.4 cm) sauté pan or deep-fat fryer, then add the oil and heat to 350°F (175°C).

2. Pass the tortillas through the hot oil for 3 to 5 seconds to soften. (Tortillas need to be soft so they will roll without tearing.) Transfer to a paper towel–lined plate, keeping the tortillas separate or they will stick together.

3. Place 2 tablespoons of shredded pork in a strip on one side of each tortilla. Roll up the tortillas as tight as possible so they are tubes; secure each with a toothpick, if necessary. Place seam side down to seal the roll.

4. Fry the taquitos a few at a time in the oil until crisp, 1 to 2 minutes. Drain on paper towels.

5. Arrange taquitos on shredded lettuce and top with sour cream, Guacamole (recipe follows), and Pico de Gallo (recipe follows).

Pork Deshebrada

⚜ CHEF TIP: Dried chiles should be cleaned before use. Wipe the chile with a damp cloth to remove impurities. Dried chiles are roasted or toasted so that they release their aroma and are easier to grind or puree. They can be toasted in a 350°F (175°C) oven until they begin to change color and smell toasted. They can also be toasted whole in a dry sauté pan or on a griddle until the color changes slightly and chiles become fragrant (but not to the point the aroma becomes harsh). Or you can cut the stem end off and cut down the length of one side of the chile to flatten it. Remove the seeds and veins, if desired. Then, press the flattened chiles onto a hot pan using a spatula, flipping occasionally. When the "inside" changes color and smells toasted, remove from the heat. Some recipes call for the chiles to be quickly fried instead of roasted, which requires only a small amount of oil.

AMOUNT	MEASURE	INGREDIENT
For the Puree		
15	3 ounces/85 g	Dried New Mexico red chiles
2 cups	16 ounces/470 ml	Water
1 cup	4 ounces/112 g	Onion, in chunks
2	10 g	Garlic cloves
For the Pork		
1	5–6 pounds/2.26–2.72 kg	Pork shoulder roast, bone-in
1½ cups	6 ounces/170 g	Onions, thinly sliced
4	1 ounce/28 g	Garlic cloves, finely chopped
2 teaspoons	2 g	Dried oregano
2 teaspoons	2 g	Ground cumin, preferably from toasted seeds
2 teaspoons	2 g	Salt
1 quart	32 ounces/1 L	Chicken stock
		Salt and pepper

PROCEDURE

1. Make the puree. Preheat the oven to 350°F (175°C).

2. Toast the chiles for 4 minutes or until they begin to smell toasted. Cool slightly.

3. Discard stems and seeds. Combine chiles, water, onion chucks, and whole garlic in a saucepan. Simmer until soft, about 30 minutes.

4. Remove from heat and cool slightly. In a blender or food processor, blend until smooth. Rub the puree through a fine strainer and discard residue.

5. Prepare the pork. Lay the pork, fat side up, in a braising pan. Add the onions, garlic, oregano, cumin, and salt.

6. Combine ¾ cup (6 ounces/170 ml) red chile puree and the stock. Add to the pan and bring to a simmer. Cover and braise pork for up to 4 hours, or until fork-tender. (You may also cut the meat into smaller pieces to shorten cooking time. Or use a pressure cooker, which should reduce the cooking time by at least half.)

7. Cool the pork in the braising liquid, then transfer to a cutting board. Trim away the fat and remove the bone. Shred meat with the tines of two forks, one held in each hand. Shred the meat in a downward, pulling motion.

Guacamole

CHEF TIP: Guacamole should be mixed by hand. Use a fork to blend the ingredients until the mixture has a chunky consistency. (Do not use a blender or food processor, as the consistency will be too thin.) For a more distinctive appearance, split the avocado, remove the seed, and with a paring knife, cut through the flesh, making ¼-inch (.6 cm) slices both vertically and horizontally down to the skin. Using a tablespoon, scoop the sliced flesh out of the skin. The result is a small dice that can then be mixed gently with the other ingredients. Guacamole naturally oxidizes and turns brown if stored for a while. To prevent oxidation, a little lemon juice can be spread over the top of the guacamole before storing. To use stored guacamole that has turned brown, carefully skim off and discard the oxidized portion.

AMOUNT	MEASURE	INGREDIENT
2	12 ounces/340 g	Avocados
½ cup	2 ounces/56 g	Red onion, in ¼-inch (.6 cm) dice
1	3 tablespoons/ 2.5 ounces/70 g	Jalapeño pepper, minced
¼ cup	½ ounce/15 g	Fresh cilantro leaves
½ cup	3 ounces/85 g	Tomato, peeled, in ¼-inch (.6 cm) dice
1–2 tablespoons, or to taste	½–1 ounce/15–30 ml	Lemon juice
1 tablespoon	½ ounce/5 ml	Lime juice
½ teaspoon	3 g	Salt
⅛ teaspoon	1 g	White pepper

PROCEDURE Peel and pit the avocados. Place avocado in a bowl and mash to a chunky texture. Add the remaining ingredients and mix thoroughly. Season to taste.

Pico de Gallo

CHEF TIP: Also called salsa fresca or salsa Mexicana, this salsa is typically made with chopped uncooked ingredients. White sweet onions are known for their mild, even sugary, taste. They have a thinner, lighter color than other onions and tend to be more fragile. When cut into, white sweet onions should have a creamy white interior. Texas has a number of sweet onion varieties: Sunbrero Sweet, Pecos, and the Texas 1015. Red onions also tend to have a mild to sweet flavor.

AMOUNT	MEASURE	INGREDIENT
1 tablespoon	½ ounce/15 ml	Olive oil
1	5 g	Garlic clove, minced
1 cup	4 ounces/113 g	Sweet onion, in ¼-inch (.6 cm) dice
1		Serrano chile, minced
1½ tablespoons	5 g	Fresh cilantro, minced
1 cup	6 ounces/170 g	Tomato, peeled, in, ¼-inch (.6 cm) dice
1 tablespoon	½ ounce/15 ml	Lime juice
		Salt and pepper

PROCEDURE Combine all the ingredients and correct seasoning with salt and pepper. Serve at room temperature.

Pork Taquitos with Sour Cream, Guacamole, and Pico de Gallo

Tex Mex Plate

Crayfish Tacos with Green Chile Sauce

CHEF TIP: Crayfish not purchased purged must be purged before cooking. Mud bugs, craw daddies, and crawfish are all names referring to the poplar shellfish of the southern United States. Crayfish are native to every continent excluding Africa, however. Nevertheless, Texas is a close second to Louisiana in the crayfish aquaculture industry.

AMOUNT	MEASURE	INGREDIENT
For the Sauce		
8	16 ounces/453 g	Tomatillos, husked
2 tablespoons	½ ounce/15 g	Shallots, chopped
2	10 g	Garlic cloves, chopped
1 cup	4 ounces/112 g	Poblano or Anaheim chiles, roasted, peeled, chopped
¼ cup	½ ounce/15 g	Fresh cilantro, chopped
1	3 tablespoons/2.5 ounces/70 g	Jalapeño pepper, chopped
1 tablespoon	½ ounce/15 ml	Lime juice
		Water
		Salt
For the Tacos		
¼ cup	2 ounces/60 ml	Vegetable oil
8		6-inch (15.2 cm) corn tortillas
1 cup	4 ounces/112 g	Onion, in ¼-inch (.6 cm) dice
½ cup	2 ounces/56 g	Green bell pepper, julienned
½ cup	2 ounces/56 g	Red bell pepper, julienned
1	5 g	Garlic clove, minced
1	1 teaspoon/7 g	Serrano chile, finely diced
2 cups	12 ounces/340 g	Crayfish tails, cooked, shelled, cleaned
2 cups	4 ounces/112 g	Iceberg lettuce, shredded

PROCEDURE

1. Make the sauce. Blanch half the tomatillos in boiling water for 1 minute. Cool quickly. Chop tomatillos and puree with remaining sauce ingredients in a blender. Add water to achieve the desired consistency. Adjust seasoning. Set aside.

2. Prepare the tacos. Heat the oil to 375°F (190°C) and fry the tortillas. Drain on paper towels. While tortillas are still pliable, fold in half, not too tightly as there should be an opening of about 2 inches (5 cm) between the halves at the top. Turn as the tortillas become crisp to make sure they are done on both sides and at the fold at the bottom. (It may be necessary to insert tongs in the middle to keep them from closing up. The result should be a crisp, U-shaped cup.)

3. Reheat the oil and add the onion, peppers, garlic, and serrano. Cook until limp but not soft, 3 minutes. Add the crayfish and cook until hot, approximately 1 minute.

4. Place the crayfish mixture in the tortillas. Top with warm sauce and fill with lettuce.

Cheese Enchiladas

 **CHEF TIP:** This chile gravy is essential for enchiladas, tamales, and a host of other Tex-Mex dishes. Its taste explains Tex-Mex cuisine more eloquently than words ever will. The thick brown gravy with Mexican spices is neither Mexican nor American. It wasn't created in the homes of Texas Mexicans, either. It was invented in old-fashioned Mexican restaurants that catered to Anglo tastes. But what's amazing about it today is the way it illustrates how our tastes have changed.

AMOUNT	MEASURE	INGREDIENT
For the Chile Gravy		
2 tablespoons	1 ounce/28 g	Lard or butter
½ cup	2 ounces/56 g	Onion, in ¼-inch (.6 cm) dice
1	5 g	Garlic clove, minced
¼ cup	1 ounce/28 g	All-purpose flour
2 tablespoons	½ ounce/14 g	Chili powder
2 teaspoons	4 g	Ground cumin
⅛ teaspoon		Dried oregano
2 cups	16 ounces/470 ml	Beef stock
		Salt and pepper
For the Enchiladas		
8		6-inch (15.2 cm) corn tortillas
¼ cup	2 ounces/60 ml	Vegetable oil
½ cup	2 ounces/56 g	Onion, in ¼-inch (.6 cm) dice
2 cups	8 ounces/226 g	Longhorn Cheddar cheese, grated

PROCEDURE

1. Preheat the oven to 400°F (205°C). Lightly grease an 8 x 8 inch (20.3 x 20.3 cm) baking pan or a 10-inch (25.4 cm) skillet.

2. Make the gravy. Melt the lard over medium heat. Sauté the onion and garlic until the onion is softened but not browned, 3 minutes.

3. Stir in the flour, chili powder, cumin, and oregano. Cook for 2 minutes, stirring. Then, add the stock, a little at a time, stirring well to combine. Simmer, uncovered, for 30 minutes, until mixture is reduced and thickened. Adjust thickness and season with salt and pepper.

4. Make the enchiladas. In a sauté pan, heat the oil to 350°F (175°C). Pick up a tortilla with tongs and place it into the hot oil for about 15 seconds. Remove tortilla from the oil, letting the excess oil drip back. Dip the tortilla into the chile gravy, coating both sides.

5. Place the coated tortilla on a flat surface, put a tablespoon of onion and 3 tablespoons cheese on one edge of the tortilla, and roll it up. Place the rolled tortilla seam side down in the prepared pan. Repeat with the remaining tortillas. The pan should be full.

6. Pour the remaining chile gravy on top of the enchiladas. Sprinkle the enchiladas with any remaining onion and grated cheese. Bake for 10 to 15 minutes, or until the cheese is bubbly. Serve immediately.

Arroz Mexicana

AMOUNT	MEASURE	INGREDIENT
2 tablespoons	1 ounce/30 ml	Vegetable oil
1 cup	7 ounces/198 g	Uncooked long-grain rice, rinsed twice
½ cup	2 ounces/56 g	Onion, in ¼-inch (.6 cm) dice
1	5 g	Garlic clove, minced
½ cup	2 ounces/56 g	Carrot, in ¼-inch (.6 cm) dice
1 cup	6 ounces/170 g	Tomato, peeled, in ¼-inch (.6 cm) dice
2 cups	16 ounces/470 ml	Chicken stock
		Salt and pepper

PROCEDURE

1. Heat the oil over medium-high heat. Add the rice and sauté, stirring frequently, until it begins to brown. Stir in the onion and garlic. Cook, stirring constantly, until the rice is nicely browned and has a nutty aroma.

2. Add the carrot, tomato, stock, and salt and pepper. Bring to a simmer, cover, reduce the heat to low, and simmer for approximately 20 minutes.

3. Remove cover and cook 5 minutes longer. Fluff the rice with a fork and serve.

Crayfish Tacos with Green Chile Sauce, Cheese Enchiladas, Arroz Mexicana, and Refried Beans

Refried Beans

 The bacon fat in this recipe can be replaced with a vegetable oil if a more nutritionally sound dish is desired. In the American Southwest, authentic refried beans call for smoking-hot lard to be poured over the cooked, mashed pinto beans and stirred in, thus the name refried beans. Owing to the unusually high cholesterol content of lard, we use a small amount of bacon fat and refry the beans from the bottom instead. A cast-iron frying pan yields the best results; however, a nonstick pan will also work.

AMOUNT	MEASURE	INGREDIENT
1 cup	8 ounces/226 g	Dried pinto beans
1½ quarts	48 ounces/1.5 L	Chicken stock
	2 ounces/56 g	Bacon, in ¼-inch (.6 cm) dice
½ cup	2 ounces/56 g	Onion, in ¼-inch (.6 cm) dice
1	5 g	Garlic clove, minced
		Salt and pepper
1 cup	4 ounces/112 ml	Queso fresco, grated

PROCEDURE

1. Wash and soak the beans overnight or use Quick-soak method (see page 271).

2. Drain the beans and place in a pot. Add the stock, bring to a simmer, turn down the heat, and simmer for approximately 1½ hours, or until tender.

3. Render the bacon in a 10- to 12-inch (25.4–30.5 cm) skillet over medium heat until almost crisp. Add the onion and garlic and cook 4 minutes. Add the beans. Using the back of a large wooden spoon or a potato masher, mash the beans into the bottom of the pan, stirring frequently so they do not stick. When the beans are broken up but still have visible pieces, simmer for an additional 2 to 3 minutes.

4. Season with salt and pepper, and serve with grated cheese.

Flan

**CHEF TIP:** The process of tempering is done in this recipe to prevent the eggs from cooking or scrambling when placed in the scalded milk. To temper the eggs, stir ½ to ⅓ cup (4–6 ounces/120–180 ml) of the scalded milk into the beaten eggs to warm them gradually, and then stir the egg mixture into the remaining scalded milk. Condensed milk has a unique richness and flavor.

AMOUNT	MEASURE	INGREDIENT
¾ cup	6 ounces/169 g	Sugar
1 tablespoon	½ ounce/15 ml	Water
½ teaspoon		Lemon juice
1½ cups	12 ounces/360 ml	Milk
4		Eggs
½ cup	4 ounces/120 ml	Condensed milk
1 tablespoon	½ ounce/15 ml	Vanilla extract

PROCEDURE

1. Preheat the oven to 325°F (163°C).

2. Combine ¼ cup (2 ounces/56 g) sugar, the water, and a few drops of fresh lemon juice in a pan. Over moderate heat, caramelize the sugar, cooking to golden brown. Do not overcook.

3. Pour equal amounts of the caramelized sugar into four 6-ounce (180 ml) ramekins. Set aside.

4. Heat water for a hot-water bath.

5. Heat the milk in a nonreactive pan to just before a simmer.

6. Combine the eggs, remaining ½ cup (4 ounces/120 ml) sugar, the condensed milk, and vanilla and pour in some hot milk to temper the eggs. Stir, then pour in the remainder of the warm milk and strain through a fine-mesh sieve.

7. Pour the custard into the ramekins, and place the ramekins into a baking pan. Place pan into the preheated oven and pour hot water halfway up the side of the molds. Bake until set, 30 to 45 minutes. Test by inserting the blade of a knife into the center of the custard, taking care not to pierce the bottom of the flan. If the blade comes out clean, then it is cooked.

8. Remove from heat and cool completely before unmolding. With the tip of a paring knife, go around the rim, turn the ramekin upside down onto a dessert plate, and shake the ramekin sideways to release the custard.

Caldo de Res

4 servings

 CHEF TIP: This soup is usually eaten for casual lunches; it's not a fancy dish. Caldo de Res is prepared all over Mexico and differs by region. This version is garnished with slices of corn still on the cob.

AMOUNT	MEASURE	INGREDIENT
1	8 ounces/224 g	Beef shank or chuck
2	6 ounces/168 g	Red-skin new potatoes
2	10 ounces/283 g	Carrots, peeled
1	6 ounces/168 g	Onion
1 quart	32 ounces/1 L	Cold water
1		Corn on the cob, in 1-inch (2.5 cm) slices
1 cup	5 ounces/140 g	Green cabbage, in 1-inch (2. 5 cm) dice
½ teaspoon	1 g	Dried thyme
1		Bay leaf
1		Fresh parsley sprig
½ cup	2 ounces/56 g	Zucchini, in 1-inch (2.5 cm) cubes
		Salt and pepper
1 tablespoon	½ ounce/15 ml	Lime juice
2 tablespoons	¼ ounce/7 g	Fresh cilantro, chopped
4		Corn tortillas, warm

PROCEDURE

1. Place the meat, potatoes, carrot, and onion in a large pot and add the water. Add the corn, cabbage, thyme, bay leaf, parsley, salt, and pepper. Bring to a simmer over low heat; simmer until all ingredients are cooked and tender. As ingredients become tender, remove them from the pot. The meat will take longer than the other ingredients. Skim the soup as it simmers.

2. Let the vegetables cool, and cut into 1-inch (2.5 cm) cubes or bite-size pieces. Strain the stock and reduce until very flavorful.

3. Remove the fat and cartilage from the beef. Dice the meat into ½-inch (1.2 cm) pieces.

4. Return the diced meat and chopped vegetables to the broth and bring to a simmer. Add the zucchini and season with salt and pepper. Remove the bay leaf.

5. Add the lime juice and cilantro just before serving.

6. Serve with the tortillas.

Caldo De Res

Gulf Shrimp Corn Dogs with Cabbage and Radish Slaw

4 servings

Gulf Shrimp Corn Dogs

AMOUNT	MEASURE	INGREDIENT
1½ cups	9 ounces/252 g	Cornmeal
1¾ cups	7 ounces/196 g	All-purpose flour
¾ teaspoon	3 g	Baking soda
		Salt and pepper
½ tablespoon	8 ml	Texas honey
¾ cup	6 ounces/180 ml	Buttermilk
½ cup	4 ounces/120 ml	Water
1		Egg
12	10½ ounces/294 g	Shrimp (16–20 count), peeled and deveined
As needed		Vegetable oil

PROCEDURE

1. Soak twelve 6-inch (15.2 cm) skewers in water for 30 minutes.

2. In a bowl, combine the cornmeal, ¾ cup (3 ounces/84 g) of the flour, the baking soda, and ¼ teaspoon (2 g) salt. In another bowl, combine the honey, buttermilk, water, and egg. Add the dry ingredients to the wet all at once, and stir only enough to bring the batter together; there may be lumps. Let rest 10 minutes.

3. Combine the remaining 1 cup (4 ounces/112 g) flour with some salt and pepper.

4. Skewer the shrimp lengthwise starting at the tail end. Season with salt and pepper and dredge in the seasoned flour, tapping to remove any excess. Then dip the shrimp in the batter and roll to make sure they are evenly coated.

5. Heat the oil to 350°F (177°C) in a deep-fryer or deep pot. Deep-fry the shrimp until golden brown on all sides, about 2 to 2½ minutes, until crispy and golden brown. Drain on paper towels.

6. Serve with Remoulade Sauce (recipe follows) and accompany with Cabbage and Radish Slaw (recipe follows).

Gulf Shrimp Corn Dogs with Cabbage and Radish Slaw

Remoulade Sauce

AMOUNT	MEASURE	INGREDIENT
¼ cup	½ ounce/14 g	Green onions, minced
¼ cup	1 ounce/28 g	Celery, minced
2 tablespoons	¼ ounce/7 g	Fresh parsley, minced
2 tablespoons	1 ounce/28 g	Ketchup
2 tablespoons	1 ounce/28 g	Horseradish
½ teaspoon		Tabasco
3 tablespoons	¾ ounce/22 ml	Creole mustard
1 tablespoon	½ ounce/15 ml	White vinegar
1 tablespoon	½ ounce/15 ml	Lemon juice
¼ teaspoon		Paprika
1	5 g	Garlic clove, minced
6 tablespoons	3 ounces/90 ml	Vegetable oil

PROCEDURE   Combine all the ingredients except the oil in a blender or food processor and process until well blended. Gradually add the oil; do not overprocess. Adjust seasoning with additional Tabasco as needed.

Cabbage and Radish Slaw

AMOUNT	MEASURE	INGREDIENT
2 cups	4 ounces/56 g	Green cabbage, very thinly sliced
½ cup	1 ounce/28 g	Red radishes, very thinly sliced
2 tablespoons	1 ounce/30 ml	Cider vinegar
2 tablespoons	1 ounce/30 ml	Olive oil
		Salt and pepper

PROCEDURE   Combine the cabbage and radishes in a bowl, and toss with the vinegar and oil. Season with salt and pepper; set aside to allow vegetables to slightly wilt, about 10 minutes.

Fried Chicken Livers with Bacon Hollandaise on Petite Rosemary Biscuits

✦ **CHEF TIP:** Biscuits should be delicately browned, but not hardened on the outside, moist and light on the inside, and flaky and tender. Once the flour is wet, it develops the sticky, elastic gluten, which becomes more rubbery the more it is worked. So, whereas for bread you knead to develop the gluten, you don't knead biscuit dough. Plus, the liquid added should be cold and the baking pan dusted with flour to prevent sticking but not greased.

Petite Rosemary Biscuits

AMOUNT	MEASURE	INGREDIENT
1 cup	4 ounces/112 g	All-purpose flour
1 teaspoon	4 g	Baking powder
⅛ teaspoon		Baking soda
½ teaspoon	2 g	Salt
3 tablespoons	1½ ounces/44 g	Cold unsalted butter, in small cubes
1 teaspoon	2 g	Fresh rosemary, minced
½–¾ cup	4–6 ounces/120–180 ml	Buttermilk

PROCEDURE

1. Preheat the oven to 400°F (204°C).

2. Sift the dry ingredients together. Work the butter and rosemary into the dry ingredients until mixture resembles coarse crumbs.

3. Add ½ cup (4 ounces/120 ml) buttermilk, a little at a time, mixing until all ingredients are thoroughly incorporated and a smooth ball of dough forms. Add more buttermilk if the dough is too dry but do not overwork the dough or the biscuits will not be light and fluffy.

4. On a lightly floured surface, form dough into a circle about 7 inches (17.8 cm) in diameter and ½ inch (1.3 cm) thick. Using a 1-inch (2.5 cm) round cookie cutter, cut out 12 biscuits.

5. Bake until golden on top and lightly brown on the bottom, 10 to 12 minutes.

6. When ready to serve, split biscuits in half and toast under broiler for 1 minute.

Fried Chicken Livers with Bacon Hollandaise on Petite Rosemary Biscuits

Fried Chicken Livers

AMOUNT	MEASURE	INGREDIENT
16	8 ounces/224 g	Chicken livers, deveined
1 cup	8 ounces/240 ml	Buttermilk
1 tablespoon	½ ounce/15 ml	Hot sauce
2 cups	8 ounces/224 g	All-purpose flour
		Salt and pepper
2 tablespoons		Fresh parsley, minced
As needed		Vegetable oil

PROCEDURE

1. Combine the livers, buttermilk, and hot sauce in a bowl. Marinate 2 hours or more in the refrigerator.

2. Heat the oil to 350°F (177°C) in a deep-fryer or deep pot.

3. Season the flour with a little salt and pepper.

4. Drain the livers and season with salt and pepper, dredge in the seasoned flour and shake off excess. Deep-fry livers until golden brown and livers float, about 2 to 3 minutes. Drain on a wire rack. Reserve the parsley for the garnish after assembly.

Bacon Hollandaise

AMOUNT	MEASURE	INGREDIENT
6 tablespoons	3 ounces/84 g	Unsalted butter
1 cup	4 ounces/112 g	Bacon, diced
3		Egg yolks
		Lemon juice
		Salt
2 tablespoons		Warm water
		Cayenne pepper

PROCEDURE

1. Combine the butter and bacon in a 2-quart (2 L) saucepan over low heat. Cook until bacon is rendered and pieces are crispy, about 5 minutes. Strain and reserve both the fat and crispy bacon.

2. Combine the egg yolks, lemon juice, and a pinch of salt in a stainless steel bowl. Place the bowl over a hot water bath and add the warm water; whisk until frothy, then continue whisking until mixture reaches the ribbon stage. The mixture should have a light but firm consistency and triple in volume.

3. Remove from heat and gradually add the bacon fat, whisking constantly to form an emulsified sauce. Adjust the seasoning with additional lemon juice, salt, and the cayenne pepper.

To Assemble and Serve

Spoon a small amount of Bacon Hollandaise on a plate. Place four toasted halves of biscuits on each plate and top each biscuit half with a chicken liver. Spoon the sauce over the livers and garnish with crispy bacon pieces and parsley.

Redfish on the Half Shell with Grilled Red Onion and Frisée Salad

4 servings

✦ CHEF TIP: This is a classic Texas dish: the "half shell" is the scales-on skin of the filleted fish. The dish is traditionally cooked outdoors because, in the first few minutes of cooking, the burning scales give off an aroma that is less than appetizing.

AMOUNT	MEASURE	INGREDIENT
6 tablespoons	3 ounces/84 g	Butter, softened
1 tablespoon	½ ounce/8 g	Shallots, minced
1 tablespoon	2 g	Fresh cilantro, minced
½ teaspoon		Chili powder
½ teaspoon		Paprika
4	6–8 ounces/168–224 g each	Boned redfish, snapper, drum, or sea bass, skin and scales left on
1 tablespoon	½ ounce/15 ml	Vegetable oil
		Salt and pepper
12		Lemon slices, very thin
4	8 ounces/224 g	Red onions, in ¼ inch (.6 cm) slices, grilled
2 cups	4 ounces/112 g	Frisée lettuce
4 tablespoons	2 ounces/60 ml	Balsamic vinegar

PROCEDURE

1. Preheat the grill to medium.

2. Combine the butter, shallots, cilantro, chili powder, and paprika in a bowl. Whip until fluffy or doubled in volume.

3. Brush the skin of the fish fillets with vegetable oil. Flip and season with salt and pepper. Coat with 1 tablespoon (½ ounce/28 g) of the butter mixture. Top with 3 lemon slices.

4. Place fish, skin side down, on grill and cover with a piece of aluminum foil. Cook, basting every 2 to 3 minutes, with remaining butter mixture, for 8 to 10 minutes or until fish are cooked.

5. Toss the grilled red onion and frisée lettuce with vinegar.

6. Serve each filet with warm onion salad.

Redfish on the Half Shell with Grilled Red Onion and Frisée Salad

Pecan Squares

✦ **CHEF TIP:** Pecans are the only nut native to the United States, grown on a commercial scale. The Pecan tree was designated the official state tree of Texas in 1919 (and the pecan was adopted as the state nut in 2001). Remarkably long lived, the pecan can survive more than a thousand years and grow over 100 feet tall. Many American Indians relied on pecans as an important food staple; they gathered wild pecans and combined them with fruits and vegetables (including beans, corn, and squashes), created an energy drink with pecan milk, used ground pecan meal to thicken meat stews, and included roasted pecans as part of their travel supplies to sustain them along the journey when food was scarce.

AMOUNT	MEASURE	INGREDIENT
For the Crust		
1 cup	4 ounces/120 g	All-purpose flour
¼ teaspoon		Baking powder
4 tablespoons	2 ounces/56 g	Unsalted butter, at room temperature
⅓ cup	2½ ounces/74 g	Light brown sugar
½ teaspoon		Vanilla extract
¼ cup	1 ounce/28 g	Pecans, finely chopped
For the Filling		
2		Eggs
¼ cup (packed)	2 ounces/56 g	Light brown sugar
¾ cup	6 ounces/180 ml	Dark or light corn syrup
2 tablespoons	¾ ounce/20 g	All-purpose flour
¼ teaspoon		Salt
1 teaspoon		Vanilla extract
¾ cup	2½ ounces/75 g	Pecans, chopped

PROCEDURE

1. Preheat the oven to 350°F (177°C). Grease a 9-inch (23 cm) square baking pan.

2. Make the crust. Sift together the flour and baking powder in a small bowl. In a larger bowl, cream the butter and brown sugar until soft and fluffy, 2 to 3 minutes, then add the vanilla. Add the flour mixture and combine until it resembles coarse meal; do not overmix. Sir in the pecans.

3. Press the mixture into the prepared pan and bake for 10 minutes or until lightly browned. Cool on a wire rack. Keep oven on.

4. Make the filling. Beat the eggs until foamy. Add the brown sugar, corn syrup, flour, salt, and vanilla. Pour over the baked crust and sprinkle with the pecans.

5. Bake for 25 to 30 minutes or until firm and browned. Cool in the pan before cutting into squares.

Pecan Squares

Tex-Mex Fajitas

4 servings

 CHEF TIP: Texans would love to be able to lay claim to having originated fajitas, but the honor goes to the south-of-the-border vaqueros who learned to make good use of a tough and membranous cut of beef known as "skirt steak." Before fajitas became popular throughout the United States, skirt steak was a cheap cut of meat scorned by all but the most dedicated beefeaters. The Mexican term for grilled skirt steak is *arracheras,* and its American counterpart is *fajitas.* Therefore, the term "chicken fajitas" is not truly possible. But these days, *fajita* has come to describe just about anything cooked and eaten, rolled up, in a flour tortilla.

Fajitas start with the marinade. Marinades for beef fajitas rely on acid ingredients like lime juice, not just for flavor but also to tenderize the meat. So that the marinade will have time to work, beef fajitas should be marinated several hours or up to 24 hours. The skirt steak is the traditional cut used and was reserved primarily for the chief cowboy. Other cuts of beef can be substituted, such as flank steak or sirloin, but the skirt is by far the most tender, flavorful, and authentic.

You might wonder where the cast-iron griddle with the sizzling bell peppers and onions are in this recipe. While such a serving method may be dramatic, it is an affectation developed mainly by chain restaurants and is not a part of authentic Tex-Mex fajitas.

AMOUNT	MEASURE	INGREDIENT
For Marinade I		
⅓ cup	2½ ounces/78 ml	Lime juice
¼ cup	2 ounces/55 ml	Tequila
1 teaspoon	1 g	Dried Mexican oregano
2	10 g	Garlic cloves, crushed
1 tablespoon	3 g	Fresh cilantro, minced
2 teaspoons	4 g	Ground cumin
1 teaspoon	2 g	Black pepper
For Marinade II		
1 cup	8 ounces/235 ml	Light soy sauce
¼ cup	2 ounces/156 g	Brown sugar, packed
1 teaspoon	2 g	Garlic powder
1 teaspoon	2 g	Onion powder
2 tablespoons	1 ounce/28 ml	Lemon juice
1 teaspoon	5 g	Ground ginger
For the Fajitas		
1	1 pound/453 g	Skirt steak
8		8-inch flour tortillas, warmed

1. Prepare either marinade by combining all the ingredients and refrigerating overnight.

2. Marinate the steak in either marinade for 2 hours at room temperature or overnight in the refrigerator.

3. Preheat the grill to hot.

4. Pat the meat dry and add to the grill. Sear the outside, then cook until medium-rare, 3 to 4 minutes on each side if the meat is ¾ inch (1.9 cm) thick or less. Brush the meat with the marinade two or three times while cooking

5. Transfer the meat to a cutting board. Let sit 5 minutes, then cut into thin strips.

6. Serve with warmed flour tortillas and Pico de Gallo (page 278) and Guacamole (page 277).

Braggin' Rights Brisket

8 servings

CHEF TIP: Hardwoods such as hickory, pecan, or oak are very slow burning and are the best for smoking. Mesquite, although aromatic and great for grilling, burns too hot for good barbeque and leaves an oily taste. True Texas barbeque takes place in a long, narrow pit. A fire is built at one end and the meat is put several inches from it. The meat cooks slowly at very low temperature for up to 6 hours, during which time it is basted with sauce.

AMOUNT	MEASURE	INGREDIENT
		Hickory, pecan, or mesquite chips
1	4 pounds/1.8 kg	Beef brisket
2 teaspoons	4 g	Black pepper
1 teaspoon	2 g	Cayenne pepper
1 teaspoon	2 g	Onion salt
½ teaspoon	1 g	Dry mustard
2 tablespoons	½ ounce/14 g	Salt

PROCEDURE

1. Preheat the grill or the oven to 450°F (232°C).

2. Season the brisket with the peppers, onion salt, and mustard. Sear the brisket in a roasting pan for 5 minutes on each side, until browned thoroughly.

3. Prepare the smoker.

4. Place the brisket in the smoker and smoke for 1 hour. Sprinkle with the salt and smoke for an additional 1 hour.

5. Preheat the oven to 300°F (149°C).

6. Remove brisket from the smoker, cover with foil, and roast until fork-tender, about 1 hour.

7. Remove the brisket from the oven and let rest for 25 minutes, covered loosely with aluminum foil. Reserve the rendered fat from the brisket for preparing the Barbeque Sauce (recipe follows).

8. Slice the rested brisket across the grain. Serve on hot plates and top with sauce.

Braggin' Rights Brisket

Barbeque Sauce

CHEF TIP: Hot pepper sauce comes in hundreds of varieties, flavors, and levels of heat. Tabasco is one of the most popular, but experiment until you find the one that yields the flavor for your own barbeque sauce.

AMOUNT	MEASURE	INGREDIENT
½ cup	4 ounces/112 g	Rendered fat
⅓ cup	1½ ounces/43g	Onion, in small dice
1½ cups	12 ounces/352 ml	Ketchup
½ cup	4 ounces/115 ml	Worcestershire sauce
½ cup	4 ounces/115 ml	Lemon juice
⅓ cup	2½ ounces/71g	Brown sugar
6 tablespoons	3 ounces/84 ml	Water
		Hot pepper sauce

PROCEDURE

1. Heat the rendered fat in a small saucepot. Add the onion and sauté until translucent, 3 minutes.

2. Add the ketchup, Worcestershire sauce, and lemon juice. Lower the heat and stir in the brown sugar and water. Simmer for 15 minutes. Season to taste with hot pepper sauce.

Homemade Tamales

✧ **CHEF TIP:** The shredded beef and pork here can also be prepared by simmering the meats in water until fork-tender. A chicken filling can be made by boiling chicken with seasonings such as cumin, chili powder, garlic, and salt; once cooked, the chicken meat is shredded. Simply substituting refried beans for the shredded meat can make bean tamales. A thin slice of jalapeño or a strip of fried bacon can be added to the beans for extra flavor, if desired.

Making genuine, homemade Tex-Mex tamales is a three-day process: one day to prepare the meat filling, a second day to prepare and roll the tamales, and a third day to steam and serve the tamales. However, there are ways to speed this process. One way is to substitute coarse-ground pork and/or beef for the shredded meats.

AMOUNT	MEASURE	INGREDIENT
1	12 ounces/340 g	Pork butt roast
1	6 ounces/170 g	Beef chuck roast or bottom round
5	1 ounce/28 g	Ancho chiles
1 tablespoon	½ ounce/15 g	Garlic, minced
1 cup	8 ounces/224 g	Lard
1 tablespoon	¼ ounce/7 g	Ground cumin
1 teaspoon	3 g	Black pepper
½ teaspoon	1 g	Dried oregano
		Salt
18		Cornhusks
	1½ pounds/680 g *or*	Masa *or*
	12 ounces/340 g	Masa harina
1 tablespoon	¼ ounce/7 g	Chili powder
1 tablespoon	¼ ounce/7 g	Paprika
3 tablespoons	¾ ounce/21 g	Garlic powder

PROCEDURE

DAY 1

1. Preheat the oven to 300°F (149°C).

2. Place the pork and beef in a roasting pan, cover, and roast for approximately 4 hours, or until the meats are fork-tender. While still warm, pull apart or shred the meat.

3. Remove the stems from the ancho chiles and split open the pods along one side. Rinse the chiles under cold running water. Rinse the seeds from the chiles and discard them. Place the chiles in a pot of water, cover, and simmer for 15 minutes.

4. Remove the chiles from the water and scrape the pulp from the skin. Discard the skin. Chop the pulp and reserve both the pulp and liquid until needed.

5. Sauté the garlic in 2 tablespoons (1 ounce/30 g) of the lard.

6. Combine the meat, garlic, chile pulp, and the cumin, pepper, and oregano. Season with salt. Cover and refrigerate overnight to allow the flavors to develop and permeate the meats.

(continued) →

DAY 2

1. Soak the cornhusks in water for at least 2 hours. Separate them one by one and stack them ready for use.

2. Prepare the dough by combining the masa or masa harina with the remaining ¾ cup (7 ounces/210 g) lard, the chili powder, paprika, and garlic powder. Using the reserved chile-cooking water, adjust the consistency of the dough as needed. Blend well. The more air that is incorporated into the masa dough, the better, as it will result in moist and fluffy tamales. It is impossible to overmix this dough.

3. To form the tamales, place an unbroken cornhusk on a tray or work surface in front of you with the small end away from you. Using a spatula or masa spreader, spread approximately 1 to 2 tablespoons (½–1 ounce/14–28 g) of dough on the cornhusk to cover the lower two-thirds and right 4 inches (10.2 cm). The masa should be spread thick enough so that you cannot see through to the husk.

4. Place the desired amount of meat filling in the middle of the masa. Seal by rolling it over, starting from the right side where the masa and meat are. The unspread side covers the outside of the tamale and holds it together. Fold the unfilled end at the top over to the middle. Tie the tamale, if necessary, with thin strips torn from a soaked cornhusk. Repeat to form remaining tamales, then cover the tamales and store overnight in the refrigerator.

DAY 3

1. Set up a steamer in a large saucepan with an elevated bottom and tight-fitting lid. Add water to the saucepan until it reaches just under the elevated bottom. Place the tamales on the elevated bottom, standing them shoulder to shoulder with the open ends facing up. Cover the saucepan and steam for about 1 hour or until the masa peels away from the husk. Check the water level from time to time and add water to keep the pot from boiling dry.

2. Let the tamales rest for 10 to 15 minutes to firm up before serving.

3. To serve, remove the tamales from their cornhusks. Fold the cornhusks and place one on each hot serving plate. Place 2 to 3 tamales, depending on size, on top of the husks.

Kale Chips

✤ **CHEF TIP:**   Kale is a green leafy vegetable that belongs to the same family as cabbage.

AMOUNT	MEASURE	INGREDIENT
1 cup (packed)	2½ ounces/70 g	Kale leaves
1 tablespoon	½ ounce/15 ml	Olive oil
		Sea salt
		Cayenne pepper

PROCEDURE

1. Preheat the oven to 425°F (218°C). Line a baking sheet with parchment.

2. Separate the kale leaves from the stalks and tear into large pieces. Toss with the olive oil; rub leaves between fingertips to coat both sides. Sprinkle with salt and cayenne.

3. Place kale on baking sheet, separating the leaves. Bake until the edges just begin to turn brown, approximately 5 minutes. Turn the leaves over and bake on other side for another 3 to 5 minutes, until crisp. Watch closely, as the leaves can burn quickly.

The Cuisine of the
Southwest and the
Rocky Mountain Region

Several different groups, each with its own proud history and traditions, have contributed to the Southwest's distinct character. The Native Americans in the area that are now the states of New Mexico and Arizona have had more success maintaining their languages, religions, and traditions than American Indians in other parts of the United States. The Hispanics of the region are proud of their long history. Many of their families were granted land by the Spanish Crown long before the United States existed. Although they have had to adapt to many changes over the centuries, their pride in their heritage is unwavering. In the Rocky Mountain states—Colorado, Idaho, Montana, Utah, and Wyoming—the miners, cowboys, and frontier families that ventured into this once harsh and remote land had a courage and self-reliance that is reflected in the independent streak of their sons and daughters.

Arizona   "The Grand Canyon State," where the Arizona trout is the state fish, the state reptile is the ridge-nosed rattlesnake, the state neckware is the bolo tie, and the state flower is the saguaro cactus blossom.

Colorado   "The Centennial State," where the state animal is the Rocky Mountain bighorn sheep, the state fish is the green cutthroat trout, and the state folk dance is the square dance.

Idaho   "The Gem State," known for the state fruit, which is the huckleberry; the state vegetable is the potato, and the state fish is the cutthroat trout.

Montana   "The Treasure State," also known as "Big Sky Country" and the "Mountain State," has the state fish as the blackspotted cutthroat trout and the state animal as the grizzly bear.

New Mexico   Considered the "Land of Enchantment," New Mexico has chiles and pinto beans as the state vegetables, the piñon pine as the state tree, the Rio Grande cutthroat trout as the state fish, and the roadrunner as the state bird. The state cookie is the bizcochito and the New Mexico state question is: "Red or green?" (as in the state's most famous vegetable, chile). The answer? Both!

Utah   "The Beehive State," where the state fruit includes both sweet and tart cherries, the state vegetable is the Spanish sweet onion, the state historic vegetable is the sugar beet, the state animal is the Rocky Mountain elk, and the state cooking pot is the Dutch oven.

Wyoming "The Evergreen State," also known as the "Cowboy State," "Big Wyoming," and the "Equality State," where bison is the state mammal, cutthroat trout is the state fish, and the state sport is the rodeo.

HISTORY AND MAJOR INFLUENCES

THE DEVELOPMENT OF SOUTHWESTERN CUISINE

When the Spanish first came to the Southwest, they found 98 Native American settlements, called pueblos, along the Rio Grande. The Spanish were amazed to discover that the Native Americans had already developed an irrigation system capable of bringing enough water to the desert fields to sustain a variety of local crops, primarily consisting of corn, squash, and beans. The tribes that have most significantly influenced the cuisine of this area include the Navajo, Pima, Hopi, Pueblo, and Zuni. Typically, food for the Native Americans meant much more than simple sustenance; it had religious and cultural implications as well. The Pima tribe is known to have lived in this region since the fourth century. The Pima were descendants of the ancient Hohokam tribe and were known for their expertise in growing beans—so great that they were also referred to as the Papago, or "bean people."

The Navajo tribe migrated from arctic regions in the 13th century. Originally, the Navajo were nomadic hunters and gatherers, but after arriving in the region, they adapted to some of the agrarian ways of the Pueblo tribes already living in the area. When the Europeans arrived in the region and brought with them sheep, cattle, and horses, the Navajo learned to be herders as well as farmers. The Hopi tribe is considered to have made the most significant contributions to cooking. The Hopi, descendants of the ancient Anasazi tribe, cultivated many varieties of squash, beans, and corn. They learned to cook in beehive-shaped ovens, called hornos, made of adobe clay, and frequently used cooking vessels made of fired pottery ornately decorated with geometric patterns to boil foods.

THE SPANIARDS ARRIVE

The first Europeans to venture into this region were the Spanish. In 1540, Coronado led an expedition north from Mexico in search of the Seven Cities of Cibola, where the streets were allegedly paved with gold. Finding only mud huts and hostile Indians, Coronado returned home to Mexico, discouraged and disgraced. In the following decades, the Spaniards returned and solidified their control over the area.

The introduction of meats other than wild game is attributed to the Spanish, who brought livestock with them. Capitán General Juan de Onate introduced sheep to the region in 1598, and by the 1880s, millions of sheep, cattle, and hogs were being raised, many of which were shipped to other regions of the United States. The Spanish also grew crops and introduced wheat flour to the Native Americans. Wheat became so popular that it was planted all over the region, and by the 16th century, it was more common in the American West than in Spain. Eventually, flour tortillas became as popular as corn tortillas, the original staple bread of the region. They also introduced peaches, apricots, and apples. As they had in other areas of the country, especially in Texas, the Spanish introduced many varieties of chiles that were integrated into the cuisine.

THE NATIVE AMERICANS AND THE THREE SISTERS OF FOOD

The "three sisters"—corn, beans, and squash—are the New World foods indigenous to the Southwest and Rocky Mountains. These foods supported the Native Americans and early European settlers of the region. The crops were easy to dry and store for long periods and, when eaten together, provided a complete source of protein. The farming techniques are also designed to be harmonious. When all three crops are planted together, the tall stalks of corn provide the vertical structure to which the bean plants cling, and the squash vines help provide shade and control weeds by forming a groundcover. The Native American Indians believed that corn was given to them by the corn maiden as a life-giving grain. It is the food that has the most cultural significance for them.

Corn in the region comes in six colors—red, white, blue, black, yellow, and variegated—which many Native American tribes associate with the six directions of the compass. The Zuni tribe believed that if dried corn kernels were scattered in the path of the Spanish conquistadors, they would be protected from the invaders. The Hopi tribe used each of the six colors of corn for distinctly different purposes, many religious in nature. Native Americans learned to use wood ash while cooking cornbread, and discovered that wood ash could be used as a seasoning and leavening agent.

Another of the three sisters foods is beans. Native Americans used wild beans in their diets almost 7,000 years ago. Beans, when combined and eaten with grains, seeds, or nuts, provide all the amino acids needed to create complete proteins. The Europeans, until the 15th century, were familiar with only a few varieties of beans, such as fava and broad beans, but were introduced to a large variety of New World beans by the Native Americans of the Southwest. The most common beans utilized today in the American Southwest are the pinto bean and its smaller relative, the pinquito. However, a number of ancient varieties, called "heirloom beans," are experiencing a resurgence in the United States.

The last member of the food triad is squash. Summer squash such as zucchini, yellow squash, and numerous varieties of Indian squash are all grown in the Southwest. This culturally important food staple is often referred to by its Spanish name, *calabacitas*. By the 19th century, many tribes raised a variety of fruits including peaches, figs, and apricots. Most of this fruit was dried for winter use.

Indians used a variety of implements—such as stone mortars—to grind or pulverize their foods. They shelled or hulled seeds and ground meat to tenderize it. They soaked corn in water mixed with wood ashes (forming lye) to turn the corn into hominy. Both fish and meat were pulverized and then mixed with berries and fat to form a nutrient rich, easy-to-carry food source. If it contained meat, this mixture was known as pemmican and was stored in a buffalo-skin bag.

CORN

Corn is one of the sacred plants of the Southwest; it has been cultivated by the Hopis for over 2,000 years. This grain must be planted deliberately, as corn plants cannot naturally sow their own seed. Every part of the corn was used, including the husks, which were used as the wrapping for tamales; the cornmeal dough, called "masa," was used to fill tamales and to prepare corn tortillas. Blue corn is culturally and religiously the single most important corn variety grown by the Native Americans of the Southwest. Used extensively by the Hopi, Navajo, and Pueblo tribes, the blue color occurs naturally in Indian corn. Dishes made with blue corn have a flavor that is both rich and earthy. The distinctive flavor is attributed to the drying of the kernels over a piñon wood fire. Blue corn can be used in most Southwest dishes that call for yellow corn; however, it is softer and less starchy than other Indian corns. Owing to its tendency to crumble, blue corn may need to be blended with a little wheat flour before use.

BEANS

Heirloom beans are any of the ancient wild and cultivated beans indigenous to the Southwest and once eaten by Native Americans. Heirloom beans have recently been revived in the region and are grown by specialty farmers who support and subscribe to the techniques of preservation agriculture. They include:

Anasazi Bean   Also known as "New Mexico cave beans," this bean was cultivated by the earliest Native Americans and may be the forerunner of the pinto bean. A purple, red, and white bean, it cooks in about two-thirds the time of an ordinary pinto bean and has less of the specific carbohydrate that causes gastric distress. From the Navajo word that means "ancient ones," the Anasazi bean is trademarked by Adobe Mills, a privately owned company.

More and more restaurants are taking steps toward lessening their carbon footprint on the environment—which is important, considering the restaurant industry produces a lot of waste in food, water, and energy.

Government-Backed Certifications

Energy Star   Partnered with the U.S. Environmental Protection Agency and the U.S. Department of Energy, Energy Star is a program designed to identify and advocate energy-efficient products and practices. Energy Star distinguishes environmentally friendly products based on their specifications regarding energy consumption and water usage. Energy Star also delivers technical information and educational resources to consumers looking for energy-efficient solutions in their homes or businesses.

Non-Profit Organizations

U.S. Green Building Council, LEED Green Building Rating System   The Leadership in Energy and Environmental Design (LEED) Green Building Rating System sets the national standard for the certification of high-performance green buildings. With government-backed statistics and industry-specific information, LEED provides owners and operators the resources to design, construct, and operate environmentally responsible, healthy, and cost-effective places to live and work. A LEED certification is available for buildings compliant with all aspects of the program.

Green Seal   Green Seal is a nonprofit organization promoting the manufacture, purchase, and use of ecologically responsible products and services. Green Seal provides a scientifically based certification process, evaluating the product from its production, through its use, and ending with its disposal. The application processes involve recording data, testing equipment, providing product samples, and finally an audit of the facility.

Green Restaurant Association   The Green Restaurant Association (GRA) is a nonprofit organization focused on research, education, and marketing for communities and establishments looking to go green. The GRA personally advises restaurants with economic analyses, educational material, and community coordination, all of which help direct restaurants toward a more sustainable environment.

Some of the ways these organizations award points toward their certification include:

Water Efficiency   Points in the water efficiency category are awarded for low-water landscaping, low-flow plumbing in the kitchen, water-efficient fixtures in the restrooms, Energy Star laundry facilities, on-site water treatment and more. Flow restrictors on faucets limit the amount of water used in hand washing sinks, on dish machines and dish sinks. B.R. Guests Restaurants, in New York City, saved 5 million gallons of water a year by installing flow restrictors as part of their Go Green effort.

Waste   The majority of available points in the waste category come from waste diversion techniques. Pre-consumer composting is good for 17.5 points while post-consumer composting is good for another 7.5 points. Converting grease to biodiesel can earn 2.5 points for a restaurant while diverting cardboard and paper waste is good for another eight points.

Sustainable Furnishings and Building Materials   Chairs, tables, booths, window treatments flooring, countertops, cabinetry, and all other materials used inside a restaurant are assessed when points are awarded in the sustainable furnishings and building materials categories. Products using salvaged, recycled or rapidly renewable materials can qualify for three points. FSC Certified or reused wood is also good for three points per product.

Sustainable   Food Ideally, green restaurants should serve eco-friendly food. Points are awarded for certified organic nonmeat items, free-range meats, seafood from the Monterey Bay Seafood Guide's "green list," vegan and vegetarian products, and locally sourced food items.

Energy   A restaurant's heating, cooling, ventilation, water heating, lighting, appliances and office equipment can earn

---

Appaloosa Bean   Named after the spotted horse, this bean is black and white or red and white. These beans are quick to cook and are frequently used in place of pinto beans.

Bollito Bean   Smaller than the pinto, it has a better flavor and is beige in color. This bean takes a little longer to cook than pintos and is usually boiled.

Jacob's Cattle Bean   Originating in Germany, this bean is similar to appaloosa beans but is white and maroon in color. They are fairly sweet in flavor and may be referred to as trout beans or Dalmation beans.

Pinto Bean   The most widely used bean is this country. A variation of the kidney bean, it is a pinkish beige color and slightly streaked.

Tepary Bean   This earthy-flavored bean was domesticated by prehistoric Native Indians and was of particular ceremonial importance to the Zuni. The tepary is rarely cultivated because it

points in the energy category. Additionally, using on-site renewable energy or purchasing renewable energy credits will earn a restaurant additional points. A typical restaurant can save up to $15,000 every year by using green restaurant equipment such as stoves, refrigerators, freezers, dishwashers, and more. Just installing an energy-efficient air-conditioning unit can save up to $1,500 a year. A programmable thermostat will turn off the system when it is not needed further adds to the cost savings.

Recycled and Bio-based Disposables

Restaurants that use reusable napkins and hand towels can instantly earn 13 points towards Green Restaurant Certification. In addition, a restaurant's food service disposables and tissue and office paper will be scored.

Certified Green Commercial Kitchen

Established by FoodServiceWarehouse.com, the Certified Green Commercial Kitchen program assists commercial kitchens in taking steps toward becoming more sustainable. This comprehensive program covers five keys areas: energy conservation, water conservation, waste reduction, green cleaning, and education.

Enerlogic

The Enodis Enerlogic program recognizes energy savings relative to the consumption of water, electricity and gas, and identifies the most energy-efficient Enodis commercial kitchen equipment for the environmentally minded consumer. Products qualify for the Enerlogic stamp of approval when they meet requirements set forth by outside organizations like Energy Star, CEE, the Federal Energy Management Program (FEMP), and the LEED Green Building Rating System.

Recycling

The recycling symbol has gained worldwide recognition as concerned consumers have become more committed to environmental conservation. The symbol represents a triad of sustainable activities: reduce, reuse,and recycle. Commonly seen on paper, plastic and glass containers, the recycling symbol cues people to recycle rather than simply throw things away.

The following are recyclable materials:

Aluminum Nearly everything aluminum can be made from recycled aluminum. Recycling just one ton of aluminum cans saves the energy equivalent of 1,665 gallons of gasoline.

Food Waste As much as 70 percent of all restaurant waste is food waste. Food waste can be composted to create a nutrient rich soil additive. Farms, greenhouses, and even home gardens can benefit from composted food waste.

Cardboard Old cardboard boxes can be donated to charities for reuse or sent to a recycling facility to make new cardboard and other paper products. Recycling one ton of cardboard saves 460 gallons of oil.

Glass Glass can be reused an infinite number of times. Anything made of glass can be recycled into new glass products. Recycling a single glass bottle saves enough energy to power a 100W light bulb for four hours.

Paper All non-glossy paper can be recycled into several products including newspaper, bathroom tissue, and kitty litter. Every ton of paper recycled saves energy equivalent to 185 gallons of gasoline.

Plastic Recycled plastic can be used to create several products ranging from mop heads to t-shirts. Five two-liter recycled bottles can produce enough insulation for a men's ski jacket.

Steel Recycled steel can be made into steel cans, building supplies and tools. Steel recycling saves enough energy in one year to power 18 million homes for that entire year.

Used Fryer Oil Fryer oil can be turned into biodiesel, a popular alternative fuel. Rather than paying to have your oil taken away, biodiesel companies are actually paying restaurants for this resource.

---

can harbor a mold spore that is deadly to other varieties of bean. They are variegated in color and come in a number of sizes and shapes.

SQUASH

Squashes are native to the Southwest and were cultivated by a number of Southwestern Indian tribes. As one of the "three sisters" of the Southwest, squash was of ceremonial importance. It was eaten in all stages of development and was sun-dried for winter consumption. The Spanish settlers introduced new varieties to the region that included:

Acorn Squash A sweet winter squash that is dark green on the outside with orange flesh. Often baked whole.

Butternut Squash   Tan, creamy, and sweet, it is shaped like a bowling pin.

Chayote Squash   Also known as a vegetable pear, it is pale green to cream in color, with smooth skin and a flavor similar to zucchini.

Pumpkin Squash   Familiar orange-colored squash. The seeds may be dried and salted, ground, and used as an ingredient for regional sauces.

Hubbard Squash   Oversized with yellow flesh and gray outside.

Turban Squash   A multicolored squash rich in flavor, much like pumpkin or butternut squash.

THE MEXICAN INFLUENCE

The spiciness and high seasoning of many traditional dishes are similar to those used in the Mexican states of Chihuahua and Sonora—typically, not simple but rich and complex. Flavors derived from different chiles, herbs, and seasonings are generally used to attain the characteristics of American Southwest cuisine.

MAJOR INFLUENCES IN THE ROCKY MOUNTAIN STATES

The most significant influence in the region was the rapid settlement of the American West in the mid-1800s, before the transcontinental railroad was built. Prospectors and others heading to the gold rush of California traveled two main routes: the Oregon Trail and the Santa Fe Trail. The northern route, the Oregon Trail, began in Missouri, crossed the Rocky Mountains into Utah, and veered north through Idaho and into Oregon, while the Santa Fe Trail took a more southerly route through Colorado into New Mexico. The first known group to follow the Oregon Trail left Independence, Missouri, in 1842, and, over the next two decades, hundreds of thousands of settlers left their homes to follow the quest for gold. The Mormons, however, followed the Oregon Trail for religious freedom. The Mormons left Illinois in the winter of 1846 to move their church to the west. They veered south once in the Great Basin of Utah, and by the end of 1847, some 5,000 pioneers had settled in the Salt Lake Valley.

In the 1820s, Mexico finalized its independence from Spain, and the Santa Fe Trail from Missouri to New Mexico opened. This caused the city of Santa Fe to become a trading hub for the region. During the Civil War, Congress passed the Homestead Act of 1862, offering 160 acres of land free to any citizen or intended citizen who was head of the household. From 1862 to 1900, up to 600,000 families took advantage of the government's offer. In the late 1880s, railroad companies laid their tracks across the Southwest, bringing with them improved commerce and access to new markets. Thousands of settlers from the East began to arrive in masses. The beef industry boomed, creating vast cattle kingdoms on the southeastern plains, and by the 1900s, the settlers who had brought modern tools and farming techniques had transformed over five million acres of land into fertile farms.

THE PIONEERS

The areas first tracked by trappers, prospectors, and trailblazers began to attract farmers and families and other pioneers by the 1840s. The Oregon Trail—nothing more than two wagon ruts—was blazed in 1841; by the mid-1840s, a trickle of pioneers had made that long walk west. Their daily sustenance included sourdough breads, quick breads, salt pork preparations, wild game and fish, and what could be foraged from the forests, mountain valleys, and plains. Their "prairie schooners," or covered wagons, were piled high with flour, beans, bacon, dried fruit, coffee, salt, and vinegar. Their cooking styles were similar to that of the cowboys who ate chuckwagon cooking in Texas. In the late 1800s and early 1900s, German-Russian immigrants came to homestead and farm. They found that the San Luis Valley in Colorado did not have to depend on rivers for its water supply. The valley has artesian wells that do not need pumps to bring the water to the surface. This enabled the valley to be turned into an important agricultural area, where a variety of vegetables, especially potatoes, are grown.

The Basque people who emigrated from southwestern France and northern Spain came to the West as sheepherders who worked on the ranches of Idaho, Nevada, and Wyoming. In many remote areas, thriving communities of Basque descendants developed. Hearty stews of beef, chicken, and lamb flavored with onions, garlic tomatoes, bell peppers, and herbs best describe the Basque contribution to the cooking of the region. The largest Basque community in existence today, outside of Europe, is in Boise, Idaho. The Basque restaurants found in America today are known for their family-style service and many courses of hearty food, served on long communal tables.

Much of the wild game enjoyed for its own sake today in the Rocky Mountains was first eaten out of necessity; today, game is considered a delicacy. Fowl, venison, boar, and bison thrive in the mountains of the region. But today, the game animals served in restaurants are not considered true wild game. Because the U.S. Department of Agriculture does not inspect wild game, the meat served in commercial food-service operations is raised in closely controlled environments and developed specifically for the industry by game farms and ranches. Considered to be low in fat, game available to the public is increasingly popular.

Typical **Southwestern** and **Rocky Mountain** Ingredients and Dishes

Achiote   The seed of the tropical annatto tree. Also referred to as "annatto seeds," achiote is used commercially as a natural orange coloring agent for butter and cheese. Achiote is also a useful ingredient when sautéing, as it imparts a vibrant yellow-orange tint to proteins. The seeds are available dried or crushed and can be used to flavor oil. Achiote oil can be drizzled over meat or shellfish for both color and subtle flavoring and can be added to salad dressings as a flavoring ingredient.

Agua Fresca   Originating in Mexico, a fresh fruit drink made from pureed fruit, sugar, and sparkling water. The fruits most commonly used are tamarind, watermelon, banana, strawberry, and mango.

Almendrado   An almond-flavored dessert made from beaten egg white bound with gelatin and usually served with a creamy custard sauce. The gelatin is frequently tinted with colors to resemble the Mexican flag.

Atole   An ancient soup made from ground dried corn or masa harina. Sometimes made with blue corn, atole may be thinned and sweetened and used as a beverage. It can also be found as a fermented beverage.

Buffaloberry   Used primarily to make jams and jellies, this wild berry, orange or red in color, is somewhat bitter in flavor. Found throughout the mountains and plains, it ripens in early to late fall. If picked just after a frost, the buffaloberry is sweet enough to use in pies.

Buñuelo   A pastry similar to a fried tortilla, usually served with a scoop of ice cream and a sprinkle of cinnamon sugar. They are a holiday season tradition in Mexico, but in the American Southwest they are more frequently eaten as a snack.

Capirotad   A Southwestern bread pudding made with cheese and caramel sauce. Though it is a traditional dish in the region during Lent, it is frequently found on restaurant menus throughout the year.

Chico   A dried kernel of corn, sometimes referred to as parched corn. Chicos are steamed and added to soups and stews.

Chokecherry   A small, orange-purple fruit that is a member of the plum family. It is common throughout the Rocky Mountains and is quite hardy and extremely resistant to changes in the weather. The name describes its taste—very astringent—which makes it well suited for jams, jellies, and syrups. They can be eaten from the vine when they are at their peak of ripeness; however, their leaves and pits are poisonous.

Cold Flour   A parched corn that was pounded into a coarse meal similar to polenta, mixed with sugar and cinnamon, and eaten as a cereal. This was an important provision of the chuckwagons that traveled west along the Oregon Trail.

Colorado Lamb   World renowned for its excellent flavor, low fat content, and large eye in the rack. Lamb is one of the largest agricultural products of the Rocky Mountains.

Cutthroat Trout   A variety of freshwater trout with distinctive markings on its neck.

Dandelion   A wild leafy plant with a bright yellow flower harvested by the Native American Indians. The leaves are usually blanched and served in salad. Dandelions should be eaten before they flower, after which they are bitter. Dandelion roots are used as a vegetable in Japanese cooking.

Empanada   A small, half-moon-shaped pastry stuffed with meat, fish, or cheese. Empanadas are served hot as an hors d'oeuvre or appetizer.

Epazote   A wild herb with jagged, serrated edges with a strong flavor reminiscent of kerosene. The young, small leaves are best and can be used like greens in soups or stews. It is frequently used in cooked beans of all types to reduce their gaseousness. It is also known as ambrosia, lamb's quarters, wormseed, stinkweed, and pigweed.

Fried Green Jerky   A traditional dish of the Pueblo tribe made from dried beef that is softened, fried with onions and chiles in lard, and simmered with fresh chopped tomatoes.

Game Meats   The region's game meats include the following:

>   **Buffalo**   Also called bison, a member of the Bovidae family and believed to be a descendant of wild cattle. There were over 40 million buffalo in the mid-1800s; however, the population shrank to less than 1,000 by 1900. Today there are over 150,000, as the buffalo population is strictly controlled and monitored. Buffalo is once again being raised for consumption and has become popular owing to its rich, sweet taste and low fat content compared to beef. Buffalo should be cooked at a lower temperature and for a shorter time than beef.

>   **Elk**   A very large relative of the deer. The meat is very dark and coarsely grained, without significant marbling. Smoked elk's tongue is considered a delicacy by many in the Rocky Mountains.

>   **Venison**   A generic term for any variety of deer meat. One of the most popular varieties of game, venison needs to be hung and marinated before cooking, unless the animal is very young. There are over 40 recognized species of deer. The most common venison served in the United States today is cervenna, derived from farm-raised Scottish red deer. The best venison comes from the buck, which is about two years old. The most popular cut is the haunch or leg. White-tailed deer is considered the most tender and flavorful, without the gamier taste associated with other varieties of venison.

>   **Wild Boar**   Boar meat is a deeper red than pork, and is somewhat less fatty. The meat of the young boar is tender, but older animals have considerably tougher meat with a gamier taste.

Horchata   A sweet beverage made from milk, ground raw rice, and almonds and flavored with cinnamon. It is garnished with toasted pumpkin seeds (pepitas) and is said to counteract the effects of eating very hot chiles, leaving only the essence of the flavor.

Huitalacoche   Also referred to as acuitlacoche, this is a fungus that grows on corn. The fungus is used in fairly large pieces as an ingredient in many Southwestern dishes and is prepared similarly to mushrooms.

Indian Flat Bread   Also referred to as Navajo fry bread, this all-purpose flat bread is made with corn flour by the Native Americans of the Four Corners region.

Jerky   Cured and salted, air-, or oven-dried strips of beef or bison.

Limon   A Mexican lime of the same variety as the Key lime. It is small, round, with a yellowish skin. True limons are usually found in the region's specialty markets.

Mexican Hot Chocolate   Invented by the Aztecs, this drink is derived from the beans of the cacao plant and could be drunk only by priests and important rulers for ceremonial purposes. Today, Mexican hot chocolate is a common breakfast drink and is used as a substitute for coffee and tea.

Mexican Oregano   A form of wild marjoram, it is similar in flavor to the oregano plant of the Mediterranean, but with a much stronger flavor.

Montana Whitefish   This whitefish from Flathead Lake in Montana weighs up to 9 pounds. It is known for its mild, pleasant-tasting flesh and excellent golden roe. The introduction of the whitefish in Flathead Lake was an accident. In an attempt to lure salmon, shrimp were seeded into the lake. Instead of the salmon, the whitefish came to the lake and thrived.

Nixtamal   Kernels of corn partially processed with slaked lime and similar to hominy, the ground kernels are mixed with seasonings to make a dough, like masa, to make tamales. Nixtamal is also used whole in soups and stews. It can be used as a substitute for posole. It is found packaged in the refrigerated sections of Southwest markets.

Palisade Peach   Indigenous to the western slopes of Colorado near the city of Grand Junction, Palisade peaches are world renowned for their sweet flavor and firm texture.

Panocha   This rustic dessert is a pudding originally made before sugar was available and when honey was scarce. The settlers discovered that moistened wheat kernels left in a warm place would convert to a form of sugar. This wheat could be ground and would provide sweetness to a recipe. Today, flour made from sprouted grain is still available and used to make panocha.

Pepita   The Spanish name for a pumpkin seed or squash seed of any variety. They are typically dried and roasted and eaten as a snack, used as a garnish for salads, or ground and used as a flavoring agent for regional sauces.

Piki Bread   A traditional unleavened bread made by the Hopi tribe with blue corn. It has many thin, papery layers and is cooked on heated piki stones. These stones have been seasoned with bone marrow or cooked sheep's brains and serve the same function as a cast-iron skillet or wok.

Pine Nuts   Also known as piñon nuts, they are harvested from the cones of pine trees growing at high altitudes in the Rock Mountains and the Southwest. Considered to be the largest uncultivated crop in North America, pine nuts can be roasted or ground to add a distinctive flavor to any dish.

Posole   A dried form of nixtamal, used like masa harina for making tamales and tortillas. Posole also refers to a traditional Southwestern soup or stew that uses this type of corn. Posole is available in four colors—blue, red, yellow, and white. Posole is a convenient and safe way to store corn for long periods, but it needs to be reconstituted with water prior to use. Nixtamal or hominy can be substituted for posole.

Potatoes   One of the most famous foods in the Rocky Mountains is the potato. Over 100 varieties are farmed, mostly in Idaho and Colorado. In fact, Idaho Potato is now a registered trademark. Idaho potatoes are usually grown in volcanic soil and irrigated with fresh mountain runoff water. Russet potatoes from Idaho are the most popular and common potato variety and are used primarily as baking potatoes and for the production of french fries. Colorado, while also producing Russets, is known more for its specialty potatoes that come in a variety of colors, sizes, and flavors. They include:

> **Alaskan Sweetheart Potato**   This variety of potato is slightly pink in color, with a red skin. Good for baking and boiling, it is also an excellent choice for a colorful potato salad.

> **Baby All-Blue Potato**   These potatoes are small, thin, and long. Also known as fingerling potatoes, they have a bluish-lavender flesh and are best cooked whole by steaming, roasting, or boiling.

> **Ozette Potato**   A yellow-skinned and yellow-fleshed fingerling potato best cooked by roasting or baking.

> **Purple Peruvian Potato**   A fingerling potato, originating in South America, with a purple color. The purple Peruvian potatoes have an extremely earthy flavor and are excellent either boiled or baked.

Red Bliss Potato   Also known as a Cherry Red potato, it is white fleshed, with a deep red skin and a creamy, buttery taste.

Red Sangre Potato   These medium potatoes are named after the Sangre de Cristo Mountain Range in the southern part of Colorado. They are white fleshed, with a red skin, and are excellent for both baking and boiling.

Russet Potato   This is the most popular potato in America. It is raised primarily in Idaho, where the volcanic soil and mountain runoff provide excellent growing conditions. Though not very attractive, they are large and oblong, with a slightly rough skin. Their low moisture content makes them perfect for making light and fluffy baked potatoes. Their low sugar content makes them suitable for french fries. (Americans eat more than 4.5 billion pounds of french fries annually.)

Yellow Fin or Yukon Gold Potato   A yellow-skinned and yellow-fleshed potato developed in Finland, marketed in America by Michigan farmer Jim Huston, and now grown in the San Luis Valley of Colorado. These potatoes have a creamy texture and a butter flavor suitable for any potato preparation.

Rainbow Trout   This native American trout is considered one of the world's best game fishes. Rainbow trout are easily identified by the broad reddish band, or "rainbow," that runs along the side of the fish from head to tail. This freshwater fish begins life in the rivers of Idaho. The young fish travel many hundreds of miles to the Pacific Ocean through a network of streams and rivers to live there for approximately four years. The trout return to their spawning grounds through the same rivers and streams. Modern trout farms now raise these fish for the commercial market.

Rocky Mountain Oysters   A culinary tradition of the Old West, Rocky Mountain oysters are the testicles of a sheep or young bull, roasted whole in a pan. Eating Rocky Mountain oysters was a ritual test of manhood for the cowboys of the Old West. Today, they are usually coated, breaded, then pan- or deep-fried and served with a spicy dipping sauce.

Sangria   A red wine and fresh fruit beverage first made by the Spanish priests, who introduced wine grapes to New Mexico. It is considered an excellent accompaniment to the spicy fare of the region. Tequila may be added.

Sopaipilla   A rectangle of wheat flour dough, deep-fried and served as a savory bread. It may also be filled with honey, sprinkled with powdered sugar, and served as a dessert.

Squash Blossoms   The flowers of almost any squash can be sautéed as a vegetable, deep-fried, added to soups and quesadillas, or used as a garnish. The blossom of the zucchini is most frequently seen. Squash blossoms need to be used immediately, as their quality quickly deteriorates.

Teswin   A Native American punch made from dried corn and finely ground roasted wheat. It is often flavored with anise, cloves, and cinnamon.

Tunas   The fruit of the prickly pear cactus with an orange or red flesh and a sweet, yet tart flavor. In Europe, this cactus is referred to as a Barbary fig. Tunas needs to be trimmed of its spines and outer skin before use. The cactus fruit is used in dessert preparations and as an ingredient in salads.

CROSS-REFERENCED TYPICAL INGREDIENTS AND DISHES

The following ingredients are used in both Tex-Mex and Southwestern/Rocky Mountain cooking. See Chapter 7, "Texas and Tex-Mex Cuisine," for the following:

Chiles	**Mole**	**Tamale**
Cilantro	**Nopales**	**Tomatillo**
Jícama	**Queso Fresco**	**Tortilla**
Masa and Masa Harina	**Salsa**	

Menus and Recipes from the
Cuisine of the Southwest and the Rocky Mountain Region

MENU ONE
Smoked Tomato Soup

Salad with Blood Oranges and Olive Oil Powder

Crispy Skinned Striped Bass with Ponzu Gelée

Braised Veal Cheeks (Basque)

Poached Leeks and Sautéed Radishes

Lemon Chess Pie

MENU TWO
Tortilla Chips, Tomatillo Salsa, and Salsa Fresca

Poblano and Potato Soup

Marinated Grilled Quail on Spinach Salad

Pumpkin Seed–Crusted Rainbow Trout with Calabacitas con Maize

Annatto Rice and Queso Fresco

Tres Leches Cake

MENU THREE
Navajo Fry Bread

Porrusalda (Leek Soup)

Chiles Rellenos with Roasted Tomato Salsa

Jícama Salad

Grilled Apache-Style Pork Chops with Squash Salsa and Tobacco Onions

Sopaipillas

OTHER RECIPES
Grilled Vegetable Gazpacho

Spicy Pork Empanadas

Marinated Dried Bean Salad Colorado

Lamb Shoulder with Red Chile Marinade and Cilantro Pesto

Smoked Tomato Soup

4 servings

AMOUNT	MEASURE	INGREDIENT
For the Smoked Tomatoes		
As needed		Apple, pecan, or hickory wood chips
3¾ cups	24 ounces/672 g	Plum tomatoes, halved lengthwise and seeded
1 tablespoon	½ ounce/15 ml	Olive oil
		Salt and pepper
For the Soup		
2 tablespoons	1 ounce/30 ml	Olive oil
½ cup	2 ounces/56 g	Red onion, in ¼-inch (.6 cm) dice
2	5 g	Garlic cloves, minced
1 cup	4 ounces/112 g	Red bell pepper, in ¼-inch (.6 cm) dice
2 tablespoons	½ ounce/14 g	Sun-dried tomato, chopped
½ teaspoon		Coriander seeds
1		Bay leaf
2 teaspoons		Grated fresh or prepared horseradish
1½ cups	12 ounces/360 ml	Chicken or vegetable stock
		Salt and pepper
For the Garnish		
½ cup	2 ounces/56 g	All-purpose flour
¼ cup	1 ounce/28 g	Yellow cornmeal
		Salt and pepper
	8 ounces/224 g	Asadero (Oaxaca), Monterey jack, or mozzarella cheese, cut into four 2-ounce (56 g) squares
1		Egg, lightly beaten with a pinch of salt and a little water
3 tablespoons	1½ ounces/45 ml	Vegetable oil
1 tablespoon	½ ounce/15 ml	Olive oil
⅓ cup	2 ounces/56 g	Tomato, peeled, in 1½-inch (3.6 cm) julienne
2 tablespoons		Fresh basil leaves, in chiffonade

PROCEDURE

1. Smoke the tomatoes. Heat a stovetop smoker over medium heat. Put the chips in the bottom of the smoking pan, reduce the heat to medium-low, and place the rack in the smoker.

2. Toss the tomatoes with the olive oil, salt, and pepper. Place the tomatoes, cut sides up, on the smoker rack. Cover and smoke for 3 to 5 minutes. Transfer the tomatoes to a container, seal with plastic wrap, and let cool. Rough-chop the tomatoes.

3. Make the soup. In a 3- to 4-quart (3 to 4 L) saucepan over medium heat, heat the olive oil, then add the onion, garlic, red pepper, and sun-dried tomato. Sauté until onion is translucent and soften, 3 to 5 minutes; do not brown. Add the coriander seeds, bay leaf, and horseradish, and cook 2 to 3 minutes. Add the chopped smoked tomato and the stock, then cover and cook over medium heat until tomatoes are soft, 8 to 10 minutes. Discard the bay leaf.

4. Puree the soup in a blender or food processor. It should be a little rustic; however, if desired, pass it through a fine-mesh sieve. Adjust the consistency with hot stock if necessary, and correct the seasoning with salt and pepper. Keep warm.

5. Prepare the garnish. Combine half the flour with the cornmeal and season with salt and pepper. Dip the cheese squares into the remaining plain flour, then into the beaten egg, making sure the cheese is completely covered, and then into the cornmeal-flour mixture. Press all sides of the cheese to completely cover. Refrigerate for at least 15 minutes.

6. Just before serving the soup, heat the vegetable oil over medium-high heat in a 8- to 10-inch (20.3–25.4 cm) sauté pan. Fry the cheese squares until golden brown on all sides, about 2 to 3 minutes.

7. Drain the oil from the sauté pan and add the olive oil. Toss in the julienned tomatoes to warm them and season with salt and pepper.

8. To serve, place one fried cheese square in each warmed bowl, top with the julienned tomato and basil, then ladle the soup around.

Smoked Tomato Soup

Salad with Blood Oranges and Olive Oil Powder

4 servings

AMOUNT	MEASURE	INGREDIENT
For the Dressing		
¼ cup	1 ounce/28 g	Shallots, minced
1 tablespoon	½ ounce/15 ml	Champagne vinegar
¼ cup	2 ounces/60 ml	Blood orange juice
¼ cup	2 ounces/60 ml	Olive oil
As needed		Sugar
For the Olive Oil Powder		
¼ cup plus 1 tablespoon and 2 teaspoons	2¾ fluid ounces/82 ml	Olive oil
	1 ounce/25 g	Tapioca maltodextrin
	3 g	Salt
For the Salad		
3 cups	4 ½ ounces/126 g	Boston lettuce, in large pieces, chilled
2 cups	4 ounces/56 g	Watercress, chilled
		Salt and pepper
½ cup	2 ounces/56 g	Walnuts, roughly chopped and toasted
½ cup	4 ounces/112 g	Blood orange segments, peeled and pith removed

PROCEDURE

1. Make the dressing. Combine the shallots, vinegar, and orange juice in a bowl. Let rest for 5 minutes, then whisk in the olive oil. Adjust seasoning with a bit of sugar, if necessary.

2. Make the olive oil powder. Whisk together the olive oil, maltodextrin, and salt until it converts to a powder. Pass the powder through a tamis and reserve in a sealed container.

3. Prepare the salad. Season the chilled greens with salt and pepper. Mix the dressing again, then add just enough to coat the greens.

4. Divide the greens evenly among chilled plates. Top each with the walnuts, a few orange segments, and a small mound of olive oil powder.

Salad with Blood Oranges and Olive Oil Powder

Crisp-Skinned Striped Bass with Ponzu Gelée

4 servings

CHEF TIP: Hybrid striped bass are moderately fatty and mild tasting with a firm flaky texture. The hybrids can be distinguished from wild striped bass by broken rather than solid horizontal stripes on the body. The hybrid is more resistant to temperature extremes, thus better suited to aquaculture.

AMOUNT	MEASURE	INGREDIENT
½ cup	4 ounces/120 ml	Ponzu
½ tablespoon	¼ ounce/7 g	Gelatin powder
2 tablespoons	1 ounce/30 g	Butter
1½ cups	9 ounces/252 g	Carrots, peeled, in uniform shapes (oblique or batonette)
¾ cup	6 ounces/180 ml	Chicken or vegetable stock
		Salt and pepper
½ cup	5 ounces/140 g	Tomatillos, husks removed
3	15 g	Garlic cloves
1		Serrano or jalapeño pepper
1 cup	5½ ounces/156 g	Avocado
1 tablespoon	½ ounce/15 ml	Lime juice
3 tablespoons	1½ ounces/45 ml	Vegetable oil
4	4 ounces/112 g each	Striped bass fillets, skin on
		Salt and pepper

PROCEDURE

1. Sprinkle the gelatin over the ponzu and allow to swell for 5 to 10 minutes. Slowly heat the ponzu to dissolve the gelatin, stirring. Pour into two 4-ounce (120 ml) ramekins and refrigerate.

2. Heat a 10-inch (25 cm) sauté pan over medium-high heat. Add the butter and carrots, and cook 2 minutes; do not brown. Add the stock and bring to a simmer. Cover the pan with a parchment lid and simmer on top of the stove (or in a 350°F/177°C oven) for 8 to 10 minutes or until the carrots are just tender. Remove carrots and reserve. Reduce the liquid to a glaze, then return carrots to the pan and toss to coat. Taste and adjust the seasoning with salt and pepper.

3. Preheat the broiler. Place the tomatillos, unpeeled garlic cloves, and chile on a baking pan and broil until charred, 5 to 7 minutes. Let cool, then peel the garlic and remove seeds from the chile. Puree tomatillos, garlic, chile, and the avocado and lime juice in a food processor. Season the avocado sauce to taste with salt and pepper. Unmold the ponzu gelée and cut into small cubes.

4. Heat a 10- to 12-inch (25.4–30.5 cm) sauté pan over medium-high heat, and then add vegetable oil. Pat the fish dry with paper towels, then season on both sides with salt and pepper. The oil should be shimmering, but not smoking. Add the fish skin side down and sear the fish until crisp on the bottom, 3 to 4 minutes. Turn over to finish cooking, 1 to 2 minutes more. (When the fillets hit the heat, the proteins begin to contract and they will curve upwards. Take a flexible fish spatula and press on the flesh until the fillet flattens out, which only takes a few seconds. This ensures the skin remains touching the pan and gives a crisp result.)

5. To serve, spread 2 tablespoons of the avocado sauce on each warmed plate. Place the fish skin side up on top of the sauce, and serve with the carrots and ponzu gelée cubes. (Plates must be warm to melt the gelée.)

Crisp-Skinned Striped Bass with Avocado Sauce, Carrots, and Ponzu Gelée

Braised Veal Cheeks (Basque)

4 servings

CHEF TIP: Cheeks are perhaps the toughest cut of meat on the cow because those muscles are exercised the most. Barbacoa is the Spanish term for beef cheeks that have been braised, baked, steamed, or boiled to tenderness, traditionally used in tacos. Use beef cheeks or short ribs if veal cheeks are not available.

Veal cheeks are typically about 4 to 6 ounces each. Raw, they resemble small boneless chicken-breast halves. Beef cheeks are typically 8 to 10 ounces each and take much longer to cook. After trimming the extra fat and the silverskin, each cheek has about a 60 to 65% yield.

AMOUNT	MEASURE	INGREDIENT
2 tablespoons	1 ounce/30 ml	Vegetable oil
	20 ounces/560 g	Veal cheeks, trimmed and silver skin removed
		Salt and pepper
1 cup	6 ounces/168 g	Onion, in ½-inch (1.2 cm) dice
½ cup	3 ounces/84 g	Carrot, in ½-inch (1.2 cm) dice
½ cup	3 ounces/84 g	Celery, in ½-inch (1.2 cm) dice
3	15 g	Garlic cloves, chopped
½ cup	4 ounces/120 ml	White wine
2 cups	16 ounces/480 ml	Veal stock
1		Bay leaf
1		Fresh thyme sprig
2		Star anise
1 tablespoon	¼ ounce/7 g	Black peppercorns
2 tablespoons	1 ounce/28 g	Butter
1 tablespoon	½ ounce/15 ml	Sherry vinegar

PROCEDURE

1. Preheat the oven to 360°F (182°C).

2. In a 10- to 12-inch (25.4–30.5 cm) sauté pan, heat the oil over medium-high heat. Pat veal cheeks dry with paper towels, and then season them with salt and pepper. Add to the hot oil and evenly brown on all sides, 6 to 7 minutes. Remove the meat.

3. Reduce the heat to medium low, add the onion and carrot, and sauté, stirring occasionally, until lightly caramelized, 5 to 6 minutes. Add the celery and garlic, sauté stirring occasionally, until soft and lightly browned, 3 to 4 minutes.

4. Deglaze pan with the white wine. Add the stock, bay leaf, thyme, star anise, and peppercorns. Return the meat to the pan and bring to a boil. Cover with parchment directly in contact with the meat, then cover with foil and also a pan lid. Place in the preheated oven and braise until meat is tender, 2 to 2½ hours. Veal cheeks are done when a small knife inserted in the middle slides out with no resistance. Remove veal cheeks from pan; keep warm.

5. Strain the braising liquid, then return it to the pan, skimming off any excess fat. Return to a simmer and reduce over medium heat to about 1 cup, 10 to 15 minutes. Correct the seasoning with salt and pepper, then swirl in the butter and stir in the sherry vinegar.

6. Return the cheeks to the sauce and warm through. Divide cheeks into four equal portions, place on warmed plates, and serve ¼ cup (2 ounces/60 ml) sauce with each portion.

Veal Cheeks, Sautéed Radishes, and Poached Leeks

Poached Leeks and Sautéed Radishes

4 servings

✦ **CHEF TIP:** Leeks are very cold tolerant—some varieties can withstand multiple frosts over one winter. They are also very dirty and must be cleaned thoroughly. Do not wash leeks before refrigerating them, as this accelerates their decline.

AMOUNT	MEASURE	INGREDIENT
4	14 ounces/392 g	Leeks, trim the roots, green ends, and outer leaves
1 cup	8 ounces/240 ml	Chicken or vegetable stock
1 tablespoon	½ ounce/15 ml	Olive oil
3	15 g	Garlic cloves, minced
¼ cup	1 ounce/28 g	Shallots, thinly sliced
2 tablespoons	1 ounce/28 g	Butter
1 cup	6 ounces/168 g	Red globe radishes, in quarters
		Salt and pepper

PROCEDURE

1. Cut the leeks in half lengthwise and wash thoroughly; drain. Place in parallel rows in a 10-inch (25.4 cm) sauté pan.

2. Bring the stock to a boil and pour over leeks. Cover loosely and simmer, covered, for 10 to 15 minutes or until leeks are tender. Drain well.

3. Add the olive oil, garlic and shallots, then cook 1 to 2 minutes or until vegetables are soft.

4. Add the butter and leeks, and sauté over low heat until warmed completely, 2 to 3 minutes. Remove leeks to a serving plate.

5. Add the radishes to the same sauté pan and sauté until warm. Correct the seasoning with salt and pepper, add the radishes to the leeks, and drizzle on them any leftover butter from the pan.

Lemon Chess Pie

✤ **CHEF TIP:** It is important that all ingredients for the pie be at room temperature. Otherwise, blending may be difficult, and the cold ingredients, especially the buttermilk or lemon juice, will cause the butter to resolidify and separate from the mixture.

AMOUNT	MEASURE	INGREDIENT
4		Eggs, at room temperature
1½ cups	11 ounces/308 g	Sugar
1 tablespoon	¼ ounce/7 g	White cornmeal
1 tablespoon	¼ ounce/7 g	All-purpose flour
½ teaspoon	3 g	Salt
5 tablespoons	2½ ounces/70 g	Butter, melted and cooled to room temperature
½ cup	4 ounces/120 ml	Buttermilk
5 tablespoons	2½ ounces/75 ml	Lemon juice
1 tablespoon	10 g	Lemon zest
½ teaspoon	2.5 ml	Vanilla extract
1		Unbaked 9-inch (22 cm) pre-made or frozen and defrosted piecrust
		Whipped cream (optional)

PROCEDURE

1. Preheat the oven to 350°F (175°C).

2. Whisk the eggs in a large bowl. Add the sugar, cornmeal, flour, salt, butter, buttermilk, lemon juice and zest, and vanilla, completely incorporating one before adding the next.

3. Pour the filling into the piecrust and bake in the middle of the oven for 30 to 40 minutes, until the pie is golden brown on top and almost set. The center of the pie should remain slightly loose; it will set as it cools.

4. Cool pie completely before cutting, and serve with whipped cream, if desired.

Tortilla Chips, Tomatillo Salsa, and Salsa Fresca

4 servings

Tortilla Chips

AMOUNT	MEASURE	INGREDIENT
As needed		Vegetable oil
12		8-inch (20 cm) corn tortillas
		Salt

PROCEDURE

1. Heat the oil in a deep-fryer or deep pot to 350°F (175°C).

2. Cut the corn tortillas into quarters and fry until crisp, about 2 minutes.

3. Drain on paper towels, then season with salt.

Tomatillo Salsa

AMOUNT	MEASURE	INGREDIENT
1½ cups	8 ounces/224 g	Tomatillos, husked, chopped
1½ tablespoons	¾ ounce/21 g	Red onion, in ⅛-inch (.3 cm) dice
½		Serrano chile, minced
1 tablespoon	½ ounce/15 ml	Lime juice
¼ cup (packed)	½ ounce/14 g	Fresh cilantro, roughly chopped
1 tablespoon	½ ounce/15 ml	Vegetable oil
Pinch		Sugar

PROCEDURE

1. Husk the tomatillos and wash under very hot water.

2. Rough chop and then puree in a blender or food processor. Transfer to a stainless steel bowl.

3. Add the red onion, chile, lime juice, cilantro, and oil. Add a pinch of sugar if the tomatillos are too sour. Stir well.

Salsa Fresca

AMOUNT	MEASURE	INGREDIENT
1¼ cups	8 ounces/224 g	Tomatoes, peeled, in ⅛-inch (.3 cm) dice
1 cup	4 ounces/112 g	Onion, in ⅛-inch (.3 cm) dice
1	5 g	Garlic clove, minced
1		Serrano chile, seeded, minced
¼ cup (packed)	½ ounce/14 g	Fresh cilantro leaves, finely chopped
		Salt and pepper
1 tablespoon	½ ounce/15 ml	Lime juice

PROCEDURE   Combine all the ingredients in a stainless steel bowl. Correct the seasoning.

Poblano and Potato Soup

4 servings

 **CHEF TIP:**   Sour cream, crème fraîche, and Mexican crema are all similar in taste, as they are kinds of cultured creams. Sour cream is the thickest of the three, while Mexican crema is the thinnest.

AMOUNT	MEASURE	INGREDIENT
2 tablespoons	1 ounce/30 ml	Vegetable oil
1 cup	4 ounces/112 g	Onion, in ½-inch (1.2 cm) dice
½ cup	2 ounces/56 g	Carrot, in ½-inch (1.2 cm) dice
½ cup	2 ounces/56 g	Celery, in ½-inch (1.2 cm) dice
1 teaspoon		Ground cumin
3	6 ounces/168 g	Poblano chiles, roasted, peeled, seeded, cut into ½-inch (1.2 cm) dice
2 cups	10 ounces/280 g	Russet potato, in ½-inch (1.2 cm) dice
1 quart	1 L	Chicken stock
		Salt and white pepper
¾ cup	6 ounces/180 ml	Heavy cream, warmed
1 tablespoon		Fresh cilantro leaves, chopped
¼ cup	2 ounces/60 ml	Mexican crema

PROCEDURE

1.   Heat the oil in a 3- to 4-quart (3 to 4 L) saucepan over medium heat. Add the onion, carrot, celery, and cumin and cook 5 minutes. Add the chiles, potato, and stock. Simmer for 30 minutes.

2.   Puree the soup in a blender or food processor. Bring back to a simmer and adjust the thickness to desired consistency using a little extra stock, then season with salt and pepper.

3.   Add the cream and cilantro just before serving. Serve in warmed bowls and garnish each with 1 tablespoon (½ ounce/15 ml) crema.

Marinated Grilled Quail on Spinach Salad

4 servings

AMOUNT	MEASURE	INGREDIENT
8		Bamboo skewers, soaked in water for 30 minutes
For the Vinaigrette		
¼ cup	2 ounces/60 ml	Olive oil
½ cup	4 ounces/120 ml	Vegetable oil
¼ cup	1 ounce/28 g	Shallots, minced
2 tablespoons		Fresh flat-leaf parsley, finely chopped
¼ cup	2 ounces/60 ml	Balsamic vinegar
		Salt and pepper
For the Salad		
4	8 ounces/224 g each	Quail, split at the back
½ cup	2 ounces/56 g	Roasted red bell pepper, julienned
½ cup	2 ounces/56 g	Roasted yellow bell pepper, julienned
½ cup	2 ounces/56 g	Roasted green bell pepper, julienned
¾ cup	4 ounces/112 g	Tomato, peeled, julienned
2 cups	4 ounces/112 g	Fresh spinach, cut in chiffonade

PROCEDURE

1. Soak the bamboo skewers for 30 minutes.

2. Make the dressing. Combine all ingredients in a blender and process until smooth. Correct the seasoning with more salt and pepper.

3. Prepare the quail. Place each quail on two skewers in a straight line to hold its shape. Use half the salad dressing to liberally brush the quail with the dressing. Refrigerate for 1 hour.

4. Prepare the grill.

5. Toss the peppers and tomato with ¼ cup (2 ounces/60 ml) of the vinaigrette.

6. Grill the quail for 3 to 5 minutes on each side or until the quail are completely cooked. Be careful not to burn or overcook the quail.

7. Add the spinach to the peppers mixture and toss to combine.

8. Place the salad in the center of four chilled plates. Remove the skewers from each quail and place on top of the salads. Drizzle the remaining vinaigrette over the quail.

Marinated Grilled Quail on Spinach Salad

Pumpkin Seed–Crusted Trout

4 servings

CHEF TIP: Leaving the skin on the trout helps keep the flesh moist and enhances the flavor. The meat separates easily once cooked.

Pumpkin Seed–Crusted Trout

AMOUNT	MEASURE	INGREDIENT
¾ cup	4 ounces/112 g	Green pumpkin seeds, crushed
¼ cup	1½ ounces/42 g	Cornmeal
4	5 ounces/140 g each	Trout fillets with skin, boned
		Salt and pepper
½ cup	2 ounces/56 g	All-purpose flour
2		Eggs, lightly beaten with a pinch of salt and a little water
2 tablespoons	1 ounce/30 ml	Vegetable oil
½ cup	4 ounces/112 g	Butter
1 tablespoon	3 g	Fresh flat-leaf parsley, finely chopped
1 tablespoon	½ ounce/15 ml	Lime juice

PROCEDURE

1. In a small bowl, combine the pumpkin seeds and cornmeal.

2. Season the trout with salt and pepper. Dredge the flesh side in flour, shaking off excess, then dip flesh side in egg, letting excess drip off. Coat the flesh side of the fillets with cornmeal mixture.

3. In a 10- to 12-inch (25.4–30.5 cm) sauté pan, heat the oil over medium-high heat.

4. Add the trout cornmeal mixture side down to the pan and cook until golden, 2 to 3 minutes. Turn the fillets and cook until just done, 1 minute. Transfer to warm plates, cornmeal mixture side up. (Fillets may have to be cooked in batches.)

5. In the same sauté pan, heat the butter until it starts to foam and just begins to brown. Add the parsley and lime juice, stir, and spoon over trout fillets. Serve with Calabacitas con Maize (recipe follows).

Calabacitas Con Maize

AMOUNT	MEASURE	INGREDIENT
2 tablespoons	1 ounce/28 g	Unsalted butter
½ cup	2 ounces/56 g	Onion, in ¼-inch (.6 cm) dice
1	5 g	Garlic clove, minced
2½ cups	10 ounces/280 g	Zucchini, in ½-inch (1.2 cm) dice
½ cup	2 ounces/56 g	Corn kernels
1		Serrano chile, seeded, minced
⅛ teaspoon		Dried oregano
		Salt and pepper
½ cup	3 ounces/85 g	Tomato, peeled, in ½-inch (1.2 cm) dice

PROCEDURE

1. In an 8- to 10-inch (20.3–25.4 cm) skillet, heat the butter over medium-high heat. Add the onion and garlic, and cook until the onion is translucent, 2 to 3 minutes.

2. Add the zucchini, corn, and chile. Cover the pan, lower the heat, and cook for 3 to 5 minutes or until the vegetables are tender.

3. Season with oregano, salt, and pepper.

4. Just before serving, add the tomato and toss until heated through. Correct the seasoning.

Pumpkin Seed–Crusted Trout with Calabacitas con Maize

Annatto Rice and Queso Fresco

4 servings

AMOUNT	MEASURE	INGREDIENT
1 cup	7 ounces/196 g	Uncooked long-grain rice
¼ cup	2 ounces/60 ml	Vegetable oil
½ cup	2 ounces/56 g	Onion, in ¼-inch (.6 cm) dice
1	5 g	Garlic clove, minced
¼ cup	1 ounce/28 g	Carrot, in ¼-inch (.6 cm) dice
¼ cup	1 ounce/28 g	Celery, in ¼-inch (.6 cm) dice
1 tablespoon	¼ ounce/7 g	Annatto powder
1½ cups	12 ounces/360 ml	Chicken stock
		Salt and pepper
1 cup	4 ounces/112 g	Queso fresco, grated
2 tablespoons	¼ ounce/7 g	Fresh cilantro, chopped

PROCEDURE

1. Rinse the rice in cold water and drain.

2. In a 2- to 3-quart (2 to 3 L) saucepan, heat the oil over medium heat. Add the onion, garlic, carrot, and celery, and cook for 2 minutes, stirring occasionally.

3. Add the annatto powder and mix well. Add the rice; cook stirring constantly for 3 minutes, until the rice is well coated with the oil.

4. Add the stock, season with salt and pepper, and bring to a boil, reduce the heat, and simmer for 20 minutes or until rice is tender and fluffy.

5. Let stand, covered, for 5 minutes.

6. Stir the cheese and cilantro into the rice with a fork. Serve.

Tres Leches Cake

AMOUNT	MEASURE	INGREDIENT
1½ cups	6 ounces/168 g	All-purpose flour
1 teaspoon	4 g	Baking powder
Pinch		Salt
½ cup	4 ounces/112 g	Unsalted butter
2 cups	14 ounces/392 g	Sugar
5		Eggs
1½ teaspoons		Vanilla extract
1 cup	8 ounces/240 ml	Milk
⅔ cup	7 ounces/210 ml	Sweetened condensed milk
⅔ cup	6 ounces/180 ml	Evaporated milk
⅓ cup	2⅔ ounces/80 ml	Liqueur, Frangelico, Brandy, or Chambord, (optional)
1½ cups	12 ounces/360 ml	Heavy cream

PROCEDURE

1. Preheat the oven to 350°F (175°C). Grease and flour a 9 × 13-inch (22 × 32 cm) baking pan.

2. Sift the flour, baking powder and salt together.

3. Cream the butter and half the sugar together until fluffy. Add the eggs one at a time until well combined, then add half the vanilla. Beat well.

4. Add the flour mixture to the butter mixture in three stages, mixing well until blended. Do not overmix.

5. Pour batter into the prepared pan and bake for 30 to 40 minutes, until the cake feels firm and an inserted toothpick comes out clean. Remove from oven and cool to room temperature.

6. Pierce cake with a fork or skewer 15 to 20 times.

7. Combine the milk, condensed milk, evaporated milk, and liqueur (optional) and slowly pour over the top of the cooled cake. Refrigerate for at least 1 hour before serving. (Because of the milk in the cake, it is very important that you keep the cake refrigerated until ready to serve.)

8. When ready to serve, combine the cream and the remaining vanilla and sugar, whipping until soft peaks form. Spread a layer over the top of the cake. Serve chilled.

Tres Leches Cake

Navajo Fry Bread

4 servings

CHEF TIP: When the Spanish came to America; they brought wheat, giving the native cooks an alternative to cornmeal. Navajo fry bread is also known as Indian fry bread. It can be sweet and savory, and forms the base for the Indian taco, another dish often seen at festivals and gatherings.

To grill the bread, place on a clean medium-hot grill. When bubbles form and the dough has risen slightly, turn over to finish the cooking. The bread is done when the surface appears smooth and is dry to the touch. Cooking time is around 2 to 3 minutes per side. Some browning occurs; yet generally it is blond bread.

AMOUNT	MEASURE	INGREDIENT
1 cup	4 ounces/112 g	All-purpose flour
½ teaspoon		Baking powder
¼ teaspoon		Salt
2 tablespoons	1 ounce/30 ml	Milk
5 tablespoons	2½ ounces/75 ml	Warm water
As needed		Vegetable oil

PROCEDURE

1. Combine the flour, baking powder, and salt in a mixing bowl or on a suitable, clean work surface. Make a well in the center of the flour and pour in the milk and warm water.

2. Work the flour mixture into the liquid with a wooden spoon, or use your hands. Gently work the dough into a smooth ball. Do not knead the dough, which makes for a heavy fry bread when cooked. Cover the dough and let the dough relax for a minimum of 10 minutes. (This dough is best used within a few hours.)

3. Form the dough into egg-size balls; cover and set aside for 15 minutes.

4. Heat the oil in a deep-fryer or deep pot to 375°F (190°C).

5. Form the balls using a rolling pin or floured hands, shape, stretch, pat and form a disk of about 6 to 7 inches (15 to 17.5 cm) in diameter and about ¼ inch (.6 cm) thick. It does not need to be a perfect round disk.

6. Check the temperature of the oil with a thermometer or by either dropping a small piece of dough in the hot oil and seeing if it begins to fry, or by dipping the end of a wooden spoon in and seeing if that bubbles. Add the dough rounds and press down on the dough as it fries so the top stays submersed. Fry each round in the hot oil for 2 to 3 minutes on each side. Drain on paper towels and serve. (Note: Breads can be kept warm in a 200°F/93.3°C oven for up to 1 hour. They refrigerate well and can be reheated in a 350°F/175°C oven for 10 to 15 minute before serving.)

Porrusalda (Leek Soup)

4 servings

✦ **CHEF TIP:** This soup is a traditional Basque soup recipe, whose title means "leek broth." The role of the Basques in the exploration and settlement of the Americas continues to be researched by historians and scholars.

AMOUNT	MEASURE	INGREDIENT
¼ cup	2 ounces/60 ml	Olive oil
2 cups	8 ounces/224 g	Leeks, white and light green parts, sliced
3 cups	15 ounces/425 g	Red Bliss potatoes, peeled, in ¼-inch (.6 cm) dice
2		Fresh thyme sprigs
¼ teaspoon		White pepper
2 teaspoons	10 g	Salt
1	5 g	Garlic clove, minced
2 cups	16 ounces/470 ml	Chicken stock
2		Bay leaves
2 tablespoons		Fresh flat-leaf parsley

PROCEDURE

1. In a 2- to 3-quart (2 to 3 L) pot, heat the oil over medium-high heat. Add the leeks and cook until lightly browned, about 3 to 4 minutes. Add the potatoes, seasonings, and garlic, and cook 1 minute more.

2. Add the chicken stock and bay leaves. Bring to a simmer, then cook 1 hour.

3. Remove bay leaves; correct the seasoning and stir in the parsley just before serving.

Chiles Rellenos with Roasted Tomato Salsa

Chiles Rellenos

AMOUNT	MEASURE	INGREDIENT
4		Poblano chiles
For the Filling		
2 tablespoons	1 ounce/30 ml	Vegetable oil
½ cup	2 ounces/56 g	Onion, in ¼-inch (.6 cm) dice
1	5 g	Garlic clove, minced
2 cups	8 ounces/224 g	Corn kernels
		Salt and white pepper
⅛ teaspoon		Dried oregano
¼ cup	2 ounces/60 ml	Mexican crema or sour cream
1 cup	4 ounces/112 g	Queso fresco or white farmer cheese, grated
For the Batter		
As needed		Vegetable oil
3		Eggs, separated
¼ cup	1 ounce/28 g	All-purpose flour
2 teaspoons	¼ ounce/7g	Baking powder
1½ teaspoons	¼ ounce/7 g	Salt
2 tablespoons	1 ounce/15 ml	Cold water
		All-purpose flour, for dredging

PROCEDURE

1. Roast the chiles until somewhat blackened, then put into a plastic bag or wrap with film for 10 minutes to steam, which makes them easier to peel. Once peeled slit the chilies down one side but not all the way through and remove the seeds but leave on the stem; let cool. (Remember, this is a container to be stuffed.)

2. Make the filling. In an 8- to 10-inch (20.3–25.4 cm) skillet, heat the oil, add the onion and garlic, and cook until soft but not brown, about 2 to 3 minutes.

3. Add the corn and salt, then cover the pan and cook until corn is tender (if corn is dry, you may have to add some water). Add the oregano and adjust the seasoning. Set aside to cool.

4. Blend in the crema and cheese; season with salt and pepper.

5. Stuff the chiles with the cheese mixture. Reshape and chill for 30 minutes.

6. Make the batter and fry. Heat the oil in a deep pot or deep-fryer to 350°F (175°C).

7. Beat the egg yolks and water until foamy. Add the flour, baking powder, and salt to the egg yolks and beat to combine well.

8. Whip the egg whites to soft peaks; fold the egg whites into the egg yolks. Do not overmix; it is acceptable to see a little of the egg whites.

9. Dip the stuffed chiles in a little flour and then in the batter, and fry them until golden brown on one side, about 3 to 4 minutes. Turn over and fry until golden brown on the other side, another 3 to 4 minutes. Drain on paper towels. Serve with the Roasted Tomato Salsa (recipe follows).

Roasted Tomato Salsa

AMOUNT	MEASURE	INGREDIENT
1¼ cups	8 ounces/224 g	Tomatoes, cored, quartered
1	2½ ounces/70 g	Jalapeño pepper, seeded, quartered
1 cup	6 ounces/168 g	Onion, quartered
2	10 g	Garlic cloves
Pinch		Ground cumin
2 tablespoons	1 ounce/60 ml	Vegetable oil
		Salt and pepper
		Chicken stock (optional)

PROCEDURE

1. Preheat the oven to 450°F (225°C).

2. Toss the ingredients together, place on a baking sheet, and roast for 15 to 20 minutes, until vegetables begin to brown and char. (It is important that they char; the flavor comes from the browning and charring of the vegetables.)

3. Puree the vegetables, then thin, if needed, with chicken stock. Check the seasoning.

Chiles Rellenos with Roasted Tomato Salsa

Jícama Salad

AMOUNT	MEASURE	INGREDIENT
2 cups	10 ounces/280 g	Jícama, julienned
½ cup	2 ounces/56 g	Red bell pepper, julienned
¼ cup	1 ounce/28 g	Yellow bell pepper, julienned
1 cup	4 ounces/112 g	European cucumber, peeled, julienned
¼ cup	2 ounces/60 ml	Olive oil
2 tablespoons	1 ounce/30 ml	Lime juice
½ tablespoon		Fresh flat-leaf parsley, finely chopped
		Salt and white pepper

PROCEDURE

1. Combine the vegetables with the olive oil in a bowl.

2. Season with the lime juice, parsley, salt, and pepper. Refrigerate until ready to serve.

Grilled Apache-Style Pork Chops with Squash Salsa and Tobacco Onions

4 servings

Grilled Apache-Style Pork Chops

AMOUNT	MEASURE	INGREDIENT
4	1 ounce/28 g	Garlic cloves, minced
2 teaspoons		Chili powder
1 teaspoon		Paprika
2 teaspoons		Ground cumin
½ teaspoon		Cayenne pepper
2 teaspoons		Salt
4	4 ounces/112 g each	Pork cutlets
As needed		Vegetable oil

PROCEDURE

1. Combine all the ingredients for the spice mix in a bowl and mash to a smooth paste.

2. Rub the pork with the spice mix and let marinate for 15 to 20 minutes.

3. Preheat the grill to medium heat.

4. Brush the pork with the oil, and then grill 4 to 5 minutes per side, turn onto each side twice, rotating the chops a half turn each time to get criss-cross grill marks.

5. Serve with the Squash Salsa and Tobacco Onions (recipes follow).

Squash Salsa

AMOUNT	MEASURE	INGREDIENT
½ cup	2 ounces/56 g	Red onion, minced
½ cup	2 ounces/56 g	Zucchini, in ⅛-inch (.3 cm) dice
½ cup	2 ounces/56 g	Yellow summer squash, in ⅛-inch (.3 cm) dice
¼ cup	1 ounce/28 g	Carrot, in ⅛-inch (.3 cm) dice
½ cup	3 ounces/84 g	Tomatillos, husked, in ⅛-inch (.3 cm) dice
1 cup	6 ounces/168 g	Tomato, peeled, in ⅛-inch (.3 cm) dice
1	5 g	Garlic clove, minced
1	1 teaspoon/7 g	Serrano chile, minced
1 tablespoon		Fresh marjoram, chopped
4 teaspoons	¾ ounce/22.5 ml	Olive oil
1 tablespoon	½ ounce/15 ml	Sherry vinegar
		Sugar
		Salt

PROCEDURE

1. Rinse the onion under very hot water and drain.

2. Combine the onion with the remaining ingredients.

3. Correct the seasoning. Add more chile for extra heat, if desired. Let sit for at least 1 hour at room temperature before serving.

Grilled Apache-Style Pork Chop, Squash Salsa, and Tobacco Onions

Tobacco Onions

✦ **CHEF TIP:** Tobacco onions are deep-fried onion rings seasoned with cayenne and chili powder. When cooked, they look like shredded tobacco.

AMOUNT	MEASURE	INGREDIENT
As needed		Vegetable oil
1 small	10 ounces/280 g	Red onion
1 small	10 ounces/280 g	Yellow onion
1 cup	4 ounces/112 g	All-purpose flour
		Salt and white pepper
2 tablespoons	½ ounce/14 g	Paprika
1 teaspoon		Cayenne pepper
1½ teaspoons		Chili powder

PROCEDURE

1. Heat the oil in a deep pot or deep-fat fryer to 350°F (175°C).

2. Slice the onions very thinly into rings.

3. Sift the flour and half the seasonings in a large bowl. Add the onion rings and toss until they are well coated and dry.

4. Fry the onions quickly, in small batches, until golden brown, about 1 to 2 minutes.

5. Drain on paper towels. Toss with the remaining salt and pepper, paprika, cayenne, and chili powder. Serve immediately.

Sopaipillas

✦ **CHEF TIP:** These are often called "little pillows" but the name literally means "holding soup." Sopaipillas are said to have originated in the Albuquerque, New Mexico, area over 200 years ago. Both sopaipillas and tortillas are used to soak up liquids in a dish or are stuffed with filling so they can be eaten without utensils. Here, they contain air and soak up some of the honey. If the sopaipillas do not puff properly, increase or decrease the temperature of the oil.

AMOUNT	MEASURE	INGREDIENT
½ teaspoon		Salt
½ cup plus 2 tablespoons	5 ounces/130 ml	Warm water
2 cups	8 ounces/224 g	All-purpose flour
1 teaspoon	4 g	Baking powder
2 teaspoons	10 g	Granulated sugar
2 tablespoons	1 ounce/30 ml	Vegetable shortening
As needed		Oil or shortening, for frying
¼ cup	1 ounce/28 g	Confectioners' sugar
2 tablespoons	1 ounce/30 ml	Honey

PROCEDURE

1. Dissolve the salt in the warm water.

2. Combine the flour, baking powder, and sugar. Cut in the shortening until mixture resembles very fine bread crumbs. Add the salted water to the flour and mix the dough until it forms a clean mass.

3. Turn the dough out onto a lightly floured surface and knead by folding it in half, pushing it down, and folding again. It should take 12 to 15 folds to form a soft dough that is no longer sticky. Cover and let rest for 15 minutes.

4. Divide dough into small balls approximately 1¼ inches (3.1 cm) in diameter. Cover and set aside for 10 minutes.

5. Heat the oil or shortening to 375°F (190°C).

6. Roll the dough balls to a ⅛-inch (.3 cm) thickness on a lightly floured board. The balls should roll into 5- to 5½-inch (12.7–13.9 cm) circles; they will not necessarily be evenly shaped. (Sopaipillas can be cut into any shape.) The dough should be thin, but not transparent.

7. Cut the circles into 4 triangular pieces and immediately, while the dough is still damp, put into the hot oil. Do not attempt to reform and roll the leftover dough scraps. (They do not roll out well on the second try. The scraps may be fried with the triangular pieces.)

   Submerge the pieces in the oil and they should begin to puff immediately. Fry until golden on both sides, turning once, about 2 to 3 minutes total. (If shortening is sufficiently hot, the sopaipillas will puff and become hollow shortly after being placed in the shortening. The sopaipillas will either puff or not. It is the puff that makes it a sopaipilla. Those that don't puff can still be eaten, however.)

8. Drain sopaipillas on absorbent towels, sprinkle with sugar, drizzle with honey, and serve.

Grilled Vegetable Gazpacho

4 servings

AMOUNT	MEASURE	INGREDIENT
½ cup	2 ounces/56 g	Red onion, in ½-inch (1.2 cm) slices
½ cup	2 ounces/56 g	Zucchini, in ½-inch (1.2 cm) slices
3 tablespoons	1½ ounces/45 ml	Olive oil
1 cup	5 ounces/140 g	Roasted green bell pepper, in ¼-inch (.6 cm) dice
2 cups	12 ounces/340 g	Tomato, peeled, in ¼-inch (.6 cm) dice
1 cup	4 ounces/112 g	Cucumber, peeled, in ¼-inch (.6 cm) dice
2	10 g	Garlic cloves, minced
½ cup	½ ounce/14 g	Dried bread crumbs
1 tablespoon	½ ounce/15 ml	Red wine vinegar
1½ cups	12 ounces/360 ml	Tomato juice or V8 juice
1 tablespoon	3 g	Fresh cilantro, chopped
		Salt and pepper
1 cup	8 ounces/240 ml	Chicken stock
		Corn tortillas, julienned, fried
		Green onions, sliced on the bias

PROCEDURE

1. Preheat the grill.

2. Brush the onion and zucchini slices with 1 tablespoon (½ ounce/15 ml) olive oil and grill until tender, about 4 to 6 minutes. Watch the vegetables carefully to prevent burning.

3. Place the grilled onion and zucchini and the roasted pepper into a food processor and pulse to a coarse puree. Do not overprocess, as the vegetables will become too thin and lose their natural juices and flavor.

4. Mix the tomato, cucumber, and garlic with the processed vegetables in a stainless steel bowl. Add the bread crumbs, vinegar, tomato or V8 juice, cilantro, and remaining 2 tablespoons (1 ounce/30 ml) olive oil. Season with salt and pepper. Chill thoroughly. Add chicken stock to reach desired consistency.

5. Carefully ladle the gazpacho into well-chilled soup bowls. Garnish each portion by placing a small pile of fried tortilla strips on the surface. Sprinkle the sliced green onions on top of the tortilla strips and serve.

Spicy Pork Empanadas

AMOUNT	MEASURE	INGREDIENT
For the Dough		
¼ cup	2 ounces/56 g	Butter, softened
¼ cup	2 ounces/56 g	Cream cheese, softened
¾ cup	3 ounces/84 g	All-purpose flour
¼ teaspoon		Baking powder
Dash		Cider vinegar
½ tablespoon	¼ ounce/7 ml	Vegetable oil
For the Filling		
¼ cup	2 ounces/60 ml	Vegetable oil
½ cup	4 ounces/112 g	Ground pork
¼ cup	1 ounce/28 g	Onion, in ¼-inch (.6 cm) dice
1	5 g	Garlic clove, minced
1	1 teaspoon/7 g	Serrano chile, seeded, finely diced
⅓ cup	2 ounces/56 g	Tomato, peeled, in ¼-inch (.6 cm) dice
1 tablespoon	3 g	Fresh cilantro, chopped
		Salt and pepper
As needed		Vegetable oil, for frying

PROCEDURE

1. Make the dough. Combine the butter and cream cheese. Sift the flour and baking powder together. Combine the cream cheese mixture with the dry mixture and add the vinegar. With generously floured hands, work the dough until you have a smooth, resilient dough, 3 to 4 minutes. Brush with oil and set aside.

2. Prepare the filling. Heat the oil over medium heat in a 2- to 3-quart (2–3 L) saucepan. Add the pork, onion, and garlic and cook, stirring constantly, for about 5 minutes.

3. Add the chile, tomato, cilantro, and salt and pepper, and simmer over low heat for about 10 minutes. Taste and adjust seasoning, if necessary. Cool the mixture before making the empanadas.

4. Make the empanadas. Roll out the dough to ⅛-inch (.3 cm) thickness and cut out 3-inch (7.6 cm) circles. Place a heaping tablespoon of filling in the center of each, fold over, and seal the edges. Cover with plastic so they will not dry out and refrigerate until ready to serve.

5. Heat the oil in a deep pot or deep-fryer to 350°F (175°C).

6. Fry the empanadas until golden brown, about 2 minutes. Drain on paper towels.

Marinated Dried Bean Salad Colorado

AMOUNT	MEASURE	INGREDIENT
For the Beans		
2 tablespoons	1 ounce/28 g	Dried red beans
2½ tablespoons	1 ounce/28 g	Lentils
2 tablespoons	1 ounce/28 g	Dried pinto beans
2 tablespoons	1 ounce/28 g	Dried Anasazi beans
For the Vinaigrette		
1 tablespoon	3 g	Fresh sage leaves, cut in chiffonade
2	10 g	Garlic cloves, minced
3 tablespoons	1½ ounces/45 ml	Cider vinegar
6 tablespoons	3 ounces/45 ml	Olive oil
		Salt and black pepper
For the Salad		
½ cup	2 ounces/56 g	Onion, in ½-inch (1.2 cm) dice
1	2 ounces/56 g	Roasted jalapeño, seeded, diced
1 cup	4 ounces/112 g	Roasted green bell pepper, in ½-inch (1.2 cm) dice
2½ cups	5 ounces/140 g	Leaf lettuce
½ cup	2 ounces/56 g	Green onions, sliced
2 tablespoons	1 ounce/30 ml	Heavy cream
1 teaspoon	5 ml	Cider vinegar
		Salt and black pepper
2 cups	8 ounces/224 g	Tomatoes, peeled, thinly sliced (20 slices)

PROCEDURE

1. Prepare the beans. Soak each type of bean individually overnight in water to cover. Most dried beans, except split peas and lentils, need to be soaked before cooking.

2. Drain and cook the beans individually in salted water until tender. Drain and cool, reserving the liquid from the red beans.

3. Make the dressing. Whisk together the ingredients in a small bowl.

4. Assemble the salad. Toss together the beans, onion, jalapeño, pepper, and dressing. Let the mixture marinate for 15 to 20 minutes.

5. Clean, dry, and trim the lettuce and green onions. Chop green onions finely. Combine the cream, vinegar, the green onions, and the salt and pepper in a small bowl.

6. In a large bowl, toss the lettuce with the cream mixture, divide among 4 salad plates, and overlap 5 tomato slices down the center of each plate. Season the tomatoes lightly with salt and pepper.

7. Serve about ½ cup (4 ounces/112 g) of the marinated bean salad with the greens.

Lamb Shoulder with Red Chile Marinade and Cilantro Pesto

4 servings

AMOUNT	MEASURE	INGREDIENT
For the Marinade		
½ tablespoon	5 g	Cumin seeds
1	½ ounce/14 g	Ancho chile, stemmed, seeded, halved
1	½ ounce/14 g	Pasilla chile, stemmed, seeded, halved
½ tablespoon	¼ ounce/7 g	Chipotle chile puree (from canned chile with adobo sauce)
1 tablespoon	½ ounce/15 ml	Vegetable oil
For the Pesto		
1 cup	2 ounces/56 g	Fresh cilantro leaves
1	5 g	Garlic clove, chopped
1 tablespoon	6 g	Pumpkin seeds
1 tablespoon	½ ounce/15 ml	Lime juice
1 teaspoon	5 g	Salt
¼ teaspoon	1 g	Black pepper
¼ cup	2 ounces/60 ml	Olive oil
For the Meat		
1	3 pounds/1.36 kg	Boned lamb shoulder, butterflied to a rough rectangle

PROCEDURE

1. Preheat the oven to 350°F (175°C).

2. Make the marinade. Heat a pan and add cumin seeds. Toast over medium-high heat, shaking the pan constantly until the seeds are fragrant, about 15 seconds. Grind the seeds in a coffee grinder or with a mortar and pestle.

3. Set the ancho and pasilla chiles in a small pan. Place the pan in the oven until the chile pieces develop a sheen—no more than 30 seconds. Cut the chiles into pieces small enough to grind in a coffee grinder. Grind to a powder and mix with chipotle puree and oil.

4. Make the pesto. Place the cilantro, garlic, pumpkin seeds, lime juice, salt, and pepper into a blender. Blend until the cilantro is minced. With the blender running slowly, add the oil so the pesto emulsifies.

5. Prepare the meat. Pound the lamb shoulder to a ½-inch (1.2 cm) thickness.

6. Spread two-thirds of the cilantro pesto in a thin layer over the meat, leaving at least a 1-inch (2.5 cm) border. Season and roll the lamb into a tight cylinder and truss. Rub the roast on all sides with the chile marinade; let it set out at room temperature for 1 hour.

7. Preheat the oven to 450°F (225°C).

8. Roast the lamb for 15 minutes. Reduce the heat to 350°F (175°C) and cook to medium, 135°F (57°C).

9. Let the roast rest at room temperature for 10 to 15 minutes, then slice diagonally, about ¼ inch (.6 cm) thick.

10. Serve with the remaining cilantro pesto and Jalapeño Preserves (recipe follows).

Jalapeño Preserves

AMOUNT	MEASURE	INGREDIENT
1 cup	6 ounces/170 g	Red bell pepper, finely chopped
1	2½ ounces/70 g	Jalapeño chile, seeded, finely chopped
½ cup	3½ ounces/100 g	Sugar
¼ cup	2 ounces/60 ml	Red wine vinegar
1 tablespoon	¼ ounce/7 g	Fruit pectin powder

PROCEDURE

1. In a nonreactive pan, combine the red pepper, jalapeño, sugar, and vinegar. Bring to a boil, then turn down the heat and simmer for 20 minutes, stirring periodically.

2. Remove the pan from the heat and add the fruit pectin. Return to heat and bring back to a simmer. Remove the pan from the heat and let it cool to room temperature. The jelly will be on the thin side until it chills.

The Cuisine of
California

Compared to the United States as a whole, California has a relatively young cuisine, the foundation of which is innovation. The third largest state in America and with the largest population, it has a wide variety of microclimates and geography, making it well suited for growing and raising foods of all kinds. Agriculture is the core of the state's economy and California produces more crops than any other state. Home to the largest irrigation systems built in America, it has given farmers even in the most remote deserts the opportunity to raise and harvest valuable crops.

California cuisine takes advantage of the region's abundant natural resources. With the wide variety of fresh produce and vast grazing land for livestock, its residents find obtaining fresh, local, seasonal ingredients is easy. Californians' inclination toward a healthy lifestyle has also encouraged the development of California cuisine. Foods grown and harvested naturally, prepared simply, and without preservatives and fats, along with the constant flood of aspiring chefs bringing their culinary heritage, have ensured California has its share of creativity with regard to food and food-related products. Chefs today recognize they have a commitment to the environment, to their community, and to using their talents to continue to lead the nation in fresh, new ideas that change the culinary landscape.

California's history and development have been intertwined with gold in one form or another, hence the name "The Golden State." The state flower is the golden poppy, the state tree is the California redwood, and the state animal is the grizzly bear. The state bird is the California quail, and the state fish is the golden trout. The state motto is "Eureka"—the Greek word meaning "I have found it."

HISTORY AND MAJOR INFLUENCES

The earliest residents of California were Native Americans. There were hundreds of small groups, speaking more than 100 languages, with no central government, but they existed in relative peace and isolation. Mountain tribes lived in small villages and ate deer and other small game. Coastal tribes harvested fish and shellfish from the sea. Their diets also included fruit and nuts. Acorns were an important food for almost all of California's native population. After drying the acorns and leaching out the tannin, the acorns were ground into flour to make dough that was cooked on hot rocks or made into a mush.

EUROPEAN CONTACT

The first settlers to arrive in California were the Spanish. Many were Roman Catholic missionaries who traveled to California to "civilize" and convert the natives to Christianity. Franciscan friar Junipero Serra established the first mission at San Diego in 1769, and eventually 21 California missions stretched from San Diego to Sonoma. The food in the missions reflected the Mexican and Spanish influences in the area. They grew crops such as wheat and corn and raised livestock, including cattle and pigs. The missionaries taught the Native American tribes about farming and other trades.

Along with the missionaries, a group of people known as "Californios"—Spanish-speaking people from Mexico or Spain—settled in California. These were powerful and often wealthy families who held vast territories under Spanish land grants and raised tens of thousands of cattle. They established sprawling *ranchos*, or cattle ranches, along the California coast. Most of the rancheros sold cattle hides and tallow, or animal fat used to make candles and soap. Some made wine and grew citrus fruits, which were exported. They lived and entertained in grand style. Beef was the main staple of their diet. The fortunes of the Californios changed after the Mexican-American War of 1846–48.

Mexico lost the war and, in 1848, ceded California to the United States. Though they lost their land, the Californio legacy remains. The citrus and wine trades continue to be two of California's largest industries, and the names of many California cities—including San Francisco, San Jose, Monterey, Los Angeles, and San Diego—are reminders of the Spanish-speaking people who first settled them.

THE CALIFORNIA GOLD RUSH

In 1848, shiny particles were found near a sawmill owned by German-speaking Swiss immigrant John Sutter. The particles were gold, and it was not long before more gold was found by other workers at Sutter's mill and news of the chance discovery began to spread. When the news reached San Francisco, virtually the whole town flocked to the Sacramento Valley to pan for gold. As gold fever traveled eastward, overland migration to California rose from 400 people in 1848 to over 44,000 by 1849. By the end of 1849, California's population exceeded 100,000. The rest of the world caught gold fever as well. Among the "forty-niners"—the prospectors who came to California in 1849—were people from Asia, South America, and Europe. The discovery of gold revolutionized California's economy. Gold financed the development of farming, manufacturing, shipping, and banking. Because of its location, San Francisco became the supply center of the region. Ships linked California markets to the expanding markets of the rest of the United States.

THE TRANSCONTINENTAL RAILROAD

Even after the gold rush, California remained the fastest growing state in the nation. Entrepreneurs Charles Crocker, Mark Hopkins, Collis Huntington, and Leland Stanford—known as the "Big Four"—joined together to build the western railroad link to overcome California's geographic isolation from the East Coast. Their crews laid over a thousand miles of track to join the eastern and western railroad lines. When they needed workers to lay the track, they hired primarily Chinese immigrants. By 1869, when the railroad was finished, 10,000 Chinese workers had helped to build it. After completing the job, the Chinese turned to the agriculture, mining, and manufacturing industries for work. They lived in their own neighborhoods, establishing large Chinatowns in San Francisco, Los Angeles, and other cities.

HOLLYWOOD

In the early years of the 20th century, moviemakers found their homes and fortunes in California. Southern California made outdoor filming possible during the winter months, and striking landscapes soon turned it into the glamour capital of the world. Catering to the movie studios and its stars, restaurants such as the Cocoanut Grove, the Brown Derby, and Chasen's opened and quickly learned to provide high-quality food with excellent service, setting the trend for today's modern California cuisine restaurants.

THE GEOGRAPHY AND MICROCLIMATES

When discussing any great area of agriculture, it is helpful to organize it into regions reflecting climate, geography, and culture. The coastline of California stretches 1,264 miles from the Oregon border in the north to Mexico in the south. More than half of California's population resides in the coastal region. Most live in the major cities that developed around harbors at San Francisco Bay, San Diego Bay, and the Los Angeles Basin. San Francisco Bay, one of the finest natural harbors in the world, covers about 450 square miles and is famous for its ocean breezes and the fog that rolls in from the sea. It became the gateway for newcomers heading to the states' interior in the 19th and 20th centuries. The completion of the Santa Fe Railroad in 1885 spurred population growth, as did the establishment of major army and navy bases during World War I.

The Los Angeles Basin is the largest lowland area in California, and with construction of a huge breakwater along the harbors of San Pedro and Long Beach, this bustling port overtook New York City in 1994 as America's premier gateway for foreign trade. Mountains cover most of California. The mountains guard the rich agricultural valleys from the intense heat of the desert to the east and shield the coastal valleys from the Pacific Ocean and its winds to the west.

The Central Valley lies between the coastal ranges and the Sierra Nevada. With the rich soil washed down from the surrounding mountains, this is the most productive agricultural area in California. The valley is actually two valleys in one, with the San Joaquin Valley in the south and the Sacramento Valley in the north. The climate in the San Joaquin and Sacramento valleys supports an expansive array of fruits and vegetables. After the gold rush in 1849, European settlers established vast wheat farms on the valleys' fertile soils. The great Central Valley Project, constructed in the mid-20th century, established a series of dams, reservoirs, and canals and guaranteed sufficient water for the diversification of crops. The improvements in irrigation enabled the valleys to produce tomatoes, potatoes, alfalfa, sugar beets, olives, almonds, walnuts, peaches, pears, apricots, and dozens of other fruits and vegetables.

Much of the eastern half of Southern California is a large desert triangle. Among the deserts of California are the Mojave and Colorado, as well as the notorious Death Valley. The Mojave is the largest desert in California, and Death Valley, a deep trough that is measured as the lowest point below sea level in the Western Hemisphere, was named by a group of gold seekers who struggled through the region in 1849. The Colorado Desert stretches over 4,000 miles in Southern California and includes the Coachella and Imperial valleys. In 1849, California visionary Oliver Wozencraft became convinced that these two valleys could be irrigated and turned into thriving farmland. He had a creative irrigation plan that, over the subsequent years, was modified into a chain of levees to bring water to the valleys from the Colorado River. Many settlers moved to the valleys as farming was made easier and more profitable by the constant sunshine, inexpensive water supply, and rich soil. The settlers found that in this desert area of California they could raise crops, harvest them, and sell them in the market before their competitors in the north. The nation's only commercial date palm grove grows in this desert oasis, and today the desert is known as Palm Springs and is a place of fashionable boutiques, exclusive resorts, and magnificent and opulent living.

INNOVATION IN FOOD

The largest of California's agricultural industries is dairy farming, which today produces over $3 billion worth of dairy products each year. The cheese industry of California, working with the milk of cows, goats, and sheep, is an example of the state's diversity. Small local artisans make prize-winning, hand-crafted, high-quality cheeses that compete well with their older, more established European counterparts. At the other end of the spectrum are high-tech cheese factories that produce hundreds of millions of pounds of cheese each year. Monterey jack, one of the three cheeses invented in America, is from California.

Agricultural innovation in California began with a horticulturist named Luther Burbank, who moved to Southern California from New England in the late 1800s. During a lifetime devoted to plant breeding, Luther Burbank developed more than 800 strains and varieties of plants, including 113 varieties of plums and prunes, 10 varieties of berries, 50 varieties of lilies, and the Freestone peach. In 1871, he developed the Burbank potato, which was introduced in Ireland to help combat the blight epidemic. He sold the rights to the potato and used the proceeds to travel to Santa Rosa, California. In Santa Rosa, he established a nursery garden, greenhouse, and experimental farms that have become famous throughout the world. At any one time, he maintained as many as 3,000 experiments involving millions of plants. In his work on plums, he tested about 30,000 new varieties. From this original research, California scientists began to develop new varieties of produce carefully selected for resistance to disease, bugs, and extreme weather conditions, as well as for characteristics of size, color, flavor, and shelf life.

Although a significant amount of controversy surrounds these selectively bred fruits and vegetables, especially now that some are being genetically modified, one thing is for certain: The technological advances started by Burbank in California allowed the state's produce industry to supply not only America but also the world.

MODERN CALIFORNIA CUISINE

Culinary professionals credit Alice Waters for her role in the development of California cuisine. While studying in France, Waters experienced a cuisine based on using premier ingredients grown by local farmers. She returned to America and opened her own restaurant, Chez Panisse, in Berkeley, in 1971, and partnered with local growers from Northern California. She used a single fixed-price menu that changed daily. This menu format allowed her to focus on serving not only the highest-quality products but also only when ingredients were in season, understanding that the dish is only as good as its components. As other restaurants began to adopt her philosophy, many artisan producers found opportunities to specialize in and market certain products, such as baby vegetables, varietal tomatoes, and other market-fresh produce. Chez Panisse is still considered one of the best restaurants in the United States.

About ten years later, Austrian-born chef Wolfgang Puck, the chef at Ma Maison in Los Angeles, a popular hangout for Hollywood celebrities, became one of America's first celebrity chefs. In 1982, Puck opened his own restaurant in Los Angeles, called Spago, and became known for his designer pizzas and specialty pasta dishes. He brought a lighter style of cooking to California cuisine and added an entertaining and energetic atmosphere emphasizing an "open kitchen" where guests could watch the chefs prepare their food.

Recently, fusion cuisine has become a popular innovation originating in California. Using a creative mix of flavors, techniques, and ingredients of more than one region or international cuisine, California chefs began creating dishes that both represent and serve the diverse people and cultures in the state today. California society has been shaped by many different kinds of people. From the Native Americans, to Spanish aristocrats, to gold hunters, railroad tycoons, and movie moguls, each group has left its imprint on the state. And immigration to California continues as Mexican, Japanese, Southeast Asian, Italian, French, northern European, Middle Eastern, Spanish, and Greek people contribute to the multicultural blend that keeps California cuisine fresh, imaginative, and exciting.

CALIFORNIA GRAPES

Father Junipero Serra is credited with planting the first grape vines at the San Diego Mission shortly after its founding. The early Spanish missionaries were the first to produce wine in California from local Mission grapes. However, it was not until after the 1849 gold rush that the wine industry took root. A Frenchman living in California, Jean-Louis Vignes, recognized the value of the soil and the climate, but he felt that the wines would improve if the European grape varieties grown in France could be transplanted to California.

Between the plentiful sunshine and the cooling effects of the fog that rolls in from the Pacific Ocean, California's climate was similar to the climate that vines were used to in Europe. Later, Hungarian Agoston Haraszthy took note of Vignes's success in growing French grapes. He established the first California winery, Buena Vista, in 1857. In 1861, he traveled to Europe to buy cuttings and brought over 100,000 vine cuttings representing over 300 varieties of grapes. He planted them in Sonoma Country and became known as the father of California's wine industry. Wine making in California prospered until 1916, when the vines were almost wiped out by a vine-killing root louse called phylloxera. Added to that were the 14 "dry" years during the era of Prohibition, from December 1917 until February 1933. Most of California's 713 pre-Prohibition wineries closed their doors, but a few wineries stayed in business by making legally sanctioned

The idea that evolved into Community Supported Agriculture (CSA) began in Japan, in the mid-1960s, with what is known as the Teikei movement. Japanese homemakers noticed an increase in imported foods, the consistent loss of farmland to development, and migration of farmers to the cities. A group of women approached a local farm family with an idea to address these issues and provide their families with fresh fruits and vegetables. They made a contract with the farm to finance the farm in the beginning of the season; in return, they received fresh, local produce throughout the growing season.

This idea spread to Europe in the late 1960s as an outgrowth of biodynamic farming, a process developed by Rudolph Steiner in the early 20th century based on the idea that all living organisms (land, plants, and animals) are dependent on one another. Farmers in Holland and Switzerland developed similar models as an economic and social component to these ideas of interdependence. In 1985, the first CSA program was established in the United States in Massachusetts, where it was renamed "community supported agriculture."

CSA may be formal and legal arrangements, in which members become shareholders of the farmland or garden and share in the cost of the raising the food and share what is produced on the community farm. CSA members may be required to pay for their anticipated harvest for the year up front, although some CSA groups offer monthly payment programs referred to as subscriptions. Other CSA arrangements may be less formal and more of a community than a legal arrangement, whereby community members may pledge labor and/or money to support growing produce and again share in the seasonal harvest.

Members of a CSA often receive or pick up a basket or box of produce on a weekly or monthly basis, typically from June through October. CSA offerings may include vegetables, fruits, eggs, meats, flowers. Farmers benefit from being involved in a CSA because they have the financial support needed to continue to operate the farm. Farmers enjoy better prices for their crops and farmers also have a guaranteed direct market for sales and are relieved of the additional duties of marketing their crops. CSA members share in not only the benefits of food production but also the risk of poor harvests that may result from uncontrolled pests or extreme weather.

sacramental and medicinal wines. Others survived by shipping grapes cross-country by rail to home wine-making markets. A provision of the Volstad Act allowed families to make 200 gallons annually for home consumption. Many of them also purchased "wine bricks," "wine loaves," or grape concentrate to make their wine. Vintners produced and sold concentrate with a creative label that read, "Warning: Do not add water to this product as it is likely to ferment." Public opinion eventually turned against Prohibition and the act was repealed in 1933. The California wine-making industry recovered by the 1940s; however, the existing grape-growing and wine-making techniques produced many low- to average-quality wines. After experimentation throughout the 1950s, 1960s, and 1970s, wine making in California began to reach its maturity, now yielding high-quality wines that can compete with many older, more established European wines.

Typical California Ingredients and Dishes

Abalone   The meat from a large mollusk that lives off the coast of California. There are eight species that inhabit the Pacific waters: red (the largest, and most important commercial abalone), green, black, flat (small in size and most prized), white (found in depths up to 150 feet and commercially included with the pink abalone), and the three least common species—threaded, pink, and pinto. All varieties offer meat that is extremely sweet and tasty, but it is usually tough and rubbery and requires tenderizing with a mallet prior to cooking. Their colorful, ear-shaped shells are sometimes referred to as mother of pearl. Today, the abalone industry is highly regulated, as the mollusks continue to be the favorite food of sea otters and are scarce.

Anaheim Chile   Also referred to as the California green chile, this 6- to 8-inch chile is bright green with mild to moderate heat. When this chile is grown in New Mexico, it is referred to as a New Mexico green chile. It was popularized by Emilio Ortega, a California rancher who opened the first chile cannery near Anaheim in 1900.

Artichoke A member of the thistle group of the sunflower family with a large, globular flower head. It is grown predominately in California in the town of Castroville. The Green Globe artichoke is most common to the area. Artichoke hearts have an especially appealing flavor and texture. Artichokes are served hot or cold, as an appetizer or a main dish, and as an ingredient in other dishes such as pasta sauces, vegetable dishes, and in soups and stews.

Asparagus Over 70 percent of all asparagus served in America is produced in the southern half of California's Great Central Valley. Asparagus is a member of the lily family, and the varieties include white, green, and a new breed of purple, Purple Passion.

Avocado Dating back to almost 8,000 B.C., the avocado originated in Mexico and was considered an aphrodisiac by the Aztecs. Avocados were introduced to California in 1848. Today, California produces 95 percent of the nation's crop. A single California avocado tree can produce up to 60 pounds of fresh fruit each year, approximately 120 individual avocados. The most popular varieties are the Hass and the Fuerte, which are known for their sweet, slightly nutty flavor.

Calamari Italian for "squid." Squid is found all along the California coast. It can be cooked by sautéing, frying, steaming, poaching, or broiling. Large squid are usually stuffed and braised. Squid has an ink sac in the head containing a dark black liquid that can be used (but only if the squid is extremely fresh) in sauces or as a flavoring and coloring agent for fresh pasta. Squid and octopus belong to the same family, but squid have ten arms and a long, cigar-shaped body with fins at the end; octopuses have eight arms and a stubbier body.

California Roll A form of sushi made with avocados, crab meat, cucumbers, and other ingredients wrapped in vinegared rice.

Cioppino A fish stew cooked with tomatoes, wine, and spices. This stew is associated with the Italian fishermen who came to the San Francisco Bay area in the late 1800s.

Cheese As the largest farming state in the United States, California has dairy farms and dairies processing the milk of cows, goats, and sheep all over the state.

>   **Dry Jack** A type of cheese discovered by mistake in the early 1900s by a cheese wholesaler who apparently left some in storage too long. The aged jack cheese had hardened and developed a sweet, nutty flavor. During World War I, the supply of romano and Parmesan cheeses previously imported to America became sporadic and inconsistent. Dry jack, with a texture and flavor similar to the dried Italian cheese, became popular as a substitute. It is now produced as a California artisan-style cheese.

>   **Feta Cheese** A salty, crumbly white cheese made in the style of Greek goat's milk cheese. American varieties are often made from cow's milk. After the curds are formed, the cheese is pickled in a brine solution.

>   **Goat Cheese** Called *chèvre* in France, goat cheese has become a signature ingredient in California cuisine. It is typically an intensely flavored cheese.

>   **Monterey Jack** One of the three cheeses invented in the United States (along with Colby and brick, from the Central Plains region). A mild white, semisoft cheese that originated in Monterey, California, much like the cheeses produced in the early missions. It was named after David Jacks, a dairy farmer who made the cheese just after California's gold rush years.

Chop Suey An American invention created by the cooks who fed the Chinese immigrants working to construct the Western Pacific Railroad in the mid-1800s. Considered to be "a little of this and that" from the Mandarin words *tsa tsui*, the widely varying ingredients usually include bamboo shoots, water chestnuts, bean sprouts, celery, soy sauce, and chicken or pork. Americanized Chinese dishes such as this and chow mein continue to be served in Chinese restaurants to American customers.

Citron A citrus fruit that looks like a large, lumpy lemon. Another common variety grown in California is mostly as an ornamental, called the Fingered citron or Buddha's Hand, that has formed by a half dozen or more long twisting fingers growing outward from the stem end. Only the rind is used, much like lemon rind. Citron rind is most frequently candied and often used in baking.

Cobb Salad   A chopped salad made with avocado, lettuce, celery, tomato, bacon, chicken, chives, hard-boiled egg, watercress, and Roquefort cheese. Originally created at the Brown Derby Restaurant in Los Angeles in 1934, it is now commonly used to describe many types of chopped salads.

Date   The name is from the Greek word for "finger," after the shape of the fruit. Date palm trees require at least ten years from the time the tree is planted to the time fruit can be picked. The only places in the Western Hemisphere where dates are commercially grown are the Yuma Valley in Arizona and the Coachella Valley in California, where the climate is similar to that of the Middle East and North Africa. The best dates are picked soft, and then frozen to maintain the enzymes in the fruit that produce the natural sugar powder that forms on the skin. Lower-quality dates are allowed to cure on the tree and then are softened by steaming, which destroys the enzymes.

Figs   Planted at the Spanish missions, the Mission (or Black Mission) fig has purple-black skin. Other varieties include the Brown Turkey fig, which is amber in color and milder than the Mission fig. The most commonly grown fig in California is the Calimyrna, a greenish yellow to golden colored fig more frequently seen as whole dried figs.

French Dip   The house specialty of Phillippe's, a Los Angeles restaurant dating back to 1908. The sandwich calls for thinly sliced beef, pork, or lamb served hot on a French bread roll and dipped in warm pan juices.

Garlic   A major crop from Gilroy, California, located in the San Joaquin Valley. Over 90 percent of all garlic consumed in the United States is grown here. Garlic is native to Central Asia; Japanese immigrants started garlic farming in the area in the 1920s.

Green Goddess Dressing   A mayonnaise-based salad dressing made with anchovies, tarragon, chives, and parsley, invented by the chef at the Palace Hotel in San Francisco. Green Goddess dressing was created in 1921 in honor of George Arliss, a guest of the hotel, who was starring in the play The Green Goddess, being performed in the city.

Guacamole   A dip made from the mashed pulp of avocados mixed with herbs, seasonings, and sometimes tomatoes and onions. In California, recipes for guacamole are passed down from generation to generation and guarded as stringently as chili recipes in Texas and gumbo recipes in New Orleans. Guacamole can be smooth or chunky, mild or spicy.

Kiwi   This round green fruit with black seeds and fuzzy brown skin was known as the Chinese gooseberry and originated in China. Today, 95 percent of the U.S. crop is grown in California, primarily in the San Joaquin Valley.

Olive   California has four main varieties—Mission, originally planted by the Franciscan missionaries; Manzanillo, which account for most of the acreage; and Sevillano and Ascolano, which produce the larger sizes. Approximately 75 percent of ripe olives consumed in the United States come from California. Over 90 percent of the California crop is processed as black ripe olives. The remaining olives are processed into various specialty styles or crushed for olive oil.

Oranges   After Florida, California produces the most oranges of any state. The most common varieties include:

Blood Orange   Called blood oranges because of a pigment that gives the flesh a deep red color reminiscent of blood. With the most interesting and complex flavor of any orange, the fruit's degree of red color in the flesh and peel varies according to variety, growing area, and degree of maturity. Brought to the United States by Spanish and Italian immigrants, the Ruby Blood and Moro varieties are raised in California.

Navel Orange   This variety arrived in California from Brazil in 1873. Called "navel" because of a secondary fruit at the end of the main fruit that causes a belly-button look. They are known for their large size, sweet taste, seedless flesh, and ease of peeling.

Valencia Orange   The most important of the juice oranges, this variety comes originally from Spain and is grown in large quantities in Southern California. Valencia oranges are large, thin skinned, and very juicy, with excellent flavor and few seeds.

Pacific Sole   A common flatfish found in the waters off the California coast. Several varieties of Pacific sole are available, including the English or lemon sole, rex sole, California Dover sole, rock sole, and petrale or brill sole. All of the varieties have a white, sweet-tasting flesh with a lean, fine texture. The rex and the petrale sole are two of the most sought-after fish in the region. They are frequently sautéed and served with a light sauce.

Pummelo   Two varieties of this grapefruit-like fruit were developed in California. The Chandler pummelo is large and round, with yellow skin and pink flesh. The Reinkin variety is larger and pear shaped, with white flesh.

Raisin   A sweet, dried grape. California produces the most raisins of any region of the world, mostly of the Thompson Seedless variety. It is suggested that the raisin was created by accident when a heat wave dried a farmer's grapes on the vine before he could pick them. The grape industry devotes almost 2 million tons of grapes each year to the production of raisins.

Sand Dab   A miniature relative of the flounder that is common in the waters off the California coast. They are small flatfish between 8 and 10 ounces and both eyes, brown in color and mottled with orange or black spots or blotches, are found on the same side of the fish. This fish has a sweet flesh with a fine texture and is usually pan or deep fried.

Sashimi   Very fresh, top-quality, carefully handled fish, eaten raw.

Sea Urchin   Spiky "hedgehogs of the sea" have become fashionable first-course menu items. The roe is the only edible part of the sea urchin and is considered a great delicacy.

Smoothie   A health drink that dates back to the 1970s, typically found in juice bars. Recipes for smoothies vary; however, the essential ingredients include whole fruit, fruit juice, and yogurt, which are blended together and served in tall glasses.

Sourdough Bread   A uniquely flavored bread originally made in the San Francisco Bay area beginning in 1849 by French baker Louis Boudin. Boudin's bread had a chewy texture, crisp crust, and signature sour flavor. Popular among the prospectors during the California gold rush, it is still considered a San Francisco signature.

Sourdough Starter   A fermented leavener made from a paste of flour and water, activated by yeast and used to make sourdough bread. Sourdough starter was so valuable to miners and prospectors who depended on it to survive the wilderness that they carried it in a pouch hung from their necks. They became known as "sourdoughs" themselves. Sourdough starter is usually used over and over again. Each time a batch of sourdough bread is made, a portion of the dough is reserved, then mixed with water and a little salt, which maintains the starter. It is later added to the next batch of dough in order to make it rise.

Sushi   A bite-size Japanese rice and fish preparation popularized in the United States by Californians. Two main varieties of sushi are popular: maki and niguri. Sushi maki is made with sweet, sticky rice that is rolled in seaweed with raw, cooked, or smoked fish or shellfish, or vegetables, and cut into bite-size pieces. Niguri sushi has pieces of raw fish or seafood decoratively placed on top of an oblong log of sweet, sticky rice. Sushi needs to be served freshly made from the highest quality fish or seafood available. It is typically served with soy sauce, pickled ginger slices, and wasabi, a Japanese green horseradish.

Table Grape   About one-third of the fruit and nut revenues of California come from table grapes. The Thompson Seedless grape, which is native to Iran, took its name in the United States from an Englishman named William Thompson, who planted the grapes in the Sacramento Valley in the 1860s. Today, table grapes are extensively grown from the Mexican border to many parts of the San Joaquin Valley, with over 500,000 acres of land devoted to the crop. Among the many popular table grape varieties are Ribier, Flame, Emperor, Red Globe, and Calmeria.

Wine Grape   Approximately 20 varieties of grape are used today by California wine makers, planted on more than 350,000 acres of land, primarily near the north and central coasts. The most commonly grown grape varieties for the production of white wines are the Chardonnay, French Colombard, Chenin Blanc, and Sauvignon Blanc grapes. For the production of red wines, the most common grape varieties used are the Zinfandel, Cabernet Sauvignon, Merlot, and Barbera grapes.

Menus and Recipes from
the Cuisine of California

MENU ONE

Caesar Salad

Hangtown Fry

San Francisco Cioppino

Strawberry Shortcake with Cornmeal Biscuits

MENU TWO

Tomato Panna Cotta with Candied Tomatoes and Bacon Foam

Sautéed Sand Dabs

Fennel and Sweet Onion Pizza

Monterey Jack and Green Chile Polenta with Grilled Vegetables

Lemon Mousse

MENU THREE

Cream of Garlic Soup

Baby Greens with Goat Cheese Croquette

Calamari, Artichoke, and Penne Pasta Monterey-Style

Duck with Pine Nuts and Honey

Swiss Chard with Golden Raisins

Kiwifruit and Grape Rice Pudding

OTHER RECIPES

Garden Pasta Salad

Rosemary Focaccia

Chilled Avocado and Cucumber Soup

Dilled Carrot Soup

Caesar Salad

4 servings

✦ **CHEF TIP:** Caesar salad is considered the benchmark of salads that can be prepared tableside. A wooden bowl is selected to extract the greatest amount of oil from the garlic and anchovies. It allows for a great marriage of flavors once the dressing is completed. In a typical Caesar salad bowl, no more than three portions should be made at once.

Grinding the black pepper directly onto the bare place is recommended so you can see how much pepper has been ground. Regular olive oil is recommended for maximum flavor. Extra-virgin olive oil is more expensive, has an overpowering flavor, and is slightly more acidic.

Caesar Cardini conceived this salad in 1924 at his restaurant in Tijuana, Mexico, just across the border from California. Owing to Prohibition in America, restaurants in Tijuana were popular with Hollywood stars. One evening, a group of actors entered his restaurant near closing time, and the kitchen was out of most items, including fish, chicken, and meat. Romaine lettuce, oil and vinegar, lemon, garlic, mustard, cheese, and croutons were available. In order to satisfy this Hollywood group, Caesar gathered what he had, brought it to the dining room, and assembled his new creation in front of his guests. They raved about it, and the rest is history. Shortly afterward, the International Society of Epicures in Paris named Caesar salad the greatest recipe originating from the New World in 50 years.

AMOUNT	MEASURE	INGREDIENT
For the Croutons		
¼ cup	2 ounces/60 ml	Olive oil
1	5 g	Garlic clove, crushed
2 cups	4 ounces/112 g	Sourdough bread, crusts removed, in ½-inch (1.2 cm) cubes
For the Dressing		
1	5 g	Garlic clove, minced
2 tablespoons	1 ounce/30 m	Lemon juice
2 teaspoons	10 g	Anchovy paste
		Salt
¼ teaspoon	2 g	Black pepper
1		Egg
½ cup	4 ounces/120 ml	Olive oil
For the Salad		
6 cups	12 ounces/336 g	Romaine lettuce, dark outer leaves removed, torn into bite-size pieces
½ cup	1½ ounces/42 g	Parmesan cheese, freshly grated

1. Make the croutons. In a 10- to 12-inch (25.4–30.5 cm) sauté pan, heat the oil over low-medium heat. Add the garlic, sauté 1 minute to flavor the oil, and discard garlic.

2. Increase the heat to high and add the bread cubes, turning frequently so that they brown evenly on all sides and are crisp and golden, about 1 to 2 minutes. Add more oil if necessary to keep from burning. Drain on paper towels.

3. Make the dressing. Combine the minced garlic, lemon juice, anchovy paste, salt, and pepper. Whisk to blend.

4. Immerse the egg, in shell, in a small pan of boiling water and cook for exactly 1 minute. Remove the egg and crack it into the bowl with the other ingredients. Whisk to combine.

5. Add the oil in a steady stream and whisk until smooth and emulsified.

6. Prepare the salad. Combine the lettuce, Parmesan cheese, croutons, and enough dressing to just coat the leaves. Toss and taste for seasoning.

7. Place on chilled individual plates. Serve immediately.

Hangtown Fry

AMOUNT	MEASURE	INGREDIENT
½ cup	4 ounces/112 g	Bacon, in ½-inch (1.2 cm) dice
½ cup	2 ounces/56 g	Ham, julienned
4		Eggs
¼ cup	2 ounces/60 ml	Heavy cream
2 tablespoons	1 ounce/30 ml	Water
1 tablespoon	3 g	Fresh parsley, chopped
½ cup	1½ ounces/42 g	Parmesan cheese, freshly grated
		Salt and white pepper
8	¾ cup/6 ounces/168 g	Oysters
¼ cup	1 ounce/28 g	All-purpose flour
1		Egg, lightly beaten with a little water
½ cup	2 ounces/56 g	Dried bread crumbs

PROCEDURE

1. Preheat the broiler.

2. In a 10-inch (25.4 cm) sauté pan, cook the bacon over medium heat until crisp, about 5 to 6 minutes. Drain on a paper towel, then crumble.

3. Fry the ham pieces in the bacon fat. Drain on a paper towel. Remove all but 2 tablespoons fat.

4. In a bowl, combine the eggs, cream, water, parsley, and cheese; season with pepper, but use caution with the salt; bacon and ham are both cured salty products. Coat the oysters with flour, then dip in the beaten egg and coat with bread crumbs. Fry in the bacon fat for 1 minute on both sides, adding additional fat if necessary. Stir in the bacon and ham.

5. Pour the egg and cream mixture over the oysters and let them cook over low heat, without stirring, until the eggs begin to set, 8 to 10 minutes.

6. Place the skillet under the broiler and lightly brown the top. Serve immediately.

Hangtown Fry

San Francisco Cioppino

4 servings

CHEF TIP: Cioppino is typically served with San Francisco sourdough bread or fresh-baked focaccia. Freshly made garlic croutons dipped in fresh minced herbs are also a frequent garnish. The fish and shellfish listed in this recipe are our choices. Feel free to substitute different varieties of seasonal fresh fish and shellfish to suit your taste and preferences.

Cioppino is a famous seafood recipe that originated in the North Beach area of San Francisco. Cioppino is basically a West Coast version of French bouillabaisse. The dish typically uses a tomato-based broth to stew a variety of local fish and seafood. Dungeness crab is often the featured protein in cioppino. This soup like fish stew is generally served as an entrée.

AMOUNT	MEASURE	INGREDIENT
For the Sauce		
1 tablespoon	½ ounce/15 ml	Vegetable oil
1 cup	4 ounces/112 g	Onion, in ½-inch (1.2 cm) dice
½ cup	2 ounces/56 g	Leek, in ½-inch (1.2 cm) dice
½ cup	2 ounces/56 g	Green bell pepper, in ½-inch (1.2 cm) dice
1 tablespoon	½ ounce/14 g	Garlic, minced
½ cup	2 ounces/56 g	Celery, in ½-inch (1.2 cm) dice
½ cup	2 ounces/56 g	Carrot, in ¼-inch (.6 cm) dice
1 cup	6 ounces/168 g	Plum tomato, peeled, in ¼-inch (.6 cm) dice
1 tablespoon	½ ounce/14 g	Tomato paste
2 cups	16 ounces/480 ml	Fish fumet (stock) or clam juice
½ cup	4 ounces/120 ml	Red wine
1 tablespoon	½ ounce/15 ml	Lemon juice
1		Bay leaf
1 teaspoon	1 g	Fresh oregano, chopped
1 teaspoon	1 g	Fresh basil, chopped
		Salt and black pepper
For the Cioppino		
8		Mussels, scrubbed and debearded
8		Littleneck or cherrystone clams, scrubbed
2 cups	16 ounces/480 ml	Water
4	4 ounces/112 g each	Fish fillets, firm white flesh, cut into serving-size pieces
1½ cups	8 ounces/224 g	Large shrimp (16–20 count), peeled and deveined
¾ cup	4 ounces/112 g	Sea scallops
1 tablespoon	½ ounce/15 ml	Hot sauce
2 tablespoons	¼ ounce/7 g	Fresh parsley, finely chopped

PROCEDURE

1. Make the sauce. Heat the oil in a 3- to 4-quart (3 to 4 L) saucepan over medium heat, cook the onion, leek, green pepper, garlic, celery, and carrot until tender, about 3 minutes.

2. Add the tomato and cook 3 minutes. Add the tomato paste, fish fumet, wine, lemon juice, and bay leaf. Simmer 30 minutes. Remove the bay leaf.

3. Add the fresh herbs and salt and pepper.

4. Prepare the cioppino. Clean and steam the mussels and clams in the water until the shells open. Save the cooking liquid and strain it through cheesecloth. Add the cooking liquid to the sauce.

5. Add the fish to the tomato sauce and simmer 3 minutes. Add the shrimp and scallops and simmer 2 minutes.

6. Add the hot sauce and return the mussels and clams to the pot; heat 1 minute.

7. Divide the fish and shellfish evenly into warmed soup bowls. Ladle the sauce over the seafood and sprinkle with parsley.

Cioppino

Strawberry Shortcake with Cornmeal Biscuits

4 servings

AMOUNT	MEASURE	INGREDIENT
For the Biscuits		
3 cups	12 ounces/336 g	All-purpose flour
¾ cup	4 ounces/112 g	Finely ground yellow cornmeal
1 tablespoon	½ ounce/15 g	Baking powder
1 tablespoon	½ ounce/15 g	Sugar
½ teaspoon	3 g	Salt
2 tablespoons	1 ounce/28 g	Butter, chilled, in ½-inch (1.2 cm) cubes
1½ cups	12 ounces/360 ml	Heavy cream
For the Berries		
3 cups	18 ounces/510 g	Strawberries, washed, hulled, sliced
¼ cup	2 ounces/56 g	Sugar
1 teaspoon or to taste	5 ml	Lemon juice
1 cup	8 ounces/240 ml	Heavy cream
¼ teaspoon		Vanilla extract

PROCEDURE

1. Preheat the oven to 425°F (220°C). Line a baking sheet with parchment.

2. Make the biscuits. Combine the flour, cornmeal, baking powder, sugar, and salt in a mixing bowl. Add the butter, using fingertips rub butter into flour until the mixture has the appearance of coarse meal. Add the cream; stir until a moist dough forms.

3. Place on a floured work table, dust the top with flour and gently fold dough over on itself six to eight times. Roll the dough into a rectangle approximately 6 × 9 inches (15 × 22.5 cm) long and ¾ inch (1.9 cm) thick. Cut dough into 2-inch (5 cm) uniform biscuits. Place on prepared sheet so that they just touch. Reshape the scrap dough, working it as little as possible and continue to cut biscuits.

4. Bake for approximately 20 minutes, or until the biscuits have risen and are lightly brown in color. Let cool slightly.

5. Prepare the berries. Combine the strawberries and 3 tablespoons (42 ml) of the sugar. Let stand for 15 minutes at room temperature.

6. Crush half the strawberries, adding a little lemon juice; set aside.

7. Combine the cream, remaining sugar, and vanilla. Whip to soft peaks.

8. Assemble the dessert. Split each biscuit in half horizontally and place the bottom piece of each biscuit on a chilled plate. Spoon the berry mixture onto the biscuit bottoms in equal portions. Top with a large dollop of whipped cream. Cover with the top portions of the biscuit, spoon some berry liquid on top, and serve.

Tomato Panna Cotta with Candied Tomatoes and Bacon Foam

4 servings

CHEF TIP: To serve the panna cotta, unmold the panna cotta onto plates, spoon the bacon foam on the panna cotta, then top with the candied tomato and crisp bacon bits.

Tomato Panna Cotta

AMOUNT	MEASURE	INGREDIENT
1¼ cups	10 ounces/300 ml	Heavy cream
¼ cup	2 ounces/56 g	Tomato paste
1 teaspoon		Honey
⅛ teaspoon		Tabasco
⅛ teaspoon		Red wine vinegar
		Salt and pepper
2		Sheet gelatin, bloomed in cold water and
or		squeezed dry, *or*
1½ teaspoons		Granulated gelatin
2 tablespoons	½ ounce/14 g	Bacon bits, crisped

PROCEDURE

1. Heat the cream in a 1-quart (1 L) saucepan over low heat. Whisk together the tomato paste, honey, tabasco, and vinegar in a bowl, then slowly add the warmed cream. Add the gelatin, allow to dissolve, then mix to combine.

2. Divide the mixture into four 4-ounce (120 ml) ramekins and chill in refrigerator until set, about 2 to 2½ hours.

Candied Tomatoes

AMOUNT	MEASURE	INGREDIENT
1 cup	6 ounces/168 g	Cherry tomatoes
¼ cup	2 ounces/56 g	Sugar
As needed		Vegetable oil

PROCEDURE

1. Preheat the oven to 350°F (177°C). Grease a baking sheet with vegetable oil.

2. Cut the tomatoes in half and toss in enough sugar to lightly coat. Put tomatoes cut side up on the prepared sheet and bake for 8 minutes. Cool in refrigerator for 30 minutes.

Bacon Foam

AMOUNT	MEASURE	INGREDIENT
1 tablespoon	9 g	Shallot, minced
½ cup	3 ounces/84 g	Bacon, in coarse dice
1 cup	8 ounces/240 ml	Nonfat milk

PROCEDURE

1. In a 2-quart (2 L) saucepan over medium heat, cook the shallot and bacon for 6 to 8 minutes, stirring to prevent bacon from sticking to the pan.

2. Add the milk and heat until it just starts to simmer. Turn off heat, cover pan, and let sit for 30 minutes to infuse flavor.

3. Strain out the bacon and shallot, and put milk into a clean pot. Heat until it just starts to bubble, then remove from heat and use an immersion blender or whisk to create a froth.

Tomato Panna Cotta with Candied Tomatoes and Bacon Foam

Sautéed Sand Dabs

✤ **CHEF TIP:** Sand dabs are a small flatfish native to the West Coast of North America. Sand dabs eat crustaceans and mollusks, and so they have a sweet, soft texture that is moist and mild. They are generally too small to properly fillet, so they are normally pan-dressed, scaled, and gutted. To eat, you stick a fork in where the backbone is, then push the meat outward. Over 13 species of flatfish are regularly caught in the Pacific. Common market names and substitutes for sand dabs include sole, plaice, fluke, flounder, and halibut. Pacific flatfish, like their Atlantic cousins, are known as *hirame* when prepared for sushi.

AMOUNT	MEASURE	INGREDIENT
4	8 to 10 ounces/224 g to 280 g each	Sand dabs, pan-dressed
		Salt and pepper
1		Egg, lightly beaten
¼ cup	2 ounces/60 ml	Milk
		All-purpose flour, for dusting
¼ cup	2 ounces/60 ml	Butter, clarified
1 teaspoon		Lemon juice

PROCEDURE

1. Season the fish with salt and pepper. Combine the egg and milk in a bowl. Dredge the fish in a little flour, then dip in the egg mixture and roll in the bread crumbs until thoroughly coated.

2. Heat a 10- to 12-inch (25.4–30.5 cm) sauté pan over medium heat. Add the butter and sauté the fish 2 to 3 minutes per side, depending on the thickness. To test for doneness, try to slip a skewer between the fillets and bones from the head end. If it penetrates with little resistance, the fish is cooked.

3. Transfer the fish to a warmed plate. Add the lemon juice to the pan and pour the buttery pan juices over fish.

Fennel and Sweet Onion Pizza

4 servings (2 small pizzas)

 **CHEF TIP:** A fennel bulb has a mild anise flavor.

AMOUNT	MEASURE	INGREDIENT
For the Crust		
2½ teaspoons	¼ ounce/7 g	Active dry yeast
1 teaspoon		Honey
1 tablespoon		Dry milk
¾ cup	6 ounces/180 ml	Lukewarm water (110°F/43°C)
2½ cups, plus more for dusting	10 ounces/280 g	All-purpose flour
½ cup	2 ounces/6 g	Whole wheat flour
2 tablespoons, plus more for brushing	1 ounce/30 ml	Olive oil
1¼ teaspoons	8 g	Salt
For the Topping		
2 tablespoons	1 ounce/30 ml	Olive oil
1		Fennel bulb, cut into 8 wedges
¼ cup	2 ounces/60 ml	White wine
1 cup	8 ounces/240 ml	Chicken or vegetable stock
		Salt and pepper
2 cups	12 ounces/336 g	Sweet onion, thinly sliced
3 cups	12 ounces/336 g	Asiago or Gruyère cheese
1 cup	4 ounces/112 g	Green olives, pitted, coarsely chopped
¼ cup	½ ounce/14 g	Basil leaves

PROCEDURE

1. Make the crust. In the bowl of a standing mixer fitted with the dough hook, combine the yeast, honey, dry milk, and warm water. Let stand until foaming, about 4 minutes.

2. Combine the flours and add along with the olive oil and salt, then mix at medium speed until a smooth dough forms, about 5 minutes. Divide the dough in half, cover with lightly greased plastic wrap, and let rest and relax for 15 minutes or up to 1 hour.

3. Grease two 12-inch (30.5 cm) squares of parchment. Use your greased fingers to press each piece of dough on the parchment into an 11- to 12-inch (27.9–30.5 cm) round about ⅛ inch thick (.3 cm). Brush the crust with olive oil, and let rest for 30 minutes.

4. Preheat the oven to 450°F (232°C), with a pizza stone, if possible.

5. Transfer pizza crusts to the pizza stone or a baking sheet and bake until the edges start to brown, about 4 minutes.

6. Prepare the toppings. Heat a 10- to 12-inch (25.4–30.5 cm) sauté pan over medium heat, add 1 tablespoon (½ ounce/15 ml) olive oil and the fennel wedges and cook, turning once, until lightly browned, 5 minutes. Add the wine and cook 2 minutes. Add the stock, cover, and simmer over moderately low heat, turning the fennel once, until very tender and the liquid is almost evaporated, 15 minutes. Season with salt and pepper. Transfer fennel to a cutting board and rough chop.

7. Clean the sauté pan and heat over medium heat. Add the remaining 1 tablespoon (½ ounce/15 ml) olive oil and the onion slices, cover, and cook 2 minutes until soft. Uncover and cook until the onion is caramelized, 20 to 30 minutes more. If necessary, add a few drops of water to prevent scorching.

8. Add the toppings to the crusts. Sprinkle half the cheese on each pizza, follow with half the chopped fennel, half the caramelized onions and half the green olives. Return pizza to the oven and bake an additional 6 minutes, until the toppings are hot.

9. Transfer the pizzas to a cutting board, sprinkle with basil, and cut into wedges.

Fennel and Sweet Onion Pizza

Monterey Jack and Green Chile Polenta with Grilled Vegetables

Monterey Jack and Green Chile Polenta

AMOUNT	MEASURE	INGREDIENT
½ cup plus 2 tablespoons	5 ounces/150 ml	Chicken stock
½ cup plus 2 tablespoons	5 ounces/150 ml	Milk
2 tablespoons	1 ounce/28 g	Butter
1 teaspoon	5 g	Granulated sugar
½ teaspoon	2.5 g	Salt
½ cup	3 ounces/84 g	Polenta
½ cup	2 ounces/56 g	Monterey Jack cheese, grated
1	3 tablespoons/2 ounces/56 g	Poblano chile, roasted, peeled, seeded, in ½-inch (.6 cm) dice
		Salt and white pepper

PROCEDURE

1. In a 3- to 4-quart (3 to 4 L) pot, bring the chicken stock to a boil. Reduce to a simmer and stir in the milk, butter, sugar, and salt.

2. Slowly add the polenta in a thin stream, whisking constantly. Lower the heat and continue stirring for 15 to 20 minutes, or until the mixture starts to thicken.

3. Stir in the cheese and the chile. Continue to stir while cooking over low heat until the mixture is thick and easily falls away from the sides of the pan.

4. Correct seasoning with the salt and white pepper.

Grilled Vegetables

AMOUNT	MEASURE	INGREDIENT
1		Green bell pepper, cut in quarters, pith and seeds removed
1		Red bell pepper, cut in quarters, pith and seeds removed
	8 ounces/224 g	Asparagus, ends trimmed and peeled
	8 ounces/224 g	Zucchini, cut on the bias into ½-inch (1.2 cm) pieces
	8 ounces/224 g	Japanese eggplant, sliced lengthwise into ½-inch (1.2 cm) thick rectangles
	6 ounces/168 g	Cremini mushrooms, washed and cut in half
	4 ounces/112 g	Green onions, roots cut off
¼ cup	2 ounces/60 ml	Olive oil
		Salt and pepper
2		Lemons, quartered
¼ cup	1 ounce/28 g	Parmesan cheese, shredded

PROCEDURE

1. Heat the grill to medium-high. Toss the vegetables with the olive oil and season with salt and pepper. Working in batches, grill the vegetables until tender and lightly charred all over, 8 minutes for the lemons, 6 to 8 minutes for the bell peppers, 5 to 6 minutes for the zucchini, eggplant, and mushrooms, and 4 minutes for the asparagus and green onions.

2. To serve, add the Monterey Jack and green chile polenta to the bottom of a shallow bowl, add a mixture of the grilled vegetables over the polenta, squeeze the juice of the grilled lemons over the top, and sprinkle with Parmesan cheese.

Monterey Jack and Green Chile Polenta with Grilled Vegetables

Lemon Mousse

CHEF TIP: Use pasteurized eggs because the egg whites are not going to be cooked. Pasteurization is the use of heat to destroy bacteria and viruses; liquid eggs are pasteurized, but the majority of whole eggs have not been pasteurized.

AMOUNT	MEASURE	INGREDIENT
3		Pasteurized eggs, separated
½ cup	4 ounces/120 ml	Fresh lemon juice
½ cup	4 ounces/112 g	Sugar
¼ teaspoon		Cream of tartar
½ cup	4 ounces/120 ml	Heavy cream
1 tablespoon		Lemon zest, grated

PROCEDURE

1. Whisk together the yolks, lemon juice, and half the sugar. Place over simmering water, whisking constantly until the mixture thickens. Remove from heat and whip until cool. Lay a sheet of plastic wrap directly on the surface of the curd to prevent a skin from forming. Chill the lemon curd until needed, at least 1 hour.

2. When ready to serve, whip the egg whites with the cream of tartar to soft peaks. Gradually add the remaining sugar and whip to stiff peaks.

3. Whip the cream to soft peaks.

4. Whisk the lemon curd until smooth, then fold in the egg whites and then the whipped cream. (Hint: Add a little of the beaten egg whites to the lemon curd and stir to lighten, then fold in the remaining egg whites and whipped cream in several additions. The larger the spatula or whisk, the fewer strokes that will be made and the better the results.)

5. Serve cold, garnished with lemon zest.

Lemon Mousse

Cream of Garlic Soup

4 servings

 **CHEF TIP:** Gilroy, a small town in central California, is the self-proclaimed garlic capital of the world. Typically, in California cuisine, the use of roux as a thickening agent is unpopular. In this recipe, the potatoes pureed into the soup act as the thickening agent. Chive flowers make a great garnish for this soup. They can be used in addition to the minced chives or as a replacement.

AMOUNT	MEASURE	INGREDIENT
1 tablespoon	½ ounce/15 ml	Vegetable oil
½ cup	2 ounces/56 g	Onion, in ¼-inch (.6 cm) dice
⅔ cup	2 ounces/56 g	Leek, white part only, in ¼-inch (.6 cm) dice
1½ cups	8 ounces/224 g	Russet potatoes, peeled, in ½-inch (1.2 cm) dice
⅓ cup	2 ounces/56 g	Garlic, roughly chopped
1 quart	32 ounces/.95 L	Chicken stock
½ cup	4 ounces/120 ml	Heavy cream
		Salt and white pepper
1 tablespoon	3 g	Chives, finely minced

PROCEDURE

1. In a 2- to 3-quart (2 to 3 L) saucepan, heat the oil and cook the onion and leek over medium-high heat until the onion is tender and translucent, 3 to 4 minutes. Do not brown the onion.

2. Add the potatoes, garlic, and stock. Bring to a boil, and then reduce the heat to a simmer. Simmer the soup until the potatoes and garlic are tender and thoroughly cooked, about 45 to 60 minutes.

3. Puree the mixture in a food processor or blender. Return to the heat and add the cream. Correct the seasoning with salt and pepper and reheat the soup, but do not bring to a boil.

4. Serve in a warm bowl, garnish with the chives.

Baby Greens with Goat Cheese Croquettes

4 servings

AMOUNT	MEASURE	INGREDIENT
For the Croquettes		
1 cup	4 ounces/112 g	Fresh goat cheese
		All-purpose flour, for dusting
1		Egg, light beaten
½ cup	2 ounces/56 g	Panko (Japanese bread crumbs)
As needed		Vegetable oil
For the Salad		
¼ cup	2 ounces/60 ml	Red wine vinegar
1 teaspoon	6 ml	Dijon mustard
¼ cup	2 ounces/60 ml	Walnut oil
¼ cup	2 ounces/60 ml	Olive oil
		Salt and black pepper
4 cups	8 ounces/224 g	Baby greens
2 tablespoons	¼ ounce/7 g	Chives, chopped

PROCEDURE

1. Make the croquettes. Divide the goat cheese into 8 equal portions. Roll each portion into a ball and shape. Toss the croquette in the flour, then dip in the beaten egg and roll in the Panko until evenly coated. Chill for 30 to 45 minutes.

2. Heat the oil in a deep pot or deep-fryer to 350°F (176°C). Fry the croquettes, and drain on paper towels.

3. Prepare the salad. Combine the vinegar and mustard. Slowly whisk in the oils until creamy. Correct the seasoning with salt and pepper.

4. Toss the baby greens with the vinaigrette and divide evenly among chilled plates. Place 2 croquettes on top of each plate of greens, and garnish with the chives.

Baby Greens with Goat Cheese Croquettes

Calamari, Artichoke, and Penne Pasta Monterey Style

4 servings

✦ **CHEF TIP:** Baby artichokes are the lower sprouting buds on an ordinary globe artichoke plant. Technically mature, they are tender and have no hairy choke.

AMOUNT	MEASURE	INGREDIENT
3 cups	1 pounds, 16 ounces/448 g	Baby artichokes
1		Lemon, cut in half
¼ cup	2 ounces/60 ml	Olive oil
5	1 ounce/28 g	Anchovy fillets, drained
1	5 g	Garlic clove, minced
1 cup	6 ounces/168 g	Tomato, peeled, in ¼-inch (.6 cm) dice
1 tablespoon	½ ounce/14 g	Capers, drained
½ cup	3 ounces/84 g	Kalamata olives, pitted, coarsely chopped
2 cups	12 ounces/340 g	Calamari rings and tentacles, cleaned
4½ cups	12 ounces/340 g	Penne pasta
1 tablespoon	3 g	Fresh parsley, chopped
½ tablespoon	2 g	Fresh cilantro leaves, chopped
½ tablespoon	2 g	Fresh basil, chopped
½ tablespoon	2 g	Fresh thyme, chopped
⅛ teaspoon		Red pepper flakes
½ cup	1½ ounces/42 g	Parmesan cheese, shaved
		Salt and black pepper

PROCEDURE

1. Preheat the oven to 400°F (204°C).

2. Remove the tough outer leaves from the artichokes and trim the stems. Cut off the top third of each head to remove the tough tips and then quarter them. Rub with lemon juice and toss with 2 tablespoons (1 ounce/30 ml) of the olive oil.

3. Roast in the oven until the artichokes are tender, about 20 minutes.

4. Combine the anchovies and garlic. Mash thoroughly until a paste forms.

5. Heat a 10- to 12-inch (25.4–30.5 cm) sauté pan over medium heat. Add the remaining 2 tablespoons (1 ounce/30 ml) olive oil and the anchovy-garlic mixture; stir well. Add the tomato, capers, and olives. Stir and place over medium heat; heat until the mixture comes to a boil. Reduce the heat to low and simmer, uncovered, stirring occasionally, 8 to 10 minutes.

6. Add the artichokes and the calamari. Continue cooking for 30 to 60 seconds or until calamari is cooked. Do not overcook or the calamari will be tough.

7. Cook the pasta in boiling salted water until al dente. Drain well.

8. Toss the pasta with the chopped herbs and season with the red pepper flakes.

9. Add the penne to the calamari and toss well. Check seasoning.

10. Divide the pasta onto 4 warmed plates, taking care to distribute the artichoke hearts and calamari evenly among the portions. Garnish each portion with Parmesan and a sprinkling of salt and pepper.

Calamari, Artichoke, and Penne Pasta Monterey Style

Duck with Pine Nuts and Honey

4 servings

AMOUNT	MEASURE	INGREDIENT
2	16 ounces/448 g each	Muscovy drake breasts
		Salt and pepper
1 cup	8 ounces/240 ml	Chicken stock
1 cup	8 ounces/240 ml	White wine
2 tablespoons	½ ounce/14 g	Shallots, minced
¼ cup	2 ounces/60 ml	Honey
¼ cup	1 ounce/28 g	Pine nuts, toasted
¼ cup	½ ounce/14 g	Fresh cilantro leaves, chopped

PROCEDURE

1. Preheat the oven to 425°F (218°C).

2. Score the duck skin in a crosshatch pattern with a sharp knife and remove the silver skin from the meat side. Season with salt and pepper and place skin side down in an oven-safe sauté pan over medium heat. Without turning the breasts, cook about 7 minutes. Turn the breast over and finish cooking in oven, about 5 to 7 minutes or until medium rare. Remove from pan and rest for at least 5 minutes.

3. Drain fat from the pan and add the stock, wine, shallots, and honey; reduce until the liquid thickens, 5 to 6 minutes. Add the pine nuts and cilantro. Season to taste with salt and pepper.

4. Slice and serve the duck with the sauce.

Duck Breast with Pine Nuts and Honey, and Swiss Chard with Golden Raisins

Swiss Chard with Golden Raisins

4 servings

AMOUNT	MEASURE	INGREDIENT
2 tablespoons	¾ ounce/21 g	Golden raisins
3 cups	16 ounces/448 g	Swiss chard, red or white, rinsed
2 tablespoons	1 ounce/28 g	Unsalted butter
4	1 ounce/28 g	Shallots, in ¼-inch (.6 cm) dice
1	5 g	Garlic clove, minced
1 teaspoon	5 ml	Rice wine vinegar
		Salt and black pepper

PROCEDURE

1. Soak the raisins in hot water for 15 minutes. Drain.

2. Cut the ribs from the chard leaves. Chop the ribs into ¼-inch (.6 cm) pieces. Immerse in a small pan of boiling water and boil 2 minutes. Drain.

3. Melt the butter over medium heat. Sauté the shallots and garlic about 2 minutes. Add the chard leaves and sauté 2 to 3 minutes more. Cover the pan and steam 3 to 5 minutes over low heat. Mix in the cooked ribs, add the vinegar and the raisins, and correct seasoning with salt and pepper.

4. Serve immediately.

Kiwifruit and Grape Rice Pudding

4 servings

CHEF TIP: Originally from China, the kiwifruit was cultivated at the turn of the century in New Zealand and brought to California in the 1930s. Kiwis are grown all over the world, but California has the greatest kiwi production in the United States.

AMOUNT	MEASURE	INGREDIENT
3 cups	24 ounces/720 ml	Milk
¼ cup plus 1 tablespoon	1¾ ounces/49 g	Sugar
¼ teaspoon		Salt
½ cup	3 ounces/84 g	Uncooked medium-grain rice
4		Kiwis, 2 peeled, sliced, quartered and 2 sliced
½ cup	1½ ounces/42 g	Seedless red grapes, halved
1 tablespoon	½ ounce/14 g	Unsalted butter
⅛ teaspoon		Ground cinnamon

PROCEDURE

1. Combine the milk, ¼ cup (1¾ ounces/46 g) of the sugar, and the salt. Heat until small bubbles form around the edge of the pan.

2. Stir in the rice. Cover and cook over low heat for 35 to 45 minutes or until the rice is tender and most of the milk is absorbed. Stir occasionally.

3. Stir in the kiwi quarters, the grapes, and butter.

4. Combine the remaining sugar with the cinnamon. Sprinkle each serving with cinnamon sugar and garnish with the sliced kiwi fruit. Serve warm.

Garden Pasta Salad

4 servings

AMOUNT	MEASURE	INGREDIENT
For the Salad		
1 tablespoon	½ ounce/15 ml	Vegetable oil
1 teaspoon		Salt
4 cups	8 ounces/224 g	Fusilli or small shell pasta
3 cups	12 ounces/336 g	Vegetables (carrots, zucchini, broccoli, sugar snap peas, or other vegetables of choice), julienned
For the Dressing		
2 tablespoons	1 ounce/30 ml	Grainy mustard
2	10 g	Garlic cloves, minced
1½ tablespoons	¾ ounce/22 ml	Lemon juice
1½ tablespoons	¾ ounce/22 ml	Sherry vinegar
6 tablespoons	3 ounces/90 ml	Olive oil
		Salt and black pepper
1½ tablespoons	5 g	Fresh basil, chopped
½ cup	1½ ounces/42 g	Parmesan cheese, grated

PROCEDURE

1. Make the salad. Add the oil and salt to a pot of boiling water; add the pasta and cook until al dente.

2. Drain the pasta, shock in ice water, drain again, and dry thoroughly.

3. Blanch the vegetables until crisp-tender (until the vegetables just lose their raw taste). Drain and shock in ice water. Drain again and dry thoroughly.

4. Make the dressing. Combine the mustard, garlic, lemon juice, and sherry vinegar.

5. Whisk in the olive oil. Season with salt and pepper. Add the basil and Parmesan cheese.

6. Toss the pasta, vegetables, and dressing just before serving.

Rosemary Focaccia

AMOUNT	MEASURE	INGREDIENT
For the Sponge		
1 cup	8 ounces/240 ml	Water, warm (100°F/38°C)
1 teaspoon	2 g	Active dry yeast
1 cup	4 ounces/112 g	All-purpose flour
For the Dough		
½ cup	4 ounces/120 ml	Water
⅓ cup	2½ ounces/75 ml	Dry white wine
⅓ cup	2½ ounces/75 ml	Olive oil
2 tablespoons	1 ounce/28 g	Finely ground yellow cornmeal
		Kosher salt
2¾ cups	12 ounces/336 g	All-purpose flour
5 teaspoons	¾ ounce/25 ml	Extra-virgin olive oil
1	5 g	Garlic clove, minced
		Black pepper
1½ teaspoons		Rosemary, minced

PROCEDURE

1. Make the sponge. Combine the warm water and yeast and let stand 2 minutes; stir to dissolve. Stir in the flour until the mixture is smooth. Cover and let stand at room temperature for 24 hours.

2. Make the dough. Place the sponge in the bowl of a mixer fitted with a dough hook and mix at low speed. Slowly add the water, wine, olive oil, cornmeal, and 1½ teaspoons (7.5 g) salt. Mix until thoroughly incorporated.

3. Gradually mix in the flour, and mix on low speed until the dough is formed. Increase mixer to medium speed and work dough for 5 minutes.

4. Transfer dough to a greased bowl. Cover and let rise at room temperature for approximately 1½ hours or until it doubles in size.

5. Grease a baking sheet with olive oil.

6. Transfer the dough to the baking sheet and stretch it, using oiled fingers, until the dough completely fills the sheet. Let the dough rest 5 minutes; the dough will shrink.

7. Restretch the dough to completely cover the baking sheet. If it is still too elastic, let the dough rest longer and try again. Let dough rise in pan at room temperature for 1 hour.

8. Preheat the oven to 450°F (225°C).

9. Brush the focaccia with a little olive oil and sprinkle with the garlic, black pepper, rosemary, and more kosher salt to taste. Bake for approximately 15 to 20 minutes or until nicely browned.

Chilled Avocado and Cucumber Soup

❖ **CHEF TIP:** If the surface of the soup oxidizes or turns brown after being chilled, simply skim off and discard the discolored surface before serving.

AMOUNT	MEASURE	INGREDIENT
1¼ cups	8 ounces/224 g	Avocado, in ¼-inch (.6 cm) dice
1 cup	6 ounces/168 g	Cucumber, peeled, in ¼-inch (.6 cm) dice
½ cup	4 ounces/120 ml	Heavy cream
1 tablespoon	½ ounce/15 ml	Lime juice
1 cup	8 ounces/240 ml	Chicken or vegetable stock
1 cup	8 ounces/240 ml	Plain yogurt
1	5 g	Garlic clove, minced
¾ cup	6 ounces/180 ml	Sour cream
1 tablespoon	3 g	Fresh dill, coarsely chopped
1 tablespoon	3 g	Fresh parsley, coarsely chopped
		Salt and white pepper
½ cup, or more	4 ounces/120 ml	Milk
½ cup	½ ounce/14 g	Green onions, thinly sliced

PROCEDURE

1. Set aside 2 tablespoons (1 ounce/28 g) each of the avocado and cucumber for garnish. Place the remaining avocado and cucumber in a blender or food processor and add the cream, lime juice, stock, yogurt, garlic, ½ cup (4 ounces/120 ml) of the sour cream, the dill, parsley, and salt and pepper and blend until smooth.

2. Add the milk a little at a time and blend until soup is the desired consistency.

3. Pour the soup into a stainless-steel container. Place a piece of plastic wrap on the surface to prevent discoloration and store at 40°F (4°C) or lower until thoroughly chilled, about 1 to 1½ hours.

4. When ready to serve, carefully ladle the soup into chilled soup bowls or onto plates, and garnish each portion with the reserved avocado, cucumber, a dollop of the remaining sour cream, and the green onions.

Dilled Carrot Soup

AMOUNT	MEASURE	INGREDIENT
2 tablespoons	1 ounce/28 g	Butter
1 cup	4 ounces/112 g	Leeks, white part only, in thin slices
4 cups	16 ounces/448 g	Carrots, peeled, in ¼-inch (.6 cm) dice
4 cups	16 ounces/448 g	Russet potatoes, peeled, in ¼-inch (.6 cm) dice
1 quart	1 L	Chicken stock
1½ teaspoons		Fresh thyme, finely chopped
1		Bay leaf
1½ cups	12 ounces/360 ml	Half-and-half, warmed
¼ teaspoon		Grated nutmeg
2 tablespoons	1 ounce/30 ml	Lemon juice
		Salt and white pepper
		Tabasco
2 tablespoons	¼ ounce/7 g	Fresh dill, chopped

PROCEDURE

1. In a 2- to 3-quart (2 to 3 L) saucepan, heat the butter over medium heat. Sauté the leeks, stirring occasionally, until soft, about 3 to 5 minutes.

2. Add the carrots and potatoes, and sauté for 5 minutes more.

3. Add the stock and bring to a simmer. Add the thyme and bay leaf and simmer for 20 to 30 minutes or until carrots and potatoes are tender. Remove the bay leaf.

4. Puree the vegetables and liquid in a blender. Add the remaining ingredients except the dill. Correct the seasoning and bring back to almost a boil.

5. Serve hot, garnished with dill.

The Cuisine of the
Pacific Northwest

Stone fruits, apples and pears, berries and wild mushrooms, salmon and shellfish. The moist weather conditions and volcanic soil in Oregon and Washington help create one of the most fertile growing regions in the nation. And with the Pacific coastline, the abundant and varied fish and seafood of the area are the hallmarks of the region's cuisine. With a long harvest season and an accommodating climate, these areas support some of the most impressive local ingredients and offer yields unlike those found in other parts of the country. Driven by a strong mandate to save their valuable marine and forest resources, and to practice sustainable farming methods, locals hope to continue to provide future generations with the riches of the Pacific Northwest table.

Alaska   America's last frontier and "Land of the Midnight Sun," shares the bounty of the Pacific Ocean, and by an extraordinary combination of environmental and human factors, it produces vegetables that grow to enormous sizes in the Alaskan floodplain. Here, the state fish is the king salmon, the state bird is the willow ptarmigan, the state land mammal is the moose, the state marine mammal is the bowhead whale, the state tree is the Sitka spruce, and the state flower is the forget-me-not. The state sport is dog mushing.

Oregon   "The Beaver State," where the state flower is the Oregon grape, the state fish is the Chinook salmon, the state mammal is the American beaver, the state nut is the hazelnut, the state bird is the Western meadowlark, and the state tree is the Douglas fir.

Washington   "The Evergreen State," where the state fruit is the apple; the state fish is the steelhead trout; the state flower is the coast, or western, rhododendron; the state tree is the Western hemlock; and the state grass is bluebunch wheatgrass.

HISTORY AND MAJOR INFLUENCES

WASHINGTON AND OREGON

The people of the Pacific Northwest, like all Americans, are a mixture of histories and traditions. The first arrivals—mountain men from France, England, Russia, and Canada—found opportunities in fur trapping and trading. Since these newcomers were unfamiliar with the local ingredients, the Native American Indians taught them how to sustain themselves. The nomadic hunter-gatherers of the Quinault, Quileute, Chinook, and Tillamook tribes introduced the settlers to the varieties of oysters, clams, crab, shrimp, and salmon from the Puget Sound. The

Nez Perce, Cayuse, and Spokane tribes taught the new arrivals about the local berries and how to forage for mushrooms. The European settlers were also taught how to smoke their foods. They learned about the potlach. This Chinook word meaning "to give away" is used to describe a ceremonial feast connected with native rituals and important events. For the feast, each family would bring a contribution that might include salmon, clams, wild berries, greens, or other foods in season. This feast continues to be an important tradition in the area today.

Though the first settlers came to the Pacific Northwest for the valuable fur of the sea otter and beaver, they soon realized the potential of the region. Other industries such as mining, timber, fishing, cattle raising, and farming were established. In the early 1800s, Thomas Jefferson sent the party of Lewis and Clark to explore the Northwest; about the same time, Captain George Vancouver sailed into Puget Sound through the Straits of Juan de Fuca, seeking safe harbor in what is now called Port Townsend. The opening of the Oregon Trail led settlers from the Central Plains to the Pacific Northwest, many of whom were first-generation Americans still with deep roots in Europe. Discoveries of gold on the coast and in the high country led to additional exploration and settlements.

Because Oregon and Washington are so large and mountainous, the railroads did not reach the Pacific Northwest states until 1883. The offers of work building the railroads brought people from China, Italy, and Greece. They were mostly young men who planned to earn as much money as they could before returning to their homelands. But many of those who came never left. Instead, they brought over their families from the homeland or married other settlers and raised families. Large numbers of Chinese settled in Oregon and east of the Cascade Mountains. Many of them eventually opened laundries, stores, and restaurants. By the late 1800s, immigration of Chinese laborers was prohibited, and social and political discrimination forced the Chinese immigrants to live together in areas called "Chinatowns." Immigrants from southern European countries—mainly Italy and Greece—settled in the Portland area during the late 1800s. German settlers established their farm traditions in eastern Washington, planting vast wheat fields between the Cascade Mountains and Rocky Mountains.

They were the first to grow the nation's supply of hops and barley, and to initiate the beer industry. A beer-making tradition termed microbrewing began in the mid-1800s. Microbreweries were originally breweries that produced fewer than 10,000 barrels each year, and hundreds of small breweries opened throughout the remainder of the 1800s. As technology improved and production levels increased, the definition was increased to 15,000 barrels. Scandinavian settlers brought their dairy-farming expertise to the inland valleys and hillsides of that same area and continue to produce large amounts of milk. Realizing it was difficult to transport fresh milk and butter, the settlers reproduced the distinctive cheese-making processes developed in Europe. Basque and Mexican sheepherders settled in Oregon and eastern Washington. Cattle and livestock production increased dramatically owing to demand by hungry gold miners, as well as the availability of the transcontinental railroad connections to ship the cattle across the country.

In the late 1800s and early 1900s, after a series of massive earthquakes, volcanic eruptions from Mt. Fuji, and flooding that devastated homes and farmlands, a number of Japanese immigrants arrived to work on small farms. They created a strong social network to help those who lived and worked in the area. Many eventually acquired their own land and established the first berry and vegetable farms in Washington's Puget Sound area. They also brought their native Pacific and Kumamoto oysters and Manila, or Japanese Littleneck, clams to the coast.

The Asian influence in the Northwest has been strong, and most major cities in the Northwest have flourishing Asian communities. Immigrants used the ingredients native to the Pacific Northwest but prepared them using the cooking styles of their homeland. This fusion of techniques and ingredients is now known as Pacific Rim cooking. The first to populate open-air markets, the Asians brought fresh coriander, colorful basils, ginger, bitter melon, and exotic greens. Although many of these markets are no longer in operation, the influence they had on the region's cuisine continues today. Seattle's Chinatown is known today as the International District owing to the influences of its Filipino, Thai, Korean, and Vietnamese communities.

ALASKA

Since 1867, when the United States purchased Alaska from Russia, it has been a vast unknown country to the average American citizen. Frequently referred to as America's last frontier, it is one-fifth the size of the United States, with extremes of temperature, precipitation, sunlight, and wind. A considerable percentage of Alaska's population has come from countries other than the United States. Many whose ancestors were Swedish, Norwegian, Danish, English, German, Russian, or Finnish now call themselves Alaskans. These people came in the early days, when small communities were formed—when gold camps were being built during a "Gold Rush to the Klondike." Travel was tedious then. Mail was carried by dog team, and meat was available only if there was a good hunter or trapper in the family.

Alaska suffered during the Great Depression of the 1930s. The price of fish and minerals dropped. About a quarter of the people in the United States were out of work, and those who did work were not paid well. President Franklin Roosevelt had the idea that if people moved to Alaska, they could start over again in a new place. They could farm and make a living. About 1,000 people moved from northern states like Michigan and Minnesota to Alaska during this time, and the first farm colony settled in the rich and fertile Matanuska Valley.

Every year at the Alaska State Fair in the Matanuska Valley town of Palmer, the giant vegetables are the main attraction. The challenge was begun during the Great Depression of the 1930s, when the government-relocated farmers discovered that, while the growing season is short—just three months—it is offset by nearly 24 hours of sunlight. The soil is a fine mix of glacial silt and loam, and the giant vegetable competitors carefully germinate their seed, monitor moisture, and prune strategically to direct all the plant's energy into a single vegetable. This results in vegetables like Swiss chard that grows 9 feet tall, broccoli 3 feet tall, and 7-foot-wide, 98-pound cabbages, and 25-pound mushrooms. Even with this rapid growth, these giants are considered to still have all the flavor of normal size vegetables.

The most significant berry-growing regions are in the lower foothills of Alaska and western Oregon and Washington. Lingonberries and salmonberries are found along with blueberries, huckleberries, blackberries, red raspberries, and strawberries. Alaska is home to nearly all the wild salmon that is brought to market. And here, as well as up and down the coast of the Pacific Northwest, other seafood such as halibut, rockfish, Arctic char, all types of trout, sea urchins, octopus, squid, king crabs, and scallops can be found.

A DIVERSE LANDSCAPE

While the other regions of America have been significantly influenced by the history and culture of the people who live in the area, the Pacific Northwest regional cuisine is defined by the native ingredients that flourish in this diverse landscape.

PALOUSE

Along the edge of eastern Washington and western Idaho lies an area known as the Palouse (the name derives from the French word meaning "green lawn"). This region is generally considered to be the best in the world for growing lentils, peas, and chickpeas. Crop rotation of peas and lentils with soft, white winter wheat allows a second harvest of the land and organically enriches the soil. Over 200 million pounds of lentils are produced annually, and they are exported all over the world, mostly to India and the Middle East.

YAKIMA VALLEY

West across the extensive Columbia River plateau is the Yakima Valley, an active agricultural area often called the "Fruit Bowl of the Nation." A system of canals and wells supplies growers in this dry valley with ample water to carefully control irrigation of the land. In the 1880s, the first commercial apple orchards began production in the Yakima Valley. The availability of water has transformed this area into one of the largest and most productive wine regions in the Northwest. The cool temperatures also allow for an exceptional harvest of asparagus.

THE HOOD RIVER VALLEY

Mt. Hood, the tallest of Oregon's Cascade peaks, towers over the Columbia River Gorge. Runoff from its volcanic slopes enriches soil in the valleys below, which are famous for their production of pears, peaches, plums, sweet cherries, apricots, and apples. The leading cherry is the Bing cherry, developed in 1875 by Seth Luelling of Milwaukie, Oregon. The cherry was named after the owner's Chinese orchard manager and is now one of the most significant regional crops.

THE WILLAMETTE VALLEY

For the thousands of pioneers who came across the Oregon Trail, this lush valley was the promised land that they had been seeking. Nestled between the Cascade Mountains and the Coastal Ranges south of Eugene, Oregon, the valley takes its name from the river that flows through it. Historic cities and towns, settled more than a century ago by people from all over the world, are found throughout the region. But this area is best known for its diverse agriculture, which includes a wide variety of fruits, dairy, vegetables, and hops.

This is also Oregon's top berry-growing region, with blackberries, loganberries, raspberries, and strawberries found in the region. Over 90 percent of the country's hazelnuts are produced here, and the hazelnut takes the place of pecans in many of the regional recipes. Today, the valley's wine country is gaining worldwide attention as one of the Pacific Northwest's finest wine appellations, consistently turning out internationally acclaimed Pinot Noir, Pinot Gris, and Riesling.

THE COASTAL RANGES

This area is known for its rainy climate. The high precipitation supports coniferous forests along the coastal inlets, and many varieties of mushroom thrive in these conditions, as do elk, deer, and game birds. Mushroom hunting is on the rise owing to the high prices paid at market for matsutakes, morels, and porcini. The region is also known for its native truffles. White truffles and two varieties of black truffles are found in the undergrowth of the Douglas fir trees during the early fall through early spring. Corvallis, a small town in Oregon, is headquarters of the North American Truffling Society, and the truffles not consumed by the locals are sent to upscale restaurants around the country.

THE PACIFIC COASTLINE

Rivers and inlets lend their names to the region's trademark fish and shellfish. Pacific oysters are also known by their places of origin such as Yaquina, Wescott, Shoalwater, Quilcene, and Canterbury. The best known oyster bed is in Willapa Bay, a large estuary in southern Washington. The native Olympia oyster was farmed nearly to extinction in the 19th century. Today, the Japanese Pacific oyster dominates Willapa Bay, though Olympia and another Japanese oyster, the Kumamoto, are becoming more available. Shrimp, scallops, geoduck, clams, and crabs flourish along the Washington, Oregon, and Alaska coasts. The nation's oldest mussel farm, Penn Cove Mussels, is found on Whidbey Island in Washington's Puget Sound. The Olympic Peninsula is home to the popular Dungeness crab. Though this crustacean lives along much of the coast from northern California to Alaska, this area is where it was first commercially harvested. Pacific cod, lingcod, black cod, halibut, and petrale sole are some of the fishes found along the coast. The Columbia, Rogue, Copper, and Yukon rivers flow into the Pacific, and these rivers are an important thoroughfare for the five varieties of wild salmon, the river smelt, and the mild white sturgeon.

PIKE PLACE MARKET

Seattle's Pike Place Market was founded on August 17, 1907. Started as an experiment as a response to the city's high food prices, the Pike Place Market eliminated intermediaries and allowed consumers to purchase foods directly from growers. The concept proved successful, as the farmers typically sold all of their products and the consumers enjoyed the benefits of significantly lower prices. It also became a gathering place for all the food grown in the region, including foods that represent the mix of people and the ethnic groups that lived there.

In 1930, Pike Place Market reached its height of operation by issuing over 600 permits to sell local products. But in 1942 and the beginning of World War II, the Japanese Americans, who represented nearly half of the farmers, were placed in internment camps. Many never returned, and in 1949, only 53 farmers applied for permits to sell their goods. This decline continued into the 1950s as the flight to the suburbs left the cities vacant. In the late 1960s, downtown business interests formed a plan to demolish the neglected market to make way for modern commercial development. These interests were opposed, however, by a grassroots group who sought to preserve the market for its historic and cultural values. These activists were successful, and in 1971, the citizens of Seattle voted to place the market under public ownership and preserve and restore it to its place as the "Heart and Soul of Seattle."

The first Starbucks store was opened in Pike Place Market in 1971, and this company reflects Seattle's passion for coffee and the city's influence on coffee trends around the country. Espresso, cappuccino, latte, short, tall, and skinny have all become a familiar language, and "coffee breaks" have a new and significant importance in American culture. Pike Place Market today offers the best introduction to the elements of Pacific Northwest cuisine. Artisanal products and specialty foods including smoked Pacific salmon, "handmade" and "farmstead" cheese, wild mushrooms, dried cherries, organic produce, and rustic breads are proudly produced and reflect the passion of the region.

SALMON

Nearly all of the nation's wild salmon is harvested in Alaska. Native Indians recognized five "tribes" of salmon, each having its own particular characteristics. They looked upon the salmon as life, as the salmon have been a physical and spiritual source since the days when people first came to the area. Spawned in freshwater streams, the young salmon travel to the ocean where they live and grow for three or four years. In the spring, after they reach maturity, the adult salmon return to their native streams to spawn. As the salmon return home, they stop eating and live mainly on the oils stored in their bodies. They travel great distances, leaping over obstacles such as dams and waterfalls, and are able to return to the exact spot where they were hatched. The salmon were once so plentiful that the Indians would spear or club them from the river banks, and the fish would be eaten fresh, air-dried to create jerky, or smoked. Today, wild salmon are threatened and the health of the salmon runs influence the health of the area's economy.

The fish are caught two ways: in nets and on hooks during trolling. Netted salmon are caught in larger quantities, thus making the fish less expensive to purchase. However, the flesh can be damaged in the process, resulting in lower quality fish. Trolling for salmon results in the highest quality fish, as only one fish at a time can be caught on each hook. Typically, salmon caught by trolling are labeled as such and bring a higher price at market. Salmon is prepared using numerous techniques. It is said the Alaskans have as many preparations for salmon as people in the lower 48 have for beef. Descriptions of salmon indigenous to the region include:

Chum   This variety of salmon weighs about 7 pounds and is referred to by many other names, including fall, dog, silverbrite, and calico salmon. Chum salmon has a pale flesh, with moderate fat content and mild flavor. It is commonly used to produce smoked salmon via both hot and cold smoking techniques.

King   The largest of the salmon varieties, weighing between 15 and 20 pounds. King salmon, sometimes referred to as Chinook salmon, has a high oil content and a rich, full flavor, making it excellent for grilling. Some king salmon have no pigmentation of the flesh and are called "white king" salmon. White king salmon are expensive because they are rare; however, they have the same flavor and texture as normal king salmon.

Pink   This variety of salmon is the smallest, weighing only 3 to 5 pounds each. Pink salmon are found in huge numbers in the Alaskan waters and are also referred to as humpback or humpy salmon. Their flesh is light and moist but is more delicate than that of other varieties of salmon. Most pink salmon is canned and used much like canned tuna.

Silver   This variety usually weighs 7 pounds and is also referred to as coho or hooknose salmon. It has a red flesh, similar to the king salmon, but a much lower fat content, making it not quite as flavorful as other salmon. Silver salmon are often canned and used much like canned tuna.

Sockeye   These fish generally weigh 6 pounds and have an intensely red-colored flesh. Sockeye salmon are also referred to as red and bluejack salmon. The Japanese purchase the majority of the sockeye catch, as red is the color of celebration in Japan. This makes the fish more difficult to find in the United States, as well as more expensive than the other varieties of salmon.

Alaskan Halibut   The largest member of the flounder family, Alaskan halibut are known to grow as large as 500 pounds and have firm, white flesh with a mild flavor, making them excellent for grilling, baking, or sautéing. Halibut fishing in the Pacific Northwest begins in the spring and continues until mid-November. Halibut cheeks, resembling large sea scallops, are a delicacy and can weigh up to 1 pound. The most common preparation of halibut cheeks is to dredge them in flour, pan-fry them, and serve them with a simple sauce.

Apples   Washington's rich lava ash soil and plentiful sunshine create perfect conditions for growing apples. Today, Washington is the largest apple-growing region in America, producing between 10 and 12 billion apples per year. Although more than half of the orchards are dedicated to producing Red Delicious apples, other varieties are grown. Some of the most common varieties are those best for eating (Fuji, Gala, and Red Delicious) and others that are also good for cooking and baking (Golden Delicious, Granny Smith, Jonagold, Jonathan, Newton Pippin, Rome Beauty, and Winesap).

Asparagus   The Yakima and Columbia river valleys of Washington produce over 80 million pounds of asparagus annually. The asparagus season runs from April to early June and comes in both green and a milder (but more expensive) white form, the white having been blanched by being covered with soil. The most popular asparagus is called "pencil" asparagus for its long, thin shape, but the fatter, thicker asparagus are considered to be more tender and flavorful.

Berries

Blueberries   With over 160 varieties, each has its own degree of flavor and sweetness. Generally the smaller the berry, the sweeter and more flavorful it is. Huckleberries are one of the more common varieties found in the region.

Blackberries   The largest commercial crop of blackberries is a variety also known as the marionberry. Developed in Marion County, Oregon, this variety is a cross between wild and domestic blackberries. It is aromatic with a good balance of acid and sugar and is good for pies, cobblers, and jams. Other varieties include the loganberry, a highly acidic cross between a raspberry and a blackberry, and the boysenberry, a cross between the raspberry, blackberry, and loganberry. All of these are excellent for baking.

Cranberries   Similar to the cranberries of the New England region, these very tart berries grow in the bogs along the Northwest Pacific coastline. Although the region grows only a small fraction of America's cranberries, they are sought after for their high quality, excellent flavor, and deep red color. The annual harvest takes place in October.

Lingonberries   A tart, red berry related to the cranberry and indigenous to Alaska.

Raspberries   Washington and Oregon are the top producers of red raspberries in the United States. Though not as common, wild red and black raspberries are grown in the region.

Salmonberries   Plump red orange berries that resemble clusters of salmon eggs. They are related to wild raspberries.

Strawberries   The largest commercial berry harvest in Oregon. Tiny, wild strawberries are also found in the coastal regions.

Brewpub   Different from a microbrewery, the term "brewpub" indicates a pub that that makes its own beer on the premises. Typically a brewpub also serves light, casual American cuisine to accompany its beer products.

Caviar   The salted eggs of the sturgeon fish. Pacific Northwest caviar is made in the same tradition as Russian and Iranian sturgeon caviar. The egg sacs are passed along a mesh to separate the eggs, then treated by a professional experienced in how much and how long to salt the eggs. Despite an abundance of female sturgeon in the Columbia River, many regulations concerning the collection of the roe make Pacific Northwest caviar rare as well as expensive.

Cherry Bing cherries have a sweet flavor with a dark red to almost black color and are America's most popular variety. The Rainier cherry, larger in size and gold with a reddish hue, was developed in Washington and has a more delicate flavor than the Bing cherry. Other varieties common to the region are the Meteor cherry (sour and usually used for pies, cobblers, and jams) and the Lambert cherry (which has a unique heart shape). Cherries are seasonal in nature and available only in the summer months.

Cheese The Pacific Northwest is noted as an exceptional producer of cheeses. "Farmstead cheese" is the term for handmade cheeses produced by people who raise their own goats, sheep, or cows. The region is noted for exceptional gouda, manchego, goat cheese, and blue cheese.

> **Cougar Gold Cheese** A sharp, nutty white Cheddar cheese that is the result of an experiment by students on the campus at Washington State University in the 1930s. Using excess milk from the university's agricultural program, they developed this hard cheese that could be packaged in tin cans. Their goal was to create a recipe that did not produce the gases resulting from aging that caused the packaging to explode. Cougar Gold was named after the university's mascot and comes in a variety of flavors that continue to be sold in 30-ounce tins.

> **Tillamook Cheese** *Tillamook*, a Native American word meaning "land of many waters" is the name of a county in northwestern Oregon where the milk of Holstein, Jersey, and Guernsey cows is converted into a premier Cheddar cheese. Canadian cheesemaker Peter McIntosh came to the area in the late 1800s to teach the latest production techniques. A few years later, ten dairies banded together to ensure the high-quality standards established by McIntosh. Today, this 196-member dairy cooperative, known as the Tillamook County Creamery Association, produces over 50 million pounds of this name-brand natural cheese.

Clams Found in the muddy tidelands of Oregon and Washington, clams taste best when spawning, in the early summer. When purchasing clams, the shells should be tightly closed. Varieties of clams include:

> **Geoduck** From the Native American word for "digging deep," pronounced GOO-ey-duck, this famous Pacific Northwest clam is large, sometimes growing up to 10 pounds, with a long siphon that looks like a neck. It burrows deep in the sand and is difficult to find. The neck meat can be tough and is chopped up to be used in chowder or made into fritters, or sliced into "clam steaks," pounded and pan-fried. The meat from the interior, referred to as the "breast," can be sautéed or served raw as an ingredient in sushi or as sashimi.

> **Manila Clam** Originating in Asia, the Manila clam was introduced to the Pacific Northwest by Asian immigrants in the late 1800s. This small clam, only 1 inch in diameter, is the most common variety in the region, and is generally eaten in chowder or served steamed. It grows well in the wild and in oyster farms.

> **Razor Clam** Long and slightly curved, resembling the straight razor used by barbers, this clam is served steamed, chopped, or used in chowder. The razor clam is a favorite among the Japanese and is used for sushi and sashimi preparations.

Crabs Crabs are some of the most profitable commercial seafood of the Northwest. The crab season in the Pacific Northwest is in the winter months, when the water is coldest. All of these crabs are typically purchased precooked and frozen.

> **Dungeness Crab** Common along coastal waters from Mexico to the Aleutian Islands of Alaska, Dungeness crabs have unusually sweet tasting, tender meat.

> **King Crab** The largest of the crab species, typically found in the waters of Alaska. Most king crabs grow to about 6 pounds; however, they have been known to exceed 25 pounds in weight, with a leg span of over 6 feet. The legs are generally steamed and served either hot or cold with drawn butter. King crab is fished in the rough, icy waters off the Alaskan coast, and the danger involved with fishing these crabs is one reason they are so expensive. The legs of the king crab are the only part of the crab utilized in commercial food-service operations.

Snow Crab   A smaller relative of the king crab, found in the icy waters of Alaska. Unlike the king crab, the body meat is utilized as well as the leg meat. The meat is available in many forms—body meat only, leg meat only, and combinations of body and leg meat. It is used as an ingredient in other dishes but can also be prepared by steaming, as with king crab.

Hazelnut   Nearly all of America's hazelnuts are grown in the Willamette and Umpqua valleys of Oregon. Hazelnuts can be eaten whole as a snack but are more commonly used as an ingredient in cooking and in the production of baked goods and pastries. The oil derived from grinding, heating, and pressing the hazelnuts is highly regarded, and when combined with a more neutral flavored oil, is excellent for use as a salad dressing. Hazelnuts are also used in such specialty products as paste, butter, and flour. Once known as the filbert, the Oregon nut-growing industry voted to discontinue use of the name owing to the confusion it caused among consumers and industry professionals.

Lamb   The most popular variety in the region is known as Ellensburg lamb, from eastern Washington. It is known for its excellent balance of flavor, tenderness, and fat content owing to the lamb's primary diet of grass and wild herbs instead of the more common grain.

Mussels   The native mussel of the Pacific Northwest is the blue mussel, which grows in abundance attached to rocks and pilings along the coast. Most blue mussels are Penn Cove mussels, named after the bay where they are commonly grown. Recently, the Mediterranean mussel was introduced to the Pacific Northwest waters. This species is generally larger than the blue mussel and has plumper meat. Mussels deteriorate very rapidly and the beards, or stringy tendrils that protrude from the shell, must be removed before cooking.

Nettle   A perennial plant indigenous to the forests of the region and gathered by foragers in the spring. Nettles have a peppery flavor and are used as an ingredient in cooking in a manner similar to that of sorrel and spinach. Care must be taken when picking nettles, as their stems are a skin irritant.

Oysters   There are four main varieties of oysters found in the Pacific Northwest. Because oysters filter about 100 gallons of water every day, their flavor tends to take on the flavor and characteristic of the water in which they grow. They include:

Pacific Oyster   The most common in the area and often marketed under the name of the bay from which it came. Planted in the region by the Japanese, who emigrated to the area in the late 1800s, the Pacific oyster is identified by its oblong, oval shape and its deeply cupped, lightly ridged shell.

Kunamoto Oyster   Originating in southern Japan, it is small and known for its deep cup, sweet flavor, and buttery texture.

Olympia Oyster   The only oyster native to the Pacific Northwest. It is very small, measuring only about 2 inches in diameter. The shell is round in shape and the meat has a mild, delicate flavor.

European Flat Oyster   Also known as the Belon, originally from France it has a flat, round shell. Its meat has a pronounced flavor that is usually much stronger than that of the Pacific oyster.

Pears   Summer pears include Bartlett and Red Bartlett (bell shaped, good for cooking and eating raw). Winter pears are Comice (softest, juiciest, with a smooth texture), Anjou (the most common pear, crisp, sweet, and juicy, and good for cooking or eating raw), Bosc (especially good with cheese, but also the best pear for poaching), and Seckel (very sweet and smaller than other pears, good for eating raw or cooking).

Plums   Oregon and Washington are among America's top five plum-producing states. Freestone plums, also known as Italian plus, are usually cooked and are commonly used in pies, tarts, and jams. (Freestone plums get their name because the pit is not attached to the flesh of the plum and is easily removed.) The region also produces numerous varieties of plums that are eaten raw or used in fruit salad. Plums are seasonal in nature and available from June to August.

Rockfish   This fish is common to the waters along the Pacific Coast, from Baja California all the way to the Gulf of Alaska. Although dozens of varieties of rockfish exist, the most common has a bright orange skin and yellow eye. Pacific rockfish are commonly referred to as Pacific red snapper even though the fish is only remotely related to the red snapper of the Atlantic Ocean. The meat is lean and flaky, with a mild flavor, and is generally sautéed. Other varieties of rockfish common to the region include black rockfish, quillback rockfish, canary rockfish, and Pacific Ocean perch.

Smoked Salmon   Originally developed to preserve salmon throughout the winter. In the Pacific Northwest, the hot smoking technique, also referred to as kippering, is preferred to the cold smoking technique, which leaves the salmon virtually raw. Hot-smoked salmon is usually prepared by brining the fish in a wet or dry brine; the salmon is then rinsed and cooked very slowly over a smoking hardwood fire.

Stone Fruit   A fruit containing a single pit or seed. Types of stone fruit include cherry, plum, peach, and apricot.

Sturgeon   One of the oldest fish still thriving today. It is found in the waters of the Pacific Northwest. The sturgeon is a survivor of prehistoric times and can be identified by its long snout and a bone structure that is on the surface of the flesh rather than within the fish itself. Sturgeon is a meaty white fish available in the fall. It is excellent sautéed, grilled, or smoked. The egg sac of the female sturgeon is made into caviar.

Thai Black Rice   A highly glutinous rice, black in color. Thai black rice is known for its nutty flavor and distinctly pleasing aroma.

Truffle   A rare fungus that grows underground among the roots of certain trees—primarily Douglas fir in the Pacific Northwest, as opposed to oak in France and Italy. Truffles indigenous to the Pacific Northwest include the *Tuber gibbosum*, similar to the white truffles of Umbria, Italy, and two varieties of black truffles—the *Tuber magnatum* and the *Melanogaster carthusianum*—both commonly found in Perigord, France. Truffles are known for their unique flavor and aroma. Truffles from the Pacific Northwest are quite rare and very expensive, seldom reaching the commercial markets of the United States

Walla Walla Onion   Sweet onions grown in Oregon. Walla Walla onions are as prized as other special onions with distinguishing flavors, such as Vidalia onions from Georgia and Maui onions from Hawaii.

Wild Mushrooms   Of the over 2,500 varieties of wild mushroom common to the Pacific Northwest, only about 35 are considered to be of choice edible quality. The prime locations for gathering wild mushrooms are in western Oregon and Washington, as well as in many areas of Alaska. The spring and fall seasons are when the vast majority of wild mushrooms become available, starting with morels in April and ending with chanterelles as late as December.

Chanterelle Mushroom   The most plentiful of the wild mushrooms found in the area. Chanterelles are yellow or white in color. They appear as early as July and may be available as late as December. Chanterelles have a strongly characteristic flavor and are best cooked in a simple manner that allows their flavor to be fully appreciated.

Chicken of the Woods   These mushrooms are available in fall and early winter. They are flat and do not have a stem. Their name comes from their texture and flavor, which is similar to chicken meat.

Matsutaki Mushroom   Favorites in Japanese cooking, this mushroom grows within the decaying leaves and branches that cover the forest floor. Available in mid-fall, they are noted for their rich, earthy flavor. Their shape resembles the shiitake mushroom, only with a thicker and lumpier cap.

Meadow Mushroom   This wild mushroom, when mature, is tan in color with a large, flat cap and resembles a portobello mushroom. Meadow mushrooms grow in field grasses and are available from May through June. When they are immature, they are slightly pink in color and are called "pinkbottoms."

Morel A mushroom with an earthy flavor, generally found April through May. Morels are tan to black in color and have a cone-shaped, umbrella-capped stem. Their growing patterns are inconsistent and unpredictable, making them scarce as well as expensive. The wrinkled caps are attached to a woody stem with a hollow center that lends itself well to stuffing.

Oyster Mushroom Grayish in color, growing in clusters on cottonwood trees at lower elevations along rivers and lakes, this mushroom is cultivated first in May and June, and then again in September and October.

Puffball A large, spherical mushroom found in the fall. Its large size and firm texture make it well suited for cutting into steaks and either grilling or sautéing.

Porcini Mushroom Also known as cepes in France, these mushrooms have red caps and a white, bulbous base. Normally associated with French and Italian cooking, porcini grow in the region from July through mid-September.

Menus and Recipes from
the Cuisine of the Northwest

MENU ONE
Red Lentil Soup with Walla Walla Onion Marmalade
Cauliflower Tabbouleh Salad
Hot-Smoked Salmon with Salad of Apple, Dried Cherries, and Greens
Grilled Lamb Blade Chops with Prune Plum Relish
Gai Lan (Chinese Broccoli) with Crispy Garlic
Savory Bread Pudding
Chocolate Flourless Cake with Coffee Cream Anglaise

MENU TWO
Mussels in Thai Coconut Broth
Pear and Hazelnut Salad with Oregon Blue Cheese
Seared Halibut with Ginger and Wild Mushrooms
Blackberry Barbecued Chicken
Walla Walla Onion Rings
Cranberry Beans with Fresh Oregano
Cherry Clafoutis

MENU THREE
Peek Gai Nam Daeng (Spicy Thai Chicken Wings)
Lamb Keema Paratha with Green Chutney
Ramen Noodles with Tomato and Crab
Pork Belly, Mint, and Cucumber Sandwich
Chocolate-Dipped Orange Financiers

OTHER RECIPES
Blackberry Yogurt Soup
Pea Soup with Crab and Mint

Red Lentil Soup with Walla Walla Onion Marmalade

4 servings

AMOUNT	MEASURE	INGREDIENT
1 cup	7 ounces/196 g	Red lentils, picked over, rinsed
6 cups	48 ounces/1.5 L	Chicken or vegetable stock
½ cup	3 ounces/84 g	Carrots, peeled, finely diced
½ cup	2 ounces/56 g	Celery, finely diced
1	5 g	Garlic clove, finely diced
1		Bay leaf
		Salt and pepper
3 tablespoons	1½ ounces/44 g	Unsalted butter
8 cups	1½ pounds/672 g	Walla Walla or other sweet onions, chopped
1 teaspoon		Sugar
2 teaspoons		Fresh thyme, chopped
1 tablespoon	½ ounce/15 ml	Sherry vinegar

PROCEDURE

1. In a 3- to 4-quart (3 to 4 L) pot, combine the lentils and stock, and bring to a boil. Cook for a few minutes at a gentle boil and remove any foam that comes to the surface.

2. Add the carrots, celery, garlic, and bay leaf. Reduce the heat and simmer, uncovered, until very soft, 30 to 35 minutes. Remove from heat and discard bay leaf.

3. Puree the soup; if the soup is too thick, thin with additional stock, then season with salt and ½ teaspoon (2.5 ml) pepper. Keep warm.

4. While the lentils are cooking, make the marmalade. Heat the butter in a 10- to 12-inch (25.4–30.5 cm) sauté pan over medium-low heat. Add the onions, sugar, and thyme; cook, stirring often, until very soft and caramelized, 25 to 35 minutes.

5. Stir in the vinegar and correct the seasoning with salt and pepper.

6. Ladle the soup into warm bowls and top each serving with warm onion marmalade.

Red Lentil Soup with Walla Walla Onion Marmalade

Cauliflower Tabbouleh Salad

4 servings

AMOUNT	MEASURE	INGREDIENT
2 cups	12 ounces/336 g	Cauliflower florets
¼ cup	2 ounces/60 ml	Olive oil
1	5 g	Garlic clove, minced
1½ teaspoons		Ground cumin
1 teaspoon		Paprika, hot smoked or mild
1 tablespoon		Shallot, minced
1 tablespoon		Preserved lemon, rind only, minced
1 tablespoon	3 g	Fresh mint, finely chopped
3 tablespoons	10 g	Fresh parsley, chopped
3 tablespoons	10 g	Chives, chopped
¼ cup	2 ounces/56 g	Tomato, peeled, in small dice
1 tablespoon	½ ounce/15 ml	Sherry vinegar
		Salt and pepper

PROCEDURE

1. Either grate the cauliflower with a box grater or place florets in a food processor and pulse to couscous consistency.

2. Heat a 10- to 12-inch (25.4–30.5 cm) sauté pan over medium heat, and add the oil. Add garlic, cumin, paprika and shallots; stir and cook until mixture is fragrant, 1 to 2 minutes. Remove from the heat and let cool 2 minutes, then pour over the cauliflower. Add the preserved lemon rind, mint, parsley, chives, tomato, and sherry vinegar, then toss to combine well. Season with salt and pepper.

Cauliflower Tabbouleh Salad

Hot-Smoked Salmon with Salad of Apple, Dried Cherries, and Greens

4 servings

AMOUNT	MEASURE	INGREDIENT
		Apple, pecan, or hickory wood chips
4	4 ounces/112 g each	Salmon fillets, skinless, boneless, fat line removed
2 tablespoons	1 ounce/28 g	Butter, melted
		Salt and pepper
1 teaspoon		Dijon mustard
4 tablespoons	2 ounce/60 ml	Apple cider vinegar
2 teaspoons		Honey
½ cup	4 ounce/120 ml	Vegetable oil
½ cup	3 ounces/84 g	Gale apple, cored and thinly sliced
½ cup	3 ounces/84 g	Granny Smith apple, cored and thinly sliced
¼ cup	1 ounce/28 g	Dried cherries
2 cups	4 ounces/112 g	Mixed baby greens
¼ cup	1 ounce/28 g	Hazelnuts, toasted, rough chopped

PROCEDURE

1. Preheat the oven to 350°F (176°C).

2. Heat a stovetop smoker over medium heat. Put the smoking chips in the bottom of the smoking pan, reduce the heat to medium-low, and place the rack in the smoker.

3. Brush the salmon with the melted butter and season with salt and pepper. Place the salmon, presentation side up, on the smoker rack. Cover and smoke for 3 to 5 minutes. Transfer the salmon to a sheet pan and cook in the oven until just done, 3 to 4 minutes. Remove from oven and keep warm.

4. Whisk to combine mustard, vinegar, honey and vegetable oil. Adjust the seasoning with salt and pepper.

5. Combine the apples, cherries, and ½ cup (4 ounces/120 ml) of the dressing and toss well. Allow the apples and cherries to soak up flavor for 30 minutes.

6. Add the salad greens to the apples and dried cherries and toss to combine.

7. Serve the salad on chilled plates and top with a salmon fillet drizzled with a tablespoon (½ ounce/15 ml) of the remaining dressing.

Grilled Lamb Blade Chops with Prune Plum Relish

4 servings

CHEF TIP: Lamb shoulder blade chops are cut number 1207 B from the NAMP Meat Buyers Guide. Blade chops are cut from the blade portion of the shoulder and contain part of the blade bone and backbone. Lamb shoulder arm chops may be substituted.

AMOUNT	MEASURE	INGREDIENT
1½ cups	9 ounces/252 g	Prune plums, pitted and diced,
or		*or*
1 cup		Dried prunes, soaked
¼ cup	2 ounces/56 g	Red onion, in ¼-inch (.6 cm) dice
¼ cup	2 ounces/56 g	Red bell pepper, in ¼-inch (.6 cm) dice
1 tablespoon	½ ounce/15 ml	Raspberry vinegar
2 teaspoons	10 ml	Balsamic vinegar
1 tablespoon	½ ounce/15 ml	Olive oil
1 tablespoon	½ ounce/14 g	Brown sugar
		Salt and pepper
4	6 ounces/168 g each	Lamb blade chops, ½ inch (1.2 cm) thick

PROCEDURE

1. Combine the prune plums, onion, red pepper, vinegars, olive oil and brown sugar in a bowl. Let sit 1 hour at room temperature or 2 hours in the refrigerator. Correct seasoning before serving.

2. Preheat the grill to high.

3. Season the chops with salt and pepper. Grill to desired doneness, about 3 minutes per side for medium-rare, depending on the thickness.

4. Serve the chops on warmed plates with 4 tablespoons (about 2 ounces/52 g) each of the relish.

Grilled Lamb Chop with Prune Plum Relish

Gai Lan (Chinese Broccoli) with Crispy Garlic

4 servings

AMOUNT	MEASURE	INGREDIENT
2 tablespoons	1 ounce/60 ml	Vegetable oil
3	15 g	Garlic cloves, very thinly sliced
¼ teaspoon		Red pepper flakes
	1½ pounds/672 g	Gai lan, stem ends trimmed
3 tablespoons	1½ ounces/45 ml	Rice wine or dry white wine
2 tablespoons	1 ounce/30 ml	Tamari (soy sauce)

PROCEDURE

1. Heat a 12-inch (30.5 cm) sauté pan or wok over high heat. When hot, add the oil and swirl to coat bottom. When oil is hot but not smoking, add the garlic and red pepper flakes. Test the oil by adding a slice of garlic. If it sizzles, add the rest of the garlic and cook, stirring constantly, until the garlic is golden, 10 to 15 seconds. Do not overcook the garlic.

2. Use a flat slotted skimmer to keep the garlic slices from sticking together. Transfer the garlic to paper towels to drain the moment they turn color, but keep the oil in pan.

3. Add the gai lan and 2 tablespoons (28 ml) of the wine. Cook, tossing and stirring to prevent scorching, until tender, about 3 minutes.

4. Add the tamari and the remaining wine; cook 1 minute.

5. Transfer to a warm serving platter and sprinkle with the reserved garlic.

Savory Bread Pudding

AMOUNT	MEASURE	INGREDIENT
2 tablespoons	1 ounce/28 g	Unsalted butter
	2 ounces/56 g	Bacon, in ¼-inch (.6 cm) dice
1 cup	4 ounces/112 g	Onion, in ¼-inch (.6 cm) dice
1	5 g	Garlic clove, minced
3		Eggs, lightly beaten
½ cup	4 ounces/120 ml	Heavy cream
½ cup	4 ounces/120 ml	Milk
½ cup	4 ounces/120 ml	Chicken stock
¼ teaspoon		Dried rosemary
		Salt and black pepper
4 cups	16 ounces/453 g	French bread, in ½-inch (1.2 cm) cubes

PROCEDURE

1. Heat the butter in a 10- to 12-inch (25.4–30.5 cm) sauté pan over medium heat. Add the bacon, onion, and garlic; cook until lightly brown, 3 to 4 minutes. Remove from pan and let cool.

2. Combine the eggs, cream, milk, stock, and rosemary in a bowl; stir in the bacon and onion mixture, then season with salt and pepper.

3. Add the bread cubes to the mixture and toss well; let sit to absorb liquid for 30 minutes.

4. Preheat the oven to 350°F (175°C). Grease a 9-inch (22.5 cm) square baking pan or large muffin tins.

5. Pour in the bread pudding mixture, cover with foil, and bake for 20 to 30 minutes. Remove the cover and bake until browned on top and a knife inserted in the middle comes out clean.

6. Cut into servings and serve hot.

Chocolate Flourless Cake with Coffee Cream Anglaise

Makes 1 cake, 6 servings

Chocolate Flourless Cake

AMOUNT	MEASURE	INGREDIENT
2 cups	8 ounces/224 g	Semisweet chocolate, chopped
½ cup	4 ounces/112 g	Butter
6		Eggs, separated
¾ cup	5¼ ounces/147 g	Sugar

PROCEDURE

1. Preheat the oven to 350°F (175°C). Cut a piece of parchment into circles to fit the bottom of six 8-ounce (226 g) timbales or ramekins. Butter both the parchment and the sides of the ramekins.

2. Combine the chocolate and butter in a 2- to 3-quart (2 to 3 L) metal bowl. Melt the chocolate over simmering water, stirring constantly, until smooth. Remove from heat and cool slightly.

3. Using a paddle and standing mixer, whisk the egg yolks with ½ cup (113 g) of the sugar until thick and pale yellow, 6 to 8 minutes.

4. Fold the melted chocolate into the egg yolk mixture, until evenly combined.

5. Whisk the egg whites to soft peak (when you turn the whisk upside down, the peaks are just starting to hold). Add the remaining sugar gradually and beat to soft peaks.

6. In several additions, fold the egg whites into the chocolate mixture.

7. Pour the batter into the prepared pans. Bake in a hot-water bath until puffed and a tester inserted into the center comes out with moist crumbs attached, about 30 minutes.

8. Transfer pan to rack. Cool 10 minutes.

9. Using small sharp knife, cut around edge of cakes. Invert onto a rack and peel off parchment. Serve with Coffee Cream Anglaise (recipe follows).

Coffee Cream Anglaise

AMOUNT	MEASURE	INGREDIENT
½ cup	4 ounces/120 ml	Milk
½ cup	4 ounces/120 ml	Heavy cream
½ cup	3½ ounces/100 g	Sugar
3		Egg yolks
1 teaspoon	5 ml	Vanilla extract
1 tablespoon	14 g	Instant espresso coffee, dissolved in ½ tablespoon (7 ml) of water or dark rum

PROCEDURE

1. Combine the milk, cream, and sugar. Stir to begin dissolving the sugar.

2. Place the yolks in a 1-quart (1 L) bowl and whisk just enough to break them.

3. Bring the milk mixture to a full rolling boil over medium heat. Remove the pan from heat and whisk about one-third of it into the yolks. Remember to begin whisking before pouring in the hot liquid. Return the saucepan to medium heat and bring the milk mixture back to a full boil.

4. Whisk the yolk mixture into the boiling liquid, and continue whisking until it thickens slightly, about 30 seconds.

5. Immediately pour the sauce through a fine-mesh strainer, then cool quickly over a bowl of ice water, stirring occasionally.

6. Stir in the vanilla and espresso.

Chocolate Flourless Cake with Coffee Cream Anglaise

Mussels in Thai Coconut Broth

4 servings

AMOUNT	MEASURE	INGREDIENT
1½ pounds	24 ounces/672 g	Mussels, beards removed
½ cup	4 ounces/120 ml	Dry white wine
1 tablespoon	½ ounce/15ml	Vegetable oil
2 cups	8 ounces/224 g	Baby bok choy, in 1-inch (2.5 cm) pieces
2½ cups	10 ounces/280 g	Red bell pepper, julienned
6 tablespoons	1½ ounces/42 g	Shallots, thinly sliced
1 tablespoon	¼ ounce/7 g	Fresh ginger, grated
1 tablespoon	5 g	Garlic, minced
2 teaspoons		Light brown sugar
2 teaspoons		Thai red curry paste
2 teaspoons		Fish sauce (nam pla)
1 can	13 ounces/390 ml	Coconut milk (unsweetened), well shaken
		Salt and pepper
¼ cup	½ ounce/14 g	Fresh cilantro
4		Lime wedges

PROCEDURE

1. Place the mussels in a 3- to 4-quart (3 to 4 L) saucepan; discard any that fail to close to the touch. Add the wine and bring to a boil over high heat. Cover and cook, shaking, until the mussels open, about 5 minutes.

2. Save the liquid and transfer the mussels to a bowl, discarding any that failed to open; cover and keep warm.

3. Pour the liquid through a fine-mesh sieve lined with cheesecloth (muslin) and set aside.

4. Set a wok or 10- to 12-inch (25.4–30.5 cm) sauté pan over high heat until very hot. Add the oil and when the oil is hot, add the bok choy, bell pepper, shallots, ginger, and garlic. Cook, stirring, for 2 to 3 minutes or until vegetables are almost soft.

5. Stir in the brown sugar, curry paste, and fish sauce; cook 1 minute.

6. Pour in the coconut milk and reserved mussel cooking liquid; bring to a boil. Correct seasoning with salt and pepper.

7. Divide the mussels and vegetables among warmed bowls and ladle the broth over the top.

8. Sprinkle with cilantro and serve immediately with lime wedges on the side.

Mussels in Thai Coconut Broth

Pear and Hazelnut Salad with Oregon Blue Cheese

4 servings

CHEF TIP: When fruit is roasted above 330°F/165.5°C, the process of caramelization occurs, which does not happen when fruit is steamed or boiled. At the higher temperature, the natural sugars turn nutty and richly sweet. To roast pears, cut in half and core. Lightly coat fruit with vegetable oil and place in a baking dish; the fruit should fit snugly in a single layer. Roast in a 400°F/204.4°C oven until pears are golden on bottom and tender when pierced with a knife, 20 to 30 minutes.

AMOUNT	MEASURE	INGREDIENT
3 cups	6 ounces/168 g	Butter lettuce
1 cup	4 ounces/112 g	Roasted pear, peeled, chopped
¼ cup	2 ounces/60 ml	Rice vinegar
1 teaspoon		Sugar
		Salt and white pepper
¼ cup	2 ounces/60 ml	Hazelnut oil
2		Whole roasted pears (Red Bartlett, preferably), peeled
¼ cup	1 ounce/28 g	Hazelnuts, roasted, chopped
½ cup	2 ounces/56 g	Oregon blue cheese

PROCEDURE

1. Break the larger lettuce leaves into 4-inch (10.2 cm) pieces.

2. Add the chopped pear to a blender along with vinegar (to prevent browning), then add the sugar, salt, pepper, and hazelnut oil and puree until smooth.

3. Place the lettuce in a bowl and toss with enough of the pear puree to lightly coat the lettuce. Arrange the dressed lettuce on chilled plates.

4. Slice each whole pear in half and spoon out the cores. Lay the halves on a cutting board, flat side down, and slice each half on a bias into 7 or 8 even slices. Press the sliced pear halves lightly to fan them out and carefully transfer the pear fans to the lettuce.

5. Scatter the hazelnuts and blue cheese over each salad and serve.

Pear and Hazelnut Salad with Oregon Blue Cheese

Seared Halibut with Ginger and Wild Mushrooms

4 servings

AMOUNT	MEASURE	INGREDIENT
4	4 ounces/112 g each	Halibut fillets
		Salt and pepper
¼ cup	2 ounces/60 ml	Vegetable oil (grape seed or canola)
2 tablespoons	½ ounce/14 g	Shallots, minced
1 tablespoon	¼ ounce/7 g	Fresh ginger, grated
2 cup	8 ounces/224 g	Wild mushrooms (chanterelles, shiitake, or other), sliced
2 tablespoons	1 ounce/28 g	Butter
1		Lemon, zested
1 tablespoon	½ ounce/15 ml	Lemon juice
¼ cup	2 ounces/60 ml	White wine

PROCEDURE

1. Season the halibut lightly with salt and set aside at room temperature 15 minutes. Then, rinse the fish fillets and pat dry.

2. Heat a 10- to 12-inch (25.4–30.5 cm) sauté pan over medium heat; add 2 tablespoons (1 ounce/30 ml) of the oil. Add the fish to the pan and cook 2 to 4 minutes, depending on the thickness of the fillets, until golden brown. Turn the fillets and cook 2 to 4 minutes more, or until golden brown and cooked through. Remove from pan and keep warm.

3. To the same pan add the remaining oil and reduce the heat to medium low. Add the shallots and ginger, then cook 1 minute. Add the mushrooms, toss well, and add 1 tablespoon (½ ounce/14 g) butter. Cook 2 to 3 minutes, stirring often. Add the lemon zest and juice and the wine, stirring the bottom of the pan. Cook on high heat until most of the liquid has cooked off.

4. Turn off the heat, add the remaining 1 tablespoon (½ ounce/14 g) butter, and correct the seasoning. Swirl to combine.

5. Serve the sauce under the halibut on warmed plates.

Seared Halibut with Ginger and Wild Mushrooms

Blackberry Barbecued Chicken

4 servings

AMOUNT	MEASURE	INGREDIENT
1 tablespoon	½ ounce/15 ml	Vegetable oil
1 cup	4 ounces/112 g	Sweet onion, in ¼-inch (.6 cm) dice
½ cup	4 ounces/120 ml	Dry red wine
2 pints	1 pound/448 g	Blackberries, fresh or frozen
¼ cup (packed)	2 ounces/56 g	Light brown sugar
1 teaspoon	5 ml	Soy sauce
1	3½ pounds/1.6 kg	Chicken, cut into 8 pieces
		Salt
		Black pepper

PROCEDURE

1. Heat the oil in a 10- to 12-inch (25.4–30.5 cm) sauté pan over medium heat. Add the onion and cook, stirring frequently, until soft, about 5 minutes.

2. Add the wine, berries, brown sugar, and soy sauce. Cook until slightly thickened, 20 to 25 minutes.

3. Pass the berry mixture through a food mill or sieve.

4. Heat the grill. Season the chicken with salt and pepper.

5. Grill the chicken skin side down for 5 minutes. Baste with the sauce, and cook an additional 3 to 5 minutes. Turn the chicken and again baste with sauce. Cook until juices run clear, 3 to 5 minutes more.

6. Baste one more time before removing from heat. Serve immediately with additional sauce.

Blackberry Barbecued Chicken with Walla Walla Onion Rings

Walla Walla Onion Rings

AMOUNT	MEASURE	INGREDIENT
As needed		Vegetable oil, for deep-frying
1	14 ounces/392 g	Sweet onion, in ¼-inch (.6 cm) slices
⅔ cup	5 ounces/150 ml	Water
⅔ cup	3½ ounces/100 g	All-purpose flour
1½ cups	3½ ounces/100 g	Panko (Japanese bread crumbs)
1 tablespoon		Lime zest
1 teaspoon		Salt
2 tablespoons	¼ ounce/7 g	Fresh cilantro, chopped
4		Lime wedges

PROCEDURE

1. Heat the oil in a deep-fryer or deep pot to 375°F (190°C). Line a baking pan with paper towels.

2. Separate the onion slices into rings.

3. Whisk together the water and flour until smooth.

4. Dip the onion rings into the flour batter, lift out, let excess drip off, and then dip the rings into the panko, coating evenly.

5. Fry until golden brown, 1 to 2 minutes. Drain on paper towels. Repeat until all the rings are cooked.

6. To serve, sprinkle the lime zest, salt, and cilantro over the fried onion rings. Serve immediately with lime wedges.

Cranberry Beans with Fresh Oregano

4 servings

AMOUNT	MEASURE	INGREDIENT
7 cups	2½ pounds/1.1 kg	Fresh cranberry (borlotti) beans, shelled
or		
1¼ cups	9 ounces/252 g	Dried cranberry beans, soaked overnight
2		Bay leaves
3	15 g	Garlic cloves
1¼ teaspoons		Salt
3 tablespoons	1½ ounces/45 ml	Extra-virgin olive oil
½ teaspoon		Black pepper
1 tablespoon	3 g	Fresh oregano, chopped

PROCEDURE

1. If using fresh beans, shell them. Cover fresh or dried beans with 2 inches (5 cm) of water. Add the bay leaves and garlic. Bring beans to a boil, reduce the heat, and simmer gently, uncovered, until beans are tender, 30 minutes for fresh beans and 1 hour for dried.

2. Add 1 teaspoon (5 ml) salt, stir well, and let stand 10 minutes.

3. Drain beans. Discard the bay leaves and mash the garlic. Stir in the olive oil, pepper, oregano, and garlic. Mix well. Serve while still warm.

Cherry Clafoutis

AMOUNT	MEASURE	INGREDIENT
2 cups	12 ounces/336 g	Cherries (Bing or other sweet), washed and pitted
3		Eggs
⅓ cup	2½ ounces/70 g	Granulated sugar
1 cup	8 ounces/240 ml	Whole milk
1 teaspoon		Vanilla extract
½ cup	2 ounces/56 g	All-purpose flour
Pinch		Salt
		Confectioners' sugar, for dusting

PROCEDURE

1. Preheat the oven to 350°F (176°C). Lightly grease a 9-inch (22.9 cm) pie pan.

2. Arrange the cherries in an even layer in the pan.

3. Whisk together the eggs and sugar until lemon colored and slightly thickened, 1 to 2 minutes. Add the milk, vanilla, and salt, and whisk to combine. Sprinkle in the flour and whisk until smooth.

4. Pour the batter over the cherries and bake until puffed and nicely browned around the edges, 45 to 50 minutes. When removed from the oven, the clafoutis will deflate as it cools.

5. Serve warm with a sprinkling of confectioners' sugar.

Cherry Clafoutis

Peek Gai Nam Daeng (Spicy Thai Chicken Wings)

4 servings

AMOUNT	MEASURE	INGREDIENT
As needed		Vegetable oil, for frying
1 pound	16 ounces/448 g	Chicken wings
½ cup	2 ounces/56 g	Cornstarch
1 tablespoon	½ ounce/15 ml	Coconut oil
2	10 g	Garlic cloves, minced
1 tablespoon		Shallot, minced
½ cup	2 ounces/56 g	Onion, minced
½ cup	3 ounces/84 g	Tomato, peeled, in ¼-inch (.6 cm) dice
½ cup	4 ounces/120 ml	Ketchup
1 tablespoon	½ ounce/15 ml	Sriracha (Asian hot sauce)
1 tablespoon	½ ounce/15 ml	Soy sauce
1 tablespoon	½ ounce/15 ml	Sugar
2 teaspoons		Oyster sauce
2 teaspoons		Mirin
2 tablespoons		Peanuts, chopped
2 tablespoons	¼ ounce/7 g	Fresh cilantro leaves
½ cup	3 ounces/84 g	Celery sticks, in ¼-inch (.6 cm) lengths

PROCEDURE

1. Heat 2 inches (5.1 cm) of the oil in a 6-quart (6 L) heavy-bottomed pan to 400°F (204°C).

2. Toss the chicken wings with the cornstarch to coat. Working in batches if necessary, fry chicken until golden brown and crisp, 8 to 10 minutes. Transfer to a wire rack to drain.

3. Heat a 10- to 12-inch (25.4–30.5 cm) sauté pan over medium-high heat. Add the coconut oil, then add the garlic, shallots, and onion; cook, stirring, until golden brown, 2 to 3 minutes. Add the tomato and cook, stirring, 3 to 4 minutes more.

4. Add the ketchup, hot sauce, soy sauce, sugar, and oyster sauce; cook, stirring, until thickened, 4 to 5 minutes. Stir in the mirin and whisk well.

5. Add the chicken wings and toss to coat with the sauce; cook 1 to 2 minutes to heat wings through.

6. Serve the wings sprinkled with the peanuts and cilantro, and serve with the celery sticks and remaining sauce on the side.

Peek Gai Nam Daeng (Spicy Thai Chicken Wings)

Lamb Keema Paratha with Green Chutney

4 servings

CHEF TIP: Keema paratha is a north Indian unleavened flatbread stuffed with spiced minced meat. "Kheem" means *spicy minced meat*, and "paratha" means *flatbread*.

Lamb Keema

AMOUNT	MEASURE	INGREDIENT
For the Filling		
3 tablespoons	1½ ounces/45 ml	Vegetable oil
1 tablespoon		Garlic, minced
2 cups	12 ounces/336 g	Ground lamb
1 teaspoon		Turmeric
1 teaspoon		Coriander seeds, toasted and crushed
1 teaspoon		Chili powder
		Salt
1 cup	8 ounces/240 ml	Plain yogurt
1 teaspoon		Ground cardamom
2 teaspoons		Fresh ginger, minced
½ cup	3 ounces/84 g	Red onion, minced
1 tablespoon		Fresh mint, finely chopped
1		Egg, lightly beaten
For the Dough		
2 cups	8 ounces/224 g	Whole wheat flour
6 tablespoons	3 ounces/90 ml	Butter, clarified
2 teaspoons		Black pepper
		Salt
½–1 cup	4–8 ounces/120–440 ml	Water
1 tablespoon	½ ounce/15 ml	Corn oil

PROCEDURE

1. Make the filling. Heat a 10- to 12-inch (25.4–30.5 cm) sauté pan over medium-high heat, then add the oil. Cook the garlic for 10 seconds. Add the lamb and turmeric, and mix well. Cook, stirring frequently, adding the coriander seeds, chili powder, and salt, for 6 to 7 minutes. Stir to break up the meat.

2. Add the yogurt and cook, stirring 2 to 3 minutes more. Cook uncovered until all the liquid has been absorbed. Let cool.

3. Add the meat mixture to a food processor and pulse the meat to break up any lumps. Add the cardamom, ginger, onion, and mint, then pulse 10 seconds. Add the egg, pulse 10 seconds, then put the mixture in a mixing bowl and refrigerate until ready to stuff the paratha.

4. Make the paratha dough. In a large bowl, using your hands, mix the flour with 3 table-spoons (1½ ounces/44 g) of the butter, the salt, and pepper. Add water a few tablespoons

at a time and knead to a soft, firm dough. If the mixture becomes dry, add a few more teaspoons of water. Add the corn oil and knead to a smooth dough. Shape into a ball and set aside to rest for 15 minutes.

5. Divide the dough into 8 rounds and roll each into a 6-inch (15.2 cm) circle. Dust with additional flour, if necessary.

6. Fill the paratha. Place 2 tablespoons of filling on the lower half of each circle. Moisten the edge with water and fold the top half over, pulling the dough gently over the filling. Seal the edge and discard any excess dough.

7. Roll out the filled rounds again to a ¼-inch (.6 cm) thickness so that they are 6 inches (15.2 cm) in diameter.

8. Heat a 10- to 12-inch (25.4–30.5 cm) sauté pan over medium heat. Add a little of the remaining butter, press the paratha lightly with a spatula and cook until golden and crisp on one side, 3 to 4 minutes. Flip over, add a little more clarified butter if necessary, and cook 3 to 4 minutes or until golden brown and crisp. Serve with Green Chutney (recipe follows)

Green Chutney

AMOUNT	MEASURE	INGREDIENT
2 cups	2 ounces/56 g	Fresh cilantro leaves
½ cup	½ ounce/28 g	Fresh mint leaves
½ cup	3 ounces/84 g	Onion, in ¼-inch (.6 cm) dice
½ teaspoon		Red chili powder
½ teaspoon		Ground cumin
2 tablespoons	1 ounce/30 ml	Lemon juice
1 teaspoon		Fresh ginger, minced
1 teaspoon		Garlic, minced
½ teaspoon		Sugar
		Salt

PROCEDURE   Place all the ingredients in a food processor and puree, or pound in mortar and pestle a little at a time.

Lamb Keema Paratha with Green Chutney

Ramen Noodles with Tomato and Crab

4 servings

AMOUNT	MEASURE	INGREDIENT
2 tablespoons	1 ounce/30 ml	Vegetable oil
½ cup	3 ounces/84 g	Onion, in ¼-inch (.6 cm) dice
1	5 g	Garlic clove, minced
2 cups	12 ounces/336 g	Tomatoes, peeled, in ¼-inch (.6 cm) dice
2 cups	12 ounces/226 g	Cooked best-quality ramen noodles
1 cup	2 ounces/56 g	Arugula, chopped
4 tablespoons	2 ounces/60 ml	Soy sauce
1 tablespoon	1 ounce/30 ml	Toasted sesame oil
1 cup	6 ounces/168 g	Crab meat, picked over
4 tablespoons	2 ounces/60 ml	Nori, shredded
4 tablespoons	2 ounces/60 ml	Green onions, chopped
3 tablespoons		Bonito flakes

PROCEDURE

1. Heat a 2-quart (2 L) saucepan over medium heat, then add 1 tablespoon (½ ounce/15 ml) of the vegetable oil. Sauté the onion and garlic until soft but not brown, 2 to 3 minutes. Add the tomatoes and increase heat to medium-high. Cook until reduced by one-third, 8 to 10 minutes. Allow to cool and then puree or pass sauce through a fine-mesh sieve. Refrigerate.

2. Toss the noodles with the remaining 1 tablespoon (½ ounce/15 ml) vegetable oil.

3. Distribute noodles and the arugula evenly in four bowls. Distribute the soy sauce and sesame oil over the bowls and top each with some of the tomato sauce and the crab meat.

4. Garnish portions with nori, green onions, and bonito flakes.

Ramen Noodles with Tomato and Crab

Pork Belly, Mint, and Cucumber Sandwich

4 servings

AMOUNT	MEASURE	INGREDIENT
For the Pork		
1½ pounds	24 ounces/696 g	Pork belly
2 tablespoons	1 ounce/30 ml	Vegetable oil
1 cup	6 ounces/168 g	Onion, rough chopped
1 cup	6 ounces/168 g	Carrot, rough chopped
½ cup	3 ounces/84 g	Celery, rough chopped
3		Whole cloves, chopped
1		Bay leaf
1		Fresh thyme sprig
⅛ teaspoon		Cayenne powder
1¼ cups	10 ounces/300 ml	Chicken stock
		Salt and pepper
For the Sandwiches		
8 slices	8 ounces/224 g	White bread
6 tablespoons	3 ounces/90 ml	Mayonnaise
2 teaspoons	10 ml	Fresh lime juice
1½ teaspoons		Red pepper flakes
1 cup	4½ ounces/126 g	Cucumber, English or hothouse, in ¹⁄₁₆-inch (.15 cm) slices
1 tablespoon	½ ounce/15 ml	Sherry vinegar
2 tablespoon	1 ounce/30 ml	Olive oil
		Salt and pepper
⅓ cup (packed)		Fresh mint leaves, rough chopped

PROCEDURE

1. Make the pork. Remove the skin from the pork belly. Tap the pork on both sides with a meat tenderizer hammer/mallet until somewhat even. If the pork is in one large piece, cut into two equal portions.

2. Using a 6-quart pressure cooker, preheat the pot over medium heat and add 1 tablespoon (½ ounce/15 ml) of the oil. Place the pork fat side down, and sear for 2 to 3 minutes. Turn over and sear the other side for 2 to 3 minutes. Remove the pork. Drain off all but 2 tablespoons (1 ounce/30 ml) of the pork fat.

3. Increase the heat to medium-high and add the onion and carrots, and sauté 2 minutes. Add the celery and cook for 2 minutes more. Then, add the cloves, bay leaf, thyme, and cayenne; stir and cook for 1 minute.

4. Add the chicken stock and scrape up any browned bits from the bottom of the pot. Add the pork belly to the pot (do not stack the meat). Lock the lid on the pressure cooker and bring to high pressure, then lower the heat to maintain the pressure and cook 35 to 40 minutes. Begin counting the cooking time when the pressure cooker has reached full pressure.

5. Remove pressure cooker from the heat and allow the pressure to reduce naturally, 15 to 20 minutes.

6. Remove the pork carefully. It should be very tender. Set the pork, fat side down, on a double layer of paper towels to drain some of the moisture.

7. Slice the pork the thickness of thick bacon, making approximately 12 slices (3 per sandwich).

8. Heat the remaining 1 tablespoon (½ ounce/15 ml) oil in a 10- to 12-inch (25.4–30.5 cm) sauté pan over medium heat. Add the pork slices and sear on both sides until crisp, about 1 minute per side. Keep hot while you assemble the sandwiches.

9. Assemble the sandwiches. Toast the bread on both sides. Combine the mayonnaise, lime juice, and red pepper flakes, and stir well to combine. (The flavor of the mayonnaise may be adjusted with additional lime juice or chili flakes.)

10. Toss the cucumber with the sherry vinegar and olive oil and season with salt and pepper.

11. Spread the lime mayonnaise evenly on one side of each toasted bread slice. Top 4 bread slices with 2 or 3 pork slices and then lay cucumber slices on top and sprinkle with mint. Top with the remaining bread slices and serve immediately.

Pork Belly, Mint, and Cucumber Sandwich

Chocolate-Dipped Orange Financiers

Makes about 12 financiers

AMOUNT	MEASURE	INGREDIENT
¾ cup	6 ounces/168 g	Butter
½ cup, plus more for dusting	2 ounces/56 g	All-purpose flour
¼		Vanilla bean, seeds scraped and reserved
	2½ ounces/70 g	Almonds, blanched and toasted
2 cups	9 ounces/252 g	Confectioners' sugar
1 teaspoon		Kosher salt
4		Egg whites, at room temperature
2 teaspoons		Orange zest
½ cup	4 ounces/112 g	Bittersweet chocolate, finely chopped
½ cup	4 ounces/120 ml	Heavy cream

PROCEDURE

1. Preheat the oven to 350°F (176°C). Grease and flour a 12-cup muffin pan.

2. Heat the butter and vanilla bean with its seeds in a 2-quart (2 L) saucepan over medium heat. Cook until the butter begins to brown, swirling constantly, 15 to 20 minutes. Remove from heat, and discard the vanilla bean. Whisk to cool, then pour into a measuring cup and set aside ½ cup plus 2 tablespoons (5 ounces/75 ml); reserve any remaining for another use.

3. Combine the flour and almonds in a food processor and process until almonds are finely ground. Transfer to a large mixing bowl and mix in the sugar and salt. Add the browned butter, the egg whites and orange zest, and whisk to combine well.

4. Pour about ¼ cup batter into each muffin cup and bake until golden brown and lightly caramelized at the edges, 20 to 25 minutes. Let cool before removing from mold to a wire rack.

5. Place the chocolate in a bowl. Bring the cream to a boil in a small pot, pour over chocolate; let sit for 1 minute. Using a rubber spatula, slowly stir from the center until chocolate is smooth.

6. Dip the top of each cake into the chocolate and then invert onto a baking sheet. Let chocolate set before serving.

Chocolate-Dipped Orange Financiers

Blackberry Yogurt Soup

4 servings

AMOUNT	MEASURE	INGREDIENT
2½ cups	12 ounces/336 g	Blackberries
¼ cup	2 ounces/60 ml	Dry white wine
¼ cup	3 ounces/90 ml	Honey
2 tablespoons	1 ounce/30 ml	Lemon juice
1½ cups	12 ounces/360 ml	Plain yogurt
¼ cup	2 ounces/60 ml	Half-and-half
4 tablespoons	2 ounces/60 ml	Sour cream

PROCEDURE

1. Combine the blackberries, wine, honey, and lemon juice in a stainless steel saucepan. Bring to a boil, cover, and reduce the heat. Slowly simmer the mixture for 15 minutes.

2. Pour the blackberry mixture into a blender or food processor and puree. Stir in the yogurt and half-and-half; refrigerate until needed.

3. To serve, carefully ladle the soup into chilled soup bowls or plates. Garnish with a small dollop of sour cream.

Pea Soup with Crab and Mint

4 servings

AMOUNT	MEASURE	INGREDIENT
2 tablespoons	1 ounce/28 g	Unsalted butter
1½ cups	6 ounces/168 g	Leeks, chopped
2 cups	10 ounces/280 g	Shelled fresh or frozen English peas
2½ cups	20 ounces/600 ml	Chicken stock
½ teaspoon		Salt
½ teaspoon		Black pepper
1 cup, loosely packed	5 ounces/140 g	Dungeness crab, picked over
1½ tablespoons	5 g	Fresh mint, chopped

PROCEDURE

1. Melt 1 tablespoon (½ ounce/14 g) butter over medium heat in a 3- to 4-quart (3 to 4 L) pot. Add the leeks and sauté until wilted, 3 to 4 minutes.

2. Add the peas, stock, and salt and pepper and bring to a boil; reduce the heat to medium low, and simmer 5 to 10 minutes.

3. In a blender or food processor, puree the soup until smooth. Return soup to the pot.

4. In a separate pan, melt the remaining 1 tablespoon (½ ounce/14 g) butter and add the crab. Cook gently until warmed through, about 1 minute. Stir the mint into the crab.

5. Ladle the soup into warmed bowls. Top each serving with a portion of crab.

Pea Soup with Crab and Mint

The Cuisine of
Hawaii

The Hawaiian Islands are some of the most recent and some of the most isolated islands on earth. Before the arrival of the first populations, the islands essentially grew nothing edible. Everything that the people of Hawaii eat has been brought in or introduced since then. From the Pacific Islanders who first reached the Hawaiian Islands, followed by the European voyages of discovery, to the migration of laborers to the sugar plantations, and now the focus on foods grown in the Islands, Hawaii offers a transparent look at the development of a society and a cuisine.

Hawaii is "The Aloha State." The word *aloha* means both "hello" and "good-bye." The state bird is the nene, or Hawaiian goose; the state flower is the yellow hibiscus; and the state tree is the kukui, or candlenut tree. The state gem is black coral, and the state marine mammal is the humpback whale. The state fish is the humuhumunukunuku apuaa (the Hawaiian alphabet has only 12 letters: a, e, i, o, u, h, k, l, m, n, p, and w), also known as the rectangular triggerfish.

HISTORY AND MAJOR INFLUENCES

HISTORY OF THE ISLANDS

The people who first lived in this part of the world are called "Polynesians"; the name means "people of the many islands." Hawaii is a chain of 132 islands that extend for more than 1,500 miles. The eight main islands are Hawaii (the Big Island), Maui, Oahu, Kauai, Molokai, Lanai, Nihau, and Kahoolawe. Almost all of the Hawaiian populations live on seven of these eight islands. The islands have absorbed wave after wave of immigrants bringing bits and pieces from their homelands to create a unique people of blended ancestry. In addition to those of Polynesian descent and whites and blacks from the mainland United States, Hawaii's population includes people of Chinese, Filipino, Japanese, Korean, and Portuguese ancestry. All have contributed customs to what has become Hawaiian culture.

THE FIRST VISITORS

It is believed that the first voyagers to Hawaii were from the Marquesas Islands and Tahiti, and they arrived in approximately A.D. 800. Expert navigators, these Polynesians explored immense stretches of ocean in sailboats made by lashing two huge canoes together and raising a sail. The early sailors used the stars, clouds, ocean currents, and even seabirds to find their way from island to island. Kings ruled separate kingdoms scattered over the Hawaiian Islands, and many chiefs ruled under each king.

In the late 1700s, Captain James Cook of the British Navy, searching for the Northwest Passage to lead from Europe to Asia, discovered Hawaii. He named it the Sandwich Islands, after the Earl of Sandwich, the First Lord of the British admiralty. Merchant vessels from all over the world stopped in the Hawaiian Islands en route to China. For many years, Hawaiians earned more money by providing whalers and traders with goods than from any other business.

During the early 19th century, the Hawaiian Islands were ruled by four chiefs. But in the 1780s, Kamehameha I—the ruling chief of Hawaii Island—defeated the other chiefs and united the islands. During Kamehameha's rule, Hawaii began to trade with other countries. Settlers, sailors, and merchants came from England, the United States, France, Portugal, Korea, the Philippines, and Russia to take advantage of Hawaii's natural resources. When King Kamehameha died in 1819, his son Liholiho ruled as Kamehameha II. As trade grew, Christian missionaries came to the islands. Political struggles between the missionaries and the Hawaiian natives weakened the established religious and social systems. In 1893, Queen Liliuokalani, a descendant of King Kamehameha, was removed from the throne by powerful U.S. and European landowners, and the Hawaiian monarchy was ended. On July 7, 1898, while pursuing the U.S. policy of manifest destiny, President William McKinley formally authorized American annexation of the Republic of Hawaii. In 1900, Hawaii was made a U.S. territory. After World War II, statehood became a major issue, and in 1959, Hawaii became the 50th state.

A MOST DIVERSE CULTURE

The Polynesian natives who came to Hawaii found tropical vegetation, fertile soil, and many species of fish and wildlife. On return visits, they brought their own foods, such as taro, breadfruit, coconuts, sweet potatoes, sugarcane, pineapples, and bananas. They also brought small pigs to start their new lives in Hawaii. When sailors traveling from the Americas to Asia stopped in Hawaii, they could rest, eat, and resupply their ships in the middle of the vast Pacific Ocean. The sailors, traders, and whalers brought with them salted meats and fish, sea biscuits, and a limited supply of fruit and vegetables. Later, in the 1820s, missionaries from the East Coast of the United States came to Hawaii in an attempt to Christianize the natives. They brought staples they were accustomed to in New England, such as potatoes, apples, salt cod, corned beef, cheese, and butter.

SUGAR AND PINEAPPLE

By the end of the 19th century, sugar and pineapple plantations run by American businessmen had taken over much of Hawaii's land, and the crops were the two most important sources of revenue for the Hawaiian economy. As the sugar crops grew, so did the demand for labor, encouraging tens of thousands of people to emigrate to Hawaii. The plantation owners hired contract workers, and substantial numbers of Chinese, Japanese, Filipinos, Koreans, and Portuguese came to work. Each group demanded its own food on the plantations, and small farms, market gardens, and fishing operations were established.

The Chinese replaced the poi—the thick, gray paste pounded from the taro root—with rice and relied on their own herbs and spices. The Japanese brought their favorite vegetables, noodle soups, and stir-fry techniques. They packed their lunches to take to the fields, and plate lunches or bento (box lunch) became common. Though many of the familiar vegetable seeds they had carried with them from Japan would not grow in Hawaii's climates, the Japanese succeeded in making tofu and soy sauce. The Portuguese introduced their favorite foods with an emphasis on pork, tomatoes, peppers, souring agents and spices, and sausages. They also built their traditional Portuguese beehive bread oven, or forno, which allowed them to make their pao doce (sweet bread). It is said they also introduced the Japanese to tempura and the Koreans to hot chiles. The Koreans brought their giant crocks of kim chee and adobo stews, and built their barbecue pits to cook their marinated meats.

The massive Hawaiian pineapple industry began when James Dole planted his first pineapple trees on the island of Oahu in 1901. In 1922, he purchased the island of Lanai for the purpose of large-scale production, and by 1950, his was the largest pineapple company in the world. But since the 1970s, with crops grown more cheaply in places such as Southeast Asia, Hawaii has taken a much more diverse posture with regard to its agricultural output. The soil in Hawaii is fertile and productive, and the climate, which offers plenty of sunshine and rain, provides excellent growing conditions for agricultural products including livestock, squash, peppers, tomatoes, and lettuce.

HAWAIIAN FOOD, LOCAL FOOD, AND THE HAWAIIAN REGIONAL FOOD MOVEMENT

When those first voyagers from the South Pacific landed on the Hawaiian Islands, they found fish, shellfish, salt, birds, and fresh water, but few edible plants. To survive and flourish, they had to bring their own edible plants. Most important to them was taro. For centuries, it was the main staple of their diet, and it is still served at luaus and important ceremonial occasions. According to a popular legend, the Hawaiian sky god Wakea and the earth god Papa produced two children. The first child died and was buried. From this spot, the taro plant grew. Their second child became the ancestor of the Hawaiian people. *Ohana*, the Hawaiian word for "family," is derived from the word *oha*, the word for the taro cormlets that branch from the stem, or corm, of the plant. The entire taro plant is edible, and there are hundreds of different varieties. The corm of the wetland taro makes the best poi, as well as taro starch or flour. The dry-land variety has a crispy texture and is used for making taro chips, and the smaller Japanese variety is used in stewed dishes. The heart-shaped, deep green leaves and stalks can be cooked as a vegetable, much like turnip greens or other leaf vegetables, or used to wrap other ingredients. The tops of the taro are saved for replanting. Where taro would not grow, sweet potatoes were planted and many varieties are available. In addition, the Marquesan settlers brought the breadfruit and the Tahitians brought the baking banana. The new settlers also introduced coconuts, sugarcane, and pineapples.

"Local food" is the term used in Hawaii to describe how the immigrants adapted to their new lives by using what were new foods to them on the sugar plantations. The food they found was unfamiliar and they had to adapt their cooking methods to create their meals from what was provided and what they brought with them. As a result, their traditional cuisines were transformed. Local food is best exemplified in the plate lunch, which is served from a plate lunch wagon that can be found around the islands, outside of office buildings, in parks, or by the beaches. Made up of two scoops of rice, a scoop of salad (usually potato salad or macaroni salad), and meat, chicken, or fish heaped on a plate to be eaten with chopsticks, salt and pepper, and soy sauce. The meat could be a large portion of kalua pig (pit-cooked pork), curry stew, Shoyu chicken (chicken simmered in soy sauce), or fried fish. Other favorites such as Portuguese sausage, Chinese sausage, Spam, sweet and sour pork, teriyaki beef, chicken katsu (a breaded and fried cutlet), Kal bi (Korean barbecued short ribs), char siu (Chinese roast pork), manapua (savory stuffed buns), and musubi (rice ball) exemplify local food. Teenagers in Hawaii consider themselves responsible for the frequently found loco moco. Designed to replace sandwiches and typical Asian foods, loco moco is now found in small local restaurants. It is two scoops of rice topped with a hamburger patty and a fried egg, then topped with a generous serving of gravy over the entire meal. Saimin, the Hawaiian version of an Asian noodle soup, is prepared many ways, typically using the somen noodle, broth, and any choice of additional ingredients and seasoning and is served for breakfast, lunch, or dinner.

The Hormel Company's canned meat product Spam (spiced ham) is still considered an important protein, a result of wartime rationing after fishing around the Islands during World War II was prohibited. Most commonly fried and served with rice, it can also be wrapped in ti leaves and roasted, used as a stuffing for wontons, skewered and deep-fried, or used in stir-fry dishes. A Spam musabi is made by using a rectangle of sticky rice, topped with a fried slice of Spam, and wrapped with a piece of dried seaweed. The most frequent snack food is any choice of preserved fruits that may be sweetened, or salted and called "crack seed." Brought by the Chinese immigrants, it refers to the seed of the fruits that are often left in, and crack for the cracking of the seed to expose the kernel.

All the ethnic cuisines rely on Hawaii's coastal and offshore fisheries. Hawaiian fish are defined in four categories:

Tuna   Tuna is the most important commercial fish in Hawaii. Varieties include skipjack or bonito (aku), the big eye or yellowfin tuna (ahi), and albacore (tombo). A large part of the catch goes to Japan to be sold for sashimi. Tunas range up to several hundred pounds in weight and their silvery bodies are darker on the top than on the bottom. In Hawaii, they are favored for sashimi or poke but are also good grilled or sautéed.

Billfish   Most common during the summer, these sport fish are known locally as au. On the mainland they are known as marlins and swordfish. Like tuna, they can be very large, from 100 to 300 pounds. The Pacific blue marlin (known as kajiki) has amber flesh that turns white when cooked. It is good barbecued or grilled, but because this fish has a very low fat content, it should not be overcooked. The broadbill swordfish (shutome) is very popular and shipped all over the continental United States. The flesh is white to pinkish, and the meat is tender and mild to the taste. This fish is high in fat and steaks may be grilled, broiled, or used in stir-fries.

Bottom Fish   The groupers or sea bass, known as hapuu, are noted for their clear white flesh and delicate taste. They are most often steamed. The ruby snapper (onaga) is small with a delicate flavor when steamed, poached, or baked. The pink snapper (opakapaka) is very popular, with a higher fat, light pink flesh, often steamed or baked and served with a light sauce.

Other Open Ocean Fish   The best known are the wahoo (known as ono), with its moist, white flesh that is good grilled or sautéed, the dolphin fish (mahimahi), which is usually cut into steaks and fried or grilled, and the moonfish (opah) with large grained flesh ranging from pink to red, and is good for broiling, smoking, and making sashimi. The moonfish is considered by the Hawaiians to be a good-luck fish and they will often give it away as a gesture of goodwill, rather than sell it.

Typical Hawaiian Ingredients and Dishes

Adobo   Spanish for "marinade," it refers to the method of preparing meat or seafood in a marinade and to the dish itself. The Mexican version is hot with chiles, the Portuguese and Philippine versions pungent with vinegar.

Azuki Beans   A dried red bean prized for its sweet flavor, mashed to make a filling for mochi, doughnuts, and other confections.

Bitter Melon   A gourd vegetable, sour in flavor, with a ridged, warty rind. They are seeded and sliced, parboiled, and then used in a variety of dishes such as stir-fries, braises, and soups. They may also be stuffed.

Bok Choy   A member of the cabbage family with thick, white stems and tasty green leaves. Most often used in soups, dumplings, or stir-fried dishes.

Butter Mochi   Local cake made of sweet rice flour (mochiko), sugar, eggs, butter, and coconut milk. Char Sui Chinese barbecued pork sold in almost every Chinese delicatessen, it is reddish and slightly sweet, and is used in many Chinese dishes and for topping saimin (Japanese noodle soup).

Chop Suey Yam   The local description of the root vegetable jícama. Eaten raw or used as a substitute for water chestnuts in Chinese dishes.

Crack Seed   A popular local snack of preserved fruits, such as rock salt plum or dried mango.

Daikon   A large mild white or sometimes black radish used in either raw or cooked form, for salads, stir-fries, and garnishes. Essential for local Japanese cooking it is steamed or pickled.

Dashi   Clear stock made from dried bonito flakes and seaweed.

Fish Cake   The paste of fresh fish of Chinese origin, and the processed fish cake of the Japanese.

Fish Sauce   Light brown to amber seasoning sauces prepared from salted, fermented fish. Known to bring all the flavoring elements into balance, the fishy smell disappears in cooking.

Five Spice Powder   A Chinese preparation with the number five possessing symbolic potency for health. It may contain star anise, fennel seeds, Sichuan peppercorns, clove, cinnamon, or nutmeg. It is used for roasted meat and poultry.

Guava   A tropical shrub with fragrant berrylike fruit. It is used for jam and jelly. The juice may be mixed with other tropical fruit juices.

Hawaiian Sea Salt   Coarse local sea salt, sometimes colored red by clay.

Hawaiian Sweet Bread (Pao Doce)   Slightly sweet Portuguese festival bread.

Hawaiian Vintage Chocolate   Using criollo cacao beans from Venezuela, Jim Walsh founded Hawaiian Vintage Chocolate believing that cacao beans are like wine grapes and that different varietals result in distinct flavors and textures and differences in soil and climate produce differences in the resulting product. Labeled by variety and when and where grown, this premium chocolate is shipped around the world.

Hoisin Sauce   A sweet and spicy brown paste of ground beans, garlic, sugar, vinegar, and sesame oil.

Imu   A traditional underground pit oven, lined with rocks and ti leaves (or banana leaves), for cooking meats such as chicken and pig.

Kale   A member of the cabbage family with dark green, crinkled leaves. Sometimes referred to as "Portuguese cabbage" because of their liking for it, particularly in their soup, caldo verde.

Kalua Pig   Pork cooked in an underground earth oven until very tender and then shredded.

Katsu   A breaded pork or chicken cutlet. Often served as a plate lunch item.

Kim Chee   A pungent Korean condiment of pickled shredded vegetables that may include Chinese cabbage, radishes, cucumber, greens, onions, garlic, and chiles, seasoned with fermented shellfish and salt. This condiment varies widely in its strength.

Kona Coffee   The only coffee commercially grown in the United States. It is prized for its wonderful, mellow aroma and robust flavor. It is hand-picked, sun-dried, and named for the area where the coffee farms are located.

Kukui Nut   From the Kukui tree, this nut was used by the early Hawaiians for oil, lighting, and other purposes. It is also still used as a relish known as inamona (the nut is roasted, pounded, and salted and served with raw fish). Not available commercially, it is very similar to macadamia nuts, which can be used as a substitute.

Lemongrass   A type of grass with long, tapered, fibrous leaves and a small tender white bulb. It is used to flavor curries, soups, and other dishes. The thick bulb can be finely chopped or ground to a paste to add to stir-fries, braises, and raw dishes.

Limu   Edible seaweed, also called "sea vegetables." Used in soups, noodle dishes, or relishes.

Loco Moco   A local fast-food menu item consisting of a hamburger patty on two scoops of rice, topped by a fried egg, and covered with brown gravy.

Lomi   To rub, press, or massage. Used for fish that has been kneaded with the fingers.

Lomilomi Salmon   Salt salmon massaged between the fingers and served chilled with tomatoes and onions as an appetizer or side dish.

Lotus Root   The root of a plant in the waterlily family that in cross-section has a delicate, lacy, starlike pattern. Thin slices of the peeled root may be used in Asian stir-fries and salads or, when fried, used as a garnish.

Luau   Traditional Hawaiian feast. The word is also used for the large green leaves of the taro plant and for the dish of chopped taro leaves with coconut milk and chicken or octopus.

Lumpia   In Philippine cooking, this thin pastry wrapper encloses a savory filling, either fresh and wrapped in a lettuce leaf, or deep-fried like an egg roll.

Lychee   The fruit of a small tree, also called the Chinese plum. The exterior of the nutlike fruit has a thin, red, scaly shell with soft, white, fleshy interior that surrounds a pit. The fruit is eaten fresh, dried, canned, or preserved in syrup both as a fruit dessert and as an accompaniment to savory foods.

Macadamia Nut   A nut from the tree native to Australia, but now cultivated mostly in Hawaii. Usually shelled and roasted before purchase, the round nut is white, sweet, and high in fat. It is used mainly for cookies, cakes, and pies.

Malasadas   Deep-fried, yeast-raised doughnuts, from the Portuguese.

Manapua   A steamed Chinese bun, usually stuffed with sweetened pork (char sui).

Mango   A tropical evergreen tree with fruit that varies in size, shape, and color. It is usually a deep green to orange color and pear shaped, with smooth orange flesh. Mangos are eaten fresh, or if still green, cooked in preserves, pickles, salads, and chutneys.

Mirin   Japanese sweet rice wine used for cooking.

Miso   Fermented soybean paste. Used in many Japanese dishes, it ranges from a mild white version to a stronger red version.

Mochi   A "cake" made of cooked, pounded mochi rice or steamed sweet rice flour. It may be filled or flavored with red azuki bean paste and eaten as a dessert.

Musubi   Rice cooked and shaped into a ball, triangle, or block, sometimes wrapped in nori, and eaten as a snack or fast-food-style item.

Maui Onion   Sweet onion, grown on the island of Maui on the slopes of Mount Haleakala. The flavor is much like the Vidalia onion from Georgia, the Walla Walla onion from Oregon, or the 1015 onion from Texas.

Nori   Thin black sheets of seaweed, used either toasted or untoasted for wrapping sushi, rice balls, and crackers, and for coating food to be deep-fried. It may also be crushed as a garnish for other Japanese dishes.

Panko   The Japanese version of bread crumbs (pan from the Portuguese word for "bread," and ko, meaning "derived from"). The larger irregular shapes make a light yet crisp coating.

Papaya   A tall tropical plant with large pear-shaped fruit that has a thin skin that turns yellow when ripe, a smooth yellow or orange flesh, and many black seeds resembling peppercorns. Unripe papaya can be cooked as a vegetable like squash; the sweet ripe fruit is eaten in many ways, like melon. It is widely used for breakfast with a squeeze of lime juice.

Passion Fruit (Lilikoi)   A climbing vine or shrub with egg-sized fruit that turns deep purple and wrinkled with ripeness. Its greenish orange flesh, which is aromatic, lemony, and intense, is eaten raw with the seeds or squeezed and bottled for juice.

Pilot Crackers (Saloon Pilots, Hardtack, Ship Biscuits)   A hard cracker that was often used for military rations because of its excellent keeping qualities. Most likely brought by the New England seamen, it is a favorite dessert when softened in hot water soaked in condensed milk and a little butter, and sprinkled with sugar.

Pineapple   Brought to Hawaii from South America in the early 1800s by the Spaniards, but the industry boomed with the importation of plants from Jamaica in 1885. Once a very important industry in Hawaii, the pineapple plantations are unable to compete with fruit grown in countries with cheaper labor.

Plate Lunch   Island lunch of the local residents consisting of two scoops of sticky rice, potato or macaroni salad, and some kind of meat.

Poi   The traditional Hawaiian porridge of cooked taro root, pounded smooth, thinned with water to the desired thickness, fermented to attain a sour flavor, and eaten with the fingers on its own or as a condiment. One of the most digestible foods, it is said to be an acquired taste.

Poke   To cut in blocks or slice crosswise. Now used to refer to fresh raw fish usually seasoned with soy salt, sesame seed paste, chiles, or seaweed. Different from sashimi, as it is rough cut and piled onto a plate and can be made with less expensive pieces of fish.

Portuguese Sausage   A spicy pork sausage. Eaten with rice, this is one of the most popular Island breakfasts.

Potstickers   Chinese meat dumplings steamed and fried in a pan, and usually served with a dipping sauce.

Pupu   A Hawaiian word used to refer to cocktail snacks or hors d'oeuvres.

Rice   One of the first major crops grown by and for the plantation workers in Hawaii to replace taro. The preferred rice is known as Calrose rice, after a variety developed for the area. When cooked, the medium to short grains cling together. It is sometimes called sticky rice and is easy to eat with chopsticks.

Saimin   Noodles in a Japanese dashi or chicken broth with a variety of toppings such as green onions, strips of omelet, char sui, fishcake, or Spam. Bamboo skewers of barbecued chicken or pork may be served on the side.

Sashimi   Literally translated as "fresh slice," in Japanese it is actually raw fish expertly sliced according to the particular variety and served with garnishes, condiments, and sauces.

Shave Ice   A Japanese favorite snack made from ice thinly shaved off a large block, mounded into a paper cone, and topped in sweet fruit-flavored syrup. It is sometimes topped with bean paste or ice cream.

Shoyu   Commonly used Japanese word for soy sauce.

Soba   A Japanese buckwheat and wheat flour noodle, brownish in color. In some parts of Japan where rice was difficult to grow, soba was the staple.

Somen   A Japanese fine wheat noodle.

Spam   Most commonly fried and served with rice or made into a musubi (a slice of teriyaki-flavored Spam fried and wrapped sushi style with rice). Hawaii consumes 5 million pounds of Spam every year, the most in the nation.

Sushi   Japanese rice flavored with a sweet vinegar. Formed into fingers or rounds, seasoned with wasabi (Japanese horseradish) or other condiment, sometimes rolled in seaweed, and garnished with raw seafood or fish, or perhaps a vegetable.

Sweet Potato   One of the first foods brought to the Islands by the first voyagers, sweet potatoes have a prominent place in the diets of different ethnic groups.

Tamarind   The pod or fruit of a large tropical tree. When fresh, its pulp is white, crisp, and sweet-sour, but when dried it turns reddish brown and very sour. It is used both as a souring agent and as a red coloring used in curries, chutneys, pickles, sauces, and refreshing drinks.

Taro   A tropical and subtropical plant used for its spinachlike leaves, asparaguslike stalks, and potatolike root. One of the most important crops in Hawaii, it can be used in soups and stews; fried into chips; or cooked, kneaded and fermented into poi. Poi is often given to babies as their first whole food, as it is easily digested and high in nutrients.

Tempura   In Japanese cooking, seafood and vegetables dredged in a light batter and quickly deep-fried in oil. Served with a dipping sauce.

Teriyaki   Japanese for poultry, fish, or meat marinated in a sweet soy sauce preparation and grilled over charcoal so that the marinade forms a glaze.

Ti   Leaves for wrapping. Ti plants were planted close to Hawaiian underground ovens (imus). The smooth, pearl-shaped leaves are used to wrap food and add flavor.

Tofu   Bean curd widely used throughout Asia. High in protein, low in calories, and free of cholesterol, tofu is made from dried soybeans processed into a "milk" that is coagulated like cheese; the molded tofu curds are kept fresh in water. Of the many types, momen (cotton) is the most common fresh tofu in the United States as well as in Japan; kinu (silk) has a finer texture. Chinese tofu is firmer than the Japanese tofu.

Udon   A thick Japanese wheat noodle.

Wasabi   A plant often called "Japanese horseradish," whose root is used as a condiment for raw fish dishes; it comes fresh, powdered, and as a paste. It is very hot in flavor and green in color.

Water Chestnut   The fruit of a long-stemmed water plant that grows inside irregularly shaped thorns beneath the floating leaves. This starchy fruit has a crisp texture and delicate taste and is widely used in Chinese dishes.

Winter Melon   A melon with hard, smooth, or furrowed skin and white to pale green or orange flesh. Varieties include casaba, honeydew, crenshaw, Santa Claus; called winter melons because they keep and travel well. Often used for soup.

Menus and Recipes from
the Cuisine of Hawaii

MENU ONE

Mango Carrot Soup

Crispy Curry Tofu

Ponzu Hanger Steak, Charred Green Onion Emulsion, Roasted Carrots, and Watercress

Grilled Ono with Pineapple Chutney on Jewels Israeli Couscous

Asian Pear and Macadamia Wontons

MENU TWO

Chicken Long Rice

Kalua Pig Spring Rolls with Pineapple Dipping Sauce

Caramelized Salmon with Orange-Shoyu Glaze, Lemongrass Beurre Blanc, Balsamic Soy
Glaze, and Fried Basil Leaves

Sautéed Mixed Vegetables

Steamed Japanese Rice

Mango Bread

MENU THREE

Ahi Tuna and Vegetable Salad with Sherry Vinaigrette

Spam Musubi

Saimin with Teriyaki Meat Sticks

Deep-Fried Calamari Salad

Pineapple Fritters with Maui Mango Sauce

OTHER RECIPES

Butternut Squash and Pumpkin Ginger Soup

Macadamia Nut–Crusted Mahimahi with Wasabi Cream Sauce

Miso Soup with Taro and Butterfish

Sautéed Pacific Snapper with Curry Kamuela Tomato Sauce

Mango Carrot Soup

4 servings

CHEF TIP: For carrot juice without a juice machine, wash 2 pounds (896 g) carrots. Process the carrots in a blender or food processor until finely chopped; add a little water if necessary. Add 2 cups (16 ounces/480 ml) hot water and stir to combine. Let steep for 30 minutes. Strain the carrot juice; press the mash to extract as much juice as possible.

AMOUNT	MEASURE	INGREDIENT
2 cups	12 ounces/336 g	Mango, rough chopped
1 tablespoon	½ ounce/15 ml	Toasted sesame oil
		Sea salt
1 cup	8 ounces/240 ml	Roasted yam, rough chopped
4 cups	32 ounces/1 L	Carrot juice
1 teaspoon	5 g	Fresh ginger, minced
2 teaspoons		Fresh lime juice
		Salt and pepper
2 tablespoons each	½ ounce/14 g each	Green, red, and yellow bell peppers, in ⅛-inch (.3 cm) dice
1 tablespoon	3 g	Fresh chives, minced

PROCEDURE

1. Puree the mango with the sesame oil and a pinch of sea salt until smooth in a blender or food processor. Place in the refrigerator to chill.

2. Combine the yam, carrot juice, ginger, and lime juice, and puree until smooth in blender or food processor. Adjust the seasoning with salt and pepper and place in refrigerator to chill for 30 minutes or more. Soup should be well chilled before serving.

3. Pour ¾ cup (60 ounces/180 ml) of carrot soup into each chilled bowl, then place 4 tablespoons (2 ounces/60 ml) mango puree in the center of each. Sprinkle with equal amounts of bell pepper and chives.

Mango Carrot Soup

Crispy Curry Tofu

AMOUNT	MEASURE	INGREDIENT
	8 ounces/224 g	Soft tofu
For the Mushrooms		
¼ cup	2 ounces/60 ml	Mirin
¼ cup	2 ounces/60 ml	Sake or water
3 tablespoons	1½ ounces/45 ml	Soy sauce
1 teaspoon		Fresh ginger, grated
⅛ teaspoon		Ground Sansho pepper
or 1 teaspoon		Sichuan peppercorns
12	4 ounces/112 g total	Fresh shiitake mushrooms, stems removed, caps whole
For the Glaze		
¼ cup	2 ounces/60 ml	Mirin
¼ cup	2 ounces/60 ml	Sake
¼ cup	2 ounces/60 ml	Yellow miso paste
2 tablespoons	1 ounce/28 g	Brown sugar
For the Curry Sauce		
2 tablespoons	1 ounce/28 g	Red curry paste
½ cup	4 ounces/120 ml	Unsweetened coconut milk
½ cup	4 ounces/120 ml	Water
2		Kaffir lime leaves
1 tablespoon	¼ ounce/7 g	Lemongrass, chopped
1 tablespoon	½ ounce/14 g	Brown sugar
For the Vegetables		
3 tablespoons	1½ ounces/45 ml	Vegetable oil
1	4 ounces/112 g	Japanese eggplant, cut in half lengthwise, then into 4 pieces on the bias
4	4 ounces/112 g	Asparagus spears, cut in half and steamed
3 cups	6 ounces/168 g	Fresh spinach
		Salt and pepper
For the Tofu		
1¼ cups	5 ounces/140 g	All-purpose flour
1 cup	8 ounces/240 ml	Cold water
1		Egg, lightly beaten
		Salt and pepper
½ cup	2 ounces/56 g	Panko bread crumbs
As needed		Vegetable oil, for deep-frying

1. Drain the tofu; wrap with paper towels and place on a flat surface. Put a plate or light weight on top and let sit for 15 to 20 minutes to drain. Dry tofu and cut into 4 pieces, each about 2 ounces/56 g. Set aside in refrigerator.

2. Make the mushrooms. Combine the mirin, sake, soy sauce, ginger, Sancho pepper, and mushrooms in a small saucepan over low heat. Bring to a simmer and cook 3 to 4 minutes or until the mushrooms are tender. Remove from the heat and let cool in the liquid for 30 minutes. Remove mushrooms from the liquid and set aside. Strain the mushroom liquid and reserve.

3. Make the miso glaze. Combine the mirin, sake, and yellow miso paste in a small saucepan, whisk well, and bring to a simmer. Cook for 20 to 25 minutes, then add the brown sugar and blend well.

4. Make the curry sauce. Combine the reserved mushroom liquid, curry paste, coconut milk, water, kaffir lime leaves, lemongrass, and brown sugar in a small saucepan and bring to a boil. Reduce to a simmer and cook 8 to 10 minutes. Strain through a fine-mesh strainer. (If sauce is too thin, correct with a mixture of cornstarch and water.) Keep warm.

5. Heat 2 tablespoons (1 ounce/30 ml) of the oil in a small sauté pan and sauté the eggplant until crisp on the outside and soft on the inside (adding additional oil, if necessary), about 3 to 4 minutes. Add the asparagus and the miso glaze, toss to coat asparagus with glaze, then set aside.

6. Heat a 10- to 12-inch (25.4–30.5 cm) sauté pan over medium-high heat. Add the remaining 1 tablespoon (½ ounce/15 ml) oil and the spinach. Sauté until wilted, about 1 to 2 minutes. Season with salt and pepper and remove from heat, draining excess moisture.

7. Fry the tofu. Heat the oil in a deep-fryer or deep pot to 350°F (176°C). Combine 1 cup (4 ounces/112 g) of the flour, the cold water, and the egg in a small bowl (use chopsticks, if possible)—do not overmix; the batter will be lumpy. Season the tofu with salt and pepper, dust with the remaining flour, dip in the batter, and then roll in the bread crumbs. Deep-fry in small batches until crisp, about 2 minutes. Drain on paper towels.

8. Place a tablespoon of the wilted spinach on each plate, top with a piece of fried tofu, then layer on a piece of eggplant, two mushrooms, and one piece of asparagus. Serve the curry sauce on the side, next to the tofu. Place any additional vegetables next to the fried piece of tofu.

Crispy Curry Tofu

Ponzu Hanger Steak, Charred Green Onion Emulsion, Roasted Carrots, and Watercress

4 servings

CHEF TIP: The hanger steak is a thick strip of meat from the underside of the cow. It hangs between the rib and the loin. It is flavorful but can be tough if not prepared correctly. There is only one hanging tender to a steer, which is why hanger and skirt steaks were called "the butcher's cut." Because there was never enough of either cut to display, butchers would take them home for their family meals.

AMOUNT	MEASURE	INGREDIENT
Hanger Steak		
¼ cup	2 ounces/60 ml	Ponzu
2 tablespoons	1 ounce/30 ml	Orange juice
1 teaspoon	5 ml	Honey
2	10 g	Garlic cloves, roughly chopped
2 teaspoons	10 ml	Rice vinegar
1 tablespoon	½ ounce/15 ml	Vegetable oil
		Salt and pepper
1 pound	16 ounces/448 g	Hanger (or flank) steak
Roasted Carrots		
1 bunch	1 pound/448 g	Carrots, unpeeled, whole
2 tablespoons	1 ounce/30 ml	Vegetable oil
		Salt and pepper
Green Onion Emulsion		
2 bunches	8 ounces/224 g	Green onions, white and 1 to 2 inches (2.5 cm–5.1 cm) of green
½ cup	4 ounces/120 ml	Vegetable oil
1 teaspoon	5 ml	Lemon juice
1 cup	2 ounces/56 g	Watercress washed and dried

PROCEDURE

1. Marinate the steak. Combine the ponzu, orange juice, honey, garlic, vinegar, 1 tablespoon (½ ounce/15 ml) of the oil, then taste and adjust seasoning with salt and pepper. Add the steak and marinate 1 hour at room temperature or refrigerate for 3 hours or overnight.

2. Prepare the carrots. Preheat the oven to 375°F (191°C). Coat the carrots with the oil and season with salt and pepper. Place the carrots on a roasting rack and roast until tender, 45 to 50 minutes. Cut into oblique pieces; keep warm.

3. Make the emulsion. Toss the green onions with 1 tablespoon (½ ounce/15 ml) of the oil. Place under a broiler or over an open flame for 3 to 5 minutes, turning the green onions until they are nicely charred on all sides. Remove from heat and allow to cool.

4. Roughly chop the green onions and place in a blender with the remaining 7 tablespoons (3½ ounces/105 ml) oil and the lemon juice. Blend until smooth. Correct seasoning with salt, pepper, and additional lemon juice, if necessary.

5. Heat a grill to high. Remove the steak from the marinate and bring to room temperature. Place on grill and cook to desired doneness, brushing occasionally with marinade, about 4 to 5 minutes on each side for medium rare. Remove from heat and allow to rest 3 to 4 minutes before slicing. Slice thinly across the grain.

6. To serve, toss the watercress with a little of the green onion emulsion. Place equal portions of watercress, roasted carrots, sliced steak, and emulsion on 4 plates.

Ponzu Hanger Steak, Charred Green Onion Emulsion, Roasted Carrots, and Watercress

Grilled Ono with Pineapple Chutney on Jewels Israeli Couscous

 **CHEF TIP:** *Ono* is a Hawaiian word meaning "good to eat." The fish of that name is more commonly known as wahoo, and is a close relative of king mackerel. All Hawaii wahoo are line-caught. Wahoo is a lean fish with a mild-sweet taste and firm texture.

Grilled Ono

AMOUNT	MEASURE	INGREDIENT
1½ cups	8 ounces/224 g	Pineapple, in ¼-inch (.6 cm) dice
¼ cup	2 ounces/60 ml	Mirin
¼ cup	2 ounces/60 ml	White balsamic vinegar
1 teaspoon	5 ml	Vanilla extract
2	2 g	Star anise
2-inch	7 g	Cinnamon stick
1	3 tablespoon/2.5 ounces/70 g	Hawaiian chile or Tabasco chile or jalapeño, seeded and minced
4	4 ounces/112 g each	Ono fillets, skinless (substitute mahimahi)
		Salt and pepper

PROCEDURE

1. Combine the pineapple, mirin, vinegar, vanilla, star anise, cinnamon, and chile in a 2- to 3-quart (2 to 3 L) saucepan over medium heat. Bring to a simmer and remove from heat. Allow favors to mellow for 1 hour.

2. Preheat a grill. Season the fish and grill for 3 to 4 minutes per side, until slightly charred and almost cooked through.

3. Serve the fillets with pineapple chutney and Jewels Israeli Couscous (recipe follows).

Grilled Ono with Pineapple Chutney on Jewels Israeli Couscous

Jewels Israeli Couscous

CHEF TIP: Israeli couscous, also called pearl couscous, is similar to regular couscous, a small whole-grain food made from semolina or wheat flour. Israeli couscous is larger than regular couscous, so it has a slightly chewy texture, with a slightly nutty flavor. In Jewels Israeli Couscous, the green edamame are the jewels.

CHEF TIP: When grilling corn, do not remove all the layers of husk; leave a few layers for protection. Soak the whole cobs in a pot of cold water for 15 minutes; be sure the ears are completely covered with water. This helps provide extra moisture for grilling and will steam the corn kernels inside the husks.

AMOUNT	MEASURE	INGREDIENT
1	½ cup/3 ounces/84 g	Ear of white corn, soaked
2 cups	16 ounces/480 ml	Chicken or vegetable stock
2	4 g	Kaffir lime leaves
1 tablespoon	¼ ounce/7 g	Lemongrass, chopped
1 cup	6 ounces/168 g	Israeli couscous
2	2 teaspoons, 14 g	Thai or Serrano chiles
1 tablespoon	½ ounce/15 ml	Vegetable oil
½ cup	3 ounces/84 g	Fresh or defrosted shelled, cooked edamame in pods (green)
		Salt and pepper

PROCEDURE

1. Heat the grill to medium.

2. Remove the corn from the soaking water and shake off excess water. Pull the husks back on the corn (leave connected to the cob) and remove and discard only the silks. Rewrap the corn with the husks and place on the grill, rotating the corn as needed to keep from becoming too charred. Grill for 15 minutes. As soon as the husk picks up the dark silhouette of the kernels and begins to pull away from the tip of the ear, the corn is ready. Cool and then cut kernels from the cobs.

3. Combine the stock, lime leaves, and lemongrass in a saucepan and simmer for 5 minutes. Strain.

4. In a 3- to 4-quart (3 to 4 L) saucepan, combine the couscous and stock, and bring to a boil. Reduce the heat and simmer until tender, 10 to 12 minutes, or until liquid has evaporated.

5. Smash the chiles until they split apart in a few places. Heat a 10-inch (25.4 cm) sauté pan and add the oil and chiles. Infuse the oil over low heat for 5 minutes, then remove the chiles and discard.

6. Turn the heat to high and add the edamame pods, continue to cook and toss until the edamame are brown and crispy, about 5 to 8 minutes. Remove the beans from the pods.

7. Stir the edamame and corn into the couscous, correct the seasoning with salt and pepper, and serve.

Asian Pear and Macadamia Wontons

4 servings

AMOUNT	MEASURE	INGREDIENT
As needed		Vegetable oil, for deep-frying
1 cup	6 ounces/168 g	Asian pear, peeled, in ¼-inch (.6 cm) dice
2 tablespoons	½ ounce/14 g	Macadamia nuts, finely chopped
½ cup	4 ounces/120 ml	Coconut milk
1 tablespoon	½ ounce/15 ml	Lemon juice
24		Wonton wrappers, cut into circles
¼ cup	1 ounce/28 g	Confectioners' sugar
¼ cup	2 ounces/60 ml	Honey

PROCEDURE

1. Combine the pear, nuts, coconut milk, and lemon juice in a 2- to 3-quart (2 to 3 L) saucepan. Simmer over low heat until almost dry, about 20 minutes. Set aside to cool.

2. Place a spoonful of the filling on each wonton circle and moisten the exposed edges with water. Top with another wonton circle, crimping the edges all the way around to seal. Place wontons on a sheet pan and freeze for 10 to 15 minutes to firm up.

3. Heat the oil in a deep-fryer or deep pot to 375°F (190°C). Deep-fry the wontons until browned and cooked through, about 1 to 2 minutes. Drain well on paper towels.

4. Dust wontons with sugar and serve with honey.

Chicken Long Rice

4 servings

AMOUNT	MEASURE	INGREDIENT
4	1½ pounds/672 g	Chicken thighs, bone-in
1½ quarts	1.4 L	Chicken stock
5 teaspoons	¾ ounce/21 g	Fresh ginger, thinly sliced
1 tablespoon	½ ounce/14 g	Salt
	6 ounces/168 g	Bean thread noodles (sai fun or mung bean noodles)
1 tablespoon	½ ounce/15 ml	Vegetable oil
1½ cups	6 ounces/168 g	Maui onion, in thin slices
1	5 g	Garlic clove, minced
1½ tablespoons	¾ ounce/23 ml	Soy sauce
3 tablespoons		Green onions, chopped

PROCEDURE

1. In a 3- to 4-quart (3 to 4 L) saucepot, cover the chicken with the stock. Add half the ginger and the salt. Cover and simmer until just cooked (do not boil), 30 minutes.

2. Allow the chicken to cool in the broth. Bone the meat, and discard the skin and bones. Cut the chicken into 1-inch (2.5 cm) cubes. Strain the stock and reserve.

3. Soak the bean thread noodles in warm water for 10 minutes or in cold water for 1 hour. Drain.

4. In a 12-inch (30.5 cm) sauté pan, heat the oil. Sauté the onion, garlic, and remaining ginger until lightly browned, about 2 to 3 minutes.

5. Add the noodles and enough reserved stock to cover. Add the soy sauce and simmer for 5 minutes. Turn off heat and let stand for 10 minutes.

6. Cut the bean thread noodles into approximately 3-inch (7.6 cm) lengths, if desired. Add the chicken meat and reheat. Top with green onions before serving.

Kalua Pig Spring Rolls with Pineapple Dipping Sauce

8 servings

AMOUNT	MEASURE	INGREDIENT
Kalua Pig Char Sui		
1	2½ pounds/1.1 kg	Boneless pork butt
2 tablespoons	1 ounce/28 g	Hawaiian or kosher salt
2 tablespoons	1 ounce/30 ml	Liquid Smoke
2	10 g	Garlic cloves, minced
8		Ti leaves, ribs removed (or aluminum foil)
Kalua Pig Spring Rolls		
As needed		Vegetable oil
¼ cup	1 ounce/28 g	Onion, in ¼- inch (.6 cm) dice
1 teaspoon		Garlic, minced
¾ cup	3 ounces/85 g	Water chestnuts, in ½-inch (1.2 cm) dice
2 cups	5 ounces/141 g	Napa cabbage, shredded
½ cup	1½ ounces/42 g	Red cabbage, shredded
¼ cup	½ ounce/14 g	Green onion, chopped
1 tablespoon	½ ounce/14 g	Carrot, finely grated
1 tablespoon	½ ounce/15 g	Oyster sauce
		Salt and white pepper
10		Spring roll wrappers, 8¾ inches (22.2 cm) in diameter
1		Egg, beaten with 1 tablespoon water

PROCEDURE

1. Preheat the oven to 400°F (205°C).

2. Roast the pork. Score the pork on all sides, making ¼-inch (.6 cm) slits about 1 inch (2.5 cm) apart.

3. Combine the salt, Liquid Smoke, and garlic. Rub mixture all over the pork butt. Wrap in ti leaves and tie with string to hold leaves in place. Place in a large roasting pan and cover tightly with lid or foil.

4. Roast for 1 hour. Lower the temperature to 350°F (175°C) and roast for 2 hours, until tender. Let cool slightly, then remove leaves. Shred the meat. Reserve 1 cup of meat for the spring rolls and set remainder aside for another use.

5. Make the spring rolls. In a 10- to 12-inch (25.4–30.5 cm) sauté pan, heat 1 tablespoon (½ ounce/15 ml) of the oil. Sauté the onion and garlic for 1 minute or until onion is translucent. Add the reserved pork and cook 1 minute. Stir in the water chestnuts, cabbages, green onion, carrot, and oyster sauce, and cook 3 minutes, until cabbage is tender. Adjust seasoning with salt and pepper. Drain excess liquid and let mixture cool.

6. Heat the remaining oil in a deep-fryer or deep pot to 375°F (190°C).

7. Separate the spring roll wrappers and keep under a slightly damp towel as you work. Place 2 tablespoons (28 g) of filling on each wrapper. Fold the nearest edge of wrapper over filling; fold left and right corners toward the center. Roll tightly and seal with the egg wash.

8. Fry the spring rolls until golden brown, about 1 to 2 minutes. Place on paper towels to drain. Serve with Pineapple Dipping Sauce (recipe follows).

Pineapple Dipping Sauce

CHEF TIP: Sambal, a spicy Malaysian condiment, can be eaten with all your Asian dishes, especially rice. Spoon some of the sambal into a small container and add fresh lime juice. This lime sambal is especially good with grilled fish.

CHEF TIP: To toast shrimp paste, compress the paste into a small disk and wrap in foil. Place the foil over an open low flame for 30 seconds to a minute on each side, until the edges of the disk are lightly browned and crisp. The paste will emit a strong smoky, burning smell, which is an indication that it is toasted correctly.

AMOUNT	MEASURE	INGREDIENT
For the Sambal		
10	2½ ounces/70 g	Hot chiles (Long Hots or 15–20 serranos)
2 tablespoons	1 ounce/28 g	Shrimp paste (toasted)
¾ teaspoon		Salt
For the Sauce		
½ cup	3 ounces/84 g	Pineapple, in ¼-inch (.6 cm) dice
¼ cup	2 ounces/56 g	Sugar
4 tablespoons	2 ounces/60 ml	Cider vinegar
4 tablespoons	2 ounces/60 ml	Water
1 tablespoon	½ ounce/15 ml	Fish sauce

PROCEDURE

1. Wash the chiles and discard stems. Air-dry or use papers towels to blot dry. Roughly chop the chiles and combine in a bowl with the shrimp paste and salt. Grind in a blender, food processor, or pound in mortar to very small pieces. Set aside 1 tablespoon (½ ounce/14 g) for the sauce and spoon remainder into a clean container for another use; keep refrigerated.

2. Combine the sambal with the pineapple, sugar, vinegar, water, and fish sauce. Chill for 1 hour before serving.

Caramelized Salmon with Orange-Shoyu Glaze

4 servings

AMOUNT	MEASURE	INGREDIENT
½ cup	4 ounces/112 g	Fresh ginger, chopped
1 tablespoon	2.5 g	Sichuan peppercorns
¼ cup	2 ounces/60 ml	Orange juice
½ cup	1 ounce/28 g	Fresh cilantro
4	4 ounces/112 g each	Salmon fillets, skin removed
½ cup	3½ ounces/98 g	Sugar
2 tablespoons	½ ounce/14 g	Black pepper, coarsely ground
1 tablespoon	½ ounce/15 ml	Peanut oil
2 tablespoons	1 ounce/30 ml	Soy sauce
2 tablespoons	1 ounce/30 ml	Grand Marnier

PROCEDURE

1. Combine the ginger, peppercorns, orange juice, and cilantro in a food processor and finely chop. Roll the salmon in the mixture; cover and marinate at room temperature for up to 2 hours.

2. Mix the sugar and black pepper.

3. Pat salmon dry and press the presentation side into the sugar-pepper mixture.

4. In a 10- to 12-inch (25.4–30.5 cm) sauté pan, heat the oil. Sauté the salmon, seasoned side down first to caramelize the sugar, 2 to 3 minutes. Do not let the sugar begin to burn.

5. Turn the salmon over and add the soy sauce and Grand Marnier, swirling and stirring well to dissolve the caramelized sugar. Lower the heat to a simmer, and finish cooking the salmon, another 2 to 3 minutes.

6. Place the salmon on warmed plates. Sauce the plates with Lemongrass Beurre Blanc (recipe follows), then drizzle with a few drops of Balsamic-Soy Glaze (recipe follows). Serve with Fried Basil Leaves (recipe follows).

Lemongrass Beurre Blanc

AMOUNT	MEASURE	INGREDIENT
½ cup	4 ounces/120 ml	White wine
1		Shallot, minced
1 stalk		Lemongrass, cut into 2-inch (5 cm) pieces, then mashed
½ cup	4 ounces/56 g	Butter, cut into 8 pieces
		Salt and white pepper

PROCEDURE

1. In a 2-quart (2 L) nonreactive saucepan, combine the wine, shallot, and lemongrass. Let the mixture soak for 30 minutes to soften the lemongrass.

2. Bring mixture to a boil, then cook over medium-high heat until the liquid is almost evaporated. Strain the liquid—you should have about 2 tablespoons (1 ounce/30 ml).

3. Return to a clean 2-quart (2 L) saucepan and bring to a boil. Remove the pan from heat and start whisking in the butter, 2 pieces at a time. If the pan gets too cool, return it to the heat. Continue moving the pan on and off the heat, whisking in the butter until all the butter is incorporated. Correct seasoning with salt and pepper.

Caramelized Salmon with Orange-Shoyu Glaze, Lemongrass Beurre Blanc, and Fried Basil Leaves

Balsamic-Soy Glaze

4 servings

AMOUNT	MEASURE	INGREDIENT
1 cup	8 ounces/240 ml	Balsamic vinegar
½ cup	4 ounces/120 ml	Soy sauce

PROCEDURE

Over medium-high heat, in a 1- to 2-quart (1 to 2 L) nonreactive saucepan, combine the vinegar and soy sauce and reduce to a syrup, about 15 minutes.

Fried Basil Leaves

4 servings

AMOUNT	MEASURE	INGREDIENT
As needed		Vegetable oil, for deep-frying
12–18		Fresh basil leaves

PROCEDURE

1. Heat the oil in a deep-fryer or deep pot to 350°F (175°C).

2. Fry the basil leaves for a few seconds, until they turn crisp and translucent. Remove and drain well. (This can be done up to 1 hour in advance.)

Sautéed Mixed Vegetables

4 servings

AMOUNT	MEASURE	INGREDIENT
2 tablespoons	1 ounce/30 ml	Vegetable oil
1 cup	4 ounces/112 g	Green beans, blanched
1 cup	4 ounces/112 g	Zucchini, in 2-inch (5 cm) sticks
1 cup	4 ounces/112 g	Red bell pepper, julienned
1 cup	4 ounces/112 g	Yellow bell pepper, julienned
		Salt and white pepper

PROCEDURE

In a 10- to 12-inch (25.4–30.5 cm) sauté pan, heat the oil over medium heat. Add the vegetables and sauté until heated through, but not browned, about 3 to 4 minutes. Season with salt and pepper to taste.

Steamed Japanese Rice

✦ **CHEF TIP:** Japanese nonglutinous short-grain rice (Calrose, Tomaki) brand is the kind most often served in the Islands. When cooked, the rice should end up moist but not mushy, the grains distinct but clinging, making it easier to be lifted on chopsticks. Because it is traditionally eaten with flavorful accompaniments, usually sour, sweet, salty, or spicy, it is cooked without salt.

AMOUNT	MEASURE	INGREDIENT
2 cups	13 ounces/364 g	Japanese short-grain rice
2 cups	16 ounces/480 ml	Water

PROCEDURE

1. Place the rice in a bowl and cover with cold water. Rub the rice with your hand and swirl it vigorously, then drain off the water. Repeat this step three or four times until the water is clear. Drain into a sieve and let it dry for 30 minutes.

2. In a 2- to 3-quart (2 to 3 L) pot, combine the rice and water, and bring to a simmer over high heat. Cover the pan, reduce the heat to medium, and cook for 15 minutes.

3. Without opening the lid, reduce the heat to its lowest point and simmer for another 5 minutes. Let the rice rest off the heat, covered, for another 5 minutes or until ready to serve.

4. Fluff the rice with a fork before serving.

Mango Bread

AMOUNT	MEASURE	INGREDIENT
1 cup	4 ounces/112 g	All-purpose flour
1 teaspoon		Baking soda
½ teaspoon		Ground cinnamon
¼ teaspoon		Salt
¾ cup	5¼ ounces/148 g	Sugar
1 cup	6 ounces/168 g	Mango, in ½-inch (1.2 cm) dice
2		Eggs, light beaten
6 tablespoons	3 ounces/90 ml	Vegetable oil
½ teaspoon		Vanilla extract
½ cup	2 ounces/56 g	Macadamia nuts, chopped

PROCEDURE

1. Preheat the oven to 350°F (175°C). Grease and flour a 9-inch loaf pan.

2. Sift the flour, baking soda, cinnamon, and salt together. Set aside.

3. Combine the sugar, mango, eggs, oil, and vanilla in a separate bowl, then whisk to combine and dissolve the sugar.

4. Add the dry ingredients to the wet ingredients, and blend together for about 1 minute. Do not overmix. Add the macadamia nuts and distribute evenly in the batter.

5. Pour the mixture into the pan. Bake for 40 to 45 minutes, or until a toothpick comes out clean. Let the bread cool before serving.

Ahi Tuna and Vegetable Salad with Sherry Vinaigrette

4 servings

AMOUNT	MEASURE	INGREDIENT
For the Vinaigrette		
1 teaspoon		Dijon mustard
2 teaspoons		Fresh lemon juice
¼ cup	2 ounces/60 ml	Aged sherry vinegar
½ cup	4 ounces/120 ml	Vegetable oil
Pinch		Granulated or palm sugar
		Salt and pepper
For the Salad		
4		Red globe radishes, thinly sliced
1 cup	6 ounces/168 g	Beets, raw, julienned, chilled
½ cup	3 ounces/84 g	Carrots, in ½-inch (1.2 cm) dice, cooked 2 minutes, chilled
1 cup	6 ounces/168 g	Green beans, cooked 2 to 3 minutes, chilled
½ cup	3 ounces/84 g	Zucchini, in ½-inch (1.2 cm) dice
1 tablespoon	3 g	Fresh parsley, chopped
		Salt and pepper
4	4 ounces/112 g each	Ahi tuna pieces, 1 inch (2.5 cm) thick
2 tablespoons	1 ounce/30 ml	Vegetable oil
1 cup	2 ounces/56 g	Mesclun salad mix
		Hawaiian pink or black lava salt (optional)

PROCEDURE

1. Make the dressing. Combine the mustard, lemon juice and vinegar in a bowl, and whisk well. Slowly whisk in the oil until emulsified. Adjust the seasoning with sugar and season with salt and pepper.

2. Make the salad. Combine the vegetables, parsley, and enough vinaigrette to coat the ingredients. Correct the seasoning with salt and pepper. Let marinate for 15 minutes.

3. Season the tuna with salt and pepper. Heat a 10- to 12-inch (25.4–30.5 cm) heavy sauté pan over medium-high heat and add the oil. Sauté the tuna on one side until it appears to be cooked half way through, about 2 to 3 minutes, then remove from pan.

4. In a bowl, combine the salad greens and vegetables, and toss with additional vinaigrette to just coat the salad greens.

5. Place equal portions of greens and vegetables on 4 plates, place a piece of tuna seared side up on top of each, and sprinkle with Hawaiian salt.

Ahi Tuna and Vegetable Salad with Sherry Vinaigrette

Spam Musubi

CHEF TIP: You can use the empty Spam can that has been opened on both sides for the musubi mold, using your hands (or a piece of Spam) to press down on the rice.

AMOUNT	MEASURE	INGREDIENT
1 can	7 ounces	Spam
3 tablespoons	1½ ounces/45 ml	Soy sauce
2 tablespoons	1 ounce/30 ml	Mirin
2 tablespoons	1 ounce/28 g	Granulated sugar
2 sheets		Nori, cut in quarters lengthwise
2 cups	13 ounces/360 g	Cooked rice

PROCEDURE

1. Open the can of Spam on both sides. Remove the Spam and cut into 8 slices.

2. In a 10- to 12-inch (25.4–30.5 cm) sauté pan over medium high heat, sauté the spam slices until slightly crisp, 2 to 3 minutes. Drain on paper towels.

3. Combine the soy sauce, mirin, and sugar in the sauté pan. Bring to a simmer over medium-high heat, then reduce to low. Add the Spam slices, coating them with the mixture. When the mixture has thickened, remove the Spam from pan and cool.

4. Lay a piece of nori lengthwise on a dry cutting board. Moisten the lower half of musubi maker (see Chef Tip) and place on lower third of nori. Fill musubi maker with rice and press flat until the rice is ¾ inch (1.9 cm) high. Top with a slice of Spam. Remove the musubi maker and keep it in a bowl of warm water to keep it clean and moist.

5. Starting at the end toward you, fold the nori over the Spam and rice stack, and keep rolling to form a ribbon. Slightly dampen the end of the nori to seal it. Repeat with the remaining nori, rice, and Spam, making sure to rinse off musubi maker after each use.

6. Serve on a plate, like sushi.

Saimin with Teryaki Meat Sticks

4 servings

Saimin

AMOUNT	MEASURE	INGREDIENT
4 cups	16 ounces/448 g	Fresh saimin, somen, or other fine white flour noodles
2 teaspoons		Dashi powder
4 cups	32 ounces/1 L	Water
4 cups	8 ounces/224 g	Fresh spinach, in 2-inch (5 cm) pieces
1 cup	4 ounces/111 g	Kamaboko (Japanese fish cake), thinly sliced
1¼ cups	8 ounces/224 g	Char sui (Chinese glazed pork roast), thinly sliced
1 tablespoon	½ ounce/15 ml	Soy sauce
½ cup	1 ounce/28 g	Green onions, thinly sliced

PROCEDURE

1. Cook the noodles in boiling water for 3 minutes or until just done. Drain and divide among 4 warmed soup bowls.

2. Make the dashi by mixing the powder with the water in a large saucepan; heat over medium heat and bring almost to a boil, but do not boil.

3. Divide the spinach among the bowls of noodles.

4. Pour a cup of dashi over the noodles and spinach in each bowl. Divide the kamaboko and char sui evenly among the bowls. Sprinkle with the soy sauce and scatter the green onions on top.

5. Serve hot with Teriyaki Meat Sticks (recipe follows).

Teriyaki Meat Sticks

CHEF TIP: Teri-anything is a plate lunch favorite, distinctly different from its Japanese origins. In Japan, the combination of soy sauce and mirin makes teriyaki, used to marinate fish and to baste broiling meats. The term derives from *teri* ("glazed") and *yaki* ("seared with heat"). In Hawaii, brown sugar is substituted for the mirin, and ginger and green onions are added. Hawaiian-style teriyaki sauce has become one of the culinary symbols of the Islands. In this recipe, chicken breast can be substituted for the beef, if desired.

AMOUNT	MEASURE	INGREDIENT
¼ cup	2 ounces/60 ml	Soy sauce
1½ tablespoons	¾ ounce/21 g	Brown sugar
1½ teaspoons		Sherry
1 teaspoon		Fresh ginger, minced
1	5 g	Garlic clove, minced
1 cup	6 ounces/170 g	Beef top round, in ½-inch (1.2 cm) slices 2 inches (5 cm) long

PROCEDURE

1. Soak four 8-inch (20 cm) wooden skewers in cold water for 30 minutes.

2. In a 2- to 3-quart (2 to 3 L) saucepan, combine the soy sauce, brown sugar, sherry, ginger, and garlic. Stir over low heat until the sugar is dissolved. Cool briefly, then add the meat and marinate for 30 minutes.

3. Preheat a grill.

4. Thread the meat onto the skewers and grill until done, about 3 to 5 minutes.

Saimin with Teriyaki Meat Sticks

Deep-Fried Calamari Salad

AMOUNT	MEASURE	INGREDIENT
For the Cilantro Vinaigrette		
2 tablespoons	¼ ounce/7g	Fresh cilantro leaves
½ cup	4 ounces/120 ml	Orange juice
½ tablespoon		Rice wine vinegar
½ tablespoon		Lime juice
¼ cup	1½ ounces/45 ml	Honey
1	5 g	Garlic clove
1 teaspoon		Fresh ginger, minced
¼ cup	2 ounces/60 ml	Vegetable oil
		Salt and pepper
For the Salad		
½ cup	2½ ounces/70 g	Red bell pepper, julienned
½ cup	2½ ounces/70 g	Yellow bell pepper, julienned
½ cup	2 ounces/56 g	Maui onion, julienned
1½ cups	9 ounces/252 g	Cucumbers, peeled, sliced
¾ cup	4 ounces/112 g	Tomato, peeled, in wedges
As needed		Vegetable oil, for deep-frying
2 cups	9 ounces/252 g	All-purpose flour
2 tablespoons	1 ounce/28 g	Paprika
2⅔ cups	16 ounces/448 g	Calamari, cut into rings
		Salt and black pepper
4 cups	8 ounces/224 g	Baby salad greens

PROCEDURE

1. Make the dressing. Combine all the ingredients and mix well.

2. Prepare the salad. Marinate the bell peppers, onion, cucumber and tomato with half the vinaigrette.

3. Heat the oil in a deep-fryer or deep pot to 350°F (175°C).

4. Combine the flour and paprika. Season the calamari with salt and pepper, then toss the calamari in the flour and paprika mixture. Dust off the excess flour.

5. Deep-fry the calamari until pale golden brown, about 2 to 3 minutes. Do not overcook or calamari will be tough and chewy. Drain on paper towels.

6. Toss the salad greens with enough vinaigrette to just coat the leaves.

7. On chilled plates, arrange the salad greens, peppers, onion, cucumber, and tomato. Place the fried calamari on top. Serve additional dressing on the side.

Deep-Fried Calamari Salad

Pineapple Fritters with Maui Mango Sauce

AMOUNT	MEASURE	INGREDIENT
For the Sauce		
1 cup	6 ounces/168 g	Mango, sliced
½ cup	3½ ounces/98 g	Sugar
1 tablespoon	½ ounce/15 ml	Lemon juice
For the Fritters		
As needed		Vegetable oil, for frying
½ cup	1½ ounces/42 g	Panko bread crumbs
¼ cup	1 ounce/28 g	Graham cracker crumbs
½ teaspoon		Ground cinnamon
8		Pineapple slices, ¼ inch (.6 cm)
¼ cup	1 ounce/28 g	All-purpose flour
1		Egg, light beaten with 1 tablespoon water and pinch of salt
¾ cup	5¼ ounces/148 g	Sugar

PROCEDURE

1. Make the sauce. Puree the mango in a food processor or blender and pass through a sieve. Add the sugar and lemon juice.

2. Heat the oil in a deep-fryer or deep pot to 350°F (175°C).

3. Mix the panko, graham crumbs, and cinnamon in a bowl. Put the flour and beaten egg into two other bowls.

4. Dip the pineapple slices first into the flour, then into the beaten egg, and then into the panko. Allow to rest 15 to 30 minutes before frying.

5. Fry the pineapple slices about 2 to 3 minutes, or until golden brown. Drain on paper towels.

6. Sprinkle pineapple with sugar and serve with the mango sauce.

Butternut Squash and Pumpkin Ginger Soup

4 servings

AMOUNT	MEASURE	INGREDIENT
1	16 ounces/448 g	Butternut squash
1	16 ounces/448 g	Small pumpkin
1 tablespoon	½ ounce/15 ml	Vegetable oil
2 tablespoons	1 ounce/28 g	Fresh ginger, minced
1½ cups	6 ounces/168 g	Maui onions, in ¼-inch (.6 cm) dice
1 tablespoon	½ ounce/14 g	Garlic, minced
1 cup	5 ounces/140 g	Carrots, in ¼-inch (.6 cm) dice
1 cup	4 ounces/112 g	Celery, in ¼-inch (.6 cm) dice
½ teaspoon		Fennel seeds
1 teaspoon		Cumin seeds
½ teaspoon		Red pepper flakes
1		Bay leaf
1		Star anise
2 tablespoons	¼ ounce/7 g	Fresh basil, chopped
1 teaspoon		Salt
½ cup	4 ounces/120 ml	Dry white wine
2 cups	16 ounces/480 ml	Chicken stock
2 slices		Fresh ginger
1		Kaffir lime leaf or regular lime leaf
1 cup	8 ounces/240 ml	Heavy cream
1 cup	2 ounces/56 g	Enoki mushrooms
2 tablespoons	¼ ounce/7g	Fresh parsley, chopped

PROCEDURE

1. Preheat the oven to 375°F (190°C).

2. Peel, seed, and chunk the squash and pumpkin, then bake, covered, until soft, about 45 minutes. In a 5- to 6-quart (5 to 6 L) pot, heat the oil and sauté the minced ginger, onions, garlic, carrots, and celery until soft, 3 to 5 minutes. Add the fennel and cumin seeds, red pepper flakes, bay leaf, star anise, basil, and salt. Cook 1 minute. Add the wine and cook 1 minute more.

3. Add the squash and pumpkin to the pot. Add the stock, and simmer 30 minutes or until the vegetables are soft. After 15 minutes, add the ginger slices and lime leaf.

4. Remove the bay leaf, lime leaf, and ginger slices.

5. Puree the soup in a food processor.

6. Place soup back in the pot and add the cream. Bring almost to a boil and correct the seasoning.

7. Heat the mushrooms and use as garnish. Serve the soup sprinkled with parsley.

Macadamia Nut–Crusted Mahimahi with Wasabi Cream Sauce

4 servings

Macadamia Nut–Crusted Mahimahi

AMOUNT	MEASURE	INGREDIENT
1 cup	4 ounces/112 g	Macadamia nuts
1¼ cups	4 ounces/112 g	Panko bread crumbs
		Salt and white pepper
4	4 ounces/112 g each	Mahimahi fillets, no skin
		All-purpose flour, for dredging
1		Egg, lightly beaten with a little water and pinch of salt
As needed		Vegetable oil, for frying

PROCEDURE

1. In a food processor, combine the macadamia nuts, panko, and salt and pepper. Blend until the mixture is finely ground.

2. Season the fish with salt and pepper, then dredge in flour, dip in the egg wash, and roll in the nut mixture, coating each fillet on both sides.

3. Heat the oil in a 10- to 12-inch (25.4–30.5 cm) sauté pan and pan-fry the fish over medium-high heat until golden brown on both sides, about 2 to 3 minutes per side, turn only once. Drain on paper towels.

4. Serve the fillets with Wasabi Cream Sauce (recipe follows).

Wasabi Cream Sauce

AMOUNT	MEASURE	INGREDIENT
1 tablespoon	½ ounce/14 g	Shallot, finely diced
½ cup	4 ounces/120 ml	Dry white wine
½ cup	4 ounces/120 ml	Fish stock
¾ cup	6 ounces/180 ml	Heavy cream
1 tablespoon	½ ounce/7 g	Wasabi powder
2 tablespoons	1 ounce/30 ml	Water
1 tablespoon	¼ ounce/7 g	Cornstarch
		Salt and white pepper

PROCEDURE

1. Combine the shallot and wine in a 2-quart (2 L) pan over medium heat; simmer until almost completely dry.

2. Add the stock and reduce the liquid by one-third.

3. Add the cream and wasabi powder, then reduce again by one-third, or to nappé consistency.

4. Combine the water and cornstarch and use to thicken the sauce, if necessary. Season with salt and pepper.

Miso Soup with Taro and Butterfish

4 servings

CHEF TIP: Butterfish is also known as black cod or sablefish.

AMOUNT	MEASURE	INGREDIENT
3 cups	24 ounces/720 ml	Water
¾ cup	3 ounces/84 g	Maui onion, in ¼-inch (.6 cm) dice
½ cup	3 ounces/84 g	Tomato, peeled, in ¼-inch (.6 cm) dice
½ tablespoon	¼ ounce/7 g	Fresh ginger, slivered
1 cup	4 ounces/112 g	Taro root, peeled, in ¼-inch (.6 cm) dice
2 tablespoons	¼ ounce/7 g	Dried shrimp
1 tablespoon	½ ounce/14 g	Dried konbu (kelp), soaked and cut into ¼-inch (.6 cm) strips
1¾ cups	4 ounces/112 g	Shiitake mushrooms, in ½-inch (1.2 cm) slices
¼ teaspoon		Dashi powder, prepared, or ¼ pkg (0.17 oz/5 g) hondashi (Japanese fish-flavored soup granules)
1 tablespoon	½ ounce/14 g	White miso
1 cup	5 ounces/140 g	Tofu, firm, in 1-inch (2.5 cm) cubes
1 cup	4 ounces/ 112 g	Butterfish fillet, in 1-inch (2.5 cm) cubes
1 teaspoon		Sugar
		Salt and white pepper

PROCEDURE

1. In a 2- to 3-quart (2 to 3 L) pot, bring the water, onion, tomato, and ginger to a boil. Reduce the heat and simmer for 20 minutes.

2. Put the taro root in a small saucepan, cover with water, and cook until tender, about 10 to 15 minutes. Drain and then add to the soup mixture.

3. Add the dried shrimp, konbu, mushrooms, and dashi to the soup. Simmer for 10 minutes.

4. Add the miso, stir to dissolve, and simmer 1 minute. Add the tofu and butterfish, and cook 1 minute more. Correct the seasoning with sugar, salt, and pepper.

5. Let the soup stand for 5 minutes before serving.

Sautéed Pacific Snapper with Curry Kamuela Tomato Sauce

4 servings

AMOUNT	MEASURE	INGREDIENT
2 tablespoons	1 ounce/30 ml	Vegetable oil
2	10 g	Garlic cloves, in ¼-inch (.6 cm) dice
1 tablespoon	½ ounce/14 g	Fresh ginger, minced
1 stalk		Lemongrass, chopped
1 tablespoon	6 g	Fennel seeds
1 tablespoon	½ ounce/14 g	Red curry paste
4 tablespoons	2 ounces/60 ml	Dry white wine
3 cups	18 ounces/504 g	Tomatoes, peeled, in ¼-inch (.6 cm) dice
½ cup	4 ounces/120 ml	Heavy cream
		Salt and black pepper
4	4 ounces/112 g each	Snapper fillets

PROCEDURE

1. In a 2- to 3-quart (2 to 3 L) pot, heat 1 tablespoon (½ ounce/15 ml) of the oil over medium heat. Add the garlic, ginger, lemongrass, fennel seeds, and curry paste. Cook and stir 2 minutes. Add the wine and reduce by half.

2. Add the tomatoes and cook 10 minutes. Add the cream and bring to a boil.

3. Let cool a few minutes, then puree the sauce and strain through a fine-mesh sieve. Correct consistency (if too thin, reduce by cooking further). Season with salt and pepper. Keep warm.

4. In a 10- to 12-inch (25.4–30.5 cm) sauté pan, heat the remaining 1 tablespoon (½ ounce/15 ml) oil and sauté the fish for 2 to 3 minutes per side, turning only once.

5. Place each fillet on a warmed plate and serve with the sauce.

Basic Culinary Vocabulary

Al dente Cooked firm, not soft or mushy. The literal meaning of *al dente* is "to the bite."

Albumin The primary protein found in egg whites. Albumin is available powdered and granulated and is frequently used as an edible glue for sealing foods together.

Allumette A classic vegetable cut that results in shapes measuring ⅛ × ⅛ × 2 inches (.3 × .3 × 5 cm). The term is used in reference to potatoes only. All other vegetables cut into this shape are referred to as julienne.

Appareil A prepared mixture of ingredients used by itself or as an ingredient in other preparations. Examples of appareils are due duxelles and pâte à choux.

Aromatics Spices, herbs, and certain vegetables added to preparations to enhance their flavor or aroma.

Aspic A clear jelly made from clarified stock and thickened with gelatin. Aspic is sometimes referred to as aspic jelly or aspic gelée and is used primarily to coat foods. In some cases, aspic is cut into uniform shapes and used as a garnish for pâtés and other charcuterie items.

Au gratin Describes foods finished under a broiler or salamander and served with a browned top. Frequently, the topping for gratinée items is made from bread crumbs, cheese, or sauce.

Au sec Describes food cooked until almost dry.

Bain marie A container that holds foods in a hot-water bath. Bain marie is also the name for a hot-water bath used to slowly cook foods or to hold them at a hot temperature until needed.

Base A widely used, commercially produced flavor base usually available in powdered, granulated, and paste forms. Bases are typically mixed with water to create instant stock or used in small quantities to enhance the flavor of soups and sauces. A number of convenient food bases are available today. The application of these convenience products greatly depends on the type of food-service establishment and the desired flavor outcomes. Some factors to consider when using bases are time, cost, storage, and flavor. Be sure to read the product's label carefully so that you know its ingredients. Taste the product to ensure that its flavor meets your expectations.

Batonnet A classic vegetable cut that results in shapes measuring ¼ × ¼ × 2 inches (.6 × .6 × 5 cm).

Blanching The process of quickly and partially cooking food items in boiling water or hot fat. Blanching is generally done as a part of a combination cooking method or to aid in the preparation of a food item. Examples of blanching uses are to remove the skin from tomatoes, to prepare french fries for final cooking, to ready food items for freezing, and to remove undesirable flavors from foods.

Bouillon French for "broth." (*See* Broth.)

Bouquet garni A selection of fresh vegetables and herbs tied into a bundle with twine. A bouquet garni is typically submerged in stocks, sauces, soups, and stews and used as a flavoring agent.

Broth The culinary definition of broth is "a flavorful liquid derived by simmering meat, vegetables, and aromatics in water." To make beef, veal, or chicken broth, simmer meat in water with vegetables and seasonings.

Brunoise A classic vegetable cut that results in shapes measuring ⅛ × ⅛ × ⅛ inch (.3 × .3 × .3 cm).

Brunoise fine A classic vegetable cut that results in shapes measuring ¹⁄₁₆ × ¹⁄₁₆ × ¹⁄₁₆ inch (.1 × .1 × .1 cm).

Caramelization The process of browning the sugars found on the surface of many foods to enhance their flavor and appearance. Browning vegetables or proteins is also referred to as *caramelizing*.

Carryover cooking What happens when roasted foods, small or large, continue to cook after being removed from the oven. Carryover cooking is normal and can dramatically alter the degree of doneness once the product is removed from the oven. The larger the food item, the greater the amount of heat it retains and the more its internal temperature rises.

Château A classic vegetable cut resulting in a small seven-sided football shape approximately 1½ inches (3.8 cm) in diameter.

Cheesecloth Cotton gauzelike cloth with a number of culinary uses, including straining liquids; enclosing spices, herbs, and other flavoring agents to be applied in a cooking process; and binding ingredients together during the cooking process. The cloth's loose weave allows for the distribution of flavor and moisture during cooking while the structural integrity of the product it encloses is maintained.

Chiffonade A vegetable cut applied to leafy greens and herbs, such as spinach and basil. It results in long, very thin strips typically used as a garnish or as a bed on which other food items are placed. This cut is accomplished by stacking the leaves, rolling the stack into a cylinder, and slicing the roll into fine strips.

Chinois A conical strainer. While this term applies to all such strainers, it is generally used to describe those that use a fine mesh rather than perforated metal to strain.

Clarification The process of turning a cloudy liquid into a clear one by removing the solid impurities or sediment from it. This process turns broth or stock into consommé by trapping the impurities in a mixture of ground meat, egg whites, and acidic product and aromatics. The term *clarification* is applied to this clarifying mixture, or clearmeat, as well as the process itself.

Clarified butter Pure butterfat rendered from whole butter (a process that removes milk solids and water). Clarified butter has a higher smoking point, or temperature at which it burns, than whole butter. This property makes it suitable for cooking food at higher temperatures and for cooking processes such as sautéing. Clarified butter has less butter flavor than whole butter and may be kept for a longer period without becoming rancid.

Clearmeat The mixture of egg white, ground meat, acidic ingredient, mirepoix, and other aromatics used in the process of clarifying stock or broth into consommé. (*See* Clarification.)

Cocotte A classic vegetable cut that results in a small seven-sided football shape approximately ¾ inch (1.9 cm) in diameter.

Compote A preparation of chilled fresh or dried fruit previously cooked slowly in a sugar syrup. Compotes are often flavored with spices or liqueur.

Concassée To pound or coarsely chop. The term is most often applied to peeled, seeded, and coarsely chopped tomatoes. The term describes the result as well as the action. For example, a chef may concassée a tomato to produce tomato concassée.

Confit Meat or poultry slowly cooked and preserved in its own fat. Classically, goose, duck, and, sometimes, pork is used to make confit.

Conical strainer Specifically, a conical strainer made of perforated metal rather than mesh. (*See* Chinois.)

Consommé A rich, clear soup made by clarifying broth or stock. Consommés are served hot or cold. A consommé reduced by half to intensify its flavor is known as a double consommé.

Coulis A thick sauce made from raw or cooked fruit or vegetables. The term *puree* is sometimes used interchangeably.

Deglaze To add a liquid, usually stock or wine, to a pot or pan after it has been used to cook a food item in order to remove the cooked food particles and their flavor from the surface of the cooking vessel. These flavorful food particles are called the fond and, once lifted from the pan, are used to enhance the flavor of a stock or sauce. (*See* Fond.)

Degraisse A French term referring to the process of removing the fat from the surface of a stock, soup, or sauce.

Depouillage A French term referring to the process of skimming the surface of a stock to remove the impurities that naturally rise to the surface while simmering.

Double and triple stocks Stocks made with a prepared stock rather than water. Double and triple stocks are not recommended, as the product cost increases significantly and the flavor is not much different from that of a properly made regular stock.

Dredge To dip or submerge an item in a dry ingredient in order to coat it. Food products are often dredged in flour to coat them prior to sautéing, pan-frying, or deep-frying. The coating keeps the product from sticking to the pan and promotes the development of a crust on the surface of the product. This crust may enhance the product by developing an appealing brown appearance and by encasing the product in a way that retains flavor and moisture.

Duxelles An appareil composed of mushrooms, shallots, and butter. The mushrooms and shallots are finely chopped and cooked in the butter until a dry, thick paste forms. Duxelles are often used to flavor items such as soups or sauces or as stuffing or a component of stuffing.

Emulsion The suspension of one liquid within another when those liquids generally do not mix. The combination of oil (or fat) and water-based liquids into a smooth mixture is the classic culinary emulsion. An emulsion has a thicker consistency than that of either liquid separately. This characteristic provides mouthfeel, cling, and general structural benefits. Emulsions may be temporary, permanent, or semipermanent. Emulsions are often aided by the addition of emulsifiers or stabilizers such as mustard or the lecithin found in egg yolks.

Enriched stock A stock made with meat as well as bones, creating a hybrid of stock and broth. For 1 gallon (128 ounces, 5.8 L) of chicken stock, it is recommended that 2 whole chickens be added to the recipe. When done, the chickens should be reserved and used in another recipe or preparation. For beef or veal stock, it is recommended that a 2-pound (1.8 kg) piece of shank meat be added to enrich the stock. Enriched stock yields a much richer flavor than plain stock and, as long as the meat is used in another preparation, should not increase cost.

Essence The fusion of a particular flavor, such as mushrooms or fennel, into a stock to derive a characteristic flavor or aroma.

Fond French for "base." In French cooking, fond refers to a stock, typically the basis for many classic and modern recipes. Fond is also used to describe the residue attached to the bottom of a cooking vessel after a food ingredient has been roasted or sautéed. A great deal of flavor is usually retained in the fond, which is removed from the cooking vessel through the process of deglazing. (*See* Deglaze.)

Fondant A classic vegetable cut that results in a small seven-sided football shape approximately 2 inches (5 cm) in diameter.

Garnish A food item added for appearance, taste, and texture. Garnish can be integral to the dish or added as an embellishing accompaniment. The term also applies to the act of adding a garnish to a dish.

Gelatin A mixture of proteins derived from boiling bones, connective tissues, and other animal parts. Gelatin, when dissolved and cooked in a hot liquid, adds a jellylike texture to the product. It is flavorless and odorless and comes in granular and sheet forms. It is used to thicken and stabilize food products.

Gelatinous Describes a liquid with jellylike properties. A gelatinous product is semisolid when cold and liquid when hot. Gelatinous properties are important for stocks and sauces due to the characteristics of richness, body, substance, and mouthfeel they provide to the food products.

Glace A quality stock reduced slowly over a prolonged period until it reaches a thick and syrupy consistency. Glace can be used to enhance or enrich soups and sauces and as a glaze to add a sheen to broiled and grilled proteins. Although some commercial food bases have a similar appearance, they may or may not achieve the same results as a fresh-made glace. Today, glace can be purchased already made, but the products vary widely in flavor and quality by manufacturer.

Glazing The process of adding sheen to a food item. Glazing can be accomplished by many means. Examples include brushing a grilled steak with glace before serving, coating an hors d'oeuvre with aspic gelée, and sautéing foods in butterfat and granulated sugar.

Grand sauce A basic classic sauce from which a number of small sauces are produced. There are five recognized grand sauces: espagnole (brown), velouté, béchamel (white), hollandaise, and tomato. In recent years, many culinarians argue that demi-glace has replaced espagnole in common use as the foundation sauce, though classic demi-glace is made from espagnole. Grand sauce is also known as *mother sauce* and *lead sauce*.

Griswold A cast-iron skillet. This heavy-gauge pan requires a seasoning process to seal it, which involves coating the pan with oil and heating it to a high temperature. The griswold is important to the production of many regional dishes. For example, it is the traditional pan used for blackening Cajun dishes, baking corn breads, and pan-frying Southern fried chicken. Its heavy gauge maintains temperature evenly once heated.

Julienne A classic vegetable cut that results in shapes measuring ⅛ × ⅛ × ½ inches (.3 × .3 × 1.2 cm).

Julienne fine A classic vegetable cut that results in shapes measuring ¹⁄₁₆ × ¹⁄₁₆ × ½ inches (.1 × .1 × 1.2 cm).

Large dice A classic vegetable cut that results in cubes measuring ¾ × ¾ × ¾ inch (1.9 × 1.9 × 1.9 cm).

Liaison A mixture of cream and egg yolk used to finish soups and sauces. The use of a liaison enriches, slightly thickens, and gives sheen to the completed soup or sauce. A liaison must be carefully incorporated into the hot product through tempering. A product containing a liaison cannot be boiled or the yolk will scramble and the item will have a curdled or broken appearance.

Marmite A stockpot, often made of earthenware. This large pot is taller than it is wide to allow prolonged periods of simmering while minimizing evaporation. Marmites sometimes have legs.

Matignon An edible mirepoix. Matignon uses the same ratio and variety of vegetables as a traditional mirepoix, but because it is intended to be consumed, the matignon should be cut into uniform shapes before cooking.

Medium dice A classic vegetable cut that results in cubes measuring ½ × ½ × ½ inch (1.2 × 1.2 × 1.2 cm).

Mince To cut or chop into very small pieces.

Mirepoix A combination of vegetables frequently used in cooking. Mirepoix typically includes 2 parts onion, 1 part carrot, and 1 part celery. The size to which mirepoix ingredients are cut varies with the intended use and is determined by the amount of time the mirepoix will be cooked. For a brown stock that cooks for 6 to 8 hours, a large dice is preferred, but for a fish stock, which cooks for 45 minutes only, a small dice yields better results.

Mise en place A culinary term meaning "everything in its place." It connotes a state of preparedness. Mise en place applies to the assembly of ingredients and equipment prior to undertaking food production. It is also a mindset brought about by thorough forethought and planning.

Nappé A liquid consistency that just coats a spoon. The term nappé also refers to the act of lightly coating a food item with sauce.

Oblique A classic vegetable cut made by cutting the vegetable on a bias. Between each cut, the vegetable is rolled 180 degrees. This cut is used primarily for carrots, but other vegetables, such as broccoli stems and asparagus, can be prepared this way.

Olivette A classic vegetable cut resulting in a small seven-sided football shape approximately ½ inch (1.2 cm) in diameter.

Onion brûlée A peeled onion cut in half and charred on the sliced side. Onion brûlée is added to stocks, soups, and sauces for added caramel color and enhanced flavor. French for "burnt onion."

Onion piqué A whole peeled onion to which a bay leaf is tacked with whole cloves. Another approach is to make a slice in the onion and secure the bay leaf within the slice, then stick cloves into the onion separately. Onion piqué is used to flavor sauces, especially white sauces such as béchamel and velouté, and soups. French for "pricked onion."

Parboil To par-cook food in boiling or simmering water.

Par-cook To partially cook a food by any method. This technique is used to bring food to a state where it can be quickly cooked to finish, especially in the case of dense foods. Par-cooking is also used to prepare a number of individual foods, which take various amounts of time to cook, to a degree of doneness whereby they can be completed together in the same amount of time.

Parisienne A classic vegetable cut resulting in perfectly round shapes. No diameter is specified, but it is very important that each of the vegetables used for the same preparation is uniform in size.

Pâte à choux A paste or batter made of milk or water, flour, butter, and eggs. It is also known as choux paste, cream-puff dough, and éclair paste. Pâte à choux is used to produce a number of hollow pastries that are often filled. It is also used as a binder or appareil for other preparations.

Paysanne   A classic vegetable cut that results in shapes measuring ½ × ½ × ⅛ inch (1.2 × 1.2 × .3 cm). Paysanne cuts can be round, triangular, or square.

Peel   To remove the outer layer or peel from fruits and vegetables. The term also describes a long-handled, spade-shaped tool used by bakers to remove baked items from the oven.

Pincé   To caramelize a product by sautéing. This term is most often applied to tomato products.

Puree   A sauce or soup made from ingredients, especially fruits or vegetables, that have been blended, processed, or sieved until a thick smooth consistency is achieved. The term also refers to the act of blending, processing, or sieving a food item to such a consistency.

Raft   Congealed clearmeat that settles at the top of a consommé during clarification.

Reduction   The product resulting when a liquid, such as a stock or sauce, is simmered or boiled to evaporate its water, reduce its volume, and concentrate its flavor. Stocks and sauces made with commercial food bases, which do not contain gelatin, will not benefit from the process of reduction.

Refresh   To submerge or run a blanched product under cold water to stop the cooking process and set the color. This is also known as shocking.

Remouillage   French for "rewetting." Remouillage is a stock made with bones previously used to make stock. The procedure for making remouillage is the same as for a regular stock, but the product is not as clear or flavorful. Remouillage is frequently used to make glace and, in the past, was used instead of regular stock to make double-strength stocks. (*See* Double stock, Glace.)

Rendering   The process of heating fatty animal products to melt and separate the fat from the remaining tissue. This process produces clear liquid fat, useful for many cooking applications, and brown, crisp connective tissue. This crisp tissue is often crumbled or cut and used as a garnish known as cracklings.

Rondeau   A heavy, wide, shallow, straight-sided pot with two loop handles.

Rondelle   A classic vegetable cut that results in round shapes, ⅛ inch (.3 cm) thick. The rondelle cut is sometimes referred to as coins.

Roux   A mixture of cooked fat and flour used to thicken soups and sauces. Often, the fat used is butter. Other fats, such as rendered animal fat and various oils, are sometimes used for their flavor and temperature characteristics. The general ratio of fat to flour is 1:1 by weight. A roux may be cooked to various degrees of doneness for desired flavor and color characteristics.

Sachet dépices   A bag of spices used to flavor soups, stocks, and sauces. The spices are generally wrapped in a piece of cheesecloth, tied with a long string, and fastened with one end of the string to the pot of the product to which it is applied. This allows the sachet ingredients to be easily added and removed when desired. A standard sachet d'épices contains cracked black peppercorns, parsley stems, bay leaf, dry thyme, and, sometimes, a crushed clove of garlic.

Sauteuse   A single-handled sauté pan with rounded, sloping sides.

Sautoir   A single-handled sauté pan with straight sides.

Shock   To submerge or run a blanched product under cold water to stop the cooking process and set the color. This is also known as refreshing.

Sieve   A wire mesh kitchen utensil used to strain liquids or sift dry ingredients, such as flour. The term also applies to the act of straining liquid or particles through a sieve.

Small dice   A classic vegetable cut that results in cubes measuring ¼ × ¼ × ¼ inch (.6 × .6 × .6 cm).

Small sauce   A derivative sauce made by altering a grand sauce with additional ingredients. Many classic small sauces can be made from each of the grand sauces.

Standard breading procedure   The sequential process of coating a food product with bread crumbs by first dredging it in flour, then egg wash, and, finally, the crumbs. This process is also used with other dry coatings, such as cracker crumbs, ground nuts, and cornmeal. Such a coating is often applied to an item before it is pan- or deep-fried.

Stir-frying   A hot, quick, dry-heat cooking method done in a skillet on the stovetop with very little fat. Traditionally, this method employs a wok as the cooking vessel. Larger items to be stir-fried are generally cut into small pieces. The method is similar to sautéing, but the food is constantly kept moving.

Sweating   The process of cooking food in a pan without browning or adding color to the food. Sweating should be done over low heat until the items are tender and begin to release moisture. The purpose of sweating is to help the food release its flavor quickly when combined and cooked with other foods. Onions are an example of a food item commonly sweated. They turn almost translucent when properly sweated.

Tempering   A process of adjustment employed when heat or acid may cause an ingredient or combination of ingredients to curdle. Heat or acid is applied to the ingredients gradually in order to adapt them to the change. Hot liquids are added slowly to a liaison, for example, to bring the temperature of the eggs up slowly so they do not scramble. This term also applies to the stabilization of chocolate through a melting and cooling process.

Tomato concassée   A rough cut or chop of peeled and seeded tomato.

Tourné   A classic vegetable cut that results in a small football shape with seven even sides.

Tranche   An angled portion slice from a fillet of fish.

Translucent Semitransparent. The term often describes the appearance of onion products cooked to the point where they are somewhat limp.

Tuber A fleshy, usually oblong or rounded thickening or outgrowth of a root, stem, or shoot beneath the ground. A common tuber is the potato.

Whisk A looped wire kitchen utensil, also called a whip, used for whipping and stirring. The term also applies to the action of whipping vigorously to incorporate ingredients or air into ingredients.

White mirepoix Standard mirepoix in which the proportion of carrots is replaced with parsnips, leeks, and mushrooms. White mirepoix is used in fish stock and fish fumet and is sometimes used in white stock when a lighter product is desired. (*See* Mirepoix.)

Zest The thin outer layer of the peel of citrus fruit. Zest is used as a flavoring agent. The term also refers to the action of cutting the zest from the citrus fruit.

AFO (Animal Feeding Operation)   EPA defines AFOs as agricultural enterprises where animals are kept and raised in confined situations. AFOs congregate animals, feed, manure and urine, dead animals, and production operations on a small land area. Feed is brought to the animals rather than the animals grazing or otherwise seeking feed in pastures, fields, or on rangeland. There are approximately 450,000 AFOs in the United States.

Agribusiness   Agribusiness is large-scale, industrialized, vertically integrated food production. It is often thought of as corporate farming, as opposed to small, family farming.

Antibiotics   Meat producers have fed growth-promoting antibiotics to food animals for years. Recently, scientists have raised concerns that, in conjunction with the general overuse of antibiotics in humans, this use of "sub-therapeutic" levels of antibiotics in food animals may lead to serious health risks for people. Banning the use of such drugs, however, would greatly reduce the efficiency of the industry, driving up the cost of meat. Some in the industry believe that the scientific evidence linking low-dose usage of antibiotics to drug-resistant illnesses in humans is too inconclusive and does not justify banning their use.

Antibiotic Free/No Antibiotics Administered   No antibiotics were administered to the animal during its lifetime.

Antibiotic resistance   Bacteria's ability to mutate in order to survive treatment with antibiotics. Over time, bacteria are able to change their characteristics so that antibiotics cannot kill them. This process happens faster when antibiotics are used very frequently, especially at low doses over long periods of time, which is common on factory farms where antibiotics are added to feed.

Arsenic   Arsenic is a natural metallic element found in low concentrations in virtually every part of the environment. It is also found in foods. There is some thought that poultry products are a potentially significant source of arsenic exposure for consumers, but studies consistently show the level of arsenic in poultry products is below the established 0.5 parts per million limit set by the Food & Drug Administration.

Bagasse   Salvaged sugar cane pulp material that can be converted into biodegradable plates, cups, and carry-out containers.

Beyond Organic   After the USDA created the "USDA Organic" label, many farms dropped their certification because they felt the new standards diluted the integrity of the label "organic." Many of these farms use methods more stringent than (i.e., beyond) organic.

Biodynamic   This holistic method is based on the philosophy that all aspects of the farm are part of an interrelated ecosystem. Biodynamic farmers work in harmony with nature and use a range of techniques to foster a sustainable, prolific environment.

Biodegradable   Able to metabolically break down into simpler compounds, including carbon dioxide, water, and biomass, leaving no toxins behind.

Biodiesel   A petroleum-free diesel fuel made from vegetable oil or other biomass. Also called *biofuel*.

Biomass   The biological matter, typically plant matter, that can be used as a potential source of energy or fuel.

Bioplastic   Disposable food service products made from vegetable or sugarcane fibers. They are designed to mimic plastic disposables but break down in commercial composting facilities or in nature without leaching any toxic chemicals into the environment.

Borax   A white, powder-like chemical compound used as a non-toxic household or commercial cleaner, deodorant, sanitizer, and pest repellant.

Brown grease   Low-grade used fryer oil removed from passive restaurant grease traps, which is mixed with dirty water; often considered unusable.

CAFO   Abbreviation for Confined Animal Feeding Operation, which is an agricultural business where animals are raised in confined situations and fed an unnatural diet, instead of allowing them to roam and graze. This operation is considered more hazardous than an AFO for one or more reasons, such as the number of animals or the location of the facility, its proximity to surface water, and potential to discharge waste into that water. The EPA determines whether an agricultural business is a CAFO based on regulations created by the Clean Water Act, and special permits have to be given for the owners to operate a CAFO legally. Enforcement of these regulations has not been very strict, which has caused many problems.

Cage-free   Birds raised without cages. What this term doesn't specify is if the birds were raised outdoors on pasture, if they had access to the outside, or if they were raised indoors in overcrowded conditions. If you want to buy eggs, poultry, or meat that was raised outdoors, look for a label that says "Pastured" or "Pasture-raised."

Clean Air Act   Set of laws passed in 1970 to regulate air pollution in the United States. The goal of this act was to improve air quality, and it was revised in 1990 to be more detailed about issues such as the hole in the ozone layer and acid rain.

Clean Water Act Set of laws passed in 1972 to regulate water pollution in the United States. This was the first-ever federal regulation of water pollution, and it gave the EPA the right to set standards and enforce them. The goal of this act was to completely stop the discharge of pollutants into the Waters of the United States and make all bodies of water in the country fishable and swimmable. It is very difficult and expensive to enforce these laws because it's not always easy to find who is polluting bodies of water.

CFL Compact Fluorescent Light, a compact version of a typical fluorescent light bulb. They last longer, produce less heat, and conserve more energy than incandescent lights.

Compost The decomposed remnants of organic matter; often used for fertilizer or landscaping purposes.

Composting The process of mixing various organic materials in a bin or heap where it leaves behind the compost, or humus. Composting diverts organic waste from landfills and can be done in-house, residentially, or in a commercial facility.

Compostable All natural and organic products or materials that are biodegradable with the help of air, moisture, and natural organisms.

Contract grower Farmer who makes an agreement with an agribusiness company, giving the company the power to make all the farm's decisions, including which animals are raised there, what these animals are fed, and how they are treated. In return, the company pays the farmer and buys the supplies.

Cover crops Crops that are grown not to be harvested for food but to cover and protect the soil surface and prevent soil erosion.

Country of Origin Labeling (COOL) If approved, this initiative would require beef, lamb, pork, fish, perishable agricultural commodities, and peanuts to be labeled with the country in which they were produced. In addition to providing consumers with valuable information about their food, Country of Origin Labeling would help to promote locally produced meat and would allow regulators to more easily trace the source of meat in the event of a recall or an outbreak of disease.

Crop rotation The practice of alternating different crops in a field in planned cycles in order to regulate nitrogen levels, prevent soil erosion, reduce fertilizer needs, and improve the overall long-term productivity of the land.

CSA Abbreviation for Community Supported Agriculture, a system in which consumers support a local farm by paying in advance for agricultural products. This reduces the financial risks for the farmer because the costs of seeds and planting crops are covered in advance by consumers. Throughout the growing season, CSA members receive a portion of the farm's harvest each week. Members share the financial risks and the bounty of the harvest—if it is a successful growing season, they receive a lot of food; if there are fewer crops, they receive less.

Dead zone An area in the Gulf of Mexico where oxygen levels are so low that most marine organisms cannot survive. One of the primary causes is runoff from farms in the Mississippi watershed.

Dioxins Dioxins are man-made pollutants that can cause an array of health risks for humans. Potent toxics, they act as endocrine disruptors (interfering with the body's natural hormone signals), damage the immune system, and may affect reproduction and childhood development. Dioxins are "persistent" compounds that drift around the world and tend to accumulate in the fatty tissues of animals and humans. At least 95% of typical human exposure comes through dietary intake of animal fats such as meat, dairy, and eggs.

Diversification Method of farming that involves more than one agricultural product.

Downers Animals that collapse during transportation or at the slaughterhouse as they are too stressed or sick to continue walking. Because normal animals fetch a higher price at the market, downers are frequently kicked or prodded to try to force them to move. Those animals that do not move may be left on the ground without food or water for days before they die. Downers are routinely processed for human consumption.

E. coli A species of bacteria that lives in the intestines of people and other vertebrates (animals with spines). Although the bacteria that naturally exist in your intestines are harmless and helpful in digestion, eating or drinking bacteria such as *E. coli* that come from outside sources (for example, polluted water or meat that has not been processed safely) can cause severe food poisoning or even death.

Eco-labeling A method of identifying products that cause less damage to the environment than other products (such as Fair Trade, organic, Food Alliance certified, raised without antibiotics, etc.). There exists a wide selection of eco-labels with different criteria and varying degrees of legitimacy. While some labels indicate that food was produced according to strict guidelines enforced and verified by third-party food-certifying agencies, other labels are self-awarded by food producers.

Efficiency An economic term for conditions that create the biggest possible profit with the smallest possible costs. This is an important idea in industry, since the goal of any business is to make as much money as possible and avoid waste—think of wastefulness as the opposite of efficiency.

Effluent Liquid waste, often from a factory or sewer. This is a term that is often used to refer to the urine and manure that is pumped into or out of a lagoon.

Electronic pasteurization or Electronically pasteurized This term means the food has been irradiated.

Environmentally preferable Another way of saying environmentally friendly, sustainable, or ecologically responsible. Some environmental certification programs use this terminology to describe green products or appliances.

EPA Environmental Protection Agency. A part of the US federal government that enforces environmental laws and provides information and guidance to policy makers.

Factory farm A large-scale industrial site where many animals (generally chickens, turkeys, cattle, or pigs) are confined and treated with hormones and antibiotics to maximize growth and prevent disease. The animals produce much more waste than the surrounding land can handle. These operations are associated with various environmental hazards as well as cruelty to animals. The government calls these facilities Concentrated (or Confined) Animal Feeding Operations (CAFOs). The EPA defines a CAFO as "new and existing operations which stable or confine and feed or maintain for a total of 45 days or more in any 12-month period more than the number of animals specified" in categories that they list. In addition, "there's no grass or other vegetation in the confinement area during the normal growing season."

Family farm/Small farm   Defined by the USDA as a farm with less than $250,000 gross receipts annually on which day-to-day labor and management is provided by the farmer and/or the farm family that owns the production or owns or leases the productive assets.

Feedlots   Buildings, lots, or a combination of buildings and lots in which animals are confined for feeding, breeding, raising, and/or holding. The concentration of hundreds or thousands of animals in a confined feedlot facility drastically reduces the welfare of these animals, creates health risks, promotes the spread of disease, and yields tremendous quantities of animal waste, which pollutes the natural environment and threatens human health.

Finishing   The process through which an animal gains weight before it is slaughtered. On factory farms, animals are generally finished on a pure grain-based diet, which induces rapid weight gain and creates the "marbled" layers of fat in beef to which consumers are accustomed. However, cows and other ruminants are naturally adapted to eat grasses; large quantities of grain cause them to develop high levels of acidity within their digestive tracts, leading to a number of health problems. Sustainably raised animals are finished on pasture, where they consume the grasses and other plants that their bodies are best adapted to digest. Research has shown that meat and dairy products from grass-fed animals are better for human health than foods from grain-fed animals. Note: Grass-fed, grain-supplemented animals are also raised on pasture, but are given access to controlled amounts of grain during the finishing period and do not encounter the health problems that animals fed a pure grain diet can face.

Fishkill   Sudden death of a significant number of fish or other aquatic life such as crabs or shrimp within one area. A fishkill can be caused by many different changes in the environment, including pollution, temperature change, and a change in acidity.

FOG   Fats, oils, and grease, which include commercial kitchen byproducts that can cause sewer damage, backups, and pollution.

Food Alliance   Meats labeled "The Food Alliance Approved" come from animals that were raised on ranches that preserve soil and water quality, and were provided access to fresh air, pasture, and comfortable living quarters, without artificial hormones, rBGH, or unnecessary antibiotics. This claim is verified by third-party inspectors. Meats are available in some farmers' markets and natural foods stores in the Northwest and Midwest; online stores also sell products.

Free range   This term refers to animals (usually poultry and the eggs that they produce) that are not confined, meaning that these animals are able to go outdoors to engage in natural behaviors. It does not necessarily mean that the products are cruelty-free or antibiotic-free, or that the animals spend the majority of their time outdoors. The use of the term "free range" is only defined by the USDA for poultry production, and need only mean that the bird has had some access to the outdoors each day, which could be a dirty or concrete feedlot. USDA considers five minutes of open-air access each day to be adequate. The term is defined by USDA, but claims are not verified by third-party inspectors.

Free walkers   These hens are housed indoors, though they can move around and have unlimited access to food. Similar to "cage-free."

Genetic engineering   The science of changing the DNA of a plant or animal to produce desirable characteristics. Examples of desirable characteristics include rapid growth and unusually large size. This is a very controversial science that many believe has not been adequately tested and studied. In addition, not everyone agrees that the plants and animals that are genetically engineered are safe for humans to eat or safe for the environment if released.

GMO (Genetically Modified Organism)   This is a plant or animal that has been genetically engineered. Many industries support the development and use of GMOs while many consumers and organizations question their safety and have called for adequate and independent testing of GMO products. It is legal for farmers in the United States and some other countries, such as Argentina, to produce and sell certain GMOs for human and animal consumption, but in other places such as Europe and Japan, they are banned until further testing can be done to prove they are safe.

GMO-Free or No GMOs   The product was produced without the use of GMOs (genetically modified organisms).

Grain-Fed   Animals were raised on grain (most commonly corn), which may be supplemented with animal byproducts and other [strange] matter such as cement dust. Unless the label says "100% Vegetarian Diet," there is no guarantee that the animal's feed was not supplemented with animal byproducts or is organic. Cattle naturally eat grass and cannot digest a diet consisting purely of grains. Many large feedlots use grains to quickly fatten the cattle, which fosters disease and the use of antibiotics.

Grain Finished   Animals are fed grain shortly before slaughter. Some producers use this method to add the fat and flavor most people are currently accustomed to.

Grass-Fed   Animals eat only grass. Most graze naturally while roaming the pasture, but, technically, they could be raised indoors. Grass-fed meats should be free of antibiotics, synthetic hormones, grain, and animal byproducts.

Grass-Fed/Grain-Supplemented   Animals are raised on grasses, but grains are added slowly into the diet. By controlling the amount of grain, the animals do not become sick or develop digestion problems that grass-fed only cattle develop.

Gray water   Slightly used water that can be reused for purposes like irrigation or cleaning. Also called *reclaimed water*.

Grease recovery devices   An improved automatic grease trap that separates water from grease more effectively, resulting in cleaner grease. *See* yellow grease.

Grease trap   A plumbing device designed to intercept greases and solid waste before they enter the sewage system. Also called a *grease interceptor*.

Green   Refers to products, equipment, practices and concepts that promote environmental sustainability.

Greenwashing   Falsely advertising a product as eco-friendly without complying with standards, testing results, or furnishing reliable proof.

Heritage   Heritage foods are derived from rare and endangered breeds of livestock and crops. These animals are purebreds and are specific breeds of animal that are near extinction. Production standards are not required by law, but true heritage farmers use sustainable production methods. This method of production saves animal breeds from extinction and preserves genetic diversity.

Groundwater   Water that exists beneath the earth's surface in underground streams and aquifers.

Heat recovery system   Technology than can be applied to water heaters in order to capture energy from otherwise wasted hot water going down the drain. The heat energy is used to preheat cold water entering the heater or water flowing to another fixture.

Heavy metals   Metallic chemicals like cadmium, arsenic, copper, and zinc that can be harmful pollutants when they enter soil and water. These chemicals are put into animal feed to make animals grow more rapidly. Heavy metals are present in human and animal waste and can enter the environment if waste is released without being treated. Animal waste is never treated to remove heavy metals. Once in the environment, heavy metals are almost impossible to get rid of because they do not decompose.

Holistic management   A decision-making framework that assists farmers and others to establish a long-term goal, a detailed financial plan, a biological plan for the landscape, and a monitoring program to assess progress toward the goal.

Hormones   Chemicals found naturally in animals' bodies that control processes such as growth and metabolism. Synthetic (man-made) hormones have been developed for a number of purposes, including treatment of hormonal disorders in people, and also for promotion of unnaturally fast growth in farm animals. One of the most well-known and controversial hormones used in farming is recombinant Bovine Growth Hormone or rBGH, which is genetically engineered and injected into dairy cattle. (*See* rBGH.) Scientists have linked excess hormones to cancer.

Hormone Free   The USDA has prohibited use of the term "Hormone Free," but meats can be labeled "No Hormones Administered."

Humus   Nutrient-rich mulch or compost resulting from mixing various organic chemicals together in a bin and allowing air, moisture, and organisms to break it down. *See* Compost.

HVAC   Heating, ventilating, and air conditioning, referring to climate control in buildings.

Impoundment   A large pond or lake, sometimes 50 to 100 acres, constructed to water the hogs at hog confinement facilities.

Independent family farm   Farm on which the ownership and management are controlled by at least one family member who lives on the farm, not by a corporation or absentee owner.

IPM (Integrated Pest Management)   Pests are controlled using natural methods, such as habitat manipulation, biological control, and pest-resistant plants. Pesticides are used in the smallest possible amounts, only when other techniques prove inadequate.

Irradiation   Exposure to radiation. Meat is sometimes irradiated to kill microorganisms and reduce the number of microbes present due to unsanitary practices, but this process alters the nutritional quality and creates new chemicals that can be harmful to humans who consume the meat. Many believe that there has not been enough testing to know whether irradiated food is safe for humans.

Lagoon   A huge, man-made hole in the ground created to hold a mixture of water and animal waste until it can be applied to land. These holes can be as large as several square acres (1 acre = 43,560 square feet) and hold 20–25 million gallons of liquid waste. This is equivalent to more than 98 Olympic-sized swimming pools. Lagoons are generally not covered and frequently leak into the surrounding soil or groundwater, so they are associated with air, water, and soil pollution.

Leaching   The process of dissolving components of a material into liquid, such as harmful chemicals leaching into groundwater.

LED   Light Emitting Diode, an energy-efficient, longer lasting, and less harmful replacement for standard incandescent lights in everyday fixtures.

Life cycle   The projected lifespan of an appliance or piece of equipment. Also pertains to the process of production, starting with extracting resources and materials from nature, manufacturing a product, consuming the product, and finally disposing of the product.

Low-flow pre-rinse valve   Pre-rinse sprayer component that allows water to flow at an increased velocity but uses fewer gallons per minute; curbs water consumption and lowers water bills.

Mad cow disease   Common name for Bovine Spongiform Encephalopathy (BSE), a cattle disease that causes the brain to waste away. It takes about 4–7 years for cattle to show symptoms of the disease after being exposed to it, but, once symptoms become visible, the cattle die within weeks. One way this disease is spread is by feeding the meat from infected cattle to other cattle (meat from infected sheep may also cause the disease). This was a common practice on factory farms until the 1980s and

1990s when it was outlawed in most countries because it was found to cause BSE. At that time, thousands of cattle believed to have been exposed to BSE were killed to prevent further spread of the disease. Consuming beef from infected cattle causes a brain-wasting disease in humans called *new variant Creutzfeldt-Jakob disease (nvCJD)*.

Methane   A gas given off by animal waste. It can be used as fuel, but the process to turn it into fuel is very expensive, so this is not done very often. Methane is a greenhouse gas, which means that it contributes to global warming.

Mobile meat processing unit   A slaughterhouse in a trailer that can be moved from one farm to another in order to accommodate small farmers and ranchers. The units drastically reduce the stress animals endure from being transported long distances.

Molting/Forced molting   Part of a hen's natural reproductive cycle. After laying eggs for about a year, a hen loses her feathers and rests for a few weeks as new feathers grow in. This is called *molting*, or *a molt*, and it usually happens at the beginning of winter. On factory farms, hens are subjected to forced molting, where farm operators cause this process to happen rapidly by depriving hens of food and water for several days and altering the schedule of light and darkness in the confinement building. This way, all the hens molt simultaneously and over a very short period.

Monoculture   Monoculture is the destruction of a diverse ecosystem and replacement with a single species or crop. This is a common practice in modern agriculture, where large acreages of crops are grown for sale to other regions or countries. Monocultures deplete the soil, and fruits and vegetables become more susceptible to pests and disease than those grown in a diverse crop environment, thus requiring larger amounts of chemical sprays.

Make-up air   The air pulled from outside the commercial kitchen to replace the air the stove hood takes in.

Microfiber   Very fine, lightweight polyester fiber used in woven and nonwoven textiles, specifically cleaning cloths or mops designed for repeated use.

Natural   Currently, no standards exist for this label except when used on meat and poultry products. USDA guidelines state that "Natural" meat and poultry products can only undergo minimal processing and cannot contain artificial colors, artificial flavors, preservatives, or other artificial ingredients. However, "natural" foods are not necessarily sustainable, organic, humanely raised, or free of hormones and antibiotics. The label "natural" is virtually meaningless.

New variant Creutzfeldt-Jakob disease (nvCJD)   Disease in humans that causes the brain to waste away, caused by eating meat infected with mad cow disease (BSE) or other related animal diseases. It was first detected in 1994, and, although it is still not known how much time it takes for symptoms to show up after a person is exposed, some scientists say it may take up to 40 years, so it is still not known how many people have been infected.

Nitrates   Chemicals made up of oxygen, nitrogen, and other elements. When chemicals containing nitrogen (for example,

ammonia) combine with water, nitrates are usually formed, and these nitrates can cause serious illness or even death if large amounts are consumed. Nitrate poisoning is usually caused by drinking water contaminated with nitrates. The primary sources of nitrate pollution are human waste and manure, especially runoff from factory farms. Processed meat also often contains nitrates, which are used to prevent the growth of harmful bacteria and to enhance the color of the meat. Eating meat that has been treated with nitrates may cause health problems, including cancer, migraines, high cholesterol, and hyperactivity.

No Antibiotics Administered, Raised Without Antibiotics, or Antibiotic-Free   No antibiotics were administered to the animal during its lifetime. If an animal becomes sick, it will be taken out of the herd and treated, but it will not be sold with this label.

No Hormones Administered or No Added Hormones   Animals were raised without added growth hormones. By law, hogs and poultry cannot be given any hormones so the use of the label on these meats is misleading. To ensure that other meats were raised without added hormones, ask your farmer or butcher.

No-till farming   The practice of planting new crops amidst cuttings of old crops and not plowing the field in order to slow the release of carbon dioxide and diminish the greenhouse effect. No-till and low-till practices also increase the retention of water and nutrients, allowing earthworms and other organisms to proliferate and keep the soil healthy.

Non-point source pollution   Harmful substances that are carried by rain and snow moving over and through the earth and that end up in groundwater, rivers, lakes, or the ocean. These substances come from various sources and can be natural or man-made. They're called *non-point source* because instead of being dumped directly from a house or factory into a body of water, the pollutant is diluted and transported by the natural cycle of precipitation.

Non-therapeutic antibiotics   Antibiotics administered to animals for purposes other than the treatment of existing illness. Factory farms routinely administer non-therapeutic antibiotics to their animals in order to boost growth rates and to prevent the outbreak of diseases that would otherwise run rampant within crowded, unsanitary factory farm facilities. The use of non-therapeutic antibiotics promotes the development of antibiotic-resistant bacteria, causing antibiotics used to treat humans to become less effective.

Nutrient pollution   Contamination of water by too many nutrients, which often come from fertilizer or waste runoff. In surface waters, this can cause overproduction of algae (this is called an *algal bloom*), which uses up all the oxygen in the water and suffocates fish and other marine life.

Organic   In order to be labeled "organic," a product, its producer, and the farmer must meet the USDA's organic standards and must be certified by a USDA-approved food-certifying agency. Organic foods cannot be grown using synthetic fertilizers, chemicals, or sewage sludge; cannot be genetically modified; and cannot be irradiated. Organic meat and poultry must be fed only organically grown feed (without any animal byproducts) and cannot be treated with hormones or antibiotics. Furthermore, the animals must have access to the outdoors, and ruminants must have access to pasture (which doesn't mean they actually have to go outdoors and graze on pasture to be considered organic).

Pastured or Pasture-Raised   Indicates the animal was raised on a pasture and that it ate grasses and food found in a pasture, rather than being fattened on grain in a feedlot or barn. Pasturing livestock and poultry is a traditional farming technique that allows animals to be raised in a humane, ecologically sustainable manner. This is basically the same as grass-fed, though the term pasture-raised indicates more clearly that the animal was raised outdoors on pasture. *See* Grass-Fed.

PLA   A processed corn starch called poly-lactic acid; it is used to form biodegradable cups and carry-out containers.

Photovoltaic   The technology surrounding the conversion of solar energy into electricity. A photovoltaic cell, for example, is a device that converts sunlight into electricity.

Post-consumer recycled content   Waste content that has been used in the consumer market and then recycled into new products.

Pre-consumer recycled content   Waste content that has never been used in the consumer market, such as products from manufacturers and processes, and has been recycled to make new products.

PSM (plant starch material)   Various vegetable starches are synthesized to form plant starch material; it is often made from mostly potato or corn starches and used to form cutlery, plates, and containers.

Raised Without the Routine Use of Antibiotics   Antibiotics were not given to the animal to promote growth or to prevent disease, but may have been administered if the animal became ill.

rBGH   Recombinant Bovine Growth Hormone, also called *recombinant Bovine Somatotropin (rBST)*. This is a genetically engineered hormone that is injected into dairy cows to increase their milk production. Cows injected with rBGH have shorter lifespans and are much more likely to suffer from udder infections. rBGH is only legal in three countries: the United States, South Africa, and Mexico. rBGH has been banned in Canada, the European Union, and elsewhere because of inadequate testing and some evidence that it leads to cancer.

rBGH-Free or rBST-Free   rBGH (recombinant bovine growth hormone; also known as recombinant bovine somatotropin [rBST]) is a genetically engineered growth hormone that is injected into dairy cows to artificially increase their milk production. The hormone has not been properly tested for safety. Milk labeled "rBGH-Free" is produced by dairy cows that never received injections of this hormone. Organic milk is rBGH free.

Rotational grazing   The practice of moving animals between two paddocks, so that each paddock undergoes a short grazing period followed by a longer rest period. The practice protects pastures from overgrazing and reduces soil erosion.

Ruminant   Ruminants are hooved animals with four-chambered stomachs that enable the animals to digest cellulose. After eating, ruminants regurgitate a semi-digested material called cud, which they chew, then eat again. Cows, goats, sheep, bison, deer, camels, llamas, and giraffes are all ruminants. These animals eat a pure vegetarian diet.

Runoff   Water from precipitation or irrigation that flows over the ground and into bodies of water. It can contribute to soil erosion and carry harmful pollutants.

Self Certified   The farmer makes claims such as "No hormones administered," but there is no outside verification of the claims, meaning the consumer must take the farmer at his or her word. Many reliable, legitimate sustainable farmers are self certified, but it's still best to know your farmer or butcher and/or to trust the brand you buy.

Small farm/Family farm   Farm that earns no more than $250,000 per year and on which the day-to-day labor and management is provided by the farmer and/or farm family that owns or leases the production or production equipment. This does not necessarily mean that the farm is organic or cruelty free, or even that it is not controlled by a major agricultural company.

Sow   Female pig that has produced a litter of piglets.

Spent hen   A hen that is no longer able to function as a factory egg-producing machine—usually about two years old. These hens, which frequently have broken bones and badly bruised bodies, are sold cheaply for use in frozen dinners or canned soups, or are discarded.

Sprayfield   Land where animal waste from the lagoon is applied. High-powered hoses are used to spray the animal waste up in the air; the waste particles can travel many miles before settling onto the land.

Steer   Castrated male cattle.

Subtherapeutic   Below the dosage levels used to treat diseases. For example, subtherapeutic feeding of penicillin to livestock.

Surface water   Water that sits or flows above the earth, including lakes, oceans, rivers, and streams.

Sustainability   The ability to provide for the needs of the world's current population without damaging the ability of future generations to provide for themselves. When a process is sustainable, it can be carried out over and over without negative environmental effects or impossibly high costs to anyone involved.

Sustainable   A product can be considered sustainable if its production enables the resources from which it was made to continue to be available for future generations. A sustainable product can thus be created repeatedly without generating negative environmental effects, without causing waste products to accumulate as pollution, and without compromising the well-being of workers or communities. Many different agricultural techniques can be used to help make food production more sustainable.

The drawback of the term *sustainable* is that it lacks a clear-cut, universally accepted, enforceable definition; thus, it can be interpreted in different ways. It is more of a philosophy or way of life than a label.

Sustainable agriculture   Farming that provides a secure living for farm families; maintains the natural environment and resources; supports the rural community; and offers respect and fair treatment to all involved, from farm workers to consumers to the animals raised for food.

T8 lighting   Lighting created by a fluorescent light with a lamp tube diameter of 8 eighths of an inch, or a 1-inch diameter. Available in a variety of lengths and shapes and more energy-efficient than T12 lighting.

T12 lighting   Lighting created by a fluorescent light with a lamp tube diameter of 12 eighths of an inch, or a 1½-inch diameter. Typically less efficient than T8 lighting.

Tail-docking   Common factory farm practice of cutting off half or more of an animal's tail, frequently performed on cattle and pigs. This prevents pigs from chewing one another's tails and cattle from hitting workers with manure-covered tails. This is a painful procedure, which is not necessary when animals are not confined since they do not exhibit these behaviors.

Third-Party Certified (or Verified)   Food inspected by a company operating independently of the producer or distributor. The third-party certification company confirms the legitimacy of claims made by food producers and distributors, thus ensuring that the food labels are meaningful. Organic and Biodynamic Certified are examples of third-party certification. Next to knowing your farmer or butcher, this is the most reliable way to trust the meat you're eating. The problem is that there are only a few third-party certified labels.

Transitional   A farm or grower who is converting to organic practices but has not yet completed the transition.

Treated by Irradiation or Treated with Radiation   The FDA requires that food treated with irradiation be labeled with one of these phrases and carry a radura symbol. Unfortunately, if you eat at a restaurant or in an institution such as a hospital, you will not know if the food has been irradiated.

USDA   United States Department of Agriculture. The USDA, which was founded by Abraham Lincoln, supports rural development, food safety, nutrition, and research for agricultural technology. The agency is also in charge of the national forests and rangelands and works to reduce hunger in the United States and internationally.

Veal   Beef from calves that are less than six months old; they are usually slaughtered at about 16 weeks of age.

Vertical integration   Economic term that is often used to describe a trend in the agriculture industry. When an agriculture corporation is vertically integrated, it is involved in more than one phase of meat production. Many of these big businesses have their own feedlots, slaughterhouses, meatpacking plants, and distributors, so they have complete control over the lives and deaths of the animals they raise.

VOCs   Volatile organic compounds. These are carbon-based molecules that give off potentially harmful gas emissions that contribute to indoor pollution. VOCs are found in paints, cleaning agents, pesticides, carpets, and some indoor furnishings.

Wastewater   Water that has been used and thrown away from residential, business, or industrial sources. It can contain a variety of waste products like soap, chemicals, or manure.

Water recovery system   Sometimes referred to as a *reclaimed water* or *gray water system,* the set-up and use for recovered water is largely situational. In the commercial kitchen, water can be captured before flowing down the drain and reused for heating purposes, steam reservoirs, or cleaning tasks.

Watershed   Area of land that contributes runoff to a particular, common body of water.

Yellow grease   Grease recovered directly from fryers or grease recovery devices, which keep grease cleaner and more valuable for grease handlers and biodiesel companies.

The Cuisine of New England

Heinrichs, Ann. *Vermont.* New York: Children's Press, 2001.
Kent, Deborah. *Maine.* New York: Children's Press, 1999.
McNair, Sylvia. *Connecticut.* New York: Children's Press, 1999.
———. *Massachusetts.* New York: Children's Press, 1998.
———. *Rhode Island.* New York: Children's Press, 2000.
Mariani, John. *The Encyclopedia of American Food and Drink.* New York: Lebhar-Friedman Books, 1999.
White, Jasper. *Jasper White's Cooking from New England.* New York: Harper & Row, 1989.

The Cuisine of the Mid-Atlantic States

Blashfield, Jean. *Delaware.* New York: Children's Press, 2000.
———. *Virginia.* New York: Children's Press, 1999.
Burgan, Michael. *Maryland.* New York: Children's Press, 1999.
Fazio, Wende. *West Virginia.* New York: Children's Press, 2000.
Heinrichs, Ann. *New York.* New York: Children's Press, 1999.
———. *Pennsylvania.* New York: Children's Press, 2000.
Stein, R. Conrad. *New Jersey.* New York: Children's Press, 1988.

The Cuisine of the Deep South

Davis, Lucille. *Alabama.* New York: Children's Press, 1999.
George, Linda. *Mississippi.* New York: Children's Press, 1999.
Hintz, Martin. *North Carolina.* New York: Children's Press, 2000.
Kent, Deborah. *Tennessee.* New York: Children's Press, 2001.
Lewis, Edna, and Scott Peacock. *The Gift of Southern Cooking.* New York: Alfred A. Knopf, 2003.
Masters, Nancy. *Georgia.* New York: Children's Press, 1999.
McNair, Sylvia. *Arkansas.* New York: Children's Press, 2001.
Stein, R. Conrad. *Kentucky.* New York: Children's Press, 1999.
———. *South Carolina.* New York: Children's Press, 1999.

Floribbean Cuisine

Heinrichs, Ann. *Florida.* New York: Children's Press, 1998.
Rodriguez, Douglas. *Nuevo Latino.* California: Ten Speed Press, 2002.
Susser, Allen. *New World Cuisine and Cookery.* New York: Doubleday, 1995.

Cajun and Creole Cuisines

Harris, Jessica B. *Beyond Gumbo.* New York: Simon and Schuster, 2003.
Hintz, Martin. *Louisiana.* New York: Children's Press, 1998.

The Cuisine of the Central Plains

Blashfield, Jean. *Wisconsin.* New York: Children's Press, 1998.
Blue, Anthony Dias. *America's Kitchen.* Georgia: Turner Publishing, Inc., 1995.
Heinrichs, Ann. *Indiana.* New York: Children's Press, 2000.
———. *Ohio.* New York: Children's Press, 1999.
Hintz, Martin. *Iowa.* New York: Children's Press, 2000.
———. *Michigan.* New York: Children's Press, 1998.
———. *Minnesota.* New York: Children's Press, 2000.
———. *Missouri.* New York: Children's Press, 1999.
———. *North Dakota.* New York: Children's Press, 2000.
Masters, Nancy. *Kansas.* New York: Children's Press, 1999.
McNari, Sylvia. *Nebraska.* New York: Children's Press, 1999.
Santella, Andrew. *Illinois.* New York: Children's Press, 1998.
Sheperd, Donna Walch. *South Dakota.* New York: Children's Press, 2001.

Texas

DeWitt, Dave, and Nancy Gerlach. *The Whole Chili Pepper Book.* Canada: Little, Brown & Company, 1990.
Griffith, Dottie. *The Contemporary Cowboy Cookbook: Recipes from the Wild West to Wall Street.* Texas: Lone Star Books, 2003.
Heinrichs, Ann. *Texas.* New York: Children's Press, 1999.
Raichlen, Steven. *BBQ USA.* New York: Workman Publishing, 2003.
Reedy, Jerry. *Oklahoma.* New York: Children's Press, 1998.

Southwestern Cuisine and The Rocky Mountain States

Blashfield, Jean. *Arizona.* New York: Children's Press, 2000.
———. *Colorado.* New York: Children's Press, 1999.
George, Linda. *Idaho.* New York: Children's Press, 2000.
———. *Montana.* New York: Children's Press, 2000.
Kent, Deborah. *New Mexico.* New York: Children's Press, 1999.
———. *Utah.* New York: Children's Press, 2000.
———. *Wyoming.* New York: Children's Press, 2000.
Stein, R. Conrad. *Nevada.* New York: Children's Press, 2000.

The Cuisine of California

Heinrichs, Ann. *California.* New York: Children's Press, 1988.
Jordan, Michele Anna. *California Home Cooking.* Boston: The Harvard Common Press, 1977.

The Cuisine of the Pacific Northwest

Blashfield, Jean. *Washington.* New York: Children's Press, 2001.
Ingram, Scott. *Oregon.* New York: Children's Press, 2000.
Nicholas, John F. *The Complete Cookbook of American Fish and Shellfish.* New York: Van Nostrand Reinhold, 1990.
Shepherd, Donna. *Alaska.* New York: Children's Press, 1999.

The Cuisine of Hawaii

Hintz, Martin. *Hawaii.* New York: Children's Press, 1999.
Laudan, Rachel. *The Food of Paradise: Exploring Hawaii's Culinary Heritage.* Hawaii: University of Hawaii Press, 1996.

Index